The Road to Nunavut

The Progress of the Eastern Arctic Inuit since the Second World War

R. QUINN DUFFY

McGill-Queen's University Press
Kingston and Montreal

©McGill-Queen's University Press 1988
ISBN 0-7735-0619-5

Legal deposit 1ˢᵗ quarter 1988
Bibliothèque nationale du Québec

Printed in Canada on acid-free paper

This book has been published with the help of
a grant from the Social Science Federation of
Canada, using funds provided by the Social
Sciences and Humanities Research Council of
Canada.

Canadian Cataloguing in Publication Data

Duffy, R. Quinn (Ronald Quinn), 1937-
  The Road to Nunavut
  Includes index. $100 3205098$
  Bibliography: p.
  ISBN 0-7735-0619-5
  1. Inuit – Canada – Social conditions. 2. Inuit –
Canada – Government relations. 3. Nunavut
(N.W.T.). I. Title.
E99.E7D84 1988   971'.00497   C87-090197-4

For my parents,
Jack and Eileen Duffy,
with love and respect

A preoccupation with one's survival is necessarily also a preoccupation with the obstacles to that survival. In earlier writers these obstacles are external – the land, the climate, and so forth. In later writers the obstacles tend to become both harder to identify and more internal; they are no longer obstacles to physical survival but obstacles to what we may call spiritual survival, to life as anything more than a minimally human being.

Margaret Atwood

We shall survive
And we shall walk

Somehow into summer ...

D.G. Jones

Contents

Acknowledgments

My interest in the Inuit dates from 1972, when I went to McGill University in Montreal as a doctoral student. Bill Kemp of the Department of Geography motivated me to study the demography of the Eastern Arctic and gave me that help and advice necessary to surmount the obstacles that bedevil the early stages of a project such as this. I am grateful to him for stimulating that interest in the Arctic that has remained with me ever since. I should also like to thank fellow student George Wenzel for his encouragement and assistance over the years.

I am indebted to McGill University for a Social Sciences Research Grant that made possible my travels in the north. I should also like to acknowledge that this book has been published with the help of a grant from the Social Science Federation of Canada, using funds provided by the Social Sciences and Humanities Research Council of Canada.

Preface

In June 1980 the magazine *Canadian Heritage* asked lawyer Marc Denhez why a small minority like the Inuit should be of concern to the rest of Canada. Denhez, a non-Inuk employed by the Inuit Tapirisat of Canada to advise on its land claims, replied, "Because they occupy one third of the country. If indeed the future of Canada is linked to the North, then we cannot postpone dealing with their problems indefinitely. That's the practical reason. From a more intellectual standpoint, how can anyone interested in Canadian culture ignore the possible extinction, under our very noses, of a unique culture which is four thousand years old."

The one-third of the country that the mere 16,000 Canadian Inuit occupy is known to them as Nunavut – "Our Land." It is a vast, empty, and silent land, a semi-continent of deeply fretted headlands and islands, some larger than several European countries. In summer it is a grey-brown monotone of bare rock and treeless tundra, speckled with lakes and pools and stippled with patches of stubborn ice and snow. The monotones of ice-scoured rock and dwarf birch and willow bushes that the traveller sees from the air are relieved at ground level by vivid splashes of colour: by the white of cotton grass, the yellow of poppies, the purple of saxifrage, and the vibrant yellow, green, and orange hues of lichens on the grey rocks. Nunavut is a wide-flung land of flat, far horizons unbroken by mountains. Only on its eastern and northern edges do mountains and glaciers rise, jagged and daunting, above the fiords of eastern and northeastern Baffin Island, of Bylot and Devon and Ellesmere and Axel Heiberg Islands. In winter the land and sea both disappear in the palling anonymity of snow and ice. They lose their separate identities. So does the north itself. It merges into the snow-covered south, reminding Canadians that they are all a northern people, inhabitants of a northern land.

Winter unites all Canadians in what is frequently referred to nowadays as their "nordicity." In the Central Arctic the annual snowfall can be as little as 30 centimetres, an amount that a one-day blizzard can dump on Montreal or Ottawa or even on Edmonton. In the Eastern Arctic snowfall is heavier but still not as much as in parts of southern Canada. Observers have measured 200 centimetres in southeast Baffin and northern Quebec, but the heaviest snow falls in the high uplands of Baffin Island, from where it decreases towards the north and west, All over the north, winter precipitation is associated with frontal activity, but because of low absolute humidities it is generally light. Travelling cyclones off the east coast of North America dominate the day-to-day pressure pattern of the Eastern Arctic. Little bad weather is associated with them. Occasionally warm, moist Atlantic air reaches Baffin Island, and the temperature rises above freezing point. When this happens it can bring cold winter rain to many lowland coastal areas. Shallow low-pressure systems crossing the southern Arctic islands from the Beaufort Sea also bring winter precipitation, but again, because they contain small amounts of water vapour, the cloud and precipitation they bring are rarely heavy.

The wind is the fiend of the Arctic. For days on end it will rage from the northwest, laden with the typically dry, hard snow of the north. The wind's wicked weapon is ground-drift: miles and miles of whirling snow that fills the air up to 50 feet above the surface of the land, cutting visibility to a few feet but making it hard to see at all because of the way it whips the eyes. The northwesterlies do their worst in the south-central Arctic islands, in Keewatin, and in the Hudson Bay area. Although the extreme low temperatures are not recorded here, this is the region of maximum wind chill in North America.

The lowest temperatures are in the west, down to a vicious −50°C, occasionally to −60 or even −65. Eastwards they rise to the highest mean winter temperatures in the Canadian Arctic, those along the Atlantic coast, though even here they are below −10°C. In the far northern islands the January mean is −35°C.

If the Eastern Arctic is spared the worst of midwinter's icy cold, it suffers worst from summer's spite. The shallow disturbances that travel in caravan eastwards across the Barren Grounds and the Arctic islands tend to find their passage blocked over southern Baffin Island and Hudson Strait. They retaliate with everything they have and vent their rage in long periods of bad weather. The air mass that holds sway over the Arctic in summer is moist and tends to be unstable. When the wind blows on shore across waters afloat with chunks of ice, it carries cloud and fog and cool temperatures to exposed coasts. In summer the highest temperatures rarely exceed 15°C in the eastern coastal and northern areas but may reach 24° inland. The more fortunate Mackenzie valley can enjoy temperatures in the low 30s, emphasizing the contrast between the cool, foggy, damp, and cloudy summer of the east and the pleasant, warm, dry summer of the west.[1]

The east is the land called Nunavut. Here, where the mainland of Canada shatters into the poleward scattering of Arctic islands, the Inuit have for thousands of years endured stoically the unkind environment of the region and adapted to it. The first people to do so came from the west four, maybe five, millennia ago. Nomadic hunters from northern Alaska, they spread eastwards across the empty Arctic barrens, carrying with them the technological assemblage that in Canada is identified as Pre-Dorset and characterized by very small, carefully and delicately chipped tools of chert and obsidian. The people who used these burins and blades and scrapers, these knife and weapon-points, were hunters of seal and caribou. In small, widely scattered nomadic bands they moved seasonally to exploit the available game resources. They persisted over large areas of the Canadian Arctic till around 800 BC, but gradually, after generations of adaptation to the harsh environment of the Eastern Arctic, a more specialized culture evolved out of the Pre-Dorset.[2] Called Dorset after the type site in Baffin Island, this new culture is distinguished by blades of ground and polished slate and by small delicate carvings in ivory, antler, and bone. But the Dorset and Pre-Dorset people lived similar lives, with the same ecological adaptation and settlement patterns.

Around 900 AD the Dorset people, or their culture, began to disappear. Between about 800 and 1300 a vast, thin drift of people from Alaska spread over Arctic Canada and coastal Greenland and down the shores of Hudson Bay. Dorset culture was almost completely buried. This second wave of migration from the west – rather than mere cultural diffusion[3] – brought the Thule people into the Canadian Eastern Arctic. Here they survived till the eighteenth century. The Thule culture evolved out of antecedents in the northern parts of Alaska. Its ecological base was whale-hunting, and whale-hunting more than anything else distinguishes the Thule from all other cultures in the Canadian Arctic, either earlier or later. The technology of the Thule people was a full range of gear for hunting the great baleen whales, but like their Dorset predecessors they hunted also caribou and seal and walrus and caught fish and birds.

On the whole the Thule made a more effective cultural adaptation to the Arctic environment than the Dorset. Their use of dogs, for instance, was a valuable aid in hunting, and harnessed to sleds the dogs enabled hunters to increase both their range and speed of travel. The Thule winter village also reflected a more effective adaptation to the Arctic. It consisted of six to thirty large houses made of stone slads and sods placed over whalebone frames. Each house had a cold-trap entrance passage, a raised flagstone sleeping-platform, a flagged floor, and various little cubicles for storage. The houses were usually constructed partly underground and often set into a gently sloping hillside facing the sea. Dorset houses had been smaller, less elaborate, and clustered in groups of only three to fifteen. Like Thule houses they were also partly sunk into the ground, but the walls probably of sod and the roofs of skin.[4] An important Eastern Arctic adaptation that the Thule people appear to have learned from their Dorset forerunners was the snow house, for snow houses are not an Alaska trait. The Thule Inuit may also have copied soapstone lamps and pots from Dorset examples.[5]

The Thule people were those whom the Europeans first encountered on the coast of Baffin Island in the late sixteenth century. The Renaissance explorers had only fitful contact with the Inuit. Constant contact began when whalemen from northwestern Europe and the northeastern United States started to fish the Davis Strait waters and intensified in the latter half of the nineteenth century, when the whaling companies introduced the practice of setting up permanent whaling stations and of overwintering in the Arctic.

The coming of the whalemen and the subsequent decline in the numbers of whales caused the collapse of Thule culture. Native whaling all but disappeared. Instead, the Inuit adopted a mixed economy of hunting seals and caribou and working for the whalemen in return for European foodstuffs and material technology. With the decline of the commercial whaling industry the Inuit, many of whom had lost their self-sufficiency and become dependent on the white men and their manufactures, turned to trapping foxes and hunting seals for individual traders or for companies.

The consequent economic and technological changes effected every aspect of Inuit society. The introduction of the English language, syllabic script, and formal education greatly altered the basis of Inuit thought and communication. The work of Anglican missionaries, who first came to the Eastern Arctic at the behest of the whalemen early in the twentieth century, accelerated these ideational changes. Missionary work led also to abandonment of the traditional religious beliefs of the Inuit, who converted to Christianity en masse.

The exchange of furs and labour for Euro-American food and man-ufactures introduced to the Arctic new economic arrangements that tied the formerly self-contained Inuit culture into the global market economy. This was to have serious repercussions in the Eastern Arctic in the mid-twentieth century. Another social change, yet to be fully resolved, was that the white man in the Arctic represented a new political force that destroyed the political independence of the Inuit as surely as trapping and wage labour destroyed their economic independence.

The whalers, the traders, and the missionaries completely shat-tered the age-old Inuit culture over most of the Eastern and Western Arctic. High-powered rifles largely superseded bows and arrows and sealing harpoons; with those old weapons went the ancient hunting skills. The kayak itself almost disappeared, and even the big skin umiak that the Inuit had used for travelling. Now they were de-manding boats with outboard motors and Peterheads powered by diesel engines. Now they were spending the long, dark winter months not in the large traditional camps, hunting seals through the ice, but in lonely family groups trapping foxes. Foxes had never had much value for the Inuit. But now the white traders were demanding them and were prepared to give in return supplies of guns and ammunition, tea and tobacco, pots and pans, and all the other items from the material inventory of southern Canada:

Their parents had relied solely on their own efforts, their own courage and skills, to supply all the needs of themselves and their kindred. They had been independent and free, possessing nothing and desiring nothing except success in hunting and fishing and a happy family life. But the present generation, the children, were dependent on strange white men who sur-rounded themselves with a multitude of strange possessions, white men who commanded mysterious knowledge and who imposed on the Eskimos tasks that seemed useless or beyond their understanding. The education that the missionaries offered them taught nothing, and explained nothing. The sky had fallen on their heads, and they stood among its ruins, unafraid but bewildered. They could not bring back the past, or foresee and plan for the future. So they drifted, uncertain of the world around them, and un-certain of themselves.[6]

The unique culture of the Canadian Inuit, which Marc Denhez described as being 4,000 years old, vanished into the Arctic mists a long, long time ago. The chapters that follow chronicle the last 40 years of cultural near-extinction of the Inuit, from the years of the Second World War to the 1980s. During those 40 years the Inuit have sunk as low as any people could in dirt, degradation, disease, and dependence. But with that tenacity of spirit that sustained them through thousands of years in the harshest environment on earth, they are fighting to regain their cultural independence, their self-respect, their identity as a unique people in the Canadian mosaic. And they are winning.

For the Inuit are survivors, and if Margaret Atwood is right, survival is the central symbol for Canada as the frontier is for the United States or the island is for England. Every country or culture, Atwood maintains, has a single unifying and informing symbol at its core – a word, a phrase, an idea, an image, or all of these – that functions like a system of beliefs, holding the country together and helping the people in it to co-operate for common ends. Survival, la survivance, performs this role for Canadians:

For early explorers and settlers, it meant bare survival in the face of "hostile" elements ... For French Canada after the English took over it became cultural survival, hanging on as a people, retaining a religion and a language under an alien government. And in English Canada now while the Americans are taking over it is acquiring a similar meaning. There is another use of the word as well: a survival can be a vestige of a vanished order which has managed to persist after its time is past ... But the main idea is the first one: hanging on, staying alive. Canadians are forever taking the national pulse like doctors at a sickbed: the aim is not to see whether the patient will live well but simply whether he will live at all.[7]

The Inuit represent all these symbolic connotations of survival. Threatened physically by hostile elements, threatened culturally, linguistically, and spiritually by a people and a government alien to their land, they have hung on, stayed alive, survived, a vestige of a vanished order. They are the Canadian survivors par excellence. This is why a small minority like the Inuit should be of concern to the rest of Canada.

Those whose story is told in the following six chapters are the Inuit of the Eastern Arctic, specifically of the Baffin administrative region of the Northwest Territories (NWT), which extends from Ellesmere Island to the northern tip of Arctic Quebec. Here 7,000 of the Arctic's 16,000 Inuit live – the largest concentration, more than half of the Eastern Arctic's Inuit population, being in the southern part of Baffin Island, with over 1,500 in the administrative centre of Ikaluit alone. For that reason southern Baffin Island features prominently in these pages.

The people of the Baffin region live in 14 isolated settlements, lonely as stars. They are widely scattered, from Grise Fiord in the north to Sanikiluaq in the south. Sanikiluaq, on the Belcher Islands in Hudson Bay, is the most southerly settlement in the Northwest Territories. The community grew around a government school, and in 1928 the Hudson's Bay Company moved its trading post here. The population in 1981 was 371 Inuit and a dozen others. They live on fishing, hunting, and trapping and on the production of unique soapstone carvings for which the settlement is now renowned.

Grise Fiord, on the south coast of Ellesmere Island, 960 miles from the North Pole, is the most northerly community in Canada. Its setting is spectacular. To the north, east, and west, the mountains of Ellesmere Island tower above the waters of Jones Sound. To the south, across the sound, Devon Island lies, its icecap a sparkling remnant of the ice sheet that covered North America to depths of thousands of feet in Pleistocene times. A hundred Inuit and a handful of people from the south live in Grise Fiord. The Inuit came in 1953 during an economic depression, when families from Port Harrison in northern Quebec and Pond Inlet on Baffin Island were moved here to take advantage of the plentiful game in what some consider the most beautiful part of the north.

As well as being the most northerly, Grise Fiord is also the smallest of the Baffin Region settlements, at least as far as total population is concerned. The smallest Inuit population, 50 out of a total of 261, lives at Nanisivik, the newest community in the north. Nanisivik means "the place where things are found." These things are minerals: lead, zinc, silver, and cadmium. To mine them, the town was built in 1974 on the shores of Strathcona Sound, not far from Arctic Bay in northwestern Baffin Island. It is thus a mining town and boasts all the modern facilities to be found in similar industrial towns: "They have taken everything of the South and put it here to make living as comfortable as possible. This is one of the few communities in the North that has a sewer system."[8]

The largest settlement in the Eastern Arctic is Iqaluit, formerly known as Frobisher Bay.[9] Designated a town in 1980, Iqaluit had a population the following year of 1,562 Inuit and 771 others. A grander place might be called the capital of the Eastern Arctic, but Iqaluit is far from grand. The main section of the town, on the site of the former Inuit camp known as Ikaluit, occupies the sloping curve of an inlet at the head of Frobisher Bay. Three miles away, across a high rocky ridge, the satellite community of Apex Hill stagnates quietly: it is small, depressing, derelict, and, like most Eastern Arctic settlements, rather untidy.

The first human settlement on the moon will look like Iqaluit.

The main town resembles a construction camp in full operation. Abandoned lumber and metal and bits of machinery lie everywhere. Heavy trucks and earth-movers rattle along the dirt roads, trailing clouds of dust when the weather is dry, splashing through mud and water when it is wet. Everywhere, like veins in a hand, a network of thin black pipes and cables pump water and power through the settlement; and heated sewers, raised above the ground on stilts, carry away the human waste and dump it in the bay.

In the midst of all the litter of construction the Inuit houses ignore the chaos around them, while up on its rock, like a feudal castle raised above a medieval village, the High Rise lords it over Iqaluit. The High Rise, known also as the Astro Complex, is a conglomerate of multi-storey buildings, the pulsing heart of the town. It houses government offices, apartments, a hotel, a post office, a bar, a dining room, a cafeteria, and a shopping mall. Through here the life-blood of Ikaluit gushes red and strong, with an artery to the airport and another to the Northern Canada Power Commission high on the bare surrounding hills.

Situated on these lunar hills another aspect of Iqaluit contrasts remarkably with the Inuit houses and the unkempt streets. Here the sterile architecture of advanced technology proliferates with incongruous science-fiction associations: groves of antennae pricking the skyline; the isolated fortress of the Power Commission, where trucks come and go continuously; the lonely, white DEW Line building, with the elegant but mysterious dome; the staring eye of the radio disc, unblinking, unmoving, but emitting a strange continuous hum; the huge silver-grey gas-tanks placed near the shore on the far edge of town, where the barren hills slide into the bay. In the town itself the white fibre-glass structures of the two schools and the arena, with their smooth, gleaming, convex walls and porthole windows, add to the futuristic incongruities of Iqaluit.

Iqaluit is the hub of communications in the Eastern Arctic. From here the airways reach out to Lake Harbour, Cape Dorset, Hall Beach, Broughton Island, Pangnirtung, and Resolute. Connections link these settlements to Clyde River, Pond Inlet, Nanisivik, to Grise Fiord, Igloolik, Arctic Bay, Sanikiluaq, to settlements in Keewatin, the central Arctic, and the west. International jets can land at Iqaluit, but the Twin Otter and the DC3 are the planes that use the small settlement airstrips, with their dirt and gravel surfaces. Bush pilots like characters from Saint-Exupéry of old Howard Hawkes movies fly the tiny, frail-looking aircraft with dedication, courage, and a sense of humour. The airstrips are the centre of the remote Arctic settlements, the placentas through which the arterial airways bring them life support from Iqaluit.

The same culture that created Iqaluit spawned these throbbing, fetal settlements. The basic family likeness is immediately striking in all of them: the prefabricated houses, the wooden shacks, the unsightly rubbish and litter. Most of them look as if they were built downwind of a garbage dump and a hurricane had just roared by. On the door of the nursing station at Pangnirtung a notice in simple cartoon style exhorts the people to put their garbage in garbage cans and not on the ground, but no one seems concerned enough to bother. Lake Harbour is comparatively clean and neat. Earth-movers scour the roads frequently in summer, removing most of the rubbish. White-painted stones edge the roads and paths. There is evidence that someone cares about the place. The habit appears to be one of long standing, for even in 1963 the Royal Canadian Mounted Police (RCMP) was commenting in its reports on "the cleanliness of the Lake Harbour Eskimo."

One family characteristic that all of the Eastern Arctic settlements share is an air of impermanence. In this respect they are like the camps they have replaced. But they do not belong here as the camps did; they do not fit into the northern environment. Architects have not yet produced a northern architecture that looks and feels northern, that gives the impression of being indigenous, durable, and permanent. The Inuit of the Eastern Arctic, the long-suffering citizens of Nunavut, deserve a native architecture worthy of the people: sturdy, adaptable, enduring, able to withstand the rigours of the uncompromising northern environment where they alone are truly at home.

This is their land, but their relationship to it has changed drastically in the last 40 years. Some southern Canadians familiar with the Arctic and its people have seen the changes coming for a long time. One such southern observer was Doug Wilkinson, author of the popular *Land of the Long Day*. In 1959 he wrote this observation on the fate of the Inuit:

A few years ago, while I was living at an Eskimo camp on north Baffin Island, I spent a week with a group of Eskimos near the bottom of Tay Sound. It was autumn in the Arctic; the lakes were covered with a thin lid of transparent ice, the air was crisp with the tang of approaching winter. The people at the camp were busy building their sod houses into which they would move at the first blizzard. Each day men sailed the decrepit whale boat onto the mirror smooth surface of the sound to hunt for seals.

There were fourteen people at the camp, the youngest aged 15 months, the eldest 56 years. One young boy, a lad of 12 attracted my attention. He was a carefree youngster, quick to laugh, quick to pout. From morn to night he was never still. He moved through the camp and over the surrounding hills with restless energy as though constantly seeking out answers to the riddles of this vast land. As I watched I couldn't help wondering what the future held for this boy and for the hundreds like him scattered across the top of the world. Although this little camp seemed a million miles from the civilized world to the south it was already evident that it was only a matter of time before the stillness of the remote fiords of north Baffin would be shattered by our encroaching mechanized civilization relentlessly probing into every corner of the Arctic seeking out the treasures of the earth.

Today I am fairly sure where that boy is going. He is a part of a great mass of people in the Canadian Arctic who will live and die watching their old way of life slip away from them while new forces slowly grind them into oblivion. The Canadian Eskimo is on the way out and you and I are slated to be interested spectators at his demise.[10]

The traditional Eskimos, whose demise we have witnessed over the last three or four decades, have been succeeded by the modern Inuit, a new breed sired from the old by the impregnation of southern Canadian culture. No clear date can be given for the birth of the modern Inuit. What people such as Doug Wilkinson saw in the Arctic in the 1950s was in a sense the prolonged and difficult labour that brought the new-born Inuit into the world. Gradually it dawned on the rest of the country that while its attention had been diverted by Cold War politics, Vietnam, the peace movement, and student rebellion, the old Eskimos had abandoned their winter camps, their igloos, dogsleds, and soapstone lamps, and disappeared into the long Arctic night. In their place the new Inuit in blue jeans and nylon parkas were living in modern houses with electric lights and television sets and buying groceries at the local supermarket.

This book tells the story of what happened in the Canadian Arctic while most of the country was looking elsewhere. Those who kept their attention fixed on the north were the federal and territorial government officials whose task was to administer the unwieldy NWT on behalf of the people of Canada. The Canadian government, in claiming political sovereignty over the Arctic archipelago, had assumed responsibility not only for the vast empty land, with the enticing promise of its hidden resources, but also for the lonely, long-neglected Eskimos who lived there, a hardy, self-reliant people with a unique way of life adapted to ice and snow and the sea's edge. These people became, without their ever having been offered any choice, the wards of the government of Canada, with the northern administration in Ottawa, and later also in Yellowknife, acting as their guardians.

This book is structured on the idea of guardianship, of bringing up children until they are old enough and mature enough to look after themselves. The introduction deals with the gradually growing but uninformed interest of the federal government in the Inuit and the reluctant assumption of the role of guardian, a role forced on Ottawa in part by concern over Arctic sovereignty. The subsequent chapters describe how the government met the normal parental tasks of providing shelter, health care, and education for the people of the Arctic, how it sought to bring the modern Inuit into a modern, technologically oriented economy, and finally how it has encouraged the Inuit to take responsibility for the running of their own affairs.

The arrangement is thus topical rather than chronological. However, many readers may want to move from chapter to chapter following concurrent events, to ascertain, for example, how housing, health, education, employment, and political evolution interact with each other at different times. To facilitate a chronological reading, I have subdivided each chapter into the same four periods: before 1945, 1945–59, 1959–71, and after 1971.

The Road to Nunavut

Reluctant Guardian

In April 1920, at Cape Crawford on the east coast of Baffin Island, a group of Inuit murdered a private trader by the name of Robert Janes. Janes had threatened to shoot the Inuit's dogs; they considered him dangerous, and they shot him. On 30 August 1921 Staff Sgt A.H. Joy of the Royal Canadian Mounted Police (RCMP) landed at the Baffin Island settlement of Pond Inlet to investigate the murder and to "reassert Canadian dominion in Baffin."[1]

Canadian dominion had been the government's main concern vis-à-vis the Arctic since the late 1890s. At the turn of the century it had become clear "that Canada intended to establish beyond any doubt, internationally, nationally, and in the minds of northern indigenous peoples themselves, that the whole of the land area between the Alaska boundary to the west, Newfoundland and Labrador to the east and the highest arctic islands to the north, formed part of national territory."[2] Suspicion about any foreign activity in the nation's northern waters had risen to the pitch of paranoia. American and European whalers, even Inuit from Danish Greenland, had been a constant source of worry, and Parliament viewed even Captain Peary's expedition to the North Pole with misgiving.

"Our interests in the Hudson Bay are increasing more and more," W.F. Maclean, Conservative MP for York South, said in the House on 18 April 1905, "and I think that the government should take some steps to keep (Peary's) expedition in their eye while it lasts, and to see that it is not merely a voyage of discovery in the interests of our neighbours to the south." The prime minister, Sir Wilfrid Laurier, assured the honourable gentleman that his government had a boat in the Arctic seas at that moment. "All right," said Maclean; "keep your eye on the captain."

On 10 July, the minister of marine and fisheries told the House that his department, jointly with the Mounted Police, intented to maintain a patrol boat on Hudson Bay: "The police will look after the policing of that vast section of the country, they will see that the customs duties are paid, that peace is maintained and that the laws of Canada are respected."

These were the government's northern priorities in the early years of this century, and all were related to the vital issue of protecting Canadian sovereignty in the Arctic. Of these three priorities – customs, peace, and the law of the land – the greatest became the maintenance of law and order. While the Danes sent doctors, nurses, teachers, and missionaries to the Inuit in their charge in Greenland, the Canadians sent policemen to the Inuit in their charge in the Canadian Arctic. Between 1905 and 1920 the then Royal Northwest Mounted Police were the main administrators of the NWT. In 1920 the government appointed the deputy minister of the interior to serve also as commissioner of the NWT and amended the Northwest Territories Act of 1905 to provide for a council of six members to assist him. But the police still carried out most of the government's work in the north.

On 24 June 1922 Parliament voted $60,000 to provide for establishment of three RCMP detachments in the High Arctic: two on Ellesmere Island and one on or near Bylot Island. Asked about the necessity for these stations, Minister of Justice and Attorney General Sir Lomer Gouin replied: "It is necessary to protect our rights against foreigners; to protect our fisheries, and to take care of our property generally."

MPs believed that it reflected the wishes of their constituents to police the empty wastes of the Arctic. Perhaps they were right. "Everyone is aware of the pride that the Canadian people have taken in maintaining justice in the extreme northern country,"Acting Minister of National Defence E.M. Macdonald said in 1923. "There are six Eskimos now in custody at Herschel Island up in the Arctic charged with murder and preparations are being made for their trial this summer. An expedition left Edmonton on the twelfth of June for that purpose taking a judge and two counsel."

It took also a hangman and the lumber to make the gallows. That was when the constituents back home began to have second thoughts about "maintaining justice in the extreme northern country." A section of the public objected. The government issued a statement and sent a messenger hurrying north to stop the proceedings. A few weeks later it sent another with the message to let things take their course. Things took their course, and the Inuit were hanged.

The case has acquired notoriety in the country. The murder of

Robert Janes at the opposite end of the Arctic is not so well known because it is less dramatic. The magistrate arrived together with the personnel needed for a full court procedure but without the gallows. The jury was selected from the crew of the ship that brought the magistrate and the lawyers. This court found one of the charged Inuit guilty of manslaughter, acquitted a second, and convicted a third of aiding and abetting. The last received a sentence of two years' close confinement in Pond Inlet; the first was sent to a southern prison for ten years.

The government ship that went north in 1922, sailing as far as the south end of Ellesmere Island, within 830 miles of the North Pole, turned out to be the first voyage of the Eastern Arctic Patrol, an annual event of far-reaching social, political, and technological consequences for the region and its people. Responsibility for overseeing the Eastern Arctic Patrol fell to a new administrative arm of the government, the Northwest Territories Branch, which, in 1923, became the Northwest Territories and Yukon Branch. This branch (the "northern administration") and the newly reconstituted council of NWT were the main agencies charged with administering and developing the Arctic islands from 1921 onwards.

They were supported by the R.C.M.P., which was responsible for on-the-spot enforcement of regulations and laws and for carrying out various government functions; by External Affairs on matters of international relations and Arctic sovereignty; by Indian Affairs, which was responsible for the Inuit as well as status Indians for a time; and by other departments such as Mines (which included the Geological Survey and the National Museum), whose contacts with the archipelago were frequent but intermittent. The fact that the Council consisted of the administrative heads of the Departments of Interior, Mines, Indian Affairs, R.C.M.P., and of External Affairs (from 1938) helped insure interdepartmental cooperation and coordination of government efforts in the Arctic.[3]

But in the 1920s the government still knew very little about the people of the north and had no idea what to do with them. "Leave them alone," Arthur Meighen said on 30 June 1924. "Make them comply with our criminal law and give them all the benefit of our civil law; in other words, treat them as everybody else is treated." Meighen, objecting to an amendment that would bring the Inuit under the Indian Act, said that he would not like to see the same policy applied to the Inuit as the government had applied to the Indians. "I object to nursing," he declared in the style of the true conservative. "I really think the nursing of our Indians has hurt them. The best policy we can adopt towards the Eskimos is to leave them alone. They are in a latitude where no-one will ever bother them."

Meighen was convinced that the white man would never move in and take away the Inuit's means of livelihood as he had the Indians'. Charles Stewart, the minister of the interior, disagreed. "It is being done at the moment," he maintained. "I am not asking that the Eskimos be placed under the department in order that they may be made wards of the government, nor is it my desire that the effect shall be to make them dependent on the people of Canada for a livelihood. But white men are going amongst them; the missionaries are beginning to require education for the children, and for that reason I think it is advisable that we have the Indian Act to apply to the Eskimos."

But the Opposition remained unconvinced. W.F. Carroll thought that bringing the Inuit under the Indian Act would only make them less ambitious to earn their own living. "The Eskimos are a thrifty people," he said, "and aside from some unforeseen occurrence, such as the loss of the animals which constitute their crop, they have done about as well as most other people."

W. Irvine had objections that appear today to have been inspired by clairvoyance. "What, for instance, are the aboriginal rights of this people? Have they any rights, for instance, to the lands they now occupy? Have they entered into consultation with the Dominion Government asking that the Superintendent General should administer their lands? If not, it might only lead to a greal deal of trouble if we were to asume the right to administer their lands without consulting with them as to their aboriginal rights."

Charles Stewart undertook to enlighten Irvine. Except in rare cases, he said, the Inuit did not live in definite localities. They followed their food "wherever it may be," though they did return to certain points for fishing "and that sort of thing." This was in contrast to the Indians, who from time immemorial had definite localities where they established themselves as tribes. "But the Eskimo does not follow that mode of life to the same extent," Stewart went on,

And so far as I know he has not laid claim to aboriginal rights or title to his land. He is established in Aklavik, which is probably the best settled district where the Eskimos congregate, has established his home there, and undoubtedly through right of tenure could lay claim to that particular locality; but there is the whole of that immense territory in the north, over which the Eskimos roam, and to which, just recently, owing to the very great increase in the price of fur, the attention of the white man has been directed.

He is trading with them, and is bringing his mode of trade and of life amongst them; there is more contact being had today than ever before with the Eskimo tribes in the north.

Arthur Meighen still refused to admit that white men were a threat to the Inuit. Canadians had moved in and taken over the territory of the Indians and therefore had to make terms with them. But Canadians were not taking over the Inuit's land; and the need for a treaty with these people did not arise. "He is in free possession of his territory," Meighen said of the Arctic hunter and trapper. "It may be he now has facility to sell what he could not sell before, but in so far as that is concerned, it has helped him, and ... "

Stewart interrupted to point out that a serious situation would arise if the government got into a dispute over the sale of the territory. "I would not cross the bridge till I got to it," said Meighen.

A year brought a significant change in the government's attitude to the Inuit. On 10 June 1925 Charles Stewart admitted in Parliament, "The Eskimos have not received very much attention at the hands of this government, but we are becoming more alive to our responsibilities in that regard."

The Opposition was not too happy about what these responsibilities might entail. M.J. Ward asked, "Is it the policy of the government to continue the legal, social and moral supervision of the Eskimos that has been carried on in the past? Is it considered wise to interfere with their traditional customs and habits, or is this not a lot of money spent to very little advantage?"

"It is quite likely," Stewart admitted, "that if it were possible to allow the natives to live in their own traditional way they would be just about as well off, although possibly the missionaries would not agree with that view; they would hold that the Eskimos ought to be given religious teaching. But you cannot keep out the white man; he will come in contact with these people, and we must take precautions to avoid such harrowing occurrences as have taken place among them from time to time in the past." Stewart was here referring to stories he had heard of whole tribes being wiped out by epidemics and of many dying from starvation. In view of this alarming situation, R.A. Hoey wanted to know if the Inuit were recognized as wards of the government. Stewart, with apparent reluctance, replied, "I am afraid we have to say they are. Were it not so, we could not very well go in and try them and imprison and execute them for infraction of our laws, as we have been doing."

So the Canadian government had, even if unofficially and unconstitutionally, assumed responsibility as guardian of the Inuit. As a surrogate father to the natives of the north, the government was remarkably ignorant about the people in its charge. "The territory is so remote that we know very little about it," the minister of the interior admitted in the House on 10 June 1925.

At this time the general belief was that the numbers of Canadian Inuit were declining while those in Alaska and Greenland were on the increase. This belief was based not on any reliable population statistics but on differences in perception of the problem and in attitudes towards it on either side of the Atlantic. These differences are all illustrated in a review by Canadian ethnologist Diamond Jenness of a statistical study of the Greenland Inuit by the Italian Giorgio Carega.[4] In his study, published in 1928, Carega attributes the increase in the numbers of Greenland Inuit "partly to the improvement in the social and economic conditions brought about by the Danish government, but mainly to the admixture of European blood, which... introduces a strengthening element that raises the birth rate, lowers the death rate, and increases longevity." Whether Carega is right or not, the important point to note is that Jenness is very much more negative. There are too many other factors relevant to the inquiry, he says and he goes on to mention the onslaught of European diseases and the widespread disturbances of population before the compilation of any censuses, as examples that "the author has not weighed sufficiently and which render his theories doubtful."

This negative attitude was typical of Canadians at that time. References were made in parliament to letters and editorials in the Toronto *Globe* "pointing out the conditions under which the Eskimo are living" and arguing that famines and seasonal starvation were causing depredations of the Canadian Inuit population while these were being alleviated elsewhere by such measures as the introduction of reindeer herding. Charles Stewart was sympathetic and agreed that something should be done for the Inuit in Canada. Distress among these people occurred in the winter season, he told the House on 6 June 1928, "and sometimes whole tribes are wiped out ... On that account we are asking for larger sums for medical attention and supplies. R.B. Bennett, the Leader of the Opposition, was not opposed to that. There were only six thousand Eskimos in all, he said: "I think the minister should state to the house very frankly that he regards the Dominion's obligation to feed and clothe them to be of such importance that he will see to it that the Eskimos are properly looked after." Stewart agreed but reminded Bennett of the need for information. "The reports we receive are usually from a year to eighteen months after the occurrence ... and we do not discover there has been distress and suffering until it is too late to apply a remedy." "Usually they are all dead," said Bennett, and Stewart agreed.

The need for information included more accurate estimates of the actual numbers of Inuit in the government's care. R.B. Bennett had declared in 1928 that there were only six thousand in all. Two years later, on 31 March 1930, Charles Stewart thought there were only "over four thousand," though he admitted to being unsure about the number.

"What is the origin of these people?" asked Hugh Guthrie. "Were they originally Indian?"

"Eskimos," replied Stewart.

"Or were they Mongolian?" Guthrie went on, as if he had not heard. "Of what race are they?"

"I am afraid my honourable friend has asked me a question I cannot answer," Mr Stewart relied.

"A good deal would depend on that," Guthrie pointed out with a quick verbal lunge, leaving the fencer's "Touché" unspoken.

"There is a difference of opinion," Stewart said in a weak attempt to parry. "Many hold that they are Mongolian, but I do not think anyone can prove it."

"Some people say they are Scotch," said Charles Avery Dunning, the minister of finance and receiver general.

The government was equally uncertain about the status of the Inuit, about whether or not they were British subjects with the right to vote in elections.

They have no treaties with us [said R.B. Bennett], they have no established reserves, as the minister knows, and I think a few moments ago he used two words which describe the situation very well. He said they were nomadic tribes. How can we, having assumed it, divest ourselves of responsibility for endeavouring to treat them as settled persons in certain communities? At the moment the responsibility for providing the Eskimos with a living rests with us, and the minister recalls that at very great expense he sent an expedition to that northern country to provide them with food and me-decine, if I remember correctly, when they were not really able to make a living for themselves. I think I can safely say that they are an uncivilized class of people; they hardly live in tribes and they have not developed any form of settled life.

Stewart did not entirely agree. "They may be broken up a great deal," he said; "one can scarcely say they are in tribes."

"I was coming to that," Bennett retorted. "When we speak of them as a tribe we must remember that they have no settled communities in which they live, and I am told by those who have visited that country that during their summer they have no settled residences at all. They have no settlements in the meaning of the term as it was used by the early pioneers with respect to the Indians. These people are not civilized as we use the word civilized."

Stewart agreed: "They are not Indians as we know Indians, with chiefs and councils and all the paraphernalia which has been set up by the Indians for the management of their affairs. These people congregate in small family groups; no doubt they have leaders but apparently in discussing matters of importance with our officials they all speak each for himself ... That is one reason for the difficulty in applying the Indian Act to the Eskimo."

The main reason, however, was that the government did not know if the Inuit were Indians or not. The confusion was due, at least in part, to the fact that the Northwest Territories Act of 1905 had made no provisions for the administration of Inuit affairs, and until 1930 the NWT Council passed no ordinances that discriminated between the Inuit and the other inhabitants of the Territories. In 1924 an amendment to the Indian Act brought the Inuit under the superintendent general of Indian affairs. Unofficially the Department of Indian Affairs had been looking after destitute Inuit since about 1880 and between 1918 and 1923 had spent $31,000, mainly for education in mission schools and for medical attention at Herschel Island in the Western Arctic.[5] The department then extended its medical services to the Eastern Arctic and by 1926 provided a full-time physician for Baffin Island.[6]

Confusion remained, however, as to who was responsible for the Inuit. The commissioner of the NWT was ostensibly looking after Inuit affairs, but certain aspects of Inuit status were irritatingly unresolved. For example, to sell liquor to Indians was illegal, but if the government considered the Inuit to be non-Indian citizens of the realm then such a law should theoretically not apply to them. Technically the Inuit were entitled to all the liquor that a white man was legally allowed in the NWT, but in fact this was not the case. The director of the Northwest Territories Branch, O.S. Finnie, wrote on 21 February 1930: "Parliament has declared that the Eskimo is neither an Indian nor is he a ward of the nation. It has always been felt that he should enjoy the full status of a white man in the Territories. However, for the present it is not considered to be in the best interest of the Eskimo to issue liquor permits for medicinal purposes."[7]

When the question of the status of the Inuit eventually went to the Supreme Court in a dispute over repayment of financial aid between Quebec and Ottawa,[8] the Court ruled, on 5 April 1939, that Eskimos were in fact Indians, "a rather astonishing pronouncement," according to Montreal anthropologist Richard Diubaldo, "since everyone knows that Eskimos are not Indians but Eskimos."

By the time the Supreme Court issued its ruling, the Inuit had been brought under the wing of a new Department of Mines and Resources, created in 1936. The Bureau of Northwest Territories and Yukon Affairs became part of the Lands, Parks and Forests Branch of the new department, thus emphasizing the fact that in spite of its willingness to act as guardian of the native people of the north, the government still appeared to regard them as part of the natural resources of the region, perhaps as the nuisance part of "our property generally" in the Arctic.

For on-site administration of the Arctic islands and for upholding the precarious prize of Canadian sovereignty, the government relied mainly on the annual voyages of the Eastern Arctic Patrol. For the first four years, from 1922, the slow, aging, and unwieldy *Arctic* carried out these duties under the command of the slow, aging, but experienced Capt. J.E. Bernier. In 1926 *Beothic* succeeded the *Arctic*. For six years the government chartered this more powerful ship from Job's Sealfishing Company of St John's.[9] By then "economy" had become the watchword, and to save money the government rented space for people and freight on the Hudson's Bay Company (HBC) supply ships plying Eastern Arctic waters. It used the *Ungava* in 1932 and the *Nascopie* from 1933 until it sank off Cape Dorset in the summer of 1947.

The disadvantage of this arrangement was that the HBC controlled the movement of the ships, allowing less time in ports of call for government business, which included supplying police posts, taking censuses, recording statistics, issuing licences, handling mail, and collecting customs, fur export, and other taxes. Special services included what medical and dental care the specialized doctors and dentists on board, often among the best in the country, could give during a short stopover. In addition to transporting medical, dental, and administrative personnel, the Eastern Arctic Patrol carried increasing numbers of private scientists, scholars, and surveyors, whose work the government considered worth supporting. The well-known Group of Seven artists A.Y. Jackson and F.H. Varley, for example, were among the prominent Canadians who made the trip.

Always on board was a complement of RCMP officers, for the chief arm of administration and government on the Arctic islands was the long reach of seven or eight police detachments. The fetch of the law stretched all the way to Dundas Harbour and Craig Harbour, where no Inuit lived and few visitors ever ventured. These outposts of "G" Division existed solely to hold on to Canadian sovereignty in the High Arctic. The policemen maintained customs and post offices, collected meteorological and other scientific data, hunted and trapped foxes, and made extensive patrols by dog team and boat around their vast northern districts.[10]

During their frequent and often dangerous patrols, the police officers enforced the range of federal laws and territorial ordinances, investigated crimes, provided relief and medical aid, and brought people "outside" for treatment or for trial. They were also the government's eyes and ears. They observed and then reported on the social, medical, and economic conditions in the Eastern Arctic, and their reports, carefully read and noted in Ottawa, often stirred political controversy and even exercised considerable influence on the government's programs and policies.

By 1940, then, the Arctic Islands had been brought effectively under Canadian authority and control. The position of the Inuit majority had been secured and safeguarded, though little was being done to relieve their hard existence or direct them towards successfully adapting to the demands of modern civilization – should it ever intrude on their homeland. The free-ranging, individualistic white adventurers and entrepreneurs had been almost entirely replaced by some 100 or 150 closely regulated employees of government, business and religious organizations who lived among the native populations and served their needs. The hardships of isolation, remoteness, barren terrain and severe climate were being relieved during the interwar decades – for the whites at least – by radio broadcasts and occasional airplane visits from outside. Improved communications were bringing the Arctic Islands nearer to the outside world, and the outside world closer to the Archipelago. Despite the best efforts of its well-intentioned, early administrators, the region and its people would be hurled totally unprepared during the 1940s into the maelstrom of modernity and of world war.[11]

The best efforts of the Eastern Arctic's early administrators, however well intentioned, fell short of the ideal in the results they achieved. Because the Canadian government fixed its attention on the wealth that the Arctic's natural resources could potentially earn, it neglected the troublesome "children of the ice" for whose support it had accepted responsibility. In the Arctic, little happened between the wars. This was the time when health, education, and other services should have been introduced and gradually improved to standards comparable with those elsewhere in the country. The government could have taken steps at the same time to encourage economic development. The Inuit in turn might then have adapted their way of life to absorb these changes while retaining a continuity of evolution and a measure of control over events. But the government let them down, did almost nothing for them, initiated little.

The laissez-faire approach of the Canadian government was in direct contrast to the Danes' managerial handling of Greenland. In Greenland the people had already given up the nomadic life and settled into permanent homes. They were no longer Inuit in a strict sense, since they had intermarried with Europeans and were themselves well on the way to becoming European. But they lived as Inuit by hunting on the sea and selling sealskins, walrus hides, blubber, and some fish to the trading posts. In the south many Greenlanders earned a living from the products of a flourishing sheep industry. The hunting economy demanded a dispersed population – less than 20,000 people in more than 200 small settlements – but this made effective administration difficult and kept social services to a minimum except in the larger centres.

There were about a dozen such places on the west coast, provided with hospital, church, school, a trading store - but no police post, for such were unknown in Greenland in those days, and there was no formal legal system ... The severity of the natural environment in this remote region was tempered by a benevolent administration, a worthy forerunner of the modern welfare state. The Danish administrators and their families lived in close contact with the native people, intermarried with them, used their language and in many ways shared their community life.[12]

In Greenland the trading stores were owned and operated by the Danish government; in the Canadian Arctic the stores were privately owned, most of them by the HBC. The federal government showed unforgivable weakness in its dealings with the HBC. If it was the reluctant, if rightful, guardian of the Inuit, the HBC was the wicked uncle, eager to take charge of the innocent orphans of the Arctic in order to exploit them for monetary gain. The company had been advancing slowly into the Eastern Arctic as the whalemen were moving out. Then, around 1910, a favourable market appeared for white fox pelts, the only fur that the Inuit's Arctic habitat produced in quantity, and the HBC rushed in to exploit this demand. In 1911 it opened its first Baffin Island post, at Lake Harbour, and it followed that with others at Cape Dorset in 1913, Frobisher Bay in 1914, Pangnirtung, Amadjuak, Pond Inlet, and Blacklead Island in 1921, and Clyde River in 1923.[13]

Meanwhile other companies were supplying agents like Wilfrid

Caron, Hiram Pitchforth, and the luckless Robert Janes, whom the Inuit murdered. These small independent companies were also in the business of providing the new necessities of life to the Inuit in return for furs and skins. The boom in fox pelts lasted well into the 1920s, encouraging still more interest in the lucrative trade. The Arctic Gold Exploration Syndicate, backed by the British and managed by Henry Toke Munn, supplied a number of posts on Baffin and Bylot islands. In 1923 the HBC swallowed this business Jonah, and it went on expanding, to Arctic Bay in 1926, Dundas Harbour in 1934, and Fort Ross in 1937. Its only major rival in the Eastern Arctic, the Sabellum Trading Company, gave up in 1927, when Hiram Pitchforth died. The HBC bought out all the others and made itself the commercial caudillo of the Eastern Arctic.

The powerful sway that the traders held over the Inuit was far from beneficial or benevolent. The government was aware of what was going on and promised to act on behalf of the Inuit but in effect did nothing. For example, Charles Stewart, the minister responsible for the native people, said in the House on 7 April 1924, "I think it is wise for us to exercise some oversight over the Canadian tribes, because as my honourable friend knows, if you do not protect them, the traders, who are not particularly anxious about the welfare of the native Eskimo, get in amongst them and debauch them, carry in liquor and exercise an evil influence among the tribes, and then the responsibility is ours. The Eskimo problem is beginning to be a rather serious one for us to handle, and we are establishing police posts at various points along the coast to protect the Eskimo and preserve their game."

But the minister did not fool MP Arthur Lewis. Lewis said in reply that his observation was "that instead of protecting the Eskimo we seem to be protecting the traders, or those who go in there. We try to enforce law and order among the Eskimos, who have never been trained along that line, and when they come into contact with the law they pay the extreme penalty whereas with their grey matter and mental development they are perhaps not able to appreciate justice in the same way we do."

The police, whom the government sent into the Arctic "to protect the Eskimo and preserve their game," were in fact on the side of the native people and defended them against the malicious greed of the traders. As early as 1927 the reports that RCMP officers sent to Ottawa from the Arctic posts condemned the traders' practice of forcing Inuit to trap in areas where fur was plentiful but food was scarce. The police continued their criticism through the war years, accusing the traders of paying low prices for furs and overcharging for supplies, especially for ammunition.

Internal criticism, such as that of the RCMP, could be shelved, filed away, forgotten. Not so the mounting censure from outsiders, from high-ranking military personnel and foreign journalists. The government immediately passed these complaints to the HBC while simultaneously making excuses for the traders. "We are inclined to feel," wrote R.A. Gibson, the deputy commissioner of the NWT, "that many visitors to the Eastern Arctic, particularly those who are only there for a short time and who are provided with all the necessities of life and many of its comforts, have all too little appreciation of the difficulties which the natives must encounter in eking out an existence in a country which has such limited and unreliable wildlife resources."[14]

But the censure continued. In the summer of 1943 the government sent observers on the annual cruise of the Eastern Arctic Patrol with instructions to check the traders' books to see if the Inuit were receiving a fair return for their furs.[15] But the HBC was not so accommodating that year. It refused to hand over "the usual information on game conditions, prices paid, debt and relief, etc., on orders direct from Winnipeg."[16] It had decided the previous year, apparently without letting government officials know, that "it would be better for all data to be supplied by the Winnipeg office."[17]

R.A. Gibson argued that the "need for regular, periodic surveys of the wild life resources and native trading through carefully prepared questionnaires is of prime importance in the administration of Eskimo affairs." Although the information that the HBC supplied from Winnipeg was "invaluable," nevertheless the officer in charge of the Eastern Arctic Patrol was entitled to "first-hand information at any trading post for the confident[ial] use of this Administration."[18] The HBC's fur trade manager "fully appreciated" the need for the surveys and questionnaires but suggested that "such questionnaires should be left at the post and picked up the following year, or alternatively sent out by some subsequent mail in cases where such facilities might exist."[19]

The Canadian government meekly accepted the HBC's defiance. A couple of months later Gibson reported to the commissioner of the RCMP: "Owing to administrative changes in the Hudson's Bay Company the information collected by the patrol will no longer be available from post managers and others connected with the fur trade."[20] The HBC, as usual, had got its own way, and the northern administration accepted the sop offered by the company. A report, wrote Gibson, "is compiled in Winnipeg from information received from district managers which is embodied in a statement officially furnished to this Administration by the Manager of the Fur Trade Department." But Maj. McKeand, the officer in charge of the Eastern Arctic Patrol, remained sceptical. He wrote to Gibson: "The Statement on (a) country produce; (b) barter prices, and (c) relief costs for the Eastern Arctic 1942–43, supplied by the Manager, Fur Trade Department, Hudson's Bay Company may be more official but no more reliable than the statements of former years."[21]

The official but careless guardian of the Inuit let the wicked uncle have his way with them. The children of the Arctic thus suffered neglect at the hands of those who should have had their welfare uppermost in mind and exploitation at the hands of those who showed few scruples about what they were doing. The actual degree of both the neglect and the exploitation became widely known only when the Second World War sent American and Canadian military personnel and civilians to the Arctic. The main task of these wartime incomers was to build and operate a chain of strategic northern air bases en route to Europe, code-named the Crimson Air Staging Route. "Airmen and construction workers returned with first-hand descriptions of the Eskimo settlements they had visited," Jenness wrote, "and foreign newspapers and magazines published accounts of Canada's north that reflected little credit to its administrators. High officials in Ottawa began to take notice."[22] They appointed Lieut. T.H. Manning, RCNVR, to act as "a sort of Liaison Officer in connection with joint defence projects in the Hudson Bay area," to relay complaints to Ottawa and to respond to American criticisms.[23]

Members of the US forces and civilian workers were "extremely critical of Eskimo living conditions and the apparent lack of interest of the Canadian government in them."[24] The Americans asked, for example, why the Canadian authorities were doing nothing about scabies, why they had done nothing to educate the Inuit, and why they allowed traders to exploit them. Citing a specific case, the Americans wanted to know why medical personnel had igored a meningitis epidemic at Southampton Island for at least two weeks and why a US plane had then to take in the sulphanilamide. Maj. D.L. McKeand of the Bureau of Northwest Territories and Yukon Affairs described the American statements as based on gossip and rumour, and the HBC dismissed them as malicious tattle by over-zealous, uninformed humanitarians who did not appreciate the harsh reality of life in the Arctic.

But the Canadian government took the criticisms more seriously and asked its geographer, J.L. Robinson, to inquire into them. In his preliminary report and recommendations Robinson outlined six problems that he saw in the Eastern Arctic.[25] The Americans had already raised most of them.

1. Controlling the contact between the native and the inevitable approaching civilization.
2. Lack of education among the Eskimo.
3. Lack of proper medical attention for the Eskimo.
4. Decrease in the number of caribou and the resulting winter clothing problem.
5. Insufficient contact of the administration with summer and winter conditions as they actually exist in the north.
6. Lack of organized information on the resources of the Eastern Arctic and lack of present or long-range planning for the land and its prople.

One of the critical problems in the north was the Inuit's lack of preparation to meet and fit into advancing civilization. The native people appeared to have two choices: preserve their traditional nomadic way of life and retreat farther and farther into less accessible and less favoured areas, or gradually change their way of life and prepare themselves "to play a part in Outside civilization." Robinson believed that some compromise was probably the best solution. But regardless of the solution, the northern administration had to take steps immediately either to preserve what remained of Inuit culture or to prepare the people for further advances of the white man.

The lack of decision about the future of the Inuit spilled over into educational policy-making. The dilemma for education was whether to provide central schools and take the children to them or to try to bring teachers to the children. To accept the first meant taking children from their home environments and removing them completely from their traditional way of life. Yet to accept the second was impossible, in view of the scattered, nomadic existence of the people. Health services had to grapple with the same dilemma, especially where tubercular patients had to be evacuated to the south for protracted stays in sanatoria.

Obviously the cultural system in the Arctic was not functioning well. Game resources, which provided both energy and materials, were declining, and the substitute store-bought foods were nutritionally inadequate. Day labour at the air bases proved not only less arduous than hunting and trapping but financially more rewarding. The more the Inuit were attracted to wage earning, the more strains and stresses appeared in the antique structure of traditional society. The unstoppable onrush of change in the Arctic alarmed and alerted the government in Ottawa:

In 1945 it transferred the care of both Eskimo and Indian health to the

Department of National Health and Welfare; and officialdom for the first time publicly recognized the Eskimos as citizens of the Dominion by distributing among them the family allowances to which a bill enacted a few months before had entitled all Canadian citizens. A year later the Commissioner of the Northwest Territories ... retired, whereupon the government ... appointed in his place Dr H.L. Keenleyside, a ranking official of the Department of External Affairs ... A freshness then began to permeate the Canadian Arctic. At long long last the winds of change were stirring.[26]

CHAPTER ONE

Supplying Shelter

TO 1945: TRADITIONAL SHELTER

"The abundance of seals found in all parts of the sea," wrote nineteenth-century anthropologist Franz Boas, "enables man to withstand the inclemency of the climate and the sterility of the soil."[1] By "man" Boas meant the Inuit of the Eastern Canadian Arctic, "the people of the seal," as Asen Balikci called them. The flesh of the seal, Boas wrote, was "almost the only food, and their blubber the indispensable fuel during the long dark winter." The skins of seals furnished "the material for summer garments and for the tent." Winter garments came from the heavy skin of the caribou, which Boas described as "scarcely less important" than the seal. "That the mode of life of the Eskimo depends wholly on the distribution of these animals will therefore be apparent, for, as already observed, they regulate their dwelling places in accordance with the migrations of the latter from place to place."

Thus the environmental conditions that determined the location of seals and caribou determined the distribution of the Inuit. In spring the seals basked in the sunshine almost everywhere along the coast and provided a good supply of food and skins. As the season advanced the ice broke up in the rivers; then the char made their way down to the sea. The Inuit moved to camps at the heads of fiords to catch the char in the shallow rivers. In July, when the snow disappeared, the Inuit moved inland to hunt caribou. The supply of food increased with the arrival of the walrus, the ground and harp seals, and the birds that left the country in the winter. As fall came and the weather grew colder, the Inuit became more dependent on the seal again, the ringed seal that lived permanently in Arctic waters. The small bays froze over, and the hunters caught the ringed seals at the edge of the newly formed ice. As the floating ice consolidated, only a few holes occurred in places where icebergs, moved by tides and strong currents, prevented the sea from freezing. Along the south coast of Baffin Island in particular "tidal currents coursing among the island-and-bay mazes" kept open lanes of water "and thereby increased the winter hunting grounds."[2] North of Cumberland Sound, however, the tides were weaker, and their effect on the ice was less noticeable. For a short time these openings in the ice offered the best hunting for the Inuit. In autumn the fiords and the narrow channels between the islands were the favourite haunt of the seal. Then later in the season they moved to more open sea where they scratched breathing holes in the ice. During the winter Inuit families came together in large camps, sometimes referred to as villages, to hunt the seal at these breathing holes. Thus the configuration of the coastline, the strength and direction of winds and tides and currents, and the seasonal movements of seal and walrus, caribou and fish controlled the annual distribution patterns and migration of the Inuit.

In following this way of life the Inuit lived in two types of dwelling: tents in summer and houses in winter. Any permanent house was called an igloo or iglu – Inuit orthography has no letter O – whether it was built of snow or of anything else; a tent was a temporary dwelling and known as a tupik. The Inuit used snow houses almost everywhere in the Eastern and Central Arctic, including Baffin Island, the Melville and Ungava peninsulas, Southampton Island, and Keewatin.[3] The Greenlanders seldom used them, except in the northwest, and west of the Mackenzie they were rare, except as temporary shelters.

In addition to constructing the well-know igloo, built of blocks of hard-packed snow, the Inuit also built houses out of stones, including the bones of whales if they happened to be handy, and adding a thick, insulating layer of turf outside the walls and over the roof. These stone and bone structures were once the most widespread of all Inuit dwellings except tents. They were found almost everywhere along the entire Arctic coast, on the mainland, and on the islands as far north as they go, including even the far limits of Ellesmere Island, the Sverdrup and Banks islands, and the Parry group, where the Inuit used to live.

The interior arrangements of all Inuit dwellings followed the same general patern. The cold-trap entrance tunnel ended in a small space, very often hardly more than room to stand in. On each side was a small bench or platform, with the stone lamp on one, the supply of meat on the other. At the back the sleeping platform, six or more feet wide, extended across the width of the house, one and a half to two feet above the level of the floor. There could be a small window of ice or seal intestines fitted above the doorway; otherwise the dwelling was in darkness save for the light from the seal-oil lamp. Stone and bone houses were warm and comfortable, for the thick layer of sod outside the walls was a good insulator and the lamps gave plenty of heat. But the Inuit, warmly dressed in caribou skin clothing, had to keep the snow houses at freezing point to avoid snow melt. Once the igloos became wet in the warmer temperatures of spring, the people moved into tents for the summer.

In the Eastern Arctic the Inuit sometimes put the summer tent to use as a lining inside the winter snow house, keeping it stretched out by thongs that passed through the walls and were held secure outside by toggles of wood or bone. This artifice allowed the interior temperature to be raised considerably without melting the walls of the igloo, to which a layer of cold air, trapped between them and the skin lining, afforded adequate protection.

In summer, skin tents were used right across the Arctic, from northeastern Greenland to Siberia. The skins were of caribou or seal, usually with the hair scraped off to lighten the weight. The tents were made in two main patterns: one ridged, the other conical. Of these the rectangular ridged tent was by far the more common and found almost everywhere in the Arctic. Poles of driftwood, a valuable possession in themselves, supported both types of tent. The sleeping area was not raised above the floor as in the snow house but was marked off from the rest of the floor space by a pole, a row of small stones, or merely by the front edge of the bedding. Otherwise the internal arrangement was much the same as in the igloo: the lamp at one side of the entrance, the meat supply at the other. Bags and boxes lined the walls. They were full of clothing, men's tools and other equipment, and women's sewing outfits. Outside, a ring of heavy stones held down the edges of the tent, for pegs would rarely hold in the rocky ground. These stone tent rings are still found in the Arctic, persistent evidence of those former campsites where the Inuit spent the long, cool, foggy days of summer.

The ecologically determined hunting and fishing way of life and the use of igloo and tent that was an integral part of it prevailed in the Eastern Arctic until the Second World War. Changes there had been. A trading post had become the centre for the few hundred Inuit who lived in each local area. These people now came to the settlements for longer or shorter stays in the summer, to meet the annual supply ship, to work as stevedores unloading the ship, and to do most of their trading. For those who had become more heavily involved in trapping, the winter distribution was determined more by the presence of foxes than of seals. It was to the traders' advantage to keep these Inuit trapping over as wide a territory as possible, and to this end they were dispersed in small camps along the coast. These camps were usually located where hunting conditions were favourable, so that the Inuit were able to supply themselves with most of their own food and clothing. But where hunting conditions were unfavourable, the traders had to grubstake the trappers who worked for them. For a small number of Inuit the year-round distribution had become fixed to places where the public and private institutions of the white man offered opportunities for permanent employment. These men were the post servants and interpreters, but at the end of the Second World War very few Inuit like these lived in the Eastern Arctic settlements.[4]

1945–59: LIVING IN SETTLEMENTS

Migration to the Settlements

The ecological changes of the war years, and in particular of the years immediately after the war, brought about changes in Inuit society and material goods. The decline of the caribou led to greater dependence on imported clothing. The decline in foxes forced Inuit more and more into unfavourable hunting areas and increased their dependence on food supplied by the traders. The disastrous post-war collapse of the world market for fur caused the purchasing power of the Inuit to decline drastically and made them more dependent on family allowances and other forms of relief. These changes, together with the provision of improved medical and educational facilities, gradually ramified throughout the Inuit cultural system and eventually affected the distribution of the more dependent Inuit by making the settlements increasingly attractive. Christensen argues from his knowledge of Greenland that the same difficulty that Greenland experienced before the improvement in the fisheries was now besetting the economy of the Canadian Inuit. This was that while the economy demanded that the Inuit live scattered along the coasts, many other forces sought to gather them into "colonies."[5] The colonies attracted Inuit not only because something was always happening there or because they held out the possibility of earning money, but because the institutions, the schools, the missions, and the health authorities wanted to have the Inuit more handily in their vicinity.

These developments set in motion a slow but perceptible flow of

Inuit families towards more or less permanent residence in the settlements. Later, as the pace of building and provision of services accelerated, the flow towards the settlements became a riptide. In many communities families made the momentous move from nomadic to sedentary living in stages. Often the children were the first to leave, sent to a residential school in a settlement while their parents remained in camp.

Most observers, like Hugh Brody, feel that the administrators put great pressure on the Inuit to move.[6] The white men were anxious to draw people into the settlements and used pressures that, in Brody's words, "were informal and diverse, both as attractions (medical service, housing, proximity to store and church) and threats (no camp schools, illness in the camps)." One Inuk summed up his own experiences this way: "I have heard some opinions. Some say that in those days it was better, living in the camps, when there were not many people, even though it was sometimes difficult to get food. That is one opinion. Another opinion is that it is a lot better living here. I myself think it used to be much better in the camps. So long as the prices at the store were all right, so long as it was possible to sell fox skins and seal skins and then buy all that we needed for camp life. Then it was really good to be there."[7]

The RCMP, watching the changes in the Inuit way of life at close quarters, became increasingly unhappy with the situation. The Inuit tried to adapt the ways of the southern Canadians whom they encountered in the settlements, but in the early stages of the transition from nomadic camps to permanent villages the attempt was unsuccessful. Housing was one aspect of the failure. In the settlements the Inuit found that new materials, the abandoned scrap of the invading culture of white North America, were available for the construction of new homes. As early as 1952 the RCMP reported: "The Frobisher Bay natives have accepted too much of the white man's civilization which does not fit well into their life, so instead of living in the clean snow house of the native they live in the squalor of a poor white man."[8]

This is RCMP romanticism. The snow house of the native was rarely clean. The French adventurer Gontran de Poncins, who lived with the Eastern Arctic Inuit just before the Second World War, had no such illusions. He described the igloo as a "witch's cave black on one side with the smoke of the lamp and sweating out on the other the damp exudation caused by the warmth of lamp and human bodies."[9] De Poncins "was too newly come from Outside to see in the igloo anything but filth: the charnel heap of frozen meat piled on the ground behind the lamp; the gnawed fish-heads strewn everywhere;

the sordid rags on the lumpish flesh, as if these Eskimos had worn their party clothes to the Post and were revealing their true selves, the maculate bodies they covered with skin and fur to hide the truth from the Whites."

In moving into the settlements the Inuit were in fact merely exchanging the squalor of the native snow house for that of a poor white man. And not all the "Whites" were blind to the truth. The welfare teacher at Cape Dorset in 1951, for example, recommended that "some authority be granted to have these homes done away with unless they met a required standard."[10] In many cases these houses were "most dreadful places."[11] Descriptions include epithets like "dirty and stinking" or "highlight of dirt,"[12] "filthy and not fit for humans to live in" or "small, dirty and stinking."[13]

In these circumstances the RCMP responsible for the people of the Arctic could no longer maintain silence. In 1951 Insp. H.A. Larsen, the officer commanding G Division, wrote a devastating letter to the commissioner of the RCMP. "Conditions generally are appalling," he charged. "Never has there existed so much destitution, filth and squalor as exists today, and in the opinion of some people the condition under which some natives live is a disgrace to Canada, surpassing the worst evils of slum areas in cities. Bad sanitary and economic conditions are gradually undermining the health of these people and if not checked will ultimately result in their extermination."[14]

Larsen was nothing if not forthright. Year by year, he continued, the Inuit were becoming more poorly dressed in store-bought clothes that were inadequate for the rigours of the Arctic climate. They did not even "begin to compare with native skin clothing," with caribou and sealskins. The Inuit were substituting rubber boots for sealskin footwear. They sold the sealskins to traders or made them up into clothing "in substantial quantities" and either donated it to the missions or exchanged it with other white residents "for some very small remuneration perhaps in the way of tobacco and cigarettes or some trinket."

Not only had clothing deteriorated but housing conditions were also steadily worsening. Many houses were made from discarded box boards and pieces of burlap or canvas or other waste materials. The accumulation of filth inside the houses was "indescribable."

James Cantley, on behalf of Arctic Services, replied to Insp. Larsen's charges in a memorandum dated 20 November 1951.[15] He pointed out that Larsen's report appeared to deal primarily with his observations in the Eastern Arctic that year, which "must of necessity have been confined to the settlements." They could not therefore have taken in "the regular native camps." In fact, Larsen had based his report not only on his own observations but on detachment reports submitted to G Division headquarters "for quite a number of years now." These reports had "stressed the appalling state of affairs occasionally," and all had been sent to the administration. So the administration should have been aware of everything in Larsen's harshly critical report. Cantley argued, however, that conditions around posts at ship time were not typical of conditions at Inuit camps in the country. "Very often, natives who come in at shiptime do not bring in their tents and other camp equipment but use any temporary shelter they can erect for the few days they are there." Therefore the statement "Conditions generally are appalling. Never has there existed so much destitution, filth and squalor as exists today" was a "gross exaggeration." However, Cantley did admit that "overall conditions among the Eskimos are not by any means as good as they might be, particularly now that their only important marketable commodity has dropped so much in value." However, "many well-fed, well-clothed people are still to be seen in the worst places."

Cantley replied to Larsen's specific complaints not by denying them but by explaining why they existed. As he said, Larsen's report was similar "to others we receive from well-meaning people who look at Eskimo problems from a 'purely humanitarian point of view' but do not go very deeply into causes or effects." So it was true, Cantley admitted, that Inuit were using more imported clothing, but this was because in the Eastern Arctic few natives had access to caribou skins with which to make winter clothing. Caribou had been unobtainable in Quebec for many years, and in Baffin Island a closed season was in effect and the Inuit were unable to kill any. Only on the west side of Hudson Bay and in the Western Arctic were caribou available. The Inuit had no choice but to get what clothing they could from the stores. As for sealskins, the Inuit considered them unsuitable for winter clothing. During the summer, too, the Inuit had come to prefer imported clothing, which, "although perhaps less picturesque and more expensive than native clothing," was probably more adequate. Cantley believed that oilskin clothes and rubber boots provided more protection while working in boats and along the shore in all kinds of weather.

It was true too that housing conditions were rapidly deteriorating. The new homes that the Inuit chose to build for themselves were no longer confined to the settlements but began to replace traditional snow houses in the winter camps as well. The RCMP reported from Iqaluit in 1956 that homes in the winter camps were "permanent ones, composed largely of a wooden frame and walls of canvas, sealskin and tundra cut in five inch layers. Inside they are dark, rather dirty in some instances, restricted in size, heated but seal-oil lamps, but fairly well suited to the needs of the Eskimos who pursue hunting and trapping."[16] This type of home was general in Baffin Island. On the south coast the "homes of practically all natives visited were tents, reinforced with scrap lumber. The floors were also of scrap lumber ... Fair natural lighting was used by having seal gut windows and in many cases, real glass."[17] In visiting all but two of the Inuit camps in the Cape Dorset area plus the camp at Aberdeen Bay in the Lake Harbour area, the RCMP officer from Lake Harbour "observed a great many Eskimo homes. In nearly all instances the houses consisted of canvas reinforced with wood and cardboard."[18] In the Cumberland Sound area all Inuit "lived in tents made of either seal skin or duck and lined with moss which serves as a good insulation."[19]

The RCMP officers who made these reports were often less negative than the Cape Dorset welfare teacher. "In most cases the homes were satisfactory," said the Lake Harbour police.[20] And at Pangnirtung the police considered sealskin tents insulated with moss to be sufficient for the Inuit's needs.[21] The RCMP used the skin tent of the Inuit to develop certain types of double-walled tents that provided "effective accommodation once properly framed with wooden members and properly floored and banked."[22]

Throughout the 1950s the winterized tents and the wood-frame, insulated, canvas homes replaced the traditional Inuit snow houses. By 1958 the snow house was "fast dying out. Both at Frobisher Bay and Lake Harbour only tents and wooden houses ... [were] used."[23] That year five "permanent snow igloos were seen in the Cape Dorset area," but a year later no Inuit were living in snow houses.[24]

Several factors account for the abandonment of the snow house. The Inuit perceived it to be inferior because it differed from the new house of the white man in materials and construction technique and in the domestic manufactures used in the interior. In the same way the Inuit abandoned the sealskin tent. "There are still not as many skin tents being used as could be," the RCMP reported in 1955, "and this is certainly not due to the fact that there has been any shortage of seals. In the district only the poorest Eskimos live in skin tents and it appears to be a matter of prestige to own a duck tent."[25] The Inuit preferred duck tents because the white men used them. So with the interior of their tents. One thing that southern Canadians noticed in particular was "the way in which the Eskimos tended to copy the interior arrangements in the houses of the NSO [Northern Service Officer] and the Technical Officer and then after a short period to go ahead on their own and add new things."[26]

Other factors involved in the abandonment of the snow house included its discomfort, coldness, and lack of space, though on these points opinions differ. A Pelly Bay woman told Ulli Steltzer: "An igloo is easier to keep up than a house. I don't remember ever being cold or uncomfortable in one. When it got too old and you had to patch it up every day, you just went ahead and built a new one."[27] Whether or not an igloo was uncomfortably cold depended more than anything on what its occupants wore. Living in an igloo was a "strenuous mode of life," one observer noted in 1948, but healthy enough if you were dressed for it.[28] It called for warm clothing inside and out because of the freezing-point temperature. In the days when the Inuit had lots of caribou skins for warm clothes and sleeping robes an igloo was a satisfactory home, but to live in one in "white man's clothes ... [was] slow suicide."[29] Even in the late 1940s many Inuit were already wearing unsuitable clothing: "cotton dresses, part-wool shawls, loose-knit sweaters that ... [did] not resist the wind."[30] For people so poorly dressed an igloo was always cold and damp. This was a factor in the high rates of tuberculosis and bronchial troubles and one of the main causes of infant mortality.

The well-being of children was another point the Inuit mentioned in their arguments for abandoning the snow house. Even the woman who spoke approvingly to Ulli Steltzer about living in one added: "Now, with seven kids, I don't think I'd ever want to live in an igloo again. The children have never known to live in one, and the space of a house is important. Even three bedrooms are not enough for us now." And a group of Inuit told the RCMP that a permanent igloo was "sufficient for an adult, but too cold for small children."[31] This group intended to get a tent in the future. The winterized tents were warmer, the Inuit said, because one could use stoves in them along with the native seal-oil lamps.[32]

Unfortunately the lack of fuel forced the Inuit to use their stone lamps most of the time, and the tent became black and greasy. When fuel did become available for stoves it made this situation worse. More fuel was needed to heat the tents, and the more kerosene the Inuit used, the more "soot and smudge" there were to blacken clothes and bedding. Further, the floorboards of the tents became "saturated with all manner of stuff," and it was common to find old skins, rags, remains of partly consumed meat, and bones of animals strewn about.[33] The lack of water made it impossible to wash out the tents as often as conditions would ordinarily demand. The snow houses of earlier times had not needed any washing: just a little scraping once in a while. If they became too dirty, the Inuit could abandon them as often as necessary and build new ones without much trouble. But the winterized tents were permanent fixtures for the long winter season. The Inuit family had to live in the same tent for all that time, filthy or not. The welfare teacher at Cape Dorset often had arguments with local Inuit on the relative merits of snow house and winter tent but never could convince the Inuit that the snow house was better. "When I have spoken to Eskimos here about life in a good snow house being better and more comfortable than in a winterized tent they argue and say that the tent is better, but I feel that this is because they never see a good snow house here."[34]

The art of building good snow houses was dying out as more and more Inuit turned to winterized tents and wood-frame construction homes. The HBC stopped stocking snow knives. It said that the Inuit didn't want to buy them, and so they didn't order them. The welfare teacher at Cape Dorset commented that if the sale of snow knives had stopped, there would be no more good igloo-builders after the present generation of experts died.[35]

So the Inuit gave up the sealskin tent and the snow house of their ancestors and drifted into the settlements where they built themselves homes of sorts from whatever scrap material came to hand. Then a new set of problems appeared. For when throngs of unsatisfactory dwellings are crowded together the housing conditions become a social issue. The problems of community responsibility first surfaced at Iqaluit.

The Rise of Iqaluit

The US Air Force had attracted Inuit labour to Iqaluit but failed to provide accommodation for either single or married Inuit. The Royal Canadian Air Force, as the controlling authority, allowed the Inuit to camp in tents or shacks or snow houses on the beach within the limits of the air base. Hefty supplies of scrap lumber were available, and many Inuit built themselves shanties, sometimes with competent advice but more often without. Large quantities of rejected food were also on hand, and the Inuit became regular visitors to the garbage dump. "All of this has resulted in a situation that is really quite deplorable," wrote the chief of Arctic Division, Northern Affairs and National Resources, in 1955. "Most people who go in and see it for the first time are shocked, but it seems that most of us get over the feeling of shock on account of such things as soon as we become familiar with them and accept them as every day."[36]

Two years later a report to the Northern Administration and Lands Branch of Northern Affairs described the conditions at Iqaluit that no longer shocked those who had become familiar with them. "This relatively large permanent settlement uses the same primitive methods that may be tolerable for small detachments," wrote Dr J.A. Hildes. "Water is from a stream, delivered to indoor tanks for gravity feed in individual houses, untreated and apparently untested. Garbage is dumped. Waste water drains on to the ground near or underneath buildings. Human waste is taken by honey buckets to local pits within the townsite. It is obvious from these remarks that these arrangements are considered grossly inadequate and potentially dangerous."[37] "Our primary objective," wrote Doug Wilkinson, then a Northern Service Officer at Iqaluit, "should be to work for the day when Eskimos can drive DNA [Department of Northern Affairs] bulldozers through the present base village and obliterate all memory of the squalor and filth it holds."[38]

The government's answer was to move the Inuit away from the Iqaluit air base and resettle them in a new townsite to be built three miles away at Apex Hill. Work began in 1955 with the construction of seven new houses. Within a year the difference between the "newly built frame construction houses erected by the government" and the "shacks in the village near the Air Base" was striking.[39] By then the Inuit families living in the houses built by the government "had a taste for a new kind of living, more commensurate with their changed way of life to a wage earning existence."[40] Gradually all the Inuit at the air base came to look favourably on the idea of moving to the Apex Hill townsite "and living in small houses in the same way as 'our' Eskimos."

By September 1955 the nursing station at Apex Hill was complete. On 1 November the school opened, with 9 pupils from the families who lived at the new town and 24 from those who lived in the village near the air base, the former Inuit camp of Ikaluit. On 29 November an anonymous official noted with obvious pride that "the initial construction program for 1955 ... was completed with the result that our departmental teacher, Miss Helen Wiltshire, is now teaching 33 children in the new school; the four-bed nursing station is operating with two National Health and Welfare nurses in charge; the workshop garage is being used for mechanical repairs and training, and all 7 Eskimo houses are occupied."[41]

That source of pride, the new townsite at Iqaluit, is now the almost derelict and depressing satellite community of Apex Hill that stagnates quietly in its once "beautiful site" three miles from the main town of Iqaluit across a high rocky ridge. What happened was that Iqaluit's offer of work, social services, housing, hospital facilities, and schools inevitably attracted Inuit from other parts of the Eastern

Arctic. In these feeder areas rapid depopulation began to cause concern. For example, in Pangnirtung the Anglican minister, Reverend Mr Graham, told the Eastern Arctic Patrol that "a potentially serious problem" was developing there.[42] The Inuit "had heard stories about the opportunities available at Frobisher Bay, and many of them wished to move there." On the south coast of Baffin Island the RCMP were reporting the complete abandonment of Inuit camps.[43] In three years some 200 people had left the Lake Harbour area alone, and the Anglican Church was actually considering closing its historic mission there.[44] "Eskimos are concentrating in the Frobisher Bay area too rapidly and in too great numbers to be absorbed," one government official complained. "Within the next five to ten years a good percentage of those people will be compelled to return to their original hunting grounds or become relief subjects."[45]

The age-old pattern of Inuit population distribution in southern Baffin Island was changed. Whereas almost half of the region's Inuit used to live along the deeply indented south coast, the same proportion in 1961 lived in Iqaluit: 858 out of 1,958. Whereas a fifth of the total used to live in the Iqaluit area, the same proportion lived along the south coast: a mere 406 people.

By 1958, however, the migration to Iqaluit had already reached its peak and begun to decline. The RCMP reported at the end of 1959: "It would now seem that the Eskimo migration from Lake Harbour to Frobisher Bay has now stopped. Lake Harbour has no natives who are considering leaving for Frobisher Bay, and in fact several familys [sic] are even considering returning to this settlement."[46] The other side of the hill was apparently not so green after all.

Two factors had dried and seared the lush green prospects. One was that by the fall of 1958 there was no longer, as was commonly believed, a "marked excess of jobs over employables."[47] The second was that the settlement itself, especially the Inuit village of Ikaluit, had become more and more overcrowded, filthy, and insanitary; it threatened the health of all who lived there.

So the government decided to turn this unhealthy and overcrowded village into a brand-new town. This decision resounded as a death knell round the buildings of the Apex Hill community, which the government's change of plan sentenced to serve "largely as an Eskimo Rehabilitation Centre" – that is, "as a transitional housing centre for Eskimos entering wage employment" – and also to provide "accommodation facilities for construction crews working on the new townsite."[48]

Preliminary work on converting the Augean slum of Ikaluit into the Eastern Arctic's latest "new townsite" began in 1961, with priority given to buildings for which the need was most urgent: a 20-bed hospital, a 16-room school and students' residence, and an apartment building with 120-occupant capacity. The daring design of these new buildings, some up to seven storeys high, set a new pattern of construction in Arctic Canada. Building on solid rock, as at Iqaluit, said the excited press releases, "can be substantially cheaper than building on the permafrost under the tundra. The use of relatively high-rise pre-cast concrete structures on a rock base and coupled with the shortest practical sewer and water lines, not only lowers initial costs but substantially reduces operating and maintenance costs and gives virtual freedom from fire hazard."[49]

In 1966 the final blow came to Apex Hill when the government decided to move the Hudson's Bay Company store, the school, the staff house, and other units into the new town rising in the former camp of Ikaluit. When these services moved, most of the people and their houses had to move too. This exodus occurred in 1969 and 1970, leaving the first-chosen Apex Hill to sleep through its baleful days ever since.

New Housing and the DEW Line

A program of improved housing in the Arctic became a high priority of the northern administration in the 1950s. But the cost of the houses had to be kept low enough to enable the Inuit, with their low average income, to achieve ownership within a reasonable period. The Department of National Health and Welfare "felt that a government subsidy covering capitalization or heating of the houses would be undesirable since it would enhance the Eskimo's dependence on the white man and hinder his development in the increasingly complex society of the modern Arctic."[50] In summary, the government's objective was to meet a minimum requirement of 50 square feet of floor space per person at a capital cost of not more than 20 cents per square foot per year during the life of the building and a heating cost related to the consumption of not more than two gallons of fuel a day.

Government engineers made their first attempt at approaching this standard of housing at Cape Dorset in 1956. Using white styrofoam, six inches thick and weighing only one pound per cubic foot, they built an igloo-type structure with wooden floors and a small door. The building was about 14 feet in diameter. The translucency of the styrofoam blocks allowed entry of a certain amount of light, and the heating was even less costly than the required standard of two gallons of fuel a day. The building, in the eyes of its southern designers, had the added advantage of conforming to a type of architecture basic to the culture of the Inuit, though the Inuit themselves would have preferred a more conventional southern design. Two more of these experimental houses were built in 1958. "Needless to say, these dwellings will be viewed with interest by other Eskimo people in the area," wrote the Lake Harbour police officer. "Should they prove themselves as a suitable dwelling, perhaps other Eskimos may take advantage of the Eskimo Loan Fund as a means of acquiring a dwelling of similar structure."[51]

But the "Starifome Igloos," as one RCMP officer called them, lacked the architectural flexibility required to meet most of the needs of the Inuit in the expanding settlements of the Eastern Arctic. A rigid frame unit evolved which the authorities considered more flexible, more responsive to the needs of individual families, and thus of a higher utility and efficiency in the northern environment.[52] These new houses were sheeted inside and out with plywood, insulated with three-or-four-inch rock-wool batts, and fitted throughout with a vapour barrier. The advantage of these houses was that they could be enhanced by adding a proper ventilation system (in 1961 still in an experimental stage); sanitary facilities, such as water containers, chemical or other toilets, cool storage, and compartments for meat and other foodstuffs; and a suitable stove, preferably a combination of heater and cooking stove.

A big impetus to the development of housing in the Arctic came from the DEW Line project. The DEW Line was a child of the Cold War of the 1950s. At that time an immediate concern of the American people was the defence of their borders against attack by long-range bombers. The evolution of the long-range bomber was for the average North American the most significant military development since the Second World War. In the past, distance had been an effective shield against foreign invasion, but by 1950 Americans and Canadians had come to realize that the rapid onrush of aircraft technology had overcome their shield's former protection and left their cities open to attack if war broke out. In 1952 the Summer Study Group of engineers and scientists associated with the Lincoln Laboratories of the Massachusettes Institute of Technology (MIT) concluded that enemy aircraft could easily approach the United States from the Arctic. But an adequate Distant Early Warning (DEW) system along the northern perimeter of the continent could give a four-to-six-hour warning. The Summer Study Group therefore recommended that the US Department of Defense promptly build a chain of radar stations across the Arctic using every new communication and detection technique available.

The proposed DEW Line was the third element in a complex early warning system for the defence of the continental United States. The first was the Pine Tree Line, confined to the northern boundary of the United States itself. The second was the Mid-Canada line, nicknamed the McGill Fence, which, by diplomatic agreement, Canada was to build along the fifty-fifth parallel. The United States was to build the DEW Line system along the Arctic shores. The route finally selected started in northwest Alaska, at Cape Lisburne, and proceeded eastwards, mainly along the Arctic coast, to the central Canadian Arctic. There it crossed over to the islands in the Arctic archipelago, traversed the Boothia and Melville peninsulas to Baffin Island, and finished up on the southeastern tip of Baffin at Cape Dyer. Late in 1954 the Department of Defense made the decision to proceed with construction of the whole DEW Line system, and in December it awarded a letter contract to the Western Electric Corporation.

A full study of the impact of the DEW Line on the people of the north has still to be written. Its repercussions on health, education, housing, and transport were powerful in comparison with its disappointing effect on unemployment. Transport development alone had far-reaching consequences. To areas that had been practically inaccessible the DEW Line builders brought dozens of airfields, regular aircraft service, and greatly improved water transport. These new facilities made fresh food, mail, and regular changes of personnel everyday phenomena. They also meant that teachers, doctors, traders, missionaries, and government administrators could move with much more ease than they had dreamed possible only a few years before. Obviously the pace of change in the Arctic was bound to accelerate, and the resulting problems were clear to all parties involved. The crucial question was: how much change could one expect the Inuit to absorb without the complete disintegration of their threatened cultural system or even the breakdown of their psychological stability?

Within the decade the answer to that question came loud and clear from almost every Inuit settlement in the Arctic. The changes already under way had proved too much. Cultural disintegration and psychological instability marked the Inuit indelibly in the 1960s. A prime cause was the crowding of too many people into settlements ill equipped to accommodate them safely or to provide meaningful work for them to do. The DEW Line helped bring this situation about, for it was an agent of concentration, luring Inuit away from the land and into centres of population. The Canadian government played a role in this process of change by agreeing to provide housing at all DEW Line stations for married Inuit workers. Maintenance of the houses would be the responsibility of the government, but the corporation's station chief would supply fuel and water and ensure sewage and garbage disposal without charge. Where there were no government-furnished quarters or where the number of Inuit employed exceeded the quarters available, Inuit employees would receive accommodation without charge in construction camp dwellings of the Atwell, Simpson, Janeway, or equivalent type.[53]

In the spring of 1958 the Canadian government announced its intention to build 47 Inuit houses at selected DEW Line stations.[54] But the planned program did not work out too well. Because of the late arrival of ships at northern sites, some of the materials were not delivered till late September, about the time construction had to stop because of the weather.[55] A report on 1958 construction operations noted that the east coast of Baffin Island "is notorious for the sudden impact of winter which is generally accompanied by heavy snows and severe conditions." For this reason the construction of housing at Broughton Island, Kivitoo, and Ekalugad Fiord was not even started, and the two houses at Padloping were only partly erected and then abandoned. Only the two at Brevoort Island and the three at Cape Dyer were completed.[56] Undeterred, the administration made provision in the 1959 – 60 estimates for the erection of 50 more houses at sites along the DEW Line.[57]

So two types of housing were available for those Inuit employed on the DEW Line. The first type, the "usual home," was the Atwell. This consisted of a frame covered by two layers of canvas with rockwool insulation between the double layers, an elaboration of the Inuit's own winterized tents. The floor inside was of wood, usually plywood. The Atwell homes were comfortable, well ventilated, easily heated in winter, and not too hot in summer. The second type of dwelling was the government-built duplex, "with one family living in each side of the building."[58] These duplexes were large enough to accommodate a family of four, "with ample room for sleeping, cooking and living conditions, such as sitting rooms, etc." These homes had "the best of furnishings inside." The Inuit living in two of them at Cape Dyer were in general "very satisfied with them." But two of the occupants maintained that in winter the wind blew through the building. One stated that the previous winter "he woke up on various occasions to find a snowdrift right across the foot of his bed."

The Federal Electric Corporation provided the first type of home, the Atwell, rent-free. The second, built by the government, was leased to the Inuit. Through 1959 a controversy surrounded the rent to be charged, The first figure to emerge unofficially was $75 a month, and Inuit paid this amount for the first few months. But several members of the administration considered this rent extremely high for such accommodation, so "a Treasury Board Minute was created lowering the rent officially to $20 per month, plus $2.50 per month for furniture, making a total of $22.50."[59] How the housing authorities arrived at this figure, however, was far from clear, and by the end of the summer of 1959 many were saying that it was too low. After a lot of study to determine the actual cost of putting up the buildings, a plan was made to amortize them over a 20-year period and adjust the rent accordingly. This "would probably mean a new figure in the vicinity of $32 to $35 per month." But this new figure was also too low. At year's end the average building costs worked out at $10,840. Amortized over 20 years without interest, this figure gave a monthly rent of $45; with interest at 6 per cent, $78.[60] The administration proposed to charge the higher rent, but the decision did not meet with general approval. Among those dissenting was the regional administrator at Iqaluit.

Firstly, many Eskimos, and particularly Easterners, have not yet swung around to the view that housing is something for which one pays money. They can acquire our way of thinking in a short time, but, apart from this fact, some of the units are still not in first class shape, and we cannot charge a full rate of seventy-eight dollars per month as yet. This is no ones fault. It is the result of inherent faults in the building ... such as ill-fitting doors, missing furniture, cold floors and various other minor defects ...

In the past Federal Electric Corporation has provided married quarters in Atwell huts, or equivalent standard of housing, warm, and furnished with, at the very least, utilitarian furniture in reasonable condition. This accommodation has been rent free. Most families, but by and large not the Westerners, are content to live in this type of building, as few of them plan to make a career of DEW Line work, and in few cases do they attempt to establish themselves as permanently or as comfortably as they would were they in their own home settlements. This is another reason why it would be difficult to impose a high rental at this time. The overall conclusion then is that a serious danger of mass 'lease-breaking' would result if rents were raised to the level under consideration. They would attempt to revert to their old Federal Electric Corporation accommodation and, failing to secure this accommodation many would resign.[61]

But the administration allowed the rent of $78 to stand and within a year became concerned about the "unusually high" turnover in

Inuit DEW Line employment. If the present high rate continues, wrote the DEW Line Northern Service Officer, "recruitment for employees could be drastically affected by the high rentals."[62] He pointed out that an Inuk starting work on the DEW Line would receive a salary of $200 a month. A rent of $78 would constitute 39 per cent of his monthly income. Three-quarters of the Inuit employed on the eastern sector of the DEW Line received $300 a month or less. Most senior officials of the Federal Electric Corporation were "frankly critical of the high rentals." They argued, first, that the Department of Northern Affairs and National Resources, in its role of aiding the Inuit in the transition to a wage economy, should subsidize the housing, and, second, that the rentals charged bore no relation to the size and quality of the houses.

The quality of the houses deteriorated even further. In 1961 a government engineer inspecting the 22 houses on the DYE sector of the DEW Line – Cape Dyer, Brevoort, Durban and Broughton islands, Kivitoo, and Cape Hooper – reported that on many of the buildings no maintenance work had been done "and consequently many units were found to be in a bad state of repair. Such items as broken windows, broken and missing door and window hardware, broken entrance steps and hand rails and missing light fixtures were very much in evidence."[63] These items of necessary emergency maintenance "applied every bit as much" to houses built in 1960 as to those built in 1958 and 1959. Under the dual strains of Arctic weather conditions and Inuit negligence, even new houses in the Eastern Arctic degenerated rapidly.

1959–71: HOUSING PROGRAMS

Resale and Rental Housing

Outside the DEW Line project and the development of Iqaluit, little economic progress had yet been made in the Eastern Arctic, and the majority of Inuit in the late 1950s were still involved in their nomadic hunting and trapping livelihood. In succeeding years the tendency of Inuit families to gather in the vicinity of trading posts and church missions accelerated. The snowballing effect of the drift from the land expanded the size of the settlements and created a new problem in the Eastern Arctic: that of providing a permanent type of accommodation for the Inuit.

But the Arctic makes brutal demands on builders and buildings alike. Not the least is the daunting lack of indigenous construction materials, so that virtually every board, plank, and nail must be brought in from the south. Once the materials are there, the season when builders can get on with the job is short and hectic and interrupted by frequent spells of bad weather. Weather is a heartless enemy of building in the Arctic. Gale-force winds rage through unprotected settlements, and fierce Arctic storms batter unmercifully every structure in their path. Houses must be as sturdy and durable as nunataks to withstand the rigours of so testing a climate.

Architecture's most insidious Arctic enemy is the permafrost. Permafrost is a double-layered phenomenon. An active upper layer freezes and thaws with the seasons, and a lower layer, often deeper than a thousand feet, remains frozen. Problems arise when heat from a poorly insulated house begins to melt the frozen soil below. The house becomes scarcely more stable than that of the biblical foolish man who built his on sand. To circumvent this destabilization, the common practice in the Arctic was to build on insulating gravel pads. But the weather was too often able to sabotage this ploy. It left ice embedded in the gravel, then allowed it slowly to melt, rendering the foundations as unstable as the melting permafrost. Prefabricated buildings in particular, like those shipped up year after year from southern Canada, were highly susceptible to the movement of their gravel pads. For many unfortunate northern families the result was gaping cracks between floors and walls, ill-fitting doors, broken window frames: the kind of mischief that Inuit and engineers alike complained about.

Yet more and more Inuit families, fleeing the harsh conditions of migrant camp life on ice and tundra, moved to the more sedentary life-style in the settlements and swelled the demand for housing, any kind of housing. Unfortunately the cash income of the average Inuit family, derived largely from the sale of furs and skins and from social assistance and family allowances, was neither sufficiently stable nor large enough to allow the conventional lending institutions to play their normal role in financing house construction. The only answer, that of a government-financed and operated housing program applicable to all Inuit, was adopted in 1959. Under this program the government resold houses to the Inuit with subsidies and Eskimo Loan Fund assistance. But only those Inuit who could demonstrate that they could meet the repayments on a house of an adequate size for their families and provide minimum services were allowed to purchase a "resale" house. To those many indigent Inuit families, unable to furnish themselves with even the most basic dwelling, the government offered minimum-sized welfare housing, generally at no cost but sometimes for a small rent.

Between 1959 and 1965 the capital cost of all resale and rental housing erected in the Arctic was $2,451,800.[64] But the fruits of such expenditure were far from satisfactory. Partly responsible was the low ceiling-price specified for the buildings. Shipping and freight difficulties, lack of skilled local construction workers, and the absence of such services as electricity, sewage disposal, and water distribution in a number of settlements created additional design obstacles.

Yet the need for housing was urgent. The most practical type of building the government could supply, within the limits of time and money, was the "rigid frame" house: a one-room structure, approximately 16 feet by 16 feet, with no toilet, stove, bath, or porch. This was obviously stop-gap housing, provided in a hurry to help ease a situation that was rapidly approaching the scale of a national emergency. Larger but more expensive house types were planned for the future, but welfare housing had to be continued for those unable to afford the more costly alternative, and this welfare housing was to be the "minimum" available under the resale plan. The administration revoked this decision in 1962[65] and submitted to Treasury Board for approval a new program that would supply housing in accordance with family size to those who could not afford to buy it themselves. Treasury Board withheld its approval pending development of a new and uniform housing policy for all the ethnic groups in the north, Inuit and Indian alike. As a result the government went on supplyind the "minimum" house to those, irrespective of family size, who were unable to purchase a home.

Criticism of the housing situation in the north gathered momentum in the 1960s. In 1960 indigent families needed about 500 houses, and prospective buyers wanted about 1,000 more. That year only 138 low-cost buildings went to 27 different settlements across the Arctic.[66] And the houses themselves were inadequate, mostly one-roomed, unequipped "match-boxes,"[67] "minimum" houses, but very far indeed from what doctors in the north regarded as minimum: that is, a house with a combined living room and kitchen; two bedrooms; a small room for toilet and tub; an economical stove, properly guarded to prevent children from getting burned; a covered 40-gallon drum with a tap, raised on a stand 18 inches high, for melting ice; a two-gallon container with a tap for drinking water mounted on a fixed wall-shelf; and a small sink with a drain.[68] This was utopian fantasy when compared with the small overcrowded government houses or the makeshift ramshackle alternatives that the Inuit built for themselves. Inuit from Iqaluit complained that housing was poor in quality, cramped, and difficult to keep clean. Cape Dorset Inuit added dampness to this list. In 1961 the federal government's Committee on Eskimo Affairs attributed high mortality and disease rates among the Inuit "to the inadequate housing in which Eskimos were living."

And yet the administration did nothing for two or three years but build more and more of the houses that more and more people condemned. It undertook no major improvements while a committee of members from Treasury Board, Citizenship and Immigration, and the Northern Administration Branch prepared a report on housing. This report did not deal with the obvious shortcomings of existing houses but merely suggested ways to eliminate the discrepancies in the housing policies of separate government departments and to regulate the size of houses to be built in northern and southern Canada, even though the housing problems in the north and the south were very different.[69] A Northern Administration spokesman denied that there had been a period of stagnation in the branch's housing policy; he preferred to call it "a period of re-assessment."

While committee members deliberated, Arctic housing became more dilapidated. Overcrowding was a major problem. By 1963 as many as 12 people were living in some houses in Iqaluit.[70] The administration's own Committee on Social Adjustment became alarmed. The correlation of substandard housing with excessive rates of tubercular morbidity and infant mortality had long been established. That such housing was also contributing to the drinking, delinquency, and general social unrest in the most afflicted settlements was also becoming apparent. The Inuit themselves complained that bad home conditions were driving children out into the streets.[71] On 20 May 1964 the Committee on Social Adjustment appointed a subcommittee "to review and report upon the low-cost and welfare housing program for Eskimos." A month later the subcommittee presented a devastating report. Both the low-cost and welfare housing schemes had failed in their primary objective of providing suitable homes for the majority of Inuit who needed them. The housing was described as low-standard, too small, inefficient to heat, and unhealthy. "In administrative terms," the report said, "the Branch appears to be on the brink of disaster. In terms of health and welfare, we may already be over the precipice."[72] Further, despite "the weight of informed opinion which supports the urgent necessity for immediate and substantial improvements, insufficient concern ... [had] been generated to undertake the necessary changes."

The report attributed most of the blame for poor housing to the faulty notion that Inuit families needed or wanted houses that offered much the same amenities of space and comfort as were available in a snow house or tent. The result of this thinking was a house that was "in reality an igloo substitute, a cramped and bare building," the main advantages of which were that it was warmer and more permanent than a snow house. Yet even these benefits were questionable when improved warmth meant a fuel bill that few could pay, and permanence created a sanitation and garbage-disposal problem that was hazardous to health.

Moreover, this assessment of the Eskimo family's wants or needs is based not on anthropological or sociological data or on the experience of informed observers, but on the questionable assumption that an Eskimo family in a new home will choose *not* to change their customary ways but continue happily to order their domestic life in much the same manner as before. This assumption is a romantic fallacy. It ignores the fact that the modern Eskimo abandons the uncomfortable aspects of his former life with alacrity, if he is given the opportunity to do so. Common features of traditional Eskimo housing: lack of privacy for copulation and defecation, a shared family bed, absence of furniture, shortage of storage space, cramped, cold, poorly-lit and badly ventilated quarters were not a product of Inuit choice, they were dictated by the physical limitations of a snowhouse and a skin tent. To perpetuate these features in a modern housing program makes as much sense as to supply the Eskimo today with a paddle-wheel steamer instead of an outboard motor, or a horseless carriage instead of a truck.

The Housing Division of Northern Administration Branch rejected the subcommittee's assumption "that the small house was selected because it provided the same amenities as an igloo."[73] Its policy was to provide as many houses as possible with the money available so that any Inuit, even those living on the land, could afford to buy and heat them. The branch still clung to the conservative philosophy of its predecessors that it must safeguard at all costs "the independence of the Eskimo." To this end the Inuit should wherever possible contribute to both the capital and the operating costs of their own housing. Thus the housing provided "was always regarded as minimal," but as the Inuit level of income rose, permitting them to buy and heat a larger home, "more accommodation units could be added." Thomas and Thompson comment that this government policy, no matter how well-meaning, was changing the form but not solving the problems of substandard housing in the north. Houses were too small, sanitation facilities were inadequate, construction materials did not hold up well over a number of years, heating left a lot to be desired, and when health factors were taken into account the houses were not a significant improvement over what the Inuit had before.

In Parliament the NWT member, Gene Rhéaume, raised, often dramatically, the plight of the Inuit. On 7 November 1963 he said in the House: "Surely a country that has the courage, foresight and the money to build highways, railways and schools can now focus its energies on the shacks, tents and igloos that still exist in the Northwest Territories to blight the mind and heart of everyone who has the eye to see them." And on 13 July 1964 he quoted from a government-sponsored report:

"Inhuman" – is the way a public health nurse described in the course of a conversation, the living conditions of the Eskimos in her community. An apt description indeed. To realize this one has to shed the romantic ideas of Eskimo life, derived from children's books and movies, and walk through a settlement of Eskimo tents on a cold September night with the wind and rain lashing against the flimsy tents, babies crying and whimpering, and children and adults alike coughing inside. Outside is the stench of human and dog excretion and of rotten food scraps ...

Substantial beginnings have been made against the odds of northern logistics in the provision of health services, housing and some means of sanitation. Nevertheless, hundreds of families still live under conditions that would not be tolerated elsewhere in a more moderate climate.

The standard of housing in the Eastern Arctic was thus kept depressingly low by a combination of accelerating Inuit migration to the settlements; the logistics of supplying isolated northern communities with building materials that could only come by ship from southern Canada; the short summer supply and building season; and the perceived need to provide only that quality of housing that Inuit could themselves afford: small, minimally equipped and furnished, and ultimately overcrowded, dilapidated, inadequate, and unhealthy. In the end the only thing to be said in favour of "minimal" resale and rental housing was that it was one low grade above the ramshackle housing and winterized tents that more and more Inuit were putting up for themselves in the swelling, insanitary settlements of the Eastern Arctic.

The Eskimo Housing Program

The year 1964 marked a critical point in the development of northern housing. By then everyone was aware that the previous policy had failed: nurses, doctors, policemen, administrators, parliamentarians, and the Inuit themselves. A subcommittee appointed to study the specific problem of Inuit housing submitted its report in

June[74] and made four recommendations:

1. An immediate survey should be undertaken to determine the answers to such basic questions as: how many houses are needed? what size and what kind? where are they needed? who needs them? how many can afford to pay how much?
2. The low-cost and welfare housing program scheduled for 1964 – 65 and following years should be cancelled immediately. No more houses should be supplied to Eskimos from government sources until a new and adequate program is devised.
3. Action at a senior level should be undertaken immediately to activate the interdepartmental committee responsible for developing a new housing program. A deadline should be set for this group to produce the necessary policy recommendations.
4. The new housing policy should go into operation in time for public housing to be shipped in the summer of 1965.

The authors of the report were obviously aware of the urgency of the problem but equally unmindful of the tardiness of bureaucracy. Officials discussed the report at length with the deputy minister, who then agreed to go to Treasury Board "with a completely revamped housing program."[75] That was not till November 1964, and the official position then was that "the major changes would not become operative before 1966." But the administration assured the Committee on Social Adjustment that it would incorporate in the Treasury Board submission "a good many if not all" of the opinions expressed in the report, including those concerning the size of houses. Indeed, the administration made progress on this particular problem in 1964 when it shipped 3 three-bedroom homes to the north and scheduled 25 more for shipping in 1965. These were resale houses to cost $5,600. Houses for the welfare housing program were still of the smaller type, but the committee received assurance that in the proposed future program "housing would be more closely related to family size."

In 1965 the government announced the new Eskimo Housing Program in which it assumed the role of landlord heading a massive rental housing development. This was a manifestation of the government's new willingness to become involved in the social development of the north. Community planning in the north actually had its beginnings in 1956 and 1957, when senior government officials, together with members of McGill University, made a study of selected northern settlements.[76] They decided that the role of government was to secure people's important needs, both aesthetic and material; that effort and cost must nevertheless be considered in every aspect of northern development, whether temporary or permanent; and that within the framework of Canada's national growth the government should try to bring about a way of living more truly related to northern conditions. This attitude, which earlier administrations would have rejected as paternalism, was endorsed at a northern conference in Ottawa in April 1964. The government applied it no more readily than in the field of housing.

The objective of the 1965 housing program was to build some 1,600 houses to replace those existing structures which the territorial administrators themselves referred to as "cracker boxes" and "packing case accommodations."[77] The plan envisioned a rental structure with the rent on a graduated scale ranging from $67.50 a month to as low as $2.[78] For this the Inuit would be able to rent a house that would contain a heater, sink, water storage tank, electric fixtures, and basic furniture. They would also be supplied with a certain amount of oil, hydro-power, water, and sewage pick-up. The kitchen would be equipped with cupboards and sink and a small cooking range which, together with the space heater, operated with fuel oil. There would also be a chemical toilet.[79] In 1966 and 1967 the government shipped slightly more than 200 of these houses to Eastern Arctic settlements. All were three-bedroom units with an approximate area of 700 square feet.[80] The RCMP reported from Cape Dorset in 1967 thet "the majority" of residents living in the new-style homes took great pride in the houses and in keeping them "clean, neat and tidy."[81] Journalist Rossi Cameron paints a picture of what the rest looked like, in this case at Eskimo Point in 1969:

The newer homes lacked years of filth, but were still unclean.

When I stepped into one of the older ones, both my sense of smell and sight were assaulted ... the place reeked.

At the opposite end of the small, cluttered room two sets of iron bunk beds, with crumpled, ragged and filthy blankets hit my eyes.

Two small children, one with a torn dirty undershirt and wet, smelling diapers, the other in equally grubby cotton clothing, sat on the kitchen table, with their smiling little faces dribbling with the chocolate bars they were munching.

The mother of the house was kneeling on the heaving floor which was littered with dirty dishes, pop cans and small parts of a motor toboggan that had obviously been brought into the house to be fixed.

She was skinning a rabbit and upon my entrance she got up, wiped her hands on her cotton dress, beamed broadly at me and offered me tea.[82]

Homeowners obviously had to be educated in the ways of living in new houses. The northern administration recognized that its tenants had little understanding of the rental program or of how it worked and knew little about the houses themselves and about the fixtures and services for which they were now answerable. To the Adult Education Division of Northern Administration Branch went "the responsibility for explaining and demonstrating these new houses."[83] Topics for instruction included the use and maintenance of the services and utilities available and the care of the house. One objective was to teach Inuit families "the do's and don'ts of renting a house, acquainting them with some of the legal aspects of leasing, and with the responsibilities of tenants in caring for rented property."[84] This ambitious adult educational program also offered instruction in budgeting a seasonal income, achieving a balanced diet, home-making ("according to 'outside' standards"), child care and community cooperation. The department recruited a number of qualified people to visit the Inuit communities, hold classes, and give instruction on the new program.[85] The NWT commissioner believed that the program was very successful, "and all across the Arctic there is tangible evidence of this."

Thomas and Thompson were more critical, both of the housing and of the educational program:

It is not surprising that there have been difficulties in implementing the housing and housing education programs. We suggest that some problems of implementation are primarily due to lack of knowledge concerning Eskimo people and their reactions to government's social and welfare programs. Rapid cultural change through imposition of a "crash" program has been attempted. This approach can lead to a break-down in the program, with goals not being achieved. The changing of existing cultural patterns is drastically different from the introducing of new traits into existing cultural patterns. The former leads to alienation and anomie, while the latter can benefit both the dispensing and recipient groups.[86]

In researching their study Thomas and Thompson found that the Inuit had retained many of their traditional cultural traits, and the authors believed that the government's programs would stand a better chance of success if these traditional ways were taken into account. Thomas and Thompson point out that although the technology of the Inuit had undergone extensive changes in the twentieth century the means for using the new material elements and the social values placed on them had not undergone a concomitant change. One example was the traditional sexual division of labour in Inuit culture. The Inuit woman was the focal point of the household. When setting up a summer camp she had the responsibility of choosing a site for the tent, setting it up, and arranging its interior. She controlled the distribution of food. The husband's role was acquiring food. Thomas and Thompson argue that adult education classes directed primarily at women should recognize that while women were responsible for preparing foods, new foods could be more effectively introduced by working through the men, since they were responsible for most buying.

As for the new houses themselves, Thomas and Thompson point out that the design provided no special areas for cutting and storing meat or for working on machinery such as the skidoos and outboard motors that most Inuit considered vital to their way of life.[87] "Seals are now often stored in the bathtubs, and cut up in the living area; skidoos are repaired indoors and the dining table is used as a work bench." The architects could have provided specific areas for these jobs in the house plans, even if it meant reducing the number of bedrooms. The belief "that persons of varying ages and of different sex require separate sleeping areas is a southern Canadian belief and not an Eskimo one ... [Within] the privacy of the home Eskimos have yet to adopt Canadian standards of bedroom morality concerning sleeping arrangements. Traditional patterns of space utilization are still employed as much as possible and a greater understanding of them on the part of the designers would result in a much different internal separation of rooms in the houses."

But the Inuit themselves gave no indication that they were displeased with the houses, at least in terms of their layout. Just the opposite. The houses proved to be an irresistible attraction, especially to the women, and the Inuit abandoned more and more camps as, one after another, families migrated permanently to the settlements. "Recent movement into the settlements," Anders observed in 1968, "was always associated closely with the progress of the federal housing program."[88]

Hugh Brody describes one household he first encountered in 1971.[89] In this house lived a hunter and trapper called Kuutuq, his wife Annie, a year-old son, two small children of about 5 and 6, and a stepdaughter of 17 with an infant of her own. They all lived "in a one-room house that measured approximately twenty-five feet by eight feet and was divided by a four-foot-wide partition into sleeping and living areas. Even by the standards of contemporary settlement conditions, that house was crowded." "To the administration it appeared a squalid failure, a blight on the community, for most of the Eskimos there lived in 'better' conditions – or less conspicuous poverty. But Kuutuq and his wife were on the whole satisfied with their life; they occasionally lamented the limitations of their small house, but they preferred to continue hunting, trapping and travelling rather than concentrating on improving it."

Some of the new tenants became owners of their houses, but not many as the administration had expected. Part of the rent was credited towards the purchase price of the homes for those tenants who did desire to become house owners. But ownership was hindered by the fact that whereas tenants had fuel-oil, electricity, water, sewage, and garbage services supplied to them, owners had to assume the full cost of providing these services themselves and this could be expensive.[90]

AFTER 1971: REHABILITATION

The Inuit continued to complain about the quality of construction work on modern houses: about draughts, poor insulation, ill-fitting windows and doors; and unfortunately they continued to compare the shoddy workmanship of their homes and the excellent work that went into houses inhabited by the white people. Wally Firth, MP for the NWT, took Inuit grievances to the House of Commons in February 1975. Speaking of Iqaluit, Firth said: "70 per cent of the population is native. The Inuit live in 35 per cent of the housing, and it is housing of a poor standard. As against that, 30 per cent of the population is made up of government employees, federal and territorial. They live in 65 per cent of the housing, and it is the best housing in Frobisher Bay ... Conditions under which native peoples live are degrading. For example, in some cases more than one family lives in a two-bedroom house. The social costs of these conditions are extremely high."[91] Among the substandard housing that Firth was referring to were those "matchboxes" that survived from the 1960s, wretched dwellings, the least dilapidated of which are still inhabited by Inuit who can just manage in them.

Rehabilitation is the word one hears most frequently in connection with these old relics of the early days when southern Canadians floundered in the mud of northern housing policy. When the Northwest Territories Housing Corporation officially took over responsability for Arctic and Subarctic housing on 1 January 1974, northerners themselves, with a mandate to make available an adequate standard of housing to all residents of the NWT, took steps to rectify the errors of their predecessors in Ottawa. One such step was the rehabilitation of the older dilapidated dwellings inherited from the dark days of the housing emergency. Extraordinary Maintenance was a program introduced in 1977 with a budget of $1.3 million and aimed specifically at improving the health, safety, and fire prevention deficiencies of "older units" in the NWT.[92] Significantly, by "older units" the Housing Corporation meant houses built prior to 1974 – that is, only three years old or more.

By the mid-1970s energy conservation had become a national obsession. Most houses in the Eastern Arctic, thrown up in haste in the balmier days before oil prices started to soar through the roof, were insufficiently insulated and far from energy efficient. Some families still use over 9,000 litres of oil a year where a southern family in a comparable home might burn only a third of that.[93] By February 1979 the Northwest Territories Housing Corporation had awakened to the energy reality facing it. It announced then that it intended to develop smaller, less expensive, energy-saving houses. It would build no more five-bedroom homes and would alter the design of its three-bedroom units to reduce the area from 1,400 to 1,000 square feet.[94] At the same time it announced that it would continue to emphasize "stick-built" construction, that is, building from the ground up instead of using prefabricated sections imported from southern Canada. Builders would also erect more houses on piles sunk deep into the frozen ground, an effective but more expensive alternative to gravel pads, which the growing scarcity of gravel was making obsolete.

To pay for these and the older houses, the corporation devised a new rental structure, launched in April 1978 but not fully introduced throughout the north till late in the year. It based the new system on 25 per cent of income less a special regional cost-of-living allowance. It thus took into account an individual's ability to pay and made allowance for the wide regional variation in the cost of living. Where such crucial factors as heating costs were higher, total rent would be lower. Rents did not, however, in any way meet the cost of providing and servicing Inuit housing. For example, in northern Quebec in 1977 most Inuit paid $74 a month in rent. Services alone were estimated to be more than $300 a month. Heating fuel cost $1.15 a gallon; water, delivered by truck, more than six cents a gallon; and electricity was expensive because it was oil generated.[95]

In 1978 a statement on housing by the Inuit Tapirisat of Canada pointed out: "Two-thirds of the houses in Inuit settlements in the Northwest Territories are in need of major repair or are in condemned condition: over half the households live in overcrowded conditions, and basic community sewage and garbage disposal are drastically in need of improvement. To compound the problem the supply of new housing cannot keep pace with new family formations."[96]

Anthropologists, sociologists, ecologists, even government representatives have added their voice to such native complaints about
housing. Architects and engineers more aware of northern needs
have suggested solutions and put forward new designs better suited
to conditions in the north. At a conference of designers and builders,
held in May 1982 at Radisson in the James Bay area of Quebec,
David T. McCann of the Northwest Territories Housing Corporation
emphasized the importance of "bearing in mind the difference between urban, industrialized people and those for whom survival is
the main priority." For most native people in the Eastern Arctic,
survival was still closely linked to traditional activities, and housing
had to be adapted to these occupations.

Improvements arose, for example, from increasing the living space
and by adding an entrance porch at each doorway and an inner
porch – this one heated – at the most frequently used entrance.[97]
This addition prevented the wind from rushing into the house and
provided storage space for snowshoes, fishing tackle, and hunting
gear. Other possible sources of improvement included planning for
inside storage, a workshop for garaging and maintaining snowmobiles and outboard motors, and a place large enough to keep the
plentiful supply of food that people have to lay in for the bad weather
when plane arrivals are notoriously uncertain.

The Northwest Territories Housing Corporation is taking note of
suggestions such as these. In 1979 it introduced its newest design:
a two-bedroom duplex of 1,000 square feet each side, adapted to
northern conditions, with an enclosed porch and unheated storage
room.[98] The basic premise of corporation planners now is that "a
house must effectively represent the needs of the hunter."[99] A series
of demonstration homes completed in the Keewatin region in 1981
is notable for its energy-conservation features. As Ottawa journalist
Gabriella Goliger describes them, "Each building is a highly insulated
airtight cube with walls 30 cm thick. Almost all windows face south
to bring in as much sunlight as possible and a large porch across the
front of the building provides a buffer against strong winds. The
porch also acts as a passive solar collector to capture the sun's heat
on bright days." Heat comes from centrally located space heaters
controlled by non-electric thermostats. These will continue to work
even during the power failures that commonly result from Arctic
storms. Triple-glazed windows, three outer doors, and airtight construction help seal the Keewatin homes against icy draughts from
outside and the escape of heat from inside. Airtightness, however,
demands a compensatory ventilation system that brings fresh air
indoors and prevents the build-up of moisture in the house. The

architects estimate that such design measures will reduce fuel consumption by 90 per cent over conventional houses.

Lack of adequate sewage and plumbing facilities will detract seriously from even the best house designs. In 1978–9 the territorial government responded to complaints by devoting $12 million to the improvement of sewer and water services in 32 communities across the NWT, including most of those in the Eastern Arctic.[100] But the absence of domestic plumbing is still a major cause of dissatisfaction. A source of many complaints is the continuing use by almost everyone, white and Inuit alike, of the "honey bag" – a plastic bag for human waste attached to a removable bowl. Once it is full it is placed outside the house for collection at regular intervals by the garbage pick-up. The procedure is inexpensive but hardly the most hygienic. In winter the intense cold practically welds the honey bags to the ground. Roving animals tear them open, and in thaws they become a health hazard and a constant offence to the eyes and nose. The new type of organic toilet that requires emptying only twice a year would be an obvious heir apparent.

But under Arctic conditions the disposal of waste and the provision of water present all communities with immense difficulties. In the NWT as a whole, responsibility for provision of water and removal of sewage and garbage shifted after 1974 from the individual to the territorial or municipal government, and native settlements were upgraded to water delivery and pick-up of waste.

A major obstacle in the path of adequate housing for every family in the Arctic – not to mention special housing for the single, the divorced, and the elderly – is cost. As Colin H. Davidson, dean of the Faculty of Interior Design at the Université de Montréal, told the Radisson conference of designers and builders in May 1982, it costs a minimum of $130,000 to $150,000 to build in the north a house that would fetch between $50,000 and $60,000 in the south. A large part of the difference derives from transport costs. The Arctic is far, far away from the industrial regions of the country, and in the north itself surface transport routes are lacking, especially in the Eastern Arctic.

Architects, engineers, and planners have not only distance and harsh physical conditions to contend with, but population characteristics as well. The initial gains of the housing program have been lost to rapid population growth and to the abandonment, around 1970, of the last remaining Inuit hunting camps. Year after year in the race for new houses the hare of demand easily speeds past the tortoise of supply. In the fable the tortoise won in the end by slow and steady plodding, and such may yet be the case in the Eastern

Arctic. In the mean time many communities continue to face overcrowding and declining, rather than improving, domestic standards. Houses buffeted outside by the implacable elements of the Arctic climate suffer inside from the heavy use of large families who crowd into their homes through much of the year. Under these conditions the average northern house, unless it undergoes rehabilitation, has a life expectancy of only about 15 years.[101]

Much of the outstanding rehabilitation work is being done by local Inuit who are receiving extensive training in the building trades. The Northwest Territories Housing Corporation is now in the process of turning housing over to the Inuit themselves through their local housing associations and through the district housing federations. The corporation will itself then function mainly as a resource organization for technical assistance, education, and funding. Education is already under way in a five-year program for Inuit to learn the trades of construction, maintenance, and management and for local contractors to master tendering procedures and the management of programs and finance. In 1982, 40 Inuit from the Baffin region took part in community housing contractor training projects.[102] The hope is that a home-grown Arctic construction industry will eventually lower the high cost of building in the north.

Without doubt the Arctic has enjoyed improvements in housing since 1978, but much remains to be done. The day is certainly still far away when every Inuit family can have what Willie Makiuk, president of the Kativik regional government, called for in September 1982: "Houses with toilets, running water and sewers. Buildings that we can afford to maintain ... and that last at least as long as the mortgage."[103]

CHAPTER TWO

Looking after Health

HEALTH CARE

To 1945: Wartime Conditions

A major criticism made by the American forces in the Eastern Arctic during the Second World War was that the Canadian government did little to look after the health of the Inuit or to provide medical assistance when it was required. The government's geographer, J.L. Robinson, in making his preliminary recommendations for the administration of the Eastern Arctic in 1943, agreed with the Americans.

The present medical and hospital organization does not appear adequate, nor give the proper medical attention. The physical handicaps of large area and inadequate transportation are the chief problems preventing this. After the war a supply of doctors should be available, and the present United States Army base should be utilized and maintained as soon as abandoned by the Americans. It is suggested that a plan be formulated to make use of the hospital and medical facilities now in the Eastern Arctic and that a planned medical program be drawn up which will give future adequate medical attention to both Eskimo and White. The hospital, being located on an air base, thus overcomes the problem of area and transportation by using planes both in bringing emergency patients to the hospital and in flying doctors out to camps for inspection and consultation. The hospitals should also become centres of research into the problems of Arctic diseases and their care.[1]

In 1943 the federal government was not directly involved in the provision of hospital services in the Arctic. At that time the federal and provincial governments were under no statutory obligation to provide medical services of any kind to Inuit or Indians anywhere in Canada. Medical attention had simply advanced from private practice and gradually extended to include the native peoples through appropriations voted by Parliament.[2] The federal government's role was limited to providing financial assistance to those religious agencies that had more willingly accepted the task of caring for the Inuit, medically as well as spiritually. In 1944 a general discussion tried to determine "whether it might not be desirable to have all schools and hospitals in the Northwest Territories owned and conducted by the government rather than by the Church missions,"[3] but the authorities involved made no firm commitment to change the situation. Expense and logistics were as always cited as the main deterrents.

The government provided, in addition to financial assistance, drugs and other medical supplies to those looking after the health of the Inuit. "At some points both the Anglican and R.C. Missionaries were supplied," an anonymous official wrote in 1944, "but as a measure of economy these medicines, etc., will now be furnished to one distributor at each point." Further, since the inauguration of the Eastern Arctic Patrol in 1922, the administration had equipped the vessel each year for medical and dental work. "A very considerable quantity of drugs and medical supplies is taken on board the vessel carrying the annual Eastern Arctic Expedition for treatment of the natives at the various ports of call," the same official reported. The doctor on board the patrol vessel also left whatever extra medicines and supplies he considered the "distributor" at each point would require "to meet conditions in his district."[4]

In 1943 the NWT had eleven hospitals, nine of them owned and operated by the missions and two by mining companies.[5] Eldorado Mining and Refining Ltd operated a small hospital or sick bay for the care of its employees at Great Bear Lake, and Consolidated Mining and Smelting Co. operated a hospital at Yellowknife primarily to look after its own workers although it did accept outside patients for treatment. But only two hospitals were located in the Eastern Arctic: one at Chesterfield Inlet, run by the Roman Catholic mission, and St Luke's Hospital and Industrial Home, which the Anglican mission operated at Pangnirtung. The area served by St Luke's covered the whole of Baffin Island and most of the northern coast of Quebec, including Ungava Bay. The population of the area, according to the 1941 census, was 2,052, which included 59 whites and half-breeds. The hospital was "electrically lighted and well-equipped with X-ray, iron lung, etc."[6] The industrial home, where the aged and infirm could be cared for, operated in conjunction with the hospital. "This institution like that operated at Chesterfield," said one medical report, "is serving a very useful purpose as it enables the natives who are able to hunt and trap to carry on their normal occupation without being handicapped by looking after their aged, sick or crippled relatives who are cared for in the home."[7] A second hospital, which the Anglican mission wanted to open at Lake Harbour, never proceeded beyond the proposal stage.[8]

The Bureau of Northwest Territories and Yukon Affairs was well aware of the deficiencies in Eastern Arctic health care even before the Americans drew world attention to them. In 1944 the bureau's chief wrote to the NWT deputy commissioner:

The need for more hospitals in the Eastern Arctic has been a burning question for more than 15 years. Bishop Fleming abandoned Lake Harbour temporarily for Pangnirtung under an agreement made in 1930. The question of a hospital in northern Quebec is outside the jurisdiction of this Administration. However, the Northwest Territories Council adopted a resolution at the One Hundred and Fifty-sixth Session dated 25th April, 1944, providing for a survey of the medical services required in both Eskimo and Indian territory of Northern Canada. It is unlikely that any steps will be taken to establish a hospital in the Northwest Territories or Quebec until the report of the survey has been received and studied.[9]

So no major change could be expected till after the end of the war. Meanwhile the Eastern Arctic remained medically backward in comparison even with the Western Arctic. In the west, at the end of 1944, 213 hospital beds served an estimated 8,000 people; in the east only 48 beds had to meet the needs of 3,762 people.[10]

The Bureau of Northwest Territories and Yukon Affairs recognized three main causes for the medical underdevelopment of the Eastern Arctic: inadequate transport, poor communications, and the "absence of any semblance of local autonomy."[11] "Until some form of local government or 'civic pride' is allowed in each government, fur trade and missionary center in the Eastern Arctic," wrote bureau chief Maj. D.L. McKeand, "misunderstandings among the semi-transient white population will persist and the health and well-being of the Eskimo suffer in consequence. Any reorganization of administration for the Eastern Arctic should provide for some form of local control of (a) food (b) clothing, and (c) shelter for the native population, otherwise any medical service will not get at the causes of mental and physical troubles."

The semi-transience of the white population arose from its inability to endure the barrenness of the Eastern Arctic environment. Doctors, nurses, and other white people could and did live indefinitely in the forested area of the Mackenzie district. They never thought of "going outside," as Maj. McKeand put it, whereas five years was about the limit for whites to live in the Eastern Arctic "if their mental and physical capacities are not to be impaired."

Poor transport was the main obstacle to development of the Eastern Arctic, not only medically but economically, and again the west did not share this disadvantage to the same extent. As McKeand said, "The Eastern Arctic ... will long remain in a somewhat similar relation to aircraft as the unplowed roads in the more civilized parts of the country are to motor vehicles in winter." "Ever since Punch Dickens made the first flight from Churchill to Chesterfield and Lake Athabasca," McKeand went on, "the use of aircraft has increased because the routes lie over comparatively level country, well watered with lakes and rivers, but conditions are different in Northern Quebec and Baffin Island where the country is not level or well-watered and, furthermore, dense fogs add to the difficulties."[12]

J.L. Robinson had realized the importance of air transport in medical services and for that reason recommended taking over the American air base hospitals. In 1941 "no regular aeroplane service to Pangnirtung or elsewhere in Baffin Island" had been established,[13] though B-17s had been scheduled to operate in the Baffin Island area in the winter of 1941–2.[14] They were based in Newfoundland and could make a return flight of 2,800 miles without refuelling. In February 1942 aircraft were at or near Pangnirtung and Lake Harbour. This was the first time that aircraft had landed in Baffin Island in the winter and the first time a mail dispatch had been made from Pangnirtung or Lake Harbour except during open navigation.[15] Emergency flights could now be authorized "when lives are in danger and there is a good chance of saving them through the delivery of drugs or toxins by aeroplane."[16] In 1944 the NWT Council discussed the possibility of using aeroplanes to carry patients to and from hospitals, a matter that Bishop Fleming, among others, believed to be worth consideration, "since after the war the use of the aeroplane will be developed tremendously."[17]

The debate on the use of the aeroplane in medical services continued. In 1946 Dr P.E. Moore, director of Indian Health Services, told a session of the NWT Council that "there should be sufficient plane service so that the natives could be brought out for treatment."[18] But northern administration, "while appreciating the need for planes," still thought that the health services should be carried to the people "to a considerable extent." The council agreed that the idea of northern health services was "to prevent disease, if possible, and educate the people to help themselves." The only way to do that was "to send in doctors and have health centres."

But finding doctors willing to venture into the Arctic was not as easy as the council made it appear. To find doctors even for as short a period as the summer cruise of the Eastern Arctic Patrol was often difficult. The Ottawa *Journal* reported on 8 July 1944: "When the Resources Department, which has the Eskimos under its charge, found it impossible to get physicians to go into the Far North to look after the Eskimos, an appeal was made to the medical profession with the result that two of its leading members volunteered their services." These were Dr George Hooper, a well-known Ottawa surgeon, who acted as medical officer of the patrol as far as Churchill, and Dr Dennis Jordan, a prominent Toronto physician, who replaced him there. D.L. McKeand, the officer in charge of the patrol that year, commented: "The Eskimo are getting better medical attention this year than ever before." The following summer, 1945, eye specialists were among the medical men on board the Eastern Arctic Patrol. At Churchill, Dr Walter Crewson of Hamilton joined optometrist Flt Lt A.H. Tweedle of Ottawa "to make a survey of eye conditions among the Eskimos."[19]

But men of the same calibre could not be found to work all year round in the Eastern Arctic settlements, and the government was glad to have the assistance of US Army medical officers. "These doctors travelled great distances to look after sick natives," the Toronto *Globe and Mail* reported on 8 August 1944. Lt T.H. Manning wrote that the American medical officers at all bases had been "of great service to the Eskimos," especially Maj. Barr at Iqaluit.[20]

1945–59: Department of National Health and Welfare

Needs of the Eastern Arctic. The northern administration did nothing officially about health care or medical facilities in the Arctic till after the Second World War. On 13 May 1946, Brooke Claxton, minister of national health and welfare, told the House of Commons that the health of Indians and Inuit had been a "matter of serious concern to the government for some time." Responsibility for health care in the Arctic had been transferred to his department from Mines and Resources in November 1945. At the time of the transfer, Mines and Resources "had prepared plans for a considerable extension of hospital and health facilities among the Indians and Eskimos." Claxton informed the House that with "regard to the health of Eskimos in the far north I may say that we had a conference here on February 8 of this year which was attended by some of the prominent doctors who have made the trip to the far north in recent years ... We have had their assistance in drawing up plans for dealing with the exceedingly difficult problems of the Eskimo and we hope to be able to do something further to extend the service that they have already been given in that field where there are some 7,700 Eskimos scattered over a territory of nearly 700,000 square miles."

The service that the Inuit already had was hardly all that good. The minister informed the House on 17 June 1946 that only nine doctors served the whole of the NWT but that his department hoped to establish more doctors and more supplementary nursing centres. The Eastern Arctic Patrol ship carried two doctors – "usually most distinguished ones" – and relief doctors and nurses were also sent up. "It would be much better," said the minister, "if the ship could stay longer at each port of call, but primarily its visits are not for reasons of health but to provide service for the Hudson's Bay Company and other people who are on it."

Opposition member Mr Case, knowing, as he said, "that the Eskimos are badly in need of medical and dental care, care for their eyes and so on," suggested that the department "give more particular attention to providing better services to the Eskimos." He proposed "as a means to that end that it acquire a suitable vessel, properly equipped as a hospital ship, and send it on its voyage so that it can play an adequate part in the health and welfare and general advancement of the Eskimos, for whose care we are largely responsible." The minister rejected the proposal because a government hospital ship would cost $250,000 a year in running costs, and he considered this too expensive for an operating period of six to ten weeks a year. However, when the new Eastern Arctic Patrol ship, the *C.D. Howe*, made its first voyage in the summer of 1950, it had "a fully modern medical section, including an operation room, a sick bay with beds for six patients, a dispensary, a complete dental office, an x-ray room and a dark room."[21]

Medical facilities in the Eastern Arctic settlements made less rapid progress than those aboard the patrol ship. Instead of receiving the hospitals proposed for Cape Dorset and Lake Harbour in January 1946, the people there had to make do with nursing stations; only Pangnirtung had a full-time medical officer.[22] Nurses were responsible for supervising health conditions in their districts and for giving first aid in cases of illness. Should hospital care be necessary the nurse called for assistance.[23] Patients needing specialized hospital treatment were flown south to Quebec City. This practice drew criticism from the Inuit and from the RCMP. Insp. H.A. Larsen maintained that the "effect on these people when being taken from their native surroundings and friends is not good."

It would be in the best interests of the Eskimos if more Government hospitals were established, especially at such places as Frobisher Bay where there are many vacant buildings formerly occupied by U.S. Army Air Force personnel. The period of recovery and convalescence might be much shorter if the Eskimos went under treatment in the environment to which they belong. Such hospitals should be much better than the present native hospitals existing at Pangnirtung and Chesterfield Inlet, which in the opinion of many persons are just disease traps and unfit for human habitation.[24]

J.G. Cantley of Northern Administration's Arctic Services agreed that it would be much more satisfactory to have the Inuit put in hospitals in their own country, but he understood "the difficulties the Department of National Health and Welfare have to contend with, particularly in regard to transportation ... and the staffing of northern institutions." Cantley added that while "some criticism may be made of the Chesterfield Inlet Hospital, I think that Inspector Larsen's comment on the Pangnirtung Hospital seems rather unjust."[25]

Nevertheless it remained the case, as an official memo informed the Advisory Committee on Northern Development in 1954, that "Medical and health services in the Yukon and Northwest Territories often fall seriously below the standards generally acceptable in Canada."[26] For example, Pangnirtung had the only hospital on Baffin Island, with 15 beds to serve a population in excess of 2,000. In addition, Cape Dorset and Lake Harbour had nursing stations. But Iqaluit could as yet boast no health-care premises of any kind. "The hospital facilities at Frobisher Bay and in Labrador have not yet been determined," the 1954 memo stated.

A close look at the difficulties of geography, of transportation, and of communications in the North, quickly leads to the conclusion that the problems to be overcome are not so much those of public health or medicine per se, as of logistics. It is not a difficult matter to have a nurse give an injection of penicillin or a dose of diphtheria toxoid to an Eskimo or to have an x-ray technician make a film of his chest, once they are on the spot. It is the business of getting them there at the right time with the facilities they need that presents the major problem.

The climate and terrain of our Canadian Northland make communication at best difficult, and sometimes impossible. These natural difficulties, combined with our limited staff and the scattered distribution of the people of nomadic habit with whom we are dealing, present an almost insurmountable problem to our service in the North.[27]

One solution, of a kind later advocated for the Western world as a whole by Ivan Illich, was more Inuit self-help. But teaching Inuit to help themselves depended on education, and programs for training native health auxiliaries did not begin for another decade.

Another factor involved in Arctic health care was the division of responsibility among departments of the federal government, the territorial governments, and private bodies. The large number of agencies involved led to duplication of services and to uneconomic use of the limited facilities available. The agencies involved included the federal departments of Northern Affairs and National Resources, National Health and Welfare, and National Defence; the two territorial governments; the Hospital Board at Yellowknife; and such private bodies as the missions and the mining companies.[28] The Advisory Committee on Northern Development studied the situation and concluded that the federal government could best resolve the administrative tangle by creating a single body with responsibility for health services throughout Yukon and the NWT. It could logically establish this new body as a Northern Health Services division of Health and Welfare. As a memo for the cabinet pointed out, the proposed Northern Health Services "would become responsible for all hospital and public health functions now carried out in the north by territorial governments, Indian Health Services, and the Department of National Defence, except possibly where the latter may wish to operate health facilities within military establishments."[29]

Confounding the efforts of northern health authorities to provide adequate care for the Inuit was the fact that the numbers of Inuit were rising rapidly year by year. Comparison between 1941 and 1951 census returns is bedevilled by a diversity of available total figures for each year. Nevertheless, the high rate of annual increase is clear. For example, in 1941 RCMP enumerations gave the total number of Inuit in Canada as 7,205.[30] However, J.L. Robinson quoted 7,392 as the "official" total but, making allowance for natives missed in the tabulations, considered 7,700 "probably a fairly accurate minimum estimate of the ... Canadian Eskimo population."[31] The same kind of discrepancy occurs in the 1951 population counts. That year the RCMP total was 9,733, whereas the official census gave only 9,493.[32] Annual rates of increase between 1941 and 1951 thus range from a low of 2.3 per cent to a high of 3.6 per cent. RCMP figures for only the NWT Inuit show a rise from 5,404 at the end of 1941 to 6,822 at the end of 1951, for an average annual increase of 2.6 per cent. This is rapid, equivalent to doubling the population in 27 years. Throughout the 1950s even this high rate accelerated, for between 1951 and 1961 the Inuit population of the Eastern Arctic grew by an average of 3.46 per cent a year.[33] This kind of uncontrolled demographic growth, in part caused by improved medical services, put a severe strain on the resources of those agencies responsible for providing medical services.

Northern Health Services and the DEW Line. After 1954 responsibility for providing medical services fell to the new administrative branch know as Northern Health Services. Envisioned by the Advisory Committee on Northern Development and presented to the cabinet by Jean Lesage, the idea of Northern Health Services received cabinet approval in December 1954, and organization pushed ahead during the following months.[34] Medical authorities foresaw further complications in co-ordinating health care in the north when in 1957 the two territorial governments assumed more of the financial burden involved. In order to head off any lack of co-ordination or co-operation between Northern Health Services and any new territorial agencies, the deputy minister of northern affairs and national resources suggested establishing a Permanent Advisory Committee on Northern Health "to serve as a co-ordinating body" between Health and Welfare and the territorial governments.[35]

The terms of reference of the committee were set out as follows:

1. to examine the implications of Northern Health Service in relation to the Governments of the Northwest Territories and Yukon Territory and their citizens;
2. to make recommendations towards the implementation of Northern Health Service and its integration with the existing health administrations of the Territorial Governments;
3. to study and make recommendations concerning the development of medical and health service facilities in the north;
4. to study the application of the principles of national health insurance to the Territories;
5. to examine ways and means for improving environmental health of Territorial citizens;
6. to conduct a continuing review of Territorial health legislation in the light of modern developments.

The Permanent Advisory Committee accepted these terms of reference at its first meeting on 26 June 1957.[36]

The establishment of Northern Health Services – the plural form was most commonly used – and the formation of the Permanent Advisory Committee solved the problems of the division of responsibility for health care in the Arctic, the duplication of facilities and services, and the lack of co-operation among all the agencies concerned. A solution to the geographic problems of distance and population distribution appeared with the coming of the DEW Line. A committee set up to consider the co-ordination of medical facilities in the Arctic "reviewed the probable effect of the establishment of the early warning lines on the medical situation in the north" and reported in November 1955:

At the present time the native population in some areas was without adequate medical service because it was widely dispersed and beyond the reach of regular transportation and communications. With the establishment of the early warning lines this situation would alter. Natives would tend to congregate around the stations, attracted by opportunities of employment or simply by curiosity. At some points the concentration of natives would increase sufficiently to warrant the establishment of some type of medical facilities. At the same time many of those who remained in camps at some distance from the lines would travel to the stations to seek medical aid when this was needed, and the camps themselves would be accessible in cases of emergency.

The Committee therefore concluded that the Department of National Health and Welfare should plan to provide facilities where they were required by the native population, rather than rely on the operating contractors.[37]

The Federal Electric Corporation, as "the operating contractors," agreed to provide medical assistance to Inuit personnel on the same basis as to other DEW Line employees. This meant that "at each sector the Office Supervisor would be a well-trained male nurse drawn from the Armed Forces. In addition, travelling the DEW Line and available to all would be three medical doctors, two dentists and a public health administrator."[38] But an earlier meeting had made it clear that the Canadian government had responsibility for the health care of the Inuit in general, and the DEW Line contractors only for the personnel manning the lines. The contractors would provide at DEW Line sites only minimum medical facilities, consisting of a medical inspection room and first aid treatment. Patients requiring more skilled treatment would be evacuated to the nearest hospital.[39] Dr Proctor of Health and Welfare told the meeting that the medical facilities the contractors would provide appeared adequate for single employees but did not include provision for the dependants of Inuit workers "or for those who would undoubtedly congregate around the stations." Experience had shown that no matter who provided the medical facilities everyone in the area would expect to use them. In fact the department had hoped that the proposed DEW Line facilities could be used to meet the needs of all the local people. If this were not to be the case, then the government would have to make provision. Late in 1959 the Federal Electric Corporation agreed that the medical, surgical, and dental care offered to all corporation employees would be extended to their dependants as out-patients and that it would also offer such care at DEW Line sites for non-employed Inuit, so long as other medical, surgical, and dental care was "not immediately available."[40] Where such care was available, the corporation would supply transport via established DEW Line routes to the nearest nursing station. The northern service officer was to co-ordinate such movement, and the Canadian government was to asume the cost.[41] This arrangement appeared to suit everyone concerned.

*1959–71: Health-Care Improvement and
Population Growth*

General satisfaction with health care arrangements along the DEW Line quickly diminished. Demands made on facilities and personnel rose alarmingly and became a matter of concern for the Federal Electric Corporation. Northern Health Services was sympathetic. "Inevitably some Eskimos have been attracted to the DEW Line," its chief noted in a memo. "The occasional DEW Line station was constructed not far from established Eskimo hunting grounds. The result has been that some Federal Electric Corporation Station Chiefs have found themselves faced with medical emergencies frequently involving young children at locations far from established settlements and hence available nursing station or hospital facilities. To the layman employed to do a technical job on the DEW Line, coping with such illness has been a trying experience, yet one which for reasons of plain humanity he has not been able to ignore."[42]

    What was a trying experience for corporation medical staff became a worrisome problem for management. By February 1962 the worry was no longer acceptable. Management directed its supervisors on the DEW Line to discontinue the delivery of medical care to Inuit not employed by the corporation. The reasons were unobjectionable. Giving such care interfered with the operation of the DEW Line, increased its cost, and added to the liability of the corporation and to the personal liability of its employees through a possible medical malpractice suit.[43]

A feasible solution was to use the DEW Line but not Federal Electric Corporation personnel. "It is proposed, therefore," wrote the chief of Northern Health Services, "that nurses should travel regularly along the line to visit every Eskimo family that can be reached. If every Eskimo family in each Sector [of the Line] were seen once a month, at least some of the medical problems would be prevented from occurring."[44] So northern health authorities saw regular home visiting by public health nurses as a means of preventing a certain amount of illness. Nurses could give babies their inoculations against polio, diphtheria, and whooping cough, check them for normal development, correct their feeding problems, and advise their mothers about cleanliness and clothing. A number of infants at various points along the line had received no such attention since birth. Nurses could also visit pregnant women. They could foresee problems likely to arise during delivery, the kind of problems that "necessitated frantic action in the past," and the patients could be transported in good time to the nearest nursing home or hospital.

The thorniest snag in this well-laid scheme was the lack of nursing homes and hospitals. On the DYE sector of the DEW Line, in eastern Baffin Island, there was no nursing station at all. The two doctors at Iqaluit were 250 miles away. The Anglican mission hospital at Pangnirtung lay across rugged, mountainous terrain 80 miles to the south. Improved transportation facilities helped to overcome these distances, but the need for improved hospital facilities remained critical. One place where improvement was most in demand was Iqaluit.

For a number of years Iqaluit had "got by with makeshift facilities," but activity there had increased to a stage where proper services were essential. At that time about 300 US servicemen, an equal number of Inuit, and about 50 Canadian servicemen and civilians lived at the air base. Dr Proctor of Northern Health Services said that if a facility were to be built at Iqaluit it should be large enough to serve as a district hospital. Pangnirtung, the only hospital on Baffin Island, was inaccessible to the Inuit from many parts of the island and was unsuitable for expansion. A hospital at Iqaluit would serve an estimated 2,280 potential users. This figure included 106 DEW Line personnel from stations on eastern Baffin Island who had no other medical facilities beyond their own inspection rooms.[45] According to Health and Welfare, this potential usage would call for a hospital of 20 to 25 beds and five bassinets, with a staff on one doctor, four

registered nurses, four nurse's aides, and ten others. When completed, Frobisher Bay General Hospital was larger than originally
planned in 1961 but, with 35 beds, was still a small hospital.[46]

A total population of 7,000 Inuit and 1,300 others needs more
than one 35-bed general hospital. To meet these needs the Medical
Services Branch of Health and Welfare, the 1962 successor to Northern Health Services, organized an extensive network of nursing stations and regional hospitals throughout northern Canada. But better
medicine, aided by improved housing and education, stimulated ever
higher rates of population growth. From 2.6 per cent a year between
1941 and 1951 and 3.46 per cent over the next decade – themselves
exceptionally high rates – the Inuit population of the Eastern Arctic
between 1961 and 1971 went on growing at an even faster rate of
4.3 per cent a year.[47] This rate, if continued, would double the
population in 16 years. It is a rate of growth found in the underdeveloped regions of Latin America. The maintenance of living
standards in a growing population requires a matching growth of
productive capital, the growth of the population alone being insufficient to produce the supplementary goods needed, the raw materials, houses, schools, teachers, doctors, nurses, and medical
facilities.

As far as the high fertility was concerned, the government did
nothing to try to counteract it. The question of population limitation
was not raised in the NWT Council till as late as 26 February 1968.[48]
The council then passed a formal notice calling for immediate implementation of a comprehensive birth control program to counter
lagging economic development. But Health and Welfare made no
special efforts in this direction and was anxious to pass the responsibility to the Education Service of the territorial government, which
in turn "appeared totally unprepared to venture into this complex
and highly technical field." At this time the Canadian Criminal Code
forbade any effective action, and both governments used this as a
justification for doing next to nothing, "rather than planning resolutely for the time when effective action could be taken to increase
the welfare of a significant number of people."[49] The only positive
action taken before the Criminal Code was amended in 1969 was to
make family planning literature available at all northern health
centres. But nothing else was done, even after passage of the amendment, "because of certain peoples' strong feelings on the subject."[50]
This quote from the NWT Council debate refers to the teachers and
the Roman Catholic Church leaders who vigorously protested the
council's attempt to disseminate birth control information through
the schools.[51] Father Van de Velde of Hall Beach demanded to know

what this information had to do with the Education Department and why it was not the responsibility of Health and Welfare.[52] Van de Velde declared that the "Eskimo considers children as wealth"; he saw the imposition of birth control programs as the "white man's self-imposed superiority raping again another of the fundamental underlayings of Eskimo society."

It is difficult to assess from Inuit speaking and writing how much of the native attitude to birth control and family size was personal or traditional and how much was due to religious pressure. At the three women's conferences in Yellowknife, Inuvik, and Pangnirtung in 1975, speakers echoed Van de Velde's sentiments. Although delegates agreed that abortion should be legalized and family planning and birth control devices be made available for those who wanted them, they were opposed to birth control in general and to abortion and tubal ligation in particular.[53] Inuit in general believed that parental permission should be essential for obtaining birth control devices because of concern that teenage girls using birth control might "become promiscuous and avoid responsibility and traditional marriage customs."[54]

The decline in population growth that did set in during the late 1960s and early 1970s appears to have been due to the availability of family planning information and birth control devices, in spite of Roman Catholic pressure against them. Native women of the Catholic faith, said Simona Arnatiaq, "handle and bear more children than they can take and many are afraid to take the pill. This is a religious pressure that is very strong today."[55] But the Catholic Church is weakly represented in the Eastern Arctic. Here parents received more inducement to restrict family size, so much so that women were encouraged to "ignore pressures around her to not have children if she feels she can't handle them."

After 1971: Health Care Today

The nursing stations set up since the 1960s form the backbone of the health-care system in the Eastern Arctic. Operated in all settlements with a population of more than 200, staffed usually by one registered nurse with one or more auxiliaries, the nursing station opens every day to give treatment, and the nurse is on call 24 hours a day for emergencies. All nursing stations have a number of beds designed for short stays of not more than two or three days. These serve for the treatment of minor illnesses or as "holding places" for more seriously ill patients prior to their evacuation to a larger treatment centre.

Resolute Bay can provide an example of one of the Eastern Arctic nursing stations. This small settlement had a population of 168 in 1981, but its total catchment is about 2,000 people, including most of the Queen Elizabeth Islands and Ellesmere Island. The station's registered nurse, who is also a midwife, provides all medical services up to surgery. Patients requiring other treatment have to go to Iqaluit or Yellowknife. The hospital at Iqaluit is still the only one in the Eastern Arctic. In December 1982 Health and Welfare transferred the running of the hospital to the territorial Department of Health, which already operated Stanton Yellowknife Hospital and the Fort Smith and Hay River health centres. The territorial government appointed an 11-member board of management with broad representation from the Baffin region to assume full responsibility for the delivery of treatment services and day-to-day operations. The hospital has been renamed the Baffin Regional Hospital.[56] The average cost of keeping patients in the hospitals at Iqaluit and Yellowknife varies from year to year, depending on the number of patients and the type of treatment provided. For example, in 1977 it ranged from $140 a day at Yellowknife to $362 at Iqaluit;[57] in 1979 the cost was $193 a day at Yellowknife and $240 at Iqaluit.[58] On average, Resolute Bay nursing station treats 50 patients a day, roughly half Inuit, half white, though in summer the number of Inuit coming to the station drops remarkably. The Inuit suffer particularly from ear and skin infections.[59]

From the operational point of view, the nursing station's main problem appears to be the singularly large responsibility that the registered nurse has to bear, often alone, in a strange environment in a harsh and hostile climate. She must keep regular clinic hours, be prepared to answer emergency calls at any time of the day or night, overcome the burden of record keeping, act as mental health counsellor, provide health education at the settlement school, win the confidence of the local people, and combat personal isolation. The crushing load of work that they have to deal with is not unique to Resolute Bay but common to all the Arctic nursing stations. For example, on 1 February 1978 Ipeelee Kilabuk, member for Central Baffin, told the NWT Council that he was worried because the only nurse based in his home community of Pangnirtung faced too heavy a work load. Pangnirtung had a population of 800. It had only one nurse on staff "with too many things to do." It had three RCMP officers "who don't have much to do."[60]

The burden placed on the registered nurses is one cause of the large turnover of nursing staff. Even in the most populous of the Arctic settlements retaining staff has proved extremely difficult. In the NWT as a whole the turnover of nurses in 1976 was 86 per cent.[61] In Keewatin in 1979 – 80 it was as high as 120 per cent.[62] Inadequate housing and salaries are partly to blame, but, in nursing stations especially, the stresses of isolation and responsibility can become unbearable. The Eastern Arctic in particular has always suffered from the difficulty of finding and keeping staff, not only on account of the intolerable strain of overwork but because of the inhospitable barrenness of the treeless tundra environment.

In the smaller settlements, with less than 200 inhabitants, too small to support a nursing station, community health auxiliaries man simple health stations supported by two-way radio or telephone communication. Iqaluit is the only Eastern Arctic settlement that benefits from full-time government-employed physicians. Other communities receive visits from a physician during the year, the number of visits varying with the size and location of the settlement but the average for all NWT communities being 9 per year.[63]

The delivery of health care to the Inuit of the Eastern Arctic has been open to criticism. Wally Firth, MP for the NWT, voiced his criticism in the House of Commons on 10 October 1975. "We desperately need programs and services that are taken for granted in other parts of the country ... Health services are not just poor; they do not exist for most people in the Northwest Territories for most of the year. The health of my constituents is surely the worst in Canada." By contrast the medical authorities in the Territories reported at the same time: "There is growing acceptance of the concept that treatment services as provided by Medical Services are approaching the point beyond which it is neither politically nor financially good sense to proceed."[64]

Since then the emphasis in northern health care has shifted from treatment, which had predominated since the Second World War, to prevention and the encouragement of self-care. But a successful preventive approach to medicine depends to a large degree on the maintenance of a healthy environment. The prime factors leading to positive health and the absence of much disease in the more highly developed parts of the world are good housing, clean water, sufficient and nutritionally adequate food, and efficient waste disposal. But the Eastern Arctic was very far from being, even in Canada in the mid-1970s, a highly developed part of the world. In most communities water was in chronically short supply. Schools had been built to plans that demanded the ready availability of water where such was unattainable. Planners had allowed settlements to grow where drainage and waste disposal were impossible. Migration had gone on unchecked to the point of overcrowding, where housing had little hope of catching up with demand. The housing and general settlement conditions were made worse by individual indifference to garbage and hazard-strewn surroundings. To take Resolute Bay again as an example, "the cemetery is located within a quarter mile of the settlement and the barren, stony terrain in the immediate vicinity of the settlement is also used for refuse disposal. While human corpses are buried, animal corpses are not, but, like the refuse and waste, remain rotting on the surface. The health risk is obvious." A policy of preventive medicine under such unfavourable circumstances was a demanding, uphill task, fraught with risk.

Medical authorities have fortunately refused to rely solely on preventive medicine but are hedging their policies with a program of improvements to the existing inadequate facilities. In 1981 an extensive review of Medical Services Branch facilities across the NWT resulted in a submission to Treasury Board for a substantial increase in the funds available for capital construction and renovations. These funds were earmarked for new nursing stations at Resolute Bay, Arctic Bay, and Repulse Bay. In addition, the territorial Department of Health planned an extensive renovation program which, over five years to 1986, would see the replacement of all trailer stations and older buildings, many of which have been braving Arctic inclemency since the 1950s. A new era of northern health care had dawned.

MORBIDITY

Tuberculosis

The single most important disease that medical services have had to contend with in the Arctic has been tuberculosis, "the scourge of the Eskimo." In 1945 Dr A. Collins, the medical officer on board the Eastern Arctic Patrol, reported:

Pulmonary and bone tuberculosis seem to be rapidly increasing particularly along both shores of Hudson Strait. Several cases were seen of each type in both young and old. It is reported that any adult native when questioned would state that at some time or other he had spat up blood, and I am informed that of a number of x-rays taken at two ports, over twenty-five per cent show evidence of either present or past pulmonary disease. It would appear that unless some measure of prevention, with isolation or care of active cases, is taken in the near future that tuberculosis will become the scourge of the North.[65]

But as competent medical authorities had argued in the past, such symptoms as coughing and bleeding were not necessarily evidence of tuberculosis. Even x-ray examination was not always reliable. Northern administration asked the medical team on the Eastern Arctic Patrol in 1945 to ascertain as best it could how prevalent tuberculosis was among the Inuit. The task was not as straightforward as administration had hoped. Most of the patients brought to the ship were suffering from "a variety of other conditions," and so the team's study of tuberculosis "was extremely limited."[66] It was able to make a definite diagnosis of the existence of tuberculosis in only 15 of 145 patients examined. "Nevertheless, there was much to make us suspicious of a high incidence of it," the doctors wrote. "The handicap of our being unable to make a wider clinical survey in the time at our disposal and of being without x-ray equipment were unfortunate." These doctors noted what others had previously reported: that most of the Inuit who suffered from tuberculosis remained ambulant even though their lesions might be quite extensive and that many recovered without rest treatment. "Possibly the pure quality of the Arctic air is partly accountable for the cures," the doctors suggested, "as well as the large amount of Vitamin D which is so bountifully supplied in the diet." Dr H.W. Lewis two years later reported: "One is impressed by the apparent remarkable resistance of these people to tubercular infections ... The Eskimo mode of living naturally would lead one to expect that individual families would be ravaged by the disease and yet the evidence so far does not so indicate."[67]

In 1946 the medical team on the Eastern Arctic Patrol was busy with tuberculosis research again, this time carrying out a major x-ray survey. Altogether it examined 1,347 films, taken from 36 per cent of the population that the survey reached.[68] From the appearance of the films and the type of lesion found, Dr Lewis felt justified in making certain observations. First, the Inuit were "pretty thoroughly tubercularized." All areas touched by the Eastern Arctic Patrol showed evidence of widespread infection, but slightly higher incidence occurred in centres around Hudson Strait compared with northern areas. However, the difference was not great enough to warrant any conclusions. Second, ample evidence suggested that the Inuit did in fact show "a marked resistance to tuberculosis." The widespread indications of previous infection that now showed gross calcification with no signs of activity seemed to bear this out. Third, further evidence seemed to indicate that the infection was universal and that it was usually a maximum dose. "How could it be otherwise," Dr Lewis asked rhetorically, "when the Eskimo is confined to a small igloo for so many months of the year? The marvel is that many do not develop the disease and succumb to it." Fourth, the data appeared to point overwhelmingly to massive infection rather than to lack of resistance, and this led to the conclusion that if infection could be controlled, tuberculosis could be controlled as readily in the Inuit as in other races.

According to Dr Lewis, the Inuit presented no special problem in the way of tuberculosis control "inherent in their particular race. They have evidently been tubercularized for many years and have survived as a race in spite of a high morbidity and mortality rate and with no attempt made to treat or segregate open cases ... Whether or not they have had longer experience as a race with tuberculosis they seem to have been better able to resist it, judging by morbidity figures and x-ray appearance of lesions."

The major difficulties in controlling the infection in the north were related to the environment, the way of life of the Inuit, and deficiencies of transport. As Lewis pointed out:

It would be a most difficult matter either to treat the Eskimo in the north, or to bring the sick ones outside for treatment. While a few who live around the settlements and are accessible to the two hospitals found in the Arctic might be treated, the only contact with many of them will be the annual visit of the Nascopie [the Eastern Arctic Patrol vessel] ... Those who have been sent out, particularly young children, lose their language and all connections with the north and become a problem of rehabilitation. They return quite unfit to take their place in the north.

Lewis's last point touched on a problem that was to dog the northern administration for many years. He himself, as many did later, suggested a sanatorium in the north, possibly at Southampton Island.

One specific environmental factor in the high incidence of tuberculosis in the Canadian Arctic was the bad housing in which the Inuit had to live. The Danes in Greenland were well aware of this and were backing up their medical program among the Inuit there by approaching tuberculosis from the welfare side as well. B.G. Sivertz wrote from Greenland: "The Danes are convinced that ... [the Greenlanders'] houses have been responsible for most of the spread of tuberculosis. They are in the middle of the task of providing every family in Greenland with a frame house, small or large in accordance with income."[69] Recognition of the relation between high rates of tubercular infection and substandard housing conditions was one of the goads that pricked the federal government into introducing low-cost housing programs into the Eastern Arctic. But officials suspected that many factors "probably contribute[d] to the spread of tuberculosis among the Eskimos," only one of which was "the close personal contact in crowded living quarters." Other contributory factors they listed included nutritional deficiencies caused by increasing dependence on white man's food; poor game conditions in some areas, which would affect both food and clothing; and delay in the isolation and removal to hospital of active cases.[70] In 1952, as a result of these and other factors, tuberculosis among the Inuit was "spreading seriously." In the following year there were 40.4 hospital admissions for tuberculosis per thousand Inuit in the NWT, compared with only 20.8 per thousand Indians.[71]

The federal government intensified its efforts to contain the spread of this disease. In addition to its housing program it provided the Eastern Arctic Patrol with better X-ray and other equipment,[72] removed more and more Inuit found to be active carriers of the disease to sanatoria in the south,[73] and in 1954–5 extended the BCG immunization program. First used by Indian Health Services in Fort Qu'Appelle in 1928, BCG was then introduced to all the provinces and territories, "with striking results in reduction of incidence and deaths."[74] At the end of 1954 the Indian Health Services, then still in charge of Inuit health care, reported to its staff with obvious pride:

Tuberculosis, which until recently has been the major problem, and continues to be the major problem in some areas, will be overcome to a great extent by the B.C.G. program combined with the increasing facilities which have been and are being so well provided for adequate regular chest surveys, combined with all of the modern means of treatment, a follow-up program which is to include assistance with rehabilitation together with the arrangements which have been made for protective foods where tuberculosis has manifested itself. The emphasis which you are placing on ways and means for bringing about a better state of nutrition for all, not only will aid in the conquest of tuberculosis but will greatly contribute to a reduction of many other ills through increasing resistance.[75]

The result of such measures was a remarkable decline in the incidence of tuberculosis. Over the 10 years ending in 1954 the rate among the Inuit dropped by 56 per cent, from 568.4 per 100,000 population to 252.5. This compares with a 90 per cent drop among the Indians, from 565.7 to only 60.2, and with a 75 per cent drop among the white population, from 40.7 to 9.8.[76] Obviously much work remained to be done among the Inuit, but northern administration remained optimistic. "It is felt that the number of active cases has now probably passed its peak," the administration reported in 1955, "and that the incidence of this disease will decline steadily over the next few years."[77] The optimism was justified. In 1956–7 the number of tuberculosis patient-days in hospitals in the NWT declined by almost 29 per cent.[78] The steady decline in the number of patients continued to the end of the decade.

The tuberculosis predicament did not improve without cost. By the end of 1956, 1,000 Inuit, nearly 10 per cent of the total Canadian Inuit population, were receiving hospital treatment in southern Canada. Most were suffering from tuberculosis. Medical banishment of this high order contributed to a major social upheaval in many Arctic communities.[79] Most northern administrators did not like the policy of removing tubercular Inuit from the north to sanatoria and hospitals in the south. The Rt Reverend Donald Marsh, (Anglican) bishop of the Arctic, was one of those most strongly opposed to the practice. He went so far as to write to the prime minister at the end of 1954 complaining about the "inhumanity of this policy."[80] He pointed out that his predecessor, A.L. Fleming, had "pressed the Department of Mines and Resources for many years to allow him to build hospitals in The Arctic (for which there were and are funds available)," but the only hospital that Bishop Fleming had been able to persuade the government to allow him to build was that at Pangnirtung, "which the Department of Mines and Resources insisted should be built in that place rather than at Lake Harbour." Bishop Marsh informed the prime minister that when he raised the matter of the enforced removal of tubercular Inuit to southern hospitals, Mines and Resources told him that the hardships to the Inuit of which he complained "would resolve themselves and would disappear in a year or two." "To the writer and to many others," Bishop Marsh went on, "it is strange that vast sums of money are to be expended upon the removal of a town [Aklavik] some 80 miles because the Government 'willy nilly' decides it should be removed, and that great sums can be spent on buildings for rehabilitation centres which would not be necessary if the people were hospitalized in their own country; yet, hospitals cannot be built to take care of them in their own country."

Bishop Marsh's position enjoyed more support in northern administration than he seems to have realized. The director himself thought that Bishop Marsh was "perfectly right in objecting to the hitherto policy of hospitalizing Eskimos in isolation from their own people."[81] Alternatives to this policy were available after the introduction of effective chemotherapy and vaccines in the 1950s. In Africa, for example, the World Health Organization dealt with tuberculosis in the home and spent the bulk of its available finances in training indigenous health-care workers. Canada stuck to a policy of evacuating and / or institutionalizing the sick while giving scant consideration to the training of native people in either self-care or health services. It was not till 1969 that the government introduced programs for training native health auxiliaries. In the mean time tubercular native patients

> were forced to live in a world in which the language, ethos, food, and lifestyle were foreign to them. Moreover, these people were often kept there in a virtual state of limbo, with little or no information about their own conditions or the fate of their families. Problems of alienation were even greater for natives from the north, as they were routinely sent to sanatoria hundreds of miles away from their homes ... It is a well-known adage in the north that many people simply never returned from these institutions, and those who did were often irrevocably changed because of their experiences.[82]

Northern administration was well aware of this deplorable situation. The director reported to his deputy minister in 1954 that Inuit patients were distributed in 24 different hospitals. In a couple of cases there was "only one Eskimo, all by himself, in a hospital among white people."

> I have discussed this with Dr. Moore [Indian Health Services] and his staff and they have agreed that we should concentrate Eskimos in groups of never less than 50. Dr. Moore is making new arrangements whereby the Mountain Sanatorium at Hamilton will be the principal Eskimo hospital in Eastern Canada. There may be one other eastern sanatorium and he will continue to use St. Boniface in Winnipeg and Charles Camsell in Edmonton. This will ensure large groups of Eskimos so that after segregating them for sex, age, etcetera, they will have lots of company. In addition we will make every effort to have substantial numbers of Eskimos on the hospital staffs.[83]

This plan obviously went only part way to meeting Bishop Marsh's criticism. He wanted hospitalization of the Inuit to be wholly within the Arctic. Concentrating them into large groups in three or four southern hospitals removed some of the more "inhuman" aspects of loneliness and isolation but did not cure the other ills of the system: the break-up of families for two years or more; the prolonged absence of the Inuit from their own environment, people, and lifestyle; and the difficulties of rehabilitation. But medical opinion was adamant. "It is utterly impossible to maintain high medical and hospital standards in small isolated units," the deputy minister of national health declared unequivocally.[84] He asked the opinion of an outstanding authority on tuberculosis about the relative chance of recovery for the average patient from treatment in a small northern hospital compared with treatment in a modern, fully equipped and staffed institution. The expert opinion was that, other things being equal, the chances of recovery would be three or four times greater in one of the larger sanatoria. Seeking statistical collaboration of this opinion, Health and Welfare researchers compared the records for five NWT hospitals with those for the Charles Camsell Indian Hospital in Edmonton. They found that deaths per hundred discharges at the former averaged 29.2, compared with 13.2 at the latter. "Admittedly some of the cases in the northern hospitals were terminal," the deputy minister wrote, "but, on the other hand is the fact that a larger proportion of the cases sent to Edmonton were for surgery, with a correspondingly high surgical risk."

In December 1954 approximately 450 Inuit were in southern hospitals for treatment and 150 in mission hospitals in the NWT. That these 600 Inuit were in hospital was used as an argument in favour of the program because their removal from their families and communities tended to reduce the incidence of tuberculosis and its spread among the Inuit at large. And in the opinion of Health and Welfare personnel, it did not make any difference if the hospitals were a hundred or a thousand miles from the Inuit's homes. "Patients in hospitals, if a hundred miles or so away from their point of origin," the deputy minister went on, "are actually as much removed from their families as they are in Quebec City, Hamilton or Edmonton. The change from an igloo or a skin tent to a hospital bed is just as marked whether that bed be on Holman Island or the city of Edmonton, and the patient discharged requires just the same readjustment to go back to his rigorous Arctic life."

Everyone was aware that the immediate diagnosis and evacuation of patients presented serious social welfare and public relations problems, the latter being exploited most expertly by Bishop Marsh; but the consensus, at least among the medical profession, was that this was "the only sensible way to deal with tuberculosis in the north."[85]

As long as housing conditions remained bad, a disease like tuberculosis would continue to flourish. A 1964 report pointed out: "All Health Authorities recognize the fact that such major diseases as Tuberculosis, Pneumonia, Enteric and Venereal disease, are concentrated in areas of poor housing, as are also high infant mortality rates, juvenile delinquency, and a host of other mental and social disorders connected with depression of the human spirit. People joined together in drab surroundings tend to lose their incentive towards good social behaviour and sense of propriety ... There is also the feeling of sordidness and hopelessness that pervades life when one's surroundings are dirty and overcrowded."[86]

The smallest dwellings were the welfare houses, and these tended to be the most overcrowded, because "the welfare type of person" was most likely to have the largest family. He or she also tended to have the least resistance to disease. Tuberculosis in particular thrived under these conditions. The high incidence of tuberculosis was costly to the government. During 1962, for example, 668 Inuit spent a total of 99,241 days in tuberculosis sanatoria, at a total cost of $1,091,651. For other acute diseases, involving as many as 2,306 Inuit, the hospital days were only 29,586, and the cost to the government was only $591,720.[87] These were only hospitalization costs. Many thousands of dollars more were spent on transporting tuberculous cases to and from sanatoria. If one takes into account also the cost of supporting ex-tuberculosis patients and their families on welfare assistance plus rehabilitation expenses, the total annual expenditure on tuberculosis must have gone into many millions of dollars.

But in alleviating the distress of tuberculosis the money was well spent. New active cases of the disease declined in the NWT from 261 in 1963 to 119 in 1964 and 90 in 1965.[88] Since then tuberculosis has dropped steadily down the list of major causes of death in the Arctic. In 1982 the incidence of this disease in the NWT was 59.02 cases per 100,000 population, the lowest rate ever recorded in the Territories, though still substantially higher than that for all of Canada.[89] The scourge of the Inuit is losing its sting. The hope is that with the continuation of good case-finding, aided by preventive programs using BCG and chemo-prophylaxis, it may one day disappear.

Infant Mortality

Another bane of the north for the past 40 years has been indefensibly high rates of infant mortality. "The death statistics which cannot be doubted," wrote R.A. Gibson, NWT deputy commissioner, in 1946, "show that a large proportion of the deaths were children at the age that they are weaned, 2 or 3 years. At the present rate the population is bound to decrease. The doctors agree that undernourishment is the cause of most infant deaths."[90] That same year J.G. Wright, officer in charge of the Eastern Arctic Patrol, reported 83 deaths in southern Baffin Island "since last ship-time."[91] Thirty-seven of these deaths were of children under 15 years of age. "The clinic has found many cases of under-nourished children," Wright remarked, "the critical period being after they are weaned."

The high mortality among children and infants in 1945–6 was

mentioned in the annual report of the medical officer at Pangnirtung. During the year ending 31 August 1946, 28 deaths occurred in the Cumberland Sound area. The majority were of children between two and three years of age, and most of these died during the "poor months" from December to March inclusive.[92] Dr G.E. Gaulton at Pangnirtung, like J.G. Wright, blamed undernourishment for the heavy mortality among children. "The fact that most of the deaths occurred during the dark season when the natives are often hungry and the fact that most of the deaths occur at the poor camps show that poor nutrition plays a very important part ... Camp sanitation is very bad. This, of course, is a matter of education, as is also the proper feeding of children."

The question of infant mortality rates among Indians and Inuit came up in the House of Commons on 17 June 1946. Brooke Claxton, the minister of national health and welfare, told the House that infant mortality among the native peoples in the north in 1942, 1943, and 1944 was "roughly" three times higher than that among white Canadians outside the NWT. Two years later the situation was no better. Interviewed in Montreal on 9 July 1948, Dr H.W. Lewis told the press that the faulty diets of Inuit mothers had "brought about an alarming increase in infant mortality."[93] Lewis, who was leaving on the Eastern Arctic Patrol, said that he planned to educate mothers in the greater use of cereals and powdered milk, which were then becoming available to the Inuit at the trading posts. He believed that too little attention was being paid to diets during the pre- and postnatal periods. One of his predecessors on the Eastern Arctic Patrol had reported the same thing in 1945. "Re infant feeding instructions," wrote Dr David Jordan, "There is need for instruction on infant feeding to reach those Eskimo mothers who cannot nurse their children. I have one example of a family at Cape Smith where there had been 6 live births and all but one died within the first 6 months of intestinal trouble, no doubt due to faulty diet."[94]

In November 1945 Health and Welfare assumed responsibility for the health care of the northern population, and, as already mentioned, health care and medical facilities began to improve. Among the actions the department took to better the lot of the Inuit was provision of funds for the payment of family allowances to Inuit children. These were paid in kind "from carefully selected lists of items designed to benefit the children."[95] In 1947 the medical officer on the Eastern Arctic Patrol reported: "For the first time in the Eastern Arctic, dry milk and pablum have been placed in supply at the several trading posts for distribution under the Family Allowances Act ... Traders, police and all the "whites" are keenly interested in this attempt at improved nutrition for small children and will help greatly in the educational effort necessary in this move toward rational auxiliary feeding."[96]

Generally the Inuit adhered to the authorized list of items, which included canned milk, pablum, cereals, and egg powder.[97] But sometimes conditions at the trading post made it difficult to do so. At Iqaluit in 1950, for example, the district registrar was issuing large quantities of flour and sugar in the family allowances, with no issues of milk, pablum, or rolled oats, because the Hudson's Bay Company was out of stock.[98] Neverthless the overall improvement in health care and social welfare showed in a noticeable improvement in the health and vital statistics of the population. According to the RCMP the Inuit themselves remarked on the changes. "The benefits derived from Family Allowances are quite in evidence," said one police report. "The general health seem[s] to have improve[d] and the children who drink milk daily have developed more resistance to sickness. Such is the concensus of opinion among the natives. In fact most children have developed a taste for milk and the parents are no longer required to more or less force the children to drink it."[99] "Early infant deaths were less frequent," the medical officer reported from the Eastern Arctic Patrol in 1947, "and this favourable condition can no doubt be credited to the plentiful supply of food for the mother, pre and ante-natal."[100]

But the optimism of reports that policemen, doctors, and others wrote from the Eastern Arctic at this time appears to have been premature. Perhaps there was an element of reporting what one wanted to see rather than what was actually happening. The introduction of a "plentiful supply of food for the mother" should have had beneficial results, so beneficial results were what everyone saw. Perhaps one could call this "the placebo effect." The true situation was not as rosy as reported. Dr Otto Schaefer, head of the Northern Medical Research Unit at the Charles Camsell Hospital in Edmonton, writes in a personal letter to the author that one "cannot help but smile about the claimed observation of improved children's health and greater resistance to diseases reported in 1949 as opposed to 1946 and attributed to more milk consumption." Schaeffer maintains that during the late 1940s and early 1950s "morbidity of children due to acute as well as chronic infectious diseases (otitis media, tuberculosis) went markedly up, not down."

Why should this have happened? It happened to a large degree because the family allowances' provision of milk, pablum, and cereals encouraged Inuit mothers to give up breast-feeding in favour of bottle-feeding, an unfortunate abandonment of age-old practice that had calamitous results for the children. Traditionally the Inuit mother fed her infant at the breast, with supplements of raw meat and fish, until the next sibling arrived about three years later. "Now the availability of milk condensates and the introduction of nursing bottles – which occurred at first and only slowly, around the trading posts, then spread rapidly with the precipitous military and civilian build-up that began in the mid-1950s – have changed feeding habits drastically."[101]

The change to bottle-feeding in the Arctic was without doubt a crucial factor in the excessive rates of infant morbidity and mortality. Dr Schaeffer has referred to a study that the Canadian Medical Service conducted between 1962 and 1965. It showed that infant mortality was constantly higher in bottle-fed infants. Schaeffer comments: "More recently I examined the relationship of infant feeding to infant morbidity in Eskimos. I found that one could demonstrate that bottle-fed children have a higher incidence not only of diseases of the gastro-intestinal tract, as might be expected, but also a greater incidence of respiratory and middle ear diseases and anemia. This association of childhood disease and the mode of infant feeding is demonstrated by one of our most frequent health problems: chronic suppurative otitis media."

Bottle-feeding thus contributed to infant mortality by reducing the infant's resistance to infection or by otherwise making them more susceptible to disease. But with regard to the actual medical cause of death, very few of the infant deaths occurred where professionnal medical attention was available, and so the causes officially given on most of the death certificates are open to question. In about 45 per cent of the cases the cause of death was unknown, and about another 45 per cent gave causes believed to involve the respiratory system.[102] For example, the Cape Dorset welfare teacher reported in October 1950: "The direct cause of the majority of these deaths appears to be pneumonia, tuberculosis and other respiratory conditions. These diseases in turn probably flourish because of low standards of living among the Eskimos, that is, inadequate shelter, poor clothing, and defective nutrition. These conditions of life, coupled with ignorance about the essentials of child care and sanitation, makes [sic] it surprising that as many children reach adulthood as seem to."[103]

This observation points up the difference between the modern and traditional Inuit. In earlier times the Inuit appear to have been healthier because they lived on fresh uncooked meat, clothed themselves in furs, and were so isolated that they rarely came in contact with sources of infection. By the late 1950s, as a result of the sudden incursion of southern Canadians and Americans into the Eastern

Arctic, the Inuit were exposed as never before to a wide range of diseases. Since most of them did not enjoy the luxury of continuous warmth and shelter, of constantly adequate nutrition, and of a sanitary environment, they were extraordinarily vulnerable to these diseases. Then, when they were laid low by infection, the circumstances of their environment aggravated their illness. Since infants suffered from the same infections as their parents, they could easily go from bad to worse because of diminished parental care. And only a few had the benefit of immediate medical attention, while many never received any such care. These factors contributed to the overall morbidity and mortality in the Eastern Arctic and in particular to infant mortality.

Of all the environmental factors contributing to high morbidity and mortality the most significant was lack of adequate shelter and warmth. Dr J.S. Willis of Indian and Northern Health Services told a meeting of the Committee on Eskimo Affairs in 1958 that the high rate of Inuit infant mortality could be attributed "to a very great extent" to bad housing. He said that in the present circumstances Health and Welfare could go on spending money indefinitely in a vain attempt to reduce the death rate. But newborn infants were too susceptible to the hazards of bad housing and consequently succumbed too quickly to allow health officials to find, remove, and treat them in time to save their lives.[104]

The result of the wretched environmental conditions of the Eastern Arctic was an infant mortality rate which the director of Northern Administration and Lands Branch noted in 1958 "exceeds that of any other ethnic group anywhere in the world for which statistics are available."[105] The highest national rate recorded by the United Nations in its *Demographic Yearbook* for 1958 was 137.7 per thousand live births in Aden, followed by 135.3 for Montserrat, 133.3 for the British Virgin Islands, and 131.9 for the coloured population of South Africa. A figure of 156.0 for the Gilbert and Ellice Islands was italicized as being unreliable or derived from incomplete data. The NWT of Canada had infant mortality rates higher than any of these except the Gilbert and Ellice Islands figure, but at 151 came close even to that.[106] This continued a high rate of infant mortality that averaged 117 between 1951 and 1955, was 149 in 1956, and 143 in 1957. These figures relate to both white and native populations together. For Canada as a whole the infant mortality rates in 1956, 1957, and 1958 were 32, 31, and 30 respectively. In Ontario they were 25 in all three years. Among the Inuit they were 230.[107] Almost a quarter of all babies born to Inuit mothers died in their first year.

Of these infant deaths neo-natal mortality was much lower than post-neo-natal mortality; in fact, in the NWT in 1962 the death rates for Inuit and Indian babies from the second to the twelfth month were nearly three times the death rates during the first month.[108] This situation was the reverse of that among the white population and reflects the overwhelming influence of environmental rather than genetic or congenital factors. Native infants were dying at excessive rates because of unhealthy living conditions. Northern Health Services in 1962 listed five main causes of high post-neo-natal mortality:

i Poor housing, lacking in shelter and inadequately heated.
ii Lack of sanitary facilities, which encouraged the spread of gastro-enteric infections.
iii Exposure to new strains of bacteria and viruses as the Eskimo family came into increasing contact with white men from many parts of the continent and even from other parts of the world.
iv Parental ignorance of the principles of hygienic living in a fixed location and of modern infant care.
v Lack of means to communicate quickly with the nearest physician or nurse when illness struck.

These same factors, with the exception of ignorance of infant care, contributed to the high rate of mortality in general, and the Eastern Arctic suffered most. As the 1962 northern health report from the Department of Northern Affairs and National Resources pointed out, the Eastern Arctic took "the highest toll of Eskimo life." As a reflection of the general situation, the average age at death for all residents in the Northwest Territories in 1963 was a very low 22 years. For Indians it was 33.16 years, for the white population 31.11 years, and for the Inuit a shocking 15.05 years. When death during the first year was excluded, these figures became 47.48, 53.0, and 35.9 years respectively. The gradual improvement in housing and other living conditions in the 1960s led to a rise in the average age at death among the Inuit. In 1965 it was 19.8, in 1966 20.9, and in 1967 21.1. This increase was due to a reduction in infant mortality which is always the first demographic statistic to respond to improved living standards.

The annual northern health reports show the declining rate of infant deaths in the Eastern Arctic. From 218 per thousand live births in 1960 they dropped to 99.2 in 1967. Further improvement, the 1967 report noted, would depend on better housing, sanitation, diet and health education, and awareness of the factors involved in healthful living. "We should still be able to reduce further the Eskimo infant mortality rate by extending treatment services into some of the remaining larger settlements which have as yet no nursing stations or resident nurses." Not surprisingly, Keewatin and Baffin had the highest infant mortality rates and crude death rates. Its own medical services in these areas, Health and Welfare admitted, "are not as well developed as in the Western Arctic, and although we have extended nursing services to Igloolik, Pond Inlet, Arctic Bay and Broughton Island within the past few years, there also appears to be a higher incidence of disease in these areas which, no doubt, accounts for the higher death rates."

In response to improved medical services and better, if still imperfect, living conditions, the death rate among Eastern Arctic infants has shown a remarkable decline, from 86.5 per thousand live births in 1971 to 38.5 in 1981. In 1978 the rate was down to as low as 17.6 in the Baffin region. The territorial Department of Health believes that the most important single factor was not better housing or medical care but "the resurgence of breast feeding especially among the Inuit. It has been shown by our department in the Northwest Territories and more recently by other workers in northern Manitoba that morbidity amongst breast fed is only a fraction of that experienced in bottle fed infants, and such decreased morbidity must naturally be reflected in lower mortality rates."[109]

The rising popularity of breast-feeding in the late 1970s was almost certainly one laudable and welcome result of the continued expansion of a number of nutrition programs established with increased co-operation between intergovernmental bodies and other agencies. In particular, infant nutrition guidelines were printed and distributed throughout the NWT to all agencies responsible for a nutrition component of community health programs.[110]

But the improvement in infant mortality statistics is no cause for complacency. In the NWT as a whole the 1981 rate of 20.8 was the lowest on record, but it gives a false impression. While Indian babies in the Western Arctic enjoyed a rate well below the average, Inuit babies in the Eastern Arctic experienced an above-average rate.[111] The rate in the Baffin zone was almost double that in the Territories as a whole and was 350 per cent higher than the rate among non-natives, recorded as 11.2. A study by Health and Welfare and the University of Alberta showed that Inuit children under one year old died at five times and Indian infants at three times the national rate.[112] This study ruled out inadequate medical care as a factor and blamed the long-standing social and economic problems of the Arctic such as low family income, alcohol, and poor housing, water-supply, sewage, nutrition, and education.

Nutrition

Poor nutrition among the Inuit has been associated with high infant mortality for decades. But general health also has suffered from bad eating habits. In 1948 Dr H.W. Lewis complained that some of the Inuit were eating too much "white men's food" and that, instead of aiding, this was harming their health.[113] During his trip on the Eastern Arctic Patrol that year he hoped to be able "to talk them into getting back to their old diet of seal and whale meat." Health authorities in the Arctic have been trying to do that ever since.

During the 1940s the Inuit consumed increasing quantities of imported foods. They acquired these foods in two ways. Those Inuit who were trappers came to "subsist largely on food bought from the store in return for white fox."[114] As more and more Inuit were attracted to trapping, more and more they grew accustomed to eating store-bought food. The administration's position was that this was "bad from the point of view of native health," but it became even more serious with the postwar depression of white fox prices because, with reduced income and greatly inflated prices for essential goods, the Inuit faced real hardship.

The second way in which the Inuit received imported food was as relief. Here again the amounts increased as the decade advanced, and the economic crisis in the north forced larger numbers of Inuit to rely on government handouts and family allowances, most of which were exchanged at the nearest Hudson's Bay Company store for food. Even as early as 1941 doctors were raising questions about the effectiveness of this kind of relief. Dr J.A. Bildfell, the medical officer at Pangnirtung, for example, wrote, "It is my private opinion that advances such as flour (white), tea, sugar, biscuits, etc., and in the quantities which have been issued for this purpose, will never save a camp from ultimate starvation in case of extreme need, and relief is to be discouraged at any other time. Of course it is always difficult to determine when a camp "is in extreme need." If relief is issued to a camp it is the custom to share it all around and there is seldom enough provision except for one fair meal."[115]

Even if the relief issues were adequate in quantity they were deficient in quality. Bildfell described the nutritional value of the ration supplied as "very unsatisfactory" and said that it only did harm unless native foods shortly replaced it. "Native foods alone," he maintained, saved the Inuit "from any dangers of starvation." "Obviously relief offers many problems," he went on, "and I am not disregarding the fact that it is our duty to prevent starvation everywhere and anywhere it exists but I am definitely of the opinion, that in extreme need ... the rations as provided will not relieve the stress and is [sic] therefore of little or no value – providing false security, encouraging a bad habit, constitutionally undermining the native and is also wasteful." Bildfell reminded the administration "that it is part of the honorable native tradition to care for their helpless and also to struggle through any crisis. This should not be interfered with to any extent."

With long-endured frustration the medical profession and others familiar with northern conditions had in the past consistently referred to the deficiency of the relief diet offered to the Inuit. But, as D.L. McKeand himself admitted, "nothing much had been done to remedy it."[116] RCMP reports going back as far as 1929[117] show that these very same foods were issued to sick and destitute natives in comparatively substantial quantities on the authority of the medical officers at Pangnirtung before St Luke's Hospital was established. A lengthy correspondence on northern nutrition and health revealed that a Dr Tisdall had "found it necessary to prepare a special vitamin tablet for Hudson's Bay Company personnel stationed in the north." An irate Maj. McKeand commented in a memo to the NWT deputy commissioner that "if Dr. Tisdall found deficiency in northern foods and prescribed a remedy, it seems reasonable for a layman to suggest that the Eskimos should have been protected against this deficiency years ago."[118]

Alarmed at last by the impact of deficient diet on morbidity and mortality in the north, especially on infant mortality, the NWT Council requested that a nutritional survey be made of the inhabitants of the Territories. Winifred Hinton of Nutrition Services in the new Department of Pensions and National Health carried out the study and prepared her report in February 1944.[119] It was not a success. Dr Hinton based her findings on a questionnaire to which she received insufficient replies. None at all came from the Eastern Arctic, "owing to unusual circumstances." So "information on the Eastern Arctic had to be obtained from officials who have visited this area." One general point that emerged from the study was "that the natives coming from a distance, that is, not living near the post, are much healthier than those at the settlements or frequent visitors." Everyone connected with the north had known this for a long time. "Medical officers of the Eastern Arctic Patrol since 1932, without exception, reported that the general health of natives remote from trading posts was better than that of those employed by white people or camped within a relatively short distance of trading centers."[120] And the NWT deputy commisioner wrote in 1947:

Medical reports over the years show that the healthiest Eskimo are those who have plentiful supplies of country produce. As the proportion of white man's food increases in the diet, the native health is found to decline. This is, no doubt, partly due to the kind of white man's food used by the natives. Flour is, of course, the main staple and this is usually cooked in the form of a bannock fried in seal oil or other grease. In recent years the flour sold to Eskimo is the high extraction variety which is supposed to retain a larger measure of vitamines and essential minerals than the former highly processed variety. Nevertheless it does not appear that an almost exclusive flour diet of this sort can sustain health.[121]

One aspect of the problem of poor nutrition among the Inuit was ignorance. The administration knew that the standard of Inuit health dropped with excessive use of white man's food, but it did not know how much or what kind of food caused the deterioration.[122] Presumably a certain amount of white man's food was permissible without an undesirable decline in health, but, the administration admitted, "we do not know where the border line lies." Doctors had been making reports on native health on the Eastern Arctic Patrol for many years. In 1946 alone they examined 1,500 Inuit and took chest x-rays. This intensive survey bore out observations made in previous years: namely, that the health at some posts, "notably in Quebec," was much below that of posts further north, "where native food conditions are better."

But the administration was guilty of operating on a double standard. It knew that "white" food was detrimental to Inuit health and also that the Inuit's health was most vulnerable at ship time each year. Yet each year the tempting prospect of issues of white man's food attracted Inuit to the settlements to work on the annual supply ship. Maj. McKeand suggested to the NWT deputy commissioner that maybe "local produce (seals, fish, etc.) should be given the native workers at ship time in preference to tinned meats, butter, biscuits, jam, tea, etc." But then he realized that there was "a danger" in denying white man's food to the Inuit at ship time – not to the Inuit but to the administration. "It would be disappointing to the natives if they were denied white man's food at ship time," McKeand remarked. "Some substitute or other form of entertainment would have to be provided otherwise the independence of the natives would assert itself and many would refuse to come to the settlement. In this event discharge of the ship would be seriously hampered."[123]

Through the 1950s the administration did much to improve the economic and material conditions of the Inuit but little to improve nutrition. Government reports suggested that the Inuit were still largely eaters of meat. "The people on Banks and Victoria Islands and in Northern Quebec, Baffin Island and the Queen Elizabeth Islands depend very largely on seals for their own consumption, and these would probably constitute from 60 to 80 per cent of total diet."[124] Inuit along the mainland coasts of Mackenzie and Keewatin, except those around the Mackenzie delta, depended very greatly on caribou, though some also engaged extensively in sealing, especially in the spring months. The only Inuit using walrus to any great extent were those around Igloolik and Southampton Island, where walrus made up probably 50 per cent of the regular diet.

But a drastic change in eating habits, especially among settlement Inuit or those convenient to a trading post, was obvious to many people working in the north. The change was from "a high protein diet of meat and fish to a high carbohydrate diet of bannock," and this "would give deficiencies of biologically valuable protein, and of minerals and vitamins, especially calcium and riboflavin."[125] Bannock is a word of Gaelic origin for various kinds of home-made bread. In the form of a thick round pancake it became a staple food for thousands of people in Arctic Canada, but its ingredients – flour, water, salt, baking powder, and whatever lard or oil was available – were not the most nutritious. "When it becomes the sole article of diet, as it often does for Eskimos around trading posts," wrote two nutritionists from Health and Welfare, "nutritional deficiencies develop."

Since 1947 most of the northern trading posts had stocked large quantities of powdered milk and pablum, and the Inuit were encouraged to use these foods as regularly as possible. Wire whippers were even provided to ease the use of powdered milk. But the Inuit continued to spend most of their money and family allowance credits on flour, pilot biscuits, and sugar, which, as a result, the administration had to limit to an acceptable ration per family.[126] It took this step not just for reasons of health but also to encourage the Inuit to hunt for their own country food and not "remain idle around the post." Nutritionists proposed to prepare for sale a bannock mix which they enriched by adding skim milk powder. This addition to bannock mix did not increase the caloric content but added 21 per cent more protein, 587 per cent more riboflavin, and 766 per cent more calcium.[127] The two government nutritionists noted: "Bannock mix costs more than flour, or than the ingredients of ordinary bannock, due to the cost of skim milk powder, and the thermoseal package. There can be no doubt that there is real health value far greater than the increased cost. No other acceptable food supplying as much food value can be shipped North." But nothing came of the bannock mix. The Hudson's Bay Company refused to stock it generally in its stores unless some type of subsidy reduced the price or unless the administration insisted on its issue for relief purposes or as family allowances.[128] The answer appeared to be to encourage the Inuit to add skim milk powder to their own recipe, but there is no indication that this was ever done.

Eating habits continued to deteriorate as more and more of the food items of southern Canada found their way on to the shelves of the Hudson's Bay Company and Inuit Cooperative stores throughout the Arctic. "People are beginning to depend upon bannock, tea, soft drinks, candy, gum and tinned foods for a diet," Anne Berndtsson, community principal at Cape Dorset, reported in 1961. "As the years go on, fewer people will hunt seal and as a result Canada will have a poorly nourished northern Canadian."

Much food that is purchased here is merely eaten from the tin or package. Food value and nutrition are unheard of. The following incident will exemplify what I have stated. This incident is one of many that occur here often if not daily.

On a visit to a summer tent home, I arrived after the mother's daily trip to the store – a daily trip in so far as daily trips can last after pay day. She had purchased the following food items: one can beets, one can asparagus, one small jar pickles, one can apricots, one can tuna fish, one dozen or more tins soft drinks, numerous packages of gum and candy, plus a twenty pound bag of flour and three pounds shortening. The tins were opened and passed out to the individuals in the tent. The person who happened to fall prey to the tin of cold, mushy asparagus – took one, tasted it, immediately discarded the entire tin with its contents outside the tent door and moved over to help young brother devour the delicious sweet pickles. These foods washed down with a tin of Mason's root beer, followed by a package of gum, would be novel for any picnic. However, I thought, surely something must be done here – something long-range, something of a permanent nature – a diet like this will kill them. This type of buying, eating and wasting lasts until the pay cheque is gone – five days to ten days after pay day. Then if hunting is not good or they have not been inspired to hunt, they go back to bannock and tea. Surely the Canadian Government cannot agree with this type of spending. Granted these people are Canadian citizens with the freedom to use their possessions as they see fit. However, if they continue in their present manner they will never have anything.[129]

The eating habits of the Inuit have improved little since then. They still eat country food – seal, caribou, fish, muktuk, duck, etc – but store-bought foods, foreign to the Inuit in substance, use, and preparation, increasingly supplement the healthier country produce. The Nutrition Canada report issued in 1974 by Health and Welfare Canada showed clearly the results of such an improper diet. A serious vitamin c deficiency was prevalent among Inuit of all ages, with over half of the adolescents and two-thirds of the adults recorded as sufferers. Inuit, especially children, adolescents, and pregnant women, also suffered from iron deficiency, and the level of calcium and vitamin D intake was very poor among all ages. Over 60 per cent of adult Inuit were found to have low levels of serum folate, a condition that leads, like iron deficiency, to anaemia. The report cited growing evidence that rapid changes in life-styles and eating habits were harming the health of the Inuit. "They have a more severe health problem than any other group we've studied," said Beth Stitchell, a Health and Welfare dietician who worked on the report.[130]

This situation was hardly encouraging, especially after more than a decade of nutritional education undertaken by the Adult Education Division. Yet it took the territorial government exactly three years to do anything about it. In February 1977 it published a report that called for a comprehensive nutritional program to improve the disheartening state of northern health.[131] Information on specific groups in the north had indicated, over and over again, that serious nutritional deficiencies were threatening the health of the native people. Studies going back more than 30 years had investigated the eating habits of the Inuit and Indians and made recommendations for their improvement. And yet in 1977 the territorial government's report was still calling for the nutritional needs of northerners to be determined.

A sense of urgency of the problem of northern nutrition has been seriously lacking. The improvement of health depends to a large degree on the reform of eating habits, but the eating habits of the Inuit have been slow to improve. Advertising of store-bought foods, especially the highly influential material on television, has tended to undermine the best efforts of nutritional educators and thus increase the improperly nourished Inuit's vulnerability to all kinds of diseases.

Epidemics

It is well established that the health and the eating habits of the Inuit both declined with increasing contact between them and the white men. The modern period of rapidly growing contact began during the Second World War, and it is no coincidence that in the 1940s epidemics of various kinds ravaged the Eastern Arctic. In 1944 J.L.

Robinson wrote: "The most serious problem facing the Eskimo ... is the sudden appearance of epidemics which wipe out numbers of their population in local areas. Since 1941 several epidemics have been chiefly instrumental in causing 304 deaths in the Eastern Arctic and thus actually reducing the population by 36 persons."[132]

During that same year a memo prepared for the NWT Council recorded: "There have been outbreaks of spinal meningitis at Southampton Island, scabies have been widespread in the same area for two years or more, there was a meningitis epidemic at Cape Dorset in 1943, the incidence of tuberculosis is generally high, and new conditions have required that consideration be given to improved methods of controlling venereal diseases."[133]

One cause of this high morbidity and resultant high mortality among the Inuit after 1941 was the greater exposure to infection from the incursion of large numbers of white men into the Eastern Arctic during the Second World War. On this topic the Ottawa *Journal* reported on 8 August 1944 that officials in the capital "feel that the Eskimo have a just grievance against the white man for all the disease he has brought among them since war started." The paper, having interviewed Maj. McKeand on his return from the Eastern Arctic Patrol, pointed out that more whites than ever before had been among the Inuit, "and almost without exception" the Inuit caught germs from the visitors. "A common cold," the paper said, "becomes serious with an Eskimo." The situation itself was not new. Every year, when the annual supply ship arrived, the local Inuit suffered severely from infections introduced from the south to which they had little or no immunity. "Colds become rapidly epidemic following the visit of any ship or plane, or dog team bringing in supplies," wrote the medical officer on board the Eastern Arctic Patrol in 1945. "It is particularly noticeable in the natives seen at Posts visited along Cumberland Sound and along Hudson Strait."[134]

What was different after 1941 was the degree of infection caused by the influx of large numbers of military and civilian personnel and the more regular arrival of aircraft. Medical reports from the Eastern Arctic year after year refer to outbreaks of influenza and pneumonia among the Inuit just after "ship-time." At best the Inuit suffered only very bad colds, at worst virulent outbreaks of respiratory infection that reached epidemic proportions. On 23 October 1941, for example, the Hudson's Bay Company post manager, James A. Thom, reported from Pangnirtung: "For the past three weeks we have been combatting the worst epidemic of influenza and pneumonia I've seen hit these people in my time up north. The hospital's maximum capacity has been estimated at 20 beds; today they have

41 patients with 20 or more natives with varying degrees of infection in tents in the settlement. To date 6 deaths have occurred, 4 male, 2 female, but only one of these in the hospital; the others died at their camps before we had a chance or reaching them."[135]

This particular epidemic was worse than Thom or even Dr Bildfell, the medical officer, realized, because neither of them was aware of the extent of the epidemic beyond Pangnirtung and the camps within motorboat range of the settlement. In fact, as Maj. McKeand explained later, two epidemics were running concurrently: one a respiratory disease with a high proportion of lobar pneumonia; the other a severe influenza or paratyphoid fever.[136] According to radio messages the casualties were as follows:

Epidemic	Patients treated	Deaths in hospital	Deaths in camps
First	42	2	20
Second	38	6	15
Totals	80	8	35

McKeand considered this "a serious matter and more so because it could have been guarded against. We have known for twenty years that epidemics of more or less severity followed the visits of ships to government stations and trading posts." His memo to the NWT deputy commissioner went on:

Our medical officers have the benefit of local radio communication and keep in touch with government, trading and mission centers. These centers are gradually being supplied with standard medical equipment and the officers in charge acting on the advice of the medical officer can readily treat white or native patients. By this means the spread of epidemics is checked.

However this service does not meet the danger from "ship's cold." This dread attack comes suddenly and when radio communication is not as reliable as in the winter months. Until the Administration asserts some authority at ship time, epidemics are bound to occur year after year. Now that the Defence Forces are penetrating the Eastern Arctic the death rate from "ship's cold" is likely to increase unless steps are taken immediately to prevent them [sic].

McKeand discussed Eastern Arctic epidemics and relief with Dr J.J. Heagerty, director of Public Services in the Department of Pensions and National Health, and reported the results to the NWT deputy commissioner.[137] Heagerty agreed with the administration's view that "the effect of the epidemic last fall would tend to impair native resistance to many forms of mental and physical depression. Consequently the natives would come to the white man for relief either by way of treatment or to receive food supplies." But the effects of the serious influenza epidemic were more far-reaching than merely to increase relief costs to the administration. The high cost of treatment and of hospitalization was catastrophic, both financially and psychologically. Even beyond the physical suffering the patients themselves endured, many families underwent the anguish of dislocation by death. Further, many of the Inuit were unable to put up fall caches of food, and many failed to prepare for the trapping season. Bildfell noted that "the local [Hudson's Bay] Company were momentarily very distressed over the outlook."[138]

In February 1943 an outbreak of cerebro-spinal fever, or spinal meningitis, affected all the camps in the Cape Dorset area. Sixteen cases developed at Ikkerashook, the largest of the local camps, and 15 at Kyruktooarluk. The RCMP reported "several" deaths and enforced isolation at all affected camps.[139] One account, which calls the outbreak "the greatest tragedy to hit Cape Dorset," says that it occurred in January 1943, sickened 50 Inuit and took the lives of 20. "The nearest doctor was at Pangnirtung, far away on the east coast of Baffin Island," this account goes on, "and the only useful medical supply was a small stock of sulfathiazole tablets in the H.B.C. medical kit ... Not until late February – more than a month after the outbreak was discovered – was an aircraft able to reach Dorset to drop medicines. By then the epidemic was dying out."[140]

One cause of concern was that a number of Igloolik Inuit were trading at Cape Dorset. White residents feared that these Inuit might "mingle in this vicinity and later return to Igloolik and perhaps be the means of spreading the disease."[141] This does not appear to have happened. The Cape Dorset area was worst hit by the epidemic. At Lake Harbour there were only five cases and two deaths; at Southampton Island seven cases and no deaths.[142] The cause of the outbreak is unknown. After examining the history of the epidemic in southern Baffin Island, the medical officer on the Eastern Arctic Patrol considered it most plausible that it "originated in the eastern section, possibly Newfoundland or Labrador, spread to isolated settlements on the coast following the more frequent course of communication, and whether carried by native contact, Nascopie or other ship, made inroads along the southern coast of Baffin Island to Southampton Island."

The Cape Dorset area continued to be hit by misfortune, a grim illustration of the precariousness of Inuit life in the mid-1940s. The Eastern Arctic Patrol in 1945 found many ill with an "intestinal trouble which may prove to be a form of paratyphoid."[143] The officer in charge of the patrol reported that 45 had died from the disease during the year, "one just after the doctors arrived." The following winter stomach flu accompanied by severe diarrhoea caused approximately 20 deaths.[144] Altogether in the Cape Dorset area between 1 April 1945 and 15 April 1946 a total of 49 deaths occurred. Influenza caused 20 of these, and typhoid fever another 9.

By the 1950s the medical authorities had succeeded in bringing serious epidemics under control. Apart from tuberculosis there was no major cause of concern, and in general health was better than during the previous decade. Around the settlements colds were a source of worry, not so much in themselves as because they tended to lead to a stubborn pneumonia in many of the small children and could have disastrous consequences when carried back to the camps, where no medical attention was available. In February 1959 the community teacher at Pangnirtung reported "a decided increase in the number of non-TB patients in the hospital, all or mostly seeming to be complications resulting from the colds, or flu, or whatever it might be."[145] Eye diseases continued to be "very prevalent," and loss of vision through corneal opacity was "common."[146] So were various skin diseases. Lice, scabies, impetigo, boils, and furuncles were described as "common at all ages in both sexes." Impetigo and boils seemed to be more prevalent in winter and tended to heal throughout the summer months, often with considerable scarring and sometimes with keloid formation. "These conditions," wrote Dr J.A. Hildes of the University of Manitoba, "seem directly related to lack of knowledge or facilities for personal cleanliness."

This criticism of Inuit habits was common and usually related to disease incidence. "The Eskimos of South Baffin Island are not particularly clean in their person or their dress," wrote the artist James Houston. "This habit they share with most Canadian Eskimos, with a few group exceptions, Pond Inlet and Pangnirtung and to a lesser extent Port Harrison. Because they have a minimum of heat in winter and summer from seal oil lamps, warm water for bathing and clothes washing is almost unobtainable. The desire to wash and be clean is clearly an educational project closely allied with health and should be stressed in the schools."[147]

Medical visitors were shocked by the lack of sanitation and hygiene. Dr J.S. Willis, who led the medical party on the Eastern Arctic Patrol in 1955, remarked that at least in summer the "toilet" seemed to be "the great outdoors" where he saw men "urinating without shame in the open before their people." The women appeared "more modest." That there seemed to be no camp rules about the disposal of excreta was borne out by the fact that he "observed dried faecal material strewn about at random all over the camp site but usually not within ten feet of a tent." Someone told him that dogs consumed the excreta, but he did not see any of them doing it. "Possibly it is only done in the winter when food is scarce."[148]

Other behavioural characteristics that appalled the medics were that chewing gum was "passed from mouth to mouth and a cigarette passed around the family circle when tobacco is in short supply. The mothers chew food for their infants. Tuberculosis is thus shared by all." Modern medical opinion does not consider the pre-mastication of food to be a factor in the spread of tuberculosis. Dr Otto Schaeffer in a personal letter argues that tuberculosis was practically always transmitted to northern natives, especially children, by inhaling tubercle bacilli contained in air-suspended droplets coughed up by infected adults in the same room or – more rarely – by inhaling tubercle bacilli whirled into the air from dried-up expectorate. By comparison, the chances of an open tuberculous mother's infecting her child with food transmitted from the mother's mouth to the infant's mouth and gastro-intestinal tract was so remote – and to Schaeffer's knowledge never documented – that the advice given to discourage this traditional practice was completely unfounded and harmful out of proportion even of imagined benefits. As a result of this advice, essential nutrients, especially iron and a number of minerals and vitamins important for healthy growth and development after the age of six months, were denied to Inuit infants. This made them less resistant to infections in general, including tuberculosis. That northern medical officers discouraged this traditional infant feeding practice for hygienic reasons is, however, understandable in an era when medicine, particularly in the north, was almost exclusively preoccupied with combating infectious diseases and chasing germs.

Changing Morbidity Patterns

In the 1960s and 1970s Inuit morbidity patterns changed significantly. At the beginning of this period pneumonia replaced tuberculosis as the primary cause of death in the Arctic. Its incidence among the Inuit was five times that among Indians and seven times that among white people.[149] By 1965 pneumonia was responsible for 20.2 per cent of deaths. The second highest cause of death that year was the multiple class of injuries, violence, and accidents. By

1967 northern health reports show that this class had risen to first place, causing 20.7 per cent of all deaths, while pneumonia slipped to second place and then in 1971 to fourth place. The top three killers of the Inuit in 1971 were, first, injuries, violence, and accidents; second, diseases of infancy, prematurity, and malformation; and third, cardiovascular disease. The association of alcohol with deaths from injuries, accidents, and violence was "estimated at between forty to fifty per cent of the total episodes."

The killer class of injuries, violence, and accidents has continued to dominate Inuit mortality, maintaining first place in the annual list of causes of death ever since. And its lead is substantial. In 1981, 41.1 per cent of Inuit deaths were due to this one class, while malignant neoplasms – in second place for the third time since they reached the top four in 1975 – caused 16.8 per cent of Inuit deaths. The cause of the high rate of death by injuries, violence, and accidents is obviously social rather than medical. It may have something to do with the fact that most "northern native communities have little or no potential for economic development and are poverty stricken. Poor educational opportunities, legal restrictions and problems of adjustment often make it difficult to move away to seek other opportunities. This produces, among other things, a high incidence of alcoholism, violence, suicide and mental disorders. Indeed, while there has been a marked decline in deaths from infectious diseases there has been a rapid increase in deaths from accidents, poisonings and violence, including suicide."[150]

The most disturbing aspect of this violent mortality is that suicide is the leader of the group, followed by drowning, crib death, gunshot wounds, asphyxia, motor vehicle accidents, and homicide, in that order.[151] Two-thirds of all NWT suicides occur among Inuit, and many are young people. Dennis Patterson, member of the territorial legislative assembly for Iqaluit, said in the House on 15 November 1979 that he was extremely concerned about the startling rate at which young people were taking their own lives in his constituency. Nine had committed suicide in one year.[152] He attributed this shocking development to his belief that the young were "angry at a society where there is no hope for them." His fear was that Iqaluit's incidence of juvenile delinquency, drug use, and suicide would be "just the beginning of what could occur across the North."

The territorial Department of Social Services was itself alarmed by the growing number of suicides and the rising incidence of drug use and tried to be as responsive as possible to community action requests. One step already taken in 1979 was the appointment of a psychiatric social worker who collaborated with a mental health coordinator at Iqaluit. This dual position received credit in the 1979 *Report on Health Conditions in the Northwest Territories* for a "marked reduction in suicides compared with previous years and particularly in the Inuit population."

Drug addiction, which reports and speeches usually coupled with suicide or crime, was not a significant problem in the NWT. The authorities paid much more attention to the abuse of alcohol, which was implicated in 85 per cent of the region's cases of child neglect.[153] On the recommendation of the Wacko Report in 1973, the territorial government set up an Alcohol and Drug Coordinating Council.[154] The functions of this council were to promote communication and co-operation between agencies involved in providing treatment and preventive services in respect to the abuse of alcohol and other drugs, and agencies involved in the distribution of alcohol; to promote the co-ordination of the policies and programs of these agencies; to serve as an advisory committee to the territorial Alcohol and Drug Programme with responsibility for allocating grants under the Community Alcohol Problems Grants Programme; and to advise the NWT Council concerning the effectiveness of territorial policies, programs, and services and the necessity for changes. The most important and beneficial of these functions was the allocation of funds to enable individual communities to set up programs aimed at combating specific local alcohol-related problems.

In tune with the changing social environment, a new health hazard appeared in the 1960s. In 1965 the incidence of gonorrhoea doubled to a rate of 2,542 per 100,000 population. This figure applies to the NWT as a whole. In Canada the national rate was 102. By 1971, after "steadily rising" for six years, the rate of gonorrhoea among NWT Inuit reached 5,162 per 100,000. This compares with 4,561 for Indians, 3,283 for others, and 159 for all of Canada. "This disease is more of a social than a medical problem," said the Department of Northern Affairs and National Resources in its 1970 health report. "Treatment is very effective, but the control is very difficult as morals and excessive use of alcohol play a significant part in the spread." The same report noted that the spread of gonorrhoea was especially increasing in the Baffin and Mackenzie zones.

The rise in the incidence of gonorrhoea continued unchecked through the 1970s. Health officials noted in 1975 that the disease "resumed its dismal upward trend ... Previously one was given to thinking that current rates were so high they could hardly get worse. This is evidently not the case. They could be very much worse and in the absence of a sense of personal responsibility for health they may well become so, especially in the face of increasing industrialization and increasing amounts of transient labour."[155] Gonorrhoea did become much worse. In 1981 the disease rate of confirmed cases was 5,577 per 100,000 Inuit, compared with just over 200 for all of Canada. The only bright spot in the dismal picture was that the incidence in Baffin Island had dropped by 8 per cent from 1980.

The changing morbidity and mortality patterns of the Inuit are clearly related to the changing social and technological environment: housing, clothing, transport, and other material elements of the Inuit cultural system were improving; education in hygiene, child care, and medicine was advancing slowly; and politically the Inuit were taking giant strides towards greater participation in the running of their own affairs. But the economic situation was still precarious, jobs were hard to find, and the ideological basis of society had crumbled. Observers noted in 1975: "Underlying the positive trends in integration and native self assertion is a pervasive social malaise. Many native northerners feel overwhelmed by foreign ideas, institutions and technology. Native institutions and often individuals cannot withstand such rapid change. The strains are manifest in critically high rates of "lifestyle" ailments: dental caries, overweight, otitis media, iron deficiency, gas-sniffing, violence and child neglect."[156] As many have already noted, chronic ill health in the Eastern Arctic is now more a social than a medical problem and as such demands the strict administration of social remedies.

CHAPTER THREE

Providing an Education

TO 1945: MISSIONARY SCHOOLING

Another of the nagging questions that American military personnel raised in the Arctic during the Second World War was why the administration was doing nothing to educate the Inuit. In the Eastern Arctic in particular the inadequacy of educational facilities, if not their almost complete absence, was remarkable. In August 1944 only four residential schools existed in the whole NWT: three Roman Catholic (Aklavik, Fort Resolution, and Fort Providence) and one Anglican (Aklavik). None of these was in the Eastern Arctic. Of nine day schools (five Anglican, two Roman Catholic, and two public) only one was in the Eastern Arctic. That was the Anglican day school at Pangnirtung. A total of 216 pupils attended these day schools out of a population, both native and non-native, of 12,028 (1941). In addition to the permanent residential and day schools, others were operated by the missions "during such times as the natives were within the settlements."[1] The Roman Catholic Church ran one of these at Lake Harbour.

The Americans were not alone in reprehending this policy. The Anglican Church in particular was severely critical of the government's lack of initiative in education. Dr A.L. Fleming, bishop of the Arctic, told the NWT deputy commissioner in 1946 that he was "perplexed and worried about ... the whole education system in the North."[2] He went on:

You will notice in the statements recorded in connection with the Commission on the Indian Act how frequently references have been made to the cumbersome Governmental machinery which involves serious and aggravating delays. Would it not be possible at this time to revamp the whole machine and bring in modern methods, placing responsible people with proper authority to deal with matters expeditiously? May I remind you that years ago when I wanted to establish a Residential School for Eskimo children we had all kinds of difficulties and your representative at Aklavik gave us no help or co-operation at first. The grants we got were hopelessly inadequate as you yourself know and this, I feel, was due to the fact that the Government at that time was simply "not interested." That day has passed, I believe, but if we are to do what seems to me to be our duty for the people in the far North then some drastic changes should be made.

The "hopelessly inadequate" government grants referred to by Bishop Fleming were $400 a year for residential schools, $200–250 for mission day schools, and $500–1,500 for public day schools.

In the face of harsh criticism, the Canadian government argued that the problem of education in the Eastern Arctic was "very complex." The thinly scattered population, the transport difficulties, the great distances, the nomadic habits of the Inuit, the necessity for Inuit children to learn the traditional way of life, the frequent changes of white personnel, and "to some extent" the linguistic and religious question all were, and largely remain, serious obstacles to an efficient educational system.

Then there is considerable difference of opinion amongst the white residents in the north as to how much education should be given to the Eskimo and how it should be provided. Some of the missionaries, of course, insist on religious schools. Those laymen who want education for the Eskimo want Government schools. Some do not think the Eskimo should be given much education or he will become dissatisfied with his lot. There is little but the fur trade to support him in the north and he would have a hard time competing with whites outside. Practically all agree that any education given should be provided in the north and that it would be a grave mistake to transport native children any distance from their homes for education since they rapidly became unfitted for the native way of life. This has been amply demonstrated in the case of children brought outside for hospitalization.[3]

And yet the Danes, facing similar environmental obstacles and perhaps the same lack of consensus among the Europeans, had succeeded in educating the Greenland Inuit to an impressive standard:

Formal schooling had been introduced everywhere in the 19th century, so that all were literate in their own language and some also in Danish. The Lutheran Church, which had responsibility also for education, was well established throughout the country, manned by hard-working and devoted

Danish pastors aided by Greenlandic catechists. The introduction of printing as long ago as 1860 had ensured a considerable literature in the native language, and the country included more than its share of authors, poets, musicians, and painters.[4]

When Trevor Lloyd went to Greenland during the Second World War, it was "a shock [to him] to find books printed by natives of the Arctic as long ago as 1860, just as it was startling to see the official radiograms sent from Godthaab to Ottawa, being transmitted by native operators." Native Greenlanders as teachers and servants of the Church were widespread, and many were craftsmen. Lloyd reported these "revelations" to Ottawa, but they had much less impact than might have been hoped. This was partly because of the difficulty of initiating reforms in the Canadian north during a time of war, but more importantly it was because "those charged with formulating northern policies were firm in the belief that there were more suitable ways of dealing with Eskimos than to turn them into Canadians – as they were demonstrably being turned into Danes in Greenland."

At the same time a growing number of Canadians did believe that their own native northerners were entitled to at least a better education than they were receiving at the time. In a letter to Bishop Fleming, the NWT deputy commissioner pointed out that "the view is held by an increasing number of people, as the north becomes better known, that we should be doing more to give our Eskimo a sufficient knowledge of English and Arithmetic to enable them to transact their business with the traders more efficiently. Coupled with this there is, of course, the opportunity offered to teach the children an elementary knowledge of hygiene without which, the doctors tell us, the natives will always be susceptible to recurring epidemics and the spread of communicable diseases."[5] Some who agreed with this point of view emphasized that any educational system in the north had to take into account the nomadic character of the Inuit, who moved about in a pattern determined by the wildlife on which they depended. "Eskimo children cannot follow a fixed school term as white children do," this argument ran, "and cannot observe strict school hours. They cannot embark on a standardized course of studies leading up to and ending in the university, unless they abandon the Eskimo way of life, and this is not desired by anyone, least of all by the Eskimos themselves. Yet it is felt that they must, in their own interest and for their own protection, be taught to write, read, and speak English; to do simple arithmetic; how to keep healthy; to appreciate the need for conservation of their wildlife resources, and to understand the nature of the social world in which they will take their place."[6]

The Dilemma of Inuit Education

When the federal government took over northern education in 1947, it made no attempt to assess the effects of the mission system on the native people's social, political, and economic welfare. Nor did it try to assess where future educational policies would lead the native peoples, or how the educational system fitted into the overall structure of development in the north. Instead the federal government adopted an incremental approach. "It was assumed that if the native peoples were illiterate, poor or otherwise backward by southern standards it was largely because they were denied the opportunity of a southern education. The emphasis was therefore placed on increasing the number of modern schools in the North, the number of students enrolled, and the number of teachers who had southern teaching certificates."[7]

A meeting of the NWT Council in May 1947 decided that, "as a matter of future policy, the Northwest Territories Administration would try and get the funds for the erection of new schools rather than ask the missions to bear this expense."[8] A month later the council recorded that Dr Andrew Moore, inspector of secondary schools in Winnipeg, had agreed "to accompany the Eastern Arctic patrol to study the problem of education in the Eastern Arctic and to report on the needs of the situation."[9]

Though Moore was supposed to have gone on this educational fact-finding mission in 1947, no mention of any report or policy in regard to Eastern Arctic schools appears in northern administration files until 1953.[10] Then there is no more than a paragraph in the minutes of the third meeting of the Sub-Committee on Eskimo Education, and it referred not to Dr Moore but to a Mr Grantham, of whom no description was given:

Mr Grantham reported on the field trip he made during the summer via the Eastern Arctic Patrol. He inspected and enquired into school situations at various points along the northern coast of Quebec, as well as on Southampton, Nottingham, Baffin, Cornwallis and Ellesmere Islands. He stressed the value of such visits and the desirability of having them on an annual basis. He suggested some form of camp lessons for Eskimo children in settlements where either no school facilities exist or [where] it would be impractical to provide regular school facilities locally. Father Laviolette also reported that his visit to Roman Catholic Missions along the Quebec coast had been very successful ... He corroborated the views expressed by Mr. Grantham concerning regular inspections and the desirability of employing some simple method of instruction for reaching camp children in remote places.[11]

In 1949 the educational authorities had established a system of territorial schools. The schools came under the aegis of the territorial administration, and all officials, including teachers, were "members of the Civil Service of Canada."[12] In the Eastern Arctic the administration provided schools at Coral Harbour, Chesterfield Inlet, and Cape Dorset in the early 1950s. In 1952 the Sub-Committee on Eskimo Education was set up under the chairmanship of J.G. Wright, chief of Northern Administration Division. It held its first meeting on 26 September to discuss the objectives of such education. One widespread attitude that the subcommittee itself had to overcome was that the Inuit did not need education. For example, it agreed "that Eskimos should not be permitted to remain illiterate even though their economy may be largely restricted to hunting, fishing and trapping."[13] "They should be furnished with that degree and kind of education," the report went on, "which will enable them to live a fuller life in their own environment and at the same time to be able to take advantage of opportunities which may arise from the encroachment of outside civilization. For the great majority of Eskimos, the present objective should be to teach them reading and writing in elementary English and simple arithmetic. There should also be both child and adult instruction in health and hygiene, coupled with some geography of the world outside, and simple social and natural sciences, all of which could be effectively taught by use of film strips."

This education was to be given in English because none of the available teachers could speak Inuktitut. Because of this linguistic incompetence, the language of instruction from Grade 1 upwards was English. In some schools Inuit children were punished for speaking their own language.[14] "Their own language, both spoken and written, will serve them well enough for their mode of life today," W.T. Larmour wrote in 1950, "but it is most certainly not always going to be sufficient."[15] The same attitude prevailed also in Greenland at this time. A special commission in January 1950 stated that "Greenlandic" could not be used as a medium for spreading modern ideas, techniques, culture, and the teaching of the professions.[16] The Danes added that printing special schoolbooks on all subjects for Greenlanders would be far too expensive for such a small population.

They advocated educating Greenlanders through Danish. This meant sending Danish teachers to Greenland with special allowances, building dozens of new primary schools, establishing special secondary schools for Greenlanders, partly in Greenland and partly in Denmark, together with other proposals all of which amounted to a solution at least 50 times more costly.

In Canada the goal of Inuit education was clear enough, but the road towards it was still undefined. Educators could discern two possible paths across the rough terrain ahead but found it difficult to decide which of the two to choose. "It is recognized that in sparsely settled Eskimo areas it is uneconomic to establish day schools, and undesirable to remove children for long intervals from their parents. Experiments are now being conducted with itinerant teachers who visit Eskimo camps periodically. It is not yet possible to make recommendations for the extension of this method of providing education."[17]

A report, *Education in Canada's Northland*, prepared apparently by the Sub-Committee on Eskimo Education in December 1954, cautiously made a choice: "The residential school is perhaps the most effective way of giving children from primitive environments, experience in education along the lines of civilization leading to vocational training to fit them for occupations in the white man's economy."[18] That qualifying "perhaps" indicates that the government was still not quite sure which way to go. But off it went, heading with noticeably unsure tread along the path to the residential school.

Residential Schools

Under the residential school system, set up in 1951 because of the lack of community schools, children were airlifted from remote settlements to larger centres such as Iqaluit, Great Whale River, Churchill, even Inuvik, Yellowknife, and Ottawa. There, for 10 months of the year, the children were housed in hostels at government expense and cared for by Roman Catholic nuns or Anglican missionaries. When the government first introduced the system, in spite of frequent assertions that it was "a grave mistake" or at least "undesirable" to remove children from their parents and their way of life, one Winnipeg newspaper accused it of kidnapping children and forcing them into schools.[19]

Opposition to the system has been vigorous and uncompromising. "Parents wept to see their children taken from them and sent to live among a different people in a foreign land. And their worst fears were rapidly realized by the disruption that such education caused to their children and to family life."[20] For those Inuit children who came from remote areas, where the traditional way of life persisted, residential schooling was disorienting and disruptive. The southern Canadian diet and the indoor warmth caused the children to suffer when they returned home to the cold and the all-meat regimen. So they resented their parents, first for sending them to such an alien situation and then later for not being able to provide the comforts of the residential school. Scorn for parents extended to the traditional way of life. Returning Inuit children tended to look down on hunting, fishing, and skin clothing, an attitude that could pose a threat to their survival.[21]

The residential school removed children not only from their parents' way of life but from their parents' control. The greatest area of concern and the first cause of dissension was this loss of parental control and the subsequent problems of child discipline that arose from the school situation. Removing a child from parents at an age when he or she was beginning important role-identification and when parental discipline and guidance came to bear on the child's social relations had serious consequences, particularly in the eyes of Inuit parents. The complaint that these parents most frequently voiced was that of loss of respect, and it seemed to be connected with the parents' awareness that they were becoming less and less influential in their own children's upbringing.[22]

Educators, from their southern perspective, had a different view of the situation. They believed that the Inuit child would make better progress if placed in the proper environment of boarding school or private, non-native home. This, of course, was progress as southern Canadians judged it. Inuit students boarding in homes with white families or guardians absorbed a large share of middle-class, southern values and behaviour patterns. The host house parents supervised them more closely, regulated their hours more strictly, discouraged absenteeism, and gave them positive inducement to achieve high standards. These students did better academically but paid a price for such success. They had to be away from their own communities for 10 months of each year. As a result they lost contact with home and widened a serious, alienating gap between themselves and their parents. They surrendered much of their language and culture and assumed many white values and white attitudes to dress, eating habits, and social activities. Subject to the combined influence of southern teachers, southern-style boarding schools or other residences, and a southern curriculum, many of these students came to disdain their own culture, their own parents, their own families in the Arctic.

Not all native people have negative feelings towards the residential school system. NWT Council member Peter Ernerk wrote in the *Edmonton Journal* that many young Inuit had benefited from being away from home, though he admitted that it was an unpleasant experience for both parents and children. But those Inuit who went away to school, according to Ernerk, were "enjoy[ing] the wage economy rather than welfare. Some are now looking after their own settlements by being community councillors or belonging to the housing associations." A man he had gone to school with 15 years earlier had just been elected to the NWT Council.[23]

Peter Ernerk is one example – and there are others – of the success of a northern educational system that had not since its inception been directed towards the northern way of life or experience. The official education policy for northern native children was that the days of the hunter were over and that the best prospects for the future lay in assimilating the children as quickly as possible into white society. At the same time the administration was uncomfortably aware of the dangers of a southern style of education for the Inuit children's readjustment to their own society when their schooling ended. The Sub-Committee on Eskimo Education agreed, though less strongly, with some of the arguments its critics had made. It recognized, for example, that several years in a residential school "sometimes" made it difficult for children to readjust to their own native way of life. In order to ease the difficulty, the school term for both residential and day schools was to be revised so that the children would be free to travel with their parents during the hunting and trapping season. This revision would ensure that that portion of the Inuit children's education would not be neglected.[24]

In originally setting up the residential schools, however, the administration had intended to give to "children from primitive environments" an education that would lead to vocational training and prepare them for work "in the white man's economy." In the mid-1950s, as a direct result of the employment demands created by the DEW Line, the government put a new emphasis on vocational training.[25] Officials quickly realized that something more than primary education was required for the benefit of those children capable of learning skilled or semi-skilled occupations. In 1955 not one technical or vocational training school existed in the NWT.[26] Inuit selected for training for work on the DEW Line had to go to a residential training centre at Leduc, Alberta, where 51 were being trained in 1958 at an approximate cost of $40,000.[27] The vocational training establishments planned for Yellowknife, Aklavik, and Iqaluit would improve the situation, but too late to benefit from the

DEW Line developments.

Day Schools

Because of the nomadic character of the people, the administration's Inuit education policy was to build day schools only where sufficient population was permanently located to justify regular school attendance. One such settlement was Pangnirtung. In 1952 about 130 children of school age lived in the area.[28] Endeavouring to teach as many as he could, "with very inadequate facilities," was the Reverend B.P. Smith of St Paul's Anglican mission, and in September 1953 his enrolment was about 30 pupils.[29] The federal day school at Cape Dorset had only 5, and no teacher. The teacher left in the fall of 1952, and the school had been closed since then.[30] The reason for the failure of Cape Dorset was the same as that advanced for Inuit education in general: "The attendance has been small (5 or 6) because the natives have to remain well dispersed along the coast to obtain their food supplies. There are over 150 children of school age in the region and their parents are anxious that they receive education." The only other school in the southern Baffin area in 1953 was at Lake Harbour with, again, about 5 pupils. Thus Iqaluit, potentially the most important settlement in the Eastern Arctic, was without any educational facilities, either missionary or federal. The administration had noted this lack in 1952 and made recommendations to rectify the situation:

It is recommended that provision be made for the establishment of a school and nursing station at Frobisher Bay. With reopening and expansion of the base at Frobisher Bay, practically all the Eskimo men of this area are employed during the summer and are camped with their families near the base. Six or eight families are employed the year round. During the greater part of the summer, there would be an enrolment of about 70 children, and about 15 – 20 during the remainder of the year. We have discussed this matter with Indian Health Services and they agree that since there is every prospect that the natives of this area will continue to have close association with whites, a school and nursing station at this point should be given high priority.[31]

At the first meeting of the Committee on Eskimo Affairs eight days later, a "recommendation that a day school and nursing station should be established near Frobisher Bay base was favourably received."[32] At the same meeting the "desirability of having at least a summer school at Pangnirtung was admitted," but as this would probably entail the use of a camp hostel the committee decided to postpone this "until such time as an overall program for education could be worked out."

But the administration did not even consider such a program for another three years. By then the new administration of the north under the recently established Department of Northern Affairs and National Resources had come to realize that the cultural system in the Arctic had been changing during the previous "few" years. "The rate of change has accelerated recently," said a memo for the cabinet in February 1955, "and the situation has now reached a serious state."[33] Up to this time the government had been following a short-sighted laissez-faire policy based on a nonchalant attitude to the needs of the Inuit. "The lack of education for most of the Indians and Eskimos in the Northwest Territories," said the same memo, "has not been too serious hitherto because nearly all of them were able to earn, and did earn their livelihood by hunting, fishing and trapping. Moreover, in the case of each group, the population was, until recent years, declining and there appeared to be good reason to think they would continue to have an adequate livelihood by following their traditional ways of life. Finally, there did not appear to be much prospect that other ways of life, for which education would equip them, would be available for any substantial number."

By 1955 it was obvious that these conditions no longer pertained. As mentioned in the previous chapter, the population in the north was increasing at an accelerating rate. The administration was well aware of the rapid demographic growth and of its implications not only for education but also for health, housing, and employment. Almost every aspect of life in the Arctic was endangered. As early as 1951 Alex Stevenson of Arctic Services, officer in charge of the Eastern Arctic Patrol, expressed his belief that a long-term policy should be developed to provide for the increasing Inuit population.[34] And in 1955 Northern Affairs warned in its annual report that population growth was intensifying the pressure on decreasing or stationary resources of game and fur-bearing animals. "At the same time this population is surprisingly youthful and is increasing at a rate which, under the present health and welfare programs, is likely to be maintained or even accelerated." The annual report brought another difficulty to public notice. "While family allowances and other social security payments have provided a new and important source of income, new means of broadening the Eskimo economy are required." This too had implications for education. Broadening the economy means providing more jobs in a greater diversity of fields. But in the technological society towards which the Arctic was moving in the mid-1950s, new jobs demanded a higher degree of education than the near-illiteracy of the Inuit, especially those in the Eastern Arctic.

The situation was very different in other Arctic regions. While not one Canadian Inuk (singular of "Inuit") in 15 could read or write, the Inuit in Greenland, Alaska, and "even Russia" had literacy rates of almost 100 per cent.[35] R.A.J. Phillips, director of Northern Administration Branch, told a conference in Toronto in 1959 that in Greenland "every citizen can read and write. The Greenlanders do not just go to school, they teach in school ... [Every] mayor of every town is a Greenlander."[36] Phillips was concerned about the illiteracy of native Canadians, and his administration proposed certain measures to improve the situation, but mostly in the Western Arctic. A 1955 memo stated:

The provision of more adequate primary education is most urgent in the Mackenzie Valley. The educational needs of the Eskimos, other than those around the mouth of the Mackenzie, will have to be met to a greater degree in the near future, but they can be deferred in part for the moment. It is accordingly recommended that all the hostels (and associated day schools) to be constructed in the next five years, except one, be in the Mackenzie Valley. The exception is a hostel at Frobisher Bay, on Baffin Island, to provide one centre for vocational training and education in that region of the Eastern Arctic which will be affected by the DEW Line and other developments there.[37]

The administration thus recognized the importance of Iqaluit, at least within the Eastern Arctic. A new school opened in Iqaluit in November 1955, but expansion of the facilities to include a hostel, vocational training, and teachers' quarters was not planned till 1959, later than similar expansion and development in western settlements like Fort Macpherson, Fort Smith, and Aklavik.[38]

1959–71: FAILURES AND SUCCESSES

Southern Curriculum, Southern Teachers

When the federal school opened in Iqaluit in 1955 it was only the second of its kind in the whole Baffin region. Another opened at Pangnirtung the following year. Others followed at Broughton Island, Arctic Bay, and Resolute Bay in 1959; Clyde River, Igloolik, and Pond Inlet in 1960; Grise Fiord and Padloping in 1962; Lake Harbour in 1963; and Hall Beach in 1967.[39] The educational system in the Eastern Arctic is thus the newest in the country.

The curriculum in these and other Arctic schools was resolutely patterned on that of the urban and rural society of southern Canada. It started in Grade 1 with Dick and Jane on the farm, a subject utterly meaningless to Inuit youngsters. And so it continued. Texts and workbooks depicted a world of which Inuit children had no concept. Stories and lessons might deal with a zoo, a milkman, traffic lights or horses, all as strange to Inuit as the far side of the moon. One teacher described the plight of the native child this way: "Learning the English language was a difficult task but learning simultaneously about the world outside compounded the problem. The child could sound out words such as street car, or newspaper but they would not know what the words referred to. Reading without meaning became a drudgery. The official view was that there were "problem students." I began to think we had problem books and a problem curriculum."[40]

Concerned educationists over and over again during the 1960s recommended the use of a curriculum that took into consideration Inuit culture and values. For too long and in too many classes Inuit pupils were made to study materials and respond to motivations based on the alien culture of white, middle-class North America. The school system attempted to introduce them to a value system that stressed individual achievement, advancement, and self-discipline in return for future rewards. This orientation often contradicted native values. "The Inuit people deplored the white man's excessive concern for self-discipline. His world was too rigid and unsensitive to human relations, and this was reflected in his education processes. Native peoples also suffered from being more present- than future-oriented: the concept of long-term education was hard to grasp."[41] The same faults bedevilled Inuit education in Alaska – and continue to cause problems there – as David Finley shows in the case of a brand-new school in Wainwright.

Despite considerable effort on the part of the school district to bring cultural relevance to the curriculum, the Wainwright school, in the final analysis, represents the societal mainstream. It is oriented towards work, success, goals, careers – and it is competitive. The Eskimos of Wainwright have had little or no exposure to such a society. Their own culture is the society they know best and in it they can function most effectively. In the village, this culture does not include competitive job markets or college classrooms. Consequently, the Eskimos often come into conflict with the school on educational matters.[42]

Part of the problem was – and still is – the cultural background of the teachers. The pseudonymous Georgia wrote in *North* in 1980:

In the Arctic, turkeys come plucked and in plastic wrappers, pumpkin comes in cans and corn is either canned or frozen. How many Inuit children who cut out pictures of turkeys, pumpkins and corn stalks to paste on school windows realize what Thanksgiving means – even semantically? In the north I have been embarrassed to see the feast of thanks unmasked as no more than a ritual, gastronomic orgy. Teachers have been among those guilty of thoughtlessly introducing symbols of a foreign festival severed from its roots and meaning.[43]

This kind of thinking, though written down in 1980, was common among those in the 1960s who wanted to see educational reform in the north. Thus another recommendation constantly repeated was that the teachers of native pupils be required to take courses that would help them understand their own culture and values and the culture and values of their pupils.

Another part of the problem facing northern education was the inadequate preparation of the teachers, most of whom came from the south with preconceived southern ideas of what they should teach in a classroom. Such prospective teachers were unaware of the special educational difficulties they would encounter with regard to cultural differences, language barriers, and limitations in the experience of children. Orientation courses ranging from only one day to two weeks were too short to train teachers for cross-cultural education.

Finding teachers to go north was often a major problem in itself. The isolation, the climate, the barren, treeless environment made recruitment of teachers difficult. When they were attracted they rarely stayed in a settlement for more than two years, and many stayed for only one year. In some cases teachers actually refused to leave the aircraft when it touched down at the isolated settlement, and the local school was unable to open till a replacement had been found.[44] These teachers have to be transported in, Paul Welsman commented, "they have to be transported out, and you have to buy housing for them, you have to pay incredible wages to them, you have to give them all kinds of benefits, you have to educate their children, and you do that at the expense of the native people in this country."[45]

But in the north the teachers remained psychologically in the south, despite their physical and cultural surroundings. Coming from the vastly different cultural milieu of the south, they often experienced difficulty in identifying with their native students. They often felt that native students were unsuited for higher academic achievements leading to better jobs and frequently equated problem students with backwardness or lack of intelligence rather than with dysfunction within the system.

A new teacher coming into a small settlement might find that the pupils had failed to progress to his or her satisfaction. For this there was often good reason unrelated to the students' ability. The normal school year was 200 days. Study of any of the enrolment records of the smaller schools in isolated settlements shows a history of schools being in session for much shorter periods, often for only 140 to 160 days in a year.[46] Children were going off to camp, and/or teachers were leaving early to get out before break-up inhibited travel. These schools were thus in operation for too short a time for children to have completed one grade in one year. So a new teacher would often put pupils back a grade to start again, sometimes on work they had covered several times before. The effect on the pupil was often understandably negative. One story, frequently told and vouched for as genuine, concerns a 15 year-old Inuk whose teacher handed him yet again a copy of *Fun with Dick and Jane*. The boy opened the book at the right page, read "Oh Dick, Oh Jane," added "Oh fuck," and walked out in disgust, never to return.

Education and Language

The southern teacher's inability to speak Inuktitut was another disadvantage of the northern educational system. In order to make the education of Inuit children in English easier, the settlement schools began to hire English-speaking Inuit classroom assistants. This marked the beginning of the native people's personal involvement in education. In 1958, 2 Inuit assistants were employed. By 1965 there were 11, and in 1968 the number jumped to 37.[47] Under the direction of the teacher, these young Inuit assistants worked with the children in their own language, interpreting class routines, giving word meanings and other instruction. The presence in the classroom of an Inuit assistant provided much security to the beginning pupil, still unaccustomed to his new English-speaking milieu.

The Inuit perceived English as the single most important requirement for dealing effectively with Euro-Canadian society. They expressed the desire for more and better teaching of English for both parents and children. "Most Eskimo, including the children," educationist David Born discovered during his fieldwork on the Belcher Islands, "felt that the Eskimo language should not be used in schools as it would inhibit the learning of English. The remainder of those interviewed felt that Eskimo could be used to advantage in the first year or two, particularly since it would help to make the introduction and acclimation of the young child to the school system less of a traumatic experience."[48] The main concern about English-language education was that of an emerging language barrier between children who spoke English and parents confined to Inuktitut. In many cases this linguistic separation was widened by the children's acquiring a different Inuit dialect at residential school from the local dialect their parents used.

Eventually northern educators themselves came to accept the fact that in spite of all their efforts language education in their Arctic schools had failed. "After several decades of struggle with the problems of developing language and community skills among the children of our indigenous people," wrote Bernard Gillie, NWT director of education, "it should be amply clear to all of us that the methods we have used, no matter how well intentioned, have produced a large number of young people with little knowledge of their mother tongue and only slightly articulate in English."[49] The Danes came to exactly the same conclusions about educating Inuit in Greenland. The Danish view, given with the benefit of hindsight 25 years later, is that the Greenland school policy failed because it "did not manage to make Greenlanders, as a people, bilingual, but rather produced a generation of people who were semi-lingual having a mastery of neither Danish nor of Greenlandic."[50] Nevertheless, Dermot Collis adds, in reviewing this Danish source for *Inuit Studies*, that the Danes in Greenland have made "a very earnest and consistent attempt to establish a school system in Greenland that is second to none. Canadian Arctic schools offer nothing remotely comparable in standard."

Eastern Arctic Education and the DEW Line

The big test of Canadian Arctic schools came with the demand for labour on the DEW Line in the 1950s and 1960s. The schools in the Western Arctic passed; those in the Eastern Arctic failed. When DEW Line recruitment reached the east the Inuit, who needed the work most, were least able to benefit from it: they were too poorly educated. The Federal Electric Corporation had to bring workers in from the Western and Central Arctic to fill vacancies at Eastern Arctic DEW Line sites for which the local labour force was unqualified.

One of the reasons advanced for the preferability of western over eastern Inuit as workers on the DEW Line, even on the eastern sector of it, was that the "men from the west" had better command of English and were thus "more desirable than men from the Eastern Arctic."[51] Although in 1961 Federal Electric officials rejected this as an excuse for the fundamental unreliability of Eastern Arctic workers,[52] a year earlier the vice-president of the corporation in a more conciliatory or diplomatic mood had himself proposed it in reference to the slow promotion of Inuit: "The basic problem seems to be the lack of ability to speak and write English. In the majority of cases Eskimos have progressed quite satisfactorily and in those cases where they have made little or no advancement, it has been due to a language barrier."[53]

Nothing could have more clearly alerted the government to the degree of its failure in providing educational facilities in the Eastern Arctic. But the administration was already well aware of the situation. On an inspection trip of the DEW Line in 1960 a government representative "was informed by all the Station Chiefs that the most pressing educational need for Eskimos is to learn English."[54] In passing this information on to the director of Northern Administration Branch, the administrator of the Mackenzie commented that this, of course, was "evident to those who contact the Eskimos in an attempt to employ them or make them employable. Without the ability to communicate they are severely handicapped."

The administrator of the Arctic agreed with the language handicap theory and extended it to what was undoubtedly the more valid underlying reason: a "lack of formal schooling." "We must remember," he wrote, " ... that in the Eastern Arctic, in particular, the potential of Eskimo employees to accept training is gravely limited by the lack of formal schooling and the lack of knowledge of English. I would hope that when we get our vocational training superintendent and our placement officers in the field, we can work much more closely with other government departments to provide training for those Eskimos whom they employ and who are capable of benefitting from such training."[55]

The Improvement of Education

The lesson of the DEW Line was that northern administration had to make a much more vigorous effort to overcome "the lack of formal schooling" in the Eastern Arctic. In this regard the 1960s marked a time of slow but perceptible improvement. The establishment of elementary schools in small communities kept the younger pupils at school but still within the family unit. Only the older children still had to go to high school in the larger centres. Working against the school-building program, however, was the fact that at this time almost half of the Eastern Arctic Inuit population was under 15 years of age, and this increasing school-age group played havoc with development plans. For example, in 1963 one two-classroom school at Pangnirtung had to accommodate 59 children. But 107 other children in the area did not attend school.[56] Planning estimates for 1964–5 called for the addition of only two more classrooms. By 1968 at least six classrooms would be needed "to accommodate children not only from the Pangnirtung area, but other children from points such as Broughton Island, Padloping and possibly Cape Dorset." Not only were more classrooms needed than originally planned, but extra hostel accommodation was equally imperative. The three small hostels already built by 1963 and housing 8 children each would have to be supplemented by 1968 with a large 50-bed hostel just for the 11-to-13-years age group. Most Arctic settlements had made similar demands for increased school and hostel buildings since at least 1961, as, for example, Broughton Island, where a second classroom was added "to provide education for the children of parents permanently employed on the DEW Line."[57] At Iqaluit the administration met the need for new accommodation by taking over buildings vacated by the departure of the US and Canadian air forces.[58]

In January 1963 the director of Northern Administration Branch was forced to admit that the "hope of giving every child in the north the opportunity for schooling by 1968 is so fast receding that it can almost be abandoned without a sharp change in present policy. Not only is our current construction program being held back by the general economic measures, but our long range forecasts of school population appears to have been low."[59] Exactly one year later approximately 800 Inuit and 400 Indian children of school-age were still not in school, "and the number of people living in the north with less than adequate educational standards to fit them for life in a modern society was far above the average for Canada as a whole."[60] To illustrate this point, the 1961 census reported that "only approximately 22% of the total population of the Northwest Territories had attained Grade VIII academic standing as opposed to approximately 38% of the population of Canada as a whole. The comparison would be even less favourable for the Northwest Territories if it were not for the large numbers of government employees, teachers, nurses and others living in the north who had obtained their education elsewhere."

Such a situation was unlikely to improve much in the near future because the rapid growth of the school-age Inuit population nullified any advances under the educational policy. Obviously the administration would have to accelerate the school construction program initiated under the policy if it were to keep ahead of the already increasing demand. To do this by the original target date of 1968 was impossible, and so the planners set a "new target date of September 1970 for completion of the basic school plant required."

The planners estimated the "basic school plant required" with the 6-to-15-years age group in mind. But a new dimension of the Arctic educational problem began to appear when the trend for Canadian children to remain longer in school became evident in the north also. To provide academic school facilities for children up to the compulsory age of 15 was no longer sufficient, because almost the entire 16-to-19-years age group and a growing proportion of the 17-to-21-year-olds were remaining in school. In all parts of Canada the encouragement and expectation were for all children to complete a secondary education of some type. This had the effect of keeping children in school an average of at least three years beyond the compulsory school period for the NWT. Belatedly the government accepted it as "evident that much greater emphasis must be placed on secondary education, both academic and vocational, if people in the north are to become self-supporting through gainful employment."

In spite of all the difficulties, the educational authorities in the north had substantially increased school enrolment. In 1955, when Northern Affairs launched its program to build schools and pupil residences throughout the Territories and to eliminate illiteracy among the native peoples of the Arctic, less than 15 per cent of the Inuit school-age population was enrolled in schools; by June 1964, "as a result of a vigorous policy of school construction," approximately 75 per cent of the 6-to-15-years-old population was at school.[61]

These children received the benefits not only of new schools in their own communities but also of an improved curriculum. In the early 1960s the Curriculum Section made the first attempts to create curricula and materials specifically for northern schools. Teachers "in the field" met with curriculum specialists from Ottawa and produced their version of suitable courses and course contents. They issued the first native-language booklets to appear in class since the syllabic gospels of the mission schools – the outstanding Arctic Reading Series that Brian Lewis wrote in the late 1960s for the Education Division of Indian Affairs and Northern Development. It is interesting, in light of the virtual neglect of the Eastern Arctic Inuit in favour of the Mackenzie valley natives, that one commentator could write peevishly: "Most such materials were produced for the Eskimos who, in the opinion of this writer, received much more attention than anyone else at that time. Schools in the lower Mackenzie Valley, on the other hand, "made do" with the Alberta Department of Education Curriculum."[62]

Many of the inadequacies of the old system were erased through improved northern school curricula and reading materials; teacher-training programs to qualify a greater number of native and non-native teachers; Inuit teaching assistants employed in many schools; financial aid from the territorial and federal governments to assist students in attaining higher education; and vocational training and kindergarten programs.

In November 1966 a program of testing showed that the grade levels registered for Inuit pupils at school did "accurately reflect academic achievement" and that Inuit pupils were reaching an educational level which in the north, for the imminent future at least, would enable them to be considered functionally literate. "This is the immediate task of the school," two educators commented in 1968, "and the area in which education can be considered to be making its greatest impact on the individual."[63] They went on:

One does not need to stretch the imagination to envisage the great significance of this fact. The achievement of functional literacy allows the individual to participate in further education or training, to gain employment, albeit at a low level, to read instructions permitting him to operate machinery or motorized vehicles, engage in commercial transactions and participate in political activities. He can enrich his mind by reading. He can travel to other communities with greater self-confidence if only because he can read safety rules or traffic signs to avoid accidents. For employment in any significant enterprise it is a first essential. Not the least important are the psychological benefits resulting from the enhancement of his status, and the boost to his self-respect he gets by mastering a process formerly monopolized by the White man.

In 1966 the Education Division, confident of its improved school system, reported: "In all aspects of operation, the northern education system aspires to standards of quality and parity of esteem with the best provincial educational systems. Through education, northern people are encouraged to take pride in the Canadian north and are fitted to share the responsibilities and bounties of Canada's growing prosperity."[64]

Others less biased viewed the northern educational situation with more critical eyes. In spite of the extensive development of facilities and programs, 60 per cent of the NWT population in 1970 had received no formal schooling, "a record which ... cannot be rationally justified in one of the world's most highly developed countries. Only seven per cent of the territorial residents had attained the level of high school or technical school, and those who had attended university were an unknown quantity unrecorded by Statistics Canada."[65]

Technical and Vocational Training

Had the government established vocational training earlier – Diamond Jenness had been advocating it strongly and repeatedly since 1925[66] – it might have avoided the extreme embarrassment and shame of the 1950s and 1960s. By then employment opportunities abounded in the Territories for people with professional, technical, and trade qualifications and for those possessing special vocational skills, but the local population was unable to take advantage of such opportunities and would not be able to do so until the educational system was expanded to equip them with the knowledge and skills required. Through the 1960s, and certainly in the latter half of the decade, employment opportunities for unskilled labour declined. This state of affairs was aggravated by the curtailment of defence activities and by the inability of resource development industries to absorb any large number of unskilled and even semi-literate labourers, especially those who could not communicate in English. A memorandum for the cabinet in 1965 stated pessimistically: "With the rapidly decreasing need for unskilled labour, the implications of this low educational standard as it affects employment possibilities for northern residents are a cause for serious concern. The economic and social consequences of educational deficiencies are already apparent in the high degree of unemployment, the need for welfare assistance and the social maladjustment now prevalent in the north. The average contribution to productivity is consequently very low."[67]

Thus the need became urgent to train the Inuit for service-type occupations in construction, merchandising, transport, communications, and tourism. In the 1960s, people brought in for the purpose from southern Canada held most of these jobs. The frustration of the Inuit and their feelings of inadequacy and inferiority are understandable. To help eradicate this inequity the NWT government instituted an apprentice-training program in 1964. Fourteen Inuit were enrolled. When an apprentice completed the minimum on-the-job training time of 8,000 hours and passed his annual theory courses he could write either the NWT exam or the interprovincial exam. The latter required a passing grade of 70 per cent but allowed the apprentice to practise his trade anywhere in Canada.

Armand Kolit, a 22-year-old from Rankin Inlet, was among the first graduates of the program and the first Inuk to receive his journeyman's certificate in carpentry. Kolit elected to write the interprovincial exam; not only did he obtain his journeyman's certificate but he did so with Inter-provincial Seal, the highest level of qualification possible in carpentry. Kolit did his apprenticeship with the Department of Indian Affairs and Northern Development in Churchill, going south in the winter for six weeks of classroom instruction at the Manitoba Institute of Technology. The *Whitehorse Star* proudly reported: "He completed the training in the minimum time allowed, although he started out with two handicaps: All his written work was in English and his education was less than what is normally required. He had to upgrade himself academically to the same level as "southern" Canadian apprentices and, at the same time, keep up with his theory courses."[68]

Few Inuit have had the drive and perseverance of Armand Kolit. The majority, largely because of their lack of education, were held down to the lower economic strata of society. Because of the low social status of their parents, the absence of educational traditions, and the lack of an adequate working knowledge of the language of instruction, the Inuit children's initial progress in school was painfully slow. Thus another need in the Arctic was for kindergarten schools as a means of easing the difficult transition from home to school. Like every other ingredient of the educational system, the establishment of kindergarten was delayed in the Arctic. Not till the administration submitted its new five-year education plan to the cabinet in 1965 was provision made for setting up kindergartens on a full-time basis in the larger settlements, where 25 or more pupils resided, and on a half-day basis wherever practical in the smaller communities.

The success of educational programs in the north, from kindergarten to secondary academic and vocational, depended on the quality of teachers, particularly those who could not only speak Inuktitut but also understand the perceptions and problems of the students and their communities. The obvious way to acquire instructors with these qualifications was to train the Inuit themselves. In 1968 Bernard Gillie, in association with Norman Macpherson, started a teacher-education program, co-sponsored by the University of Alberta, to train NWT residents to teach their own people. The pilot project began in 1969 with 15 students. Of these, 11 took NWT teaching positions, a rate of success that encouraged continuation of the program.[69]

The enrolled students had to have attained at least Grade 11. They began their studies during the winter in the NWT, taking part of their Grade 12 and getting a start on their professional courses. In May and June two instructors from the Department of Elementary Education at the University of Alberta taught two courses at Fort Smith in a kind of inter-session. The students then spent the summer session at the university, taking another Grade 12 course and two professional courses. From September to December they had an "internship" in NWT schools, where they gained teaching experience, and from January to April they were back at university taking more professional courses. Then came a second inter-session at Fort Smith in May and June, followed by one more summer session at university. By then the students had completed matriculation plus two years towards their bachelor of education degree along the elementary route. At this point they could return to university and complete the two years outstanding for a full degree or become certified by the NWT government to teach.

"Where I was schooled I figured I wasn't learning too much," Rene Otak of Igloolik told the *Edmonton Journal*, "so I got into the program because it was north-oriented. I think we're learning something from the program. I'm beginning to learn what a teacher does and how it should be."[70] Rene Otak was one of those Inuit who succeeded in the northern educational system in spite of its severely handicapping deficiencies. And success became more common as the 1960s progressed. The Inuit child in competition with southern Canadian, Indian, and Metis was moving up through the school system.[71] Even the road to university was cleared, and some young Inuit were enrolled in college courses. On 24 January 1963 the NWT approved legislation offering an almost cost-free university education to any resident student, provided that after graduation he or she returned to live in the Territories for at least three years. Many features of the scheme were patterned after Greenland and Scandinavia.[72] By 1968 one Inuit youth, "a product of the northern school system," had already completed a degree in arts and science at the University of Manitoba and gone on to study medicine.[73]

Signs were improving. Inuit were beginning to establish themselves in responsible positions as foremen, special constables, pilots. The first Inuit area administrator for Northern Affairs was working out of Spence Bay, and the Eastern Arctic was represented on the NWT Council by its own elected member, Simonie.[74] Simonie Michael, a 33-year-old carpenter and the chosen leader of the Inuit of Iqaluit, was, in September 1966, the first Inuk to be elected to the council. His maiden speech was 90 minutes long and given in Inuktitut. Another Inuk, Abe Okpik, was one of five appointed members. Simonie had been named to just about every Iqaluit council and board in which Inuit has a voice. He was also a leader in the co-operative movement and founded the housing co-operative that built 15 dwellings in Iqaluit. He had been one of two Inuit chosen to represent Canada at the coronation of Queen Elizabeth in 1953.[75]

Inuit success stories, of which this is only one, did not mean that Inuit were achieving in school as well as other Canadian children. In fact, the age at which Inuit attained their respective grades was significantly higher than the Canadian average. This age-grade retardation was due largely to the fact that Inuit pupils had had inconsistent schooling during the normal period of childhood, either because schools were unavailable or because attendance patterns were irregular. Bill Pyle, the principal of the school at Cambridge Bay in 1963, expected one in six of his 37 Inuit students to go on to Inuvik or Yellowknife for further education. "It won't be at least until the next generation that Eskimo students will move on to higher grades at about the same rate as whites," he told the *Edmonton Journal*.[76]

AFTER 1971: NORTHERN
RESPONSIBILITY FOR EDUCATION

Arctic Education for the Arctic

In 1970 administrative responsibility for northern schools was turned over to the NWT government, and since then the educational system has become increasingly responsive to Inuit cultural needs. By the early 1970s observers recognized that "the process of assimilation of native youngsters into a southern white Canadian culture, upon which was based most of the thinking not only in education but in everything else, simply does not work ... Over recent years new curricula have been developed that recognize the way of life, the language, history, heritage and culture of the native peoples. It is the policy of the government of the Northwest Territories to teach native people in their mother tongue in the primary grades. This program is just beginning."[77]

In his 1972 survey of NWT education, Bernard Gillie admitted that his own education department went about language and education the wrong way. People need to be articulate in their own tongue, he decided, before they can expect to become so in a second language. Instruction in the mother tongue during the early years of schooling, with gradual transition to a second language – likely to be the dominant language of the community – was a more effective method of developing skill in the second language than an attempt to introduce it in a forced situation that aimed at ignoring or eradicating the first language.

The Inuit Tapirisat of Canada (ITC) agreed. In 1971 this native political organization charged that the government's educational methods had failed because when young Inuit children "begin to think and wonder about the world around them, they are thinking in their own language and in terms of their own culture. But suddenly they are taken from their parents and their own culture, and are expected to think in another language. Why not let them develop their thinking ability in our own language, up to grade 3 or 4, then switch to English."[78] The NWT accepted this point of view, and a plan to educate Inuit children from kindergarten to Grade 3 in their own language went into effect in September 1972.[79]

The ITC was a prime mover of educational changes in the Arctic in the 1970s. At its annual meeting in Pangnirtung on 21 August 1972, delegates declared that education in northern Canada must be changed radically to serve the needs and preserve the culture of the native people. Elizabeth Quaki of Payne Bay, Quebec, one of only a handful of people who had become teachers, said, "As long as southern teachers and southern courses dominate schools, the Eskimo culture and heritage will continue to erode.[80]

The ITC proposed the teaching of new courses with a strong northern orientation, such as Arctic survival, hunting, fishing, trapping, and sewing. The Inuit Cultural Institute, an offshoot that the ITC sprouted to protect Inuit language and culture, declared that the NWT Department of Education was misdirected in its basic approach when it assumed, and from the beginning, that traditional Inuit training and development were secondary to the southern concept of education. "Education, especially among Inuit, is an all-embracing process, which involves training and development of knowledge, skills, mind and character ... The southern-modelled educational system has not prepared Inuit people to face modern society with confidence and efficient training, while the traditional Inuit approach has done just that – enabled Inuit to face the formidable challenge of their physical environment and their way of life. Traditional training then must be the major focus in any successful Inuit educational programme."[81]

"It's perhaps not being done as fast as it might," one delegate at Pangnirtung said, "but I don't think there's one settlement that doesn't have Eskimo people coming into the schools and telling them old legends, or showing the students how to carve and how to make bows and arrows or harpoons. In some we have been going out on the land to hunt with an Eskimo guide."[82] Norman Macpherson, NWT director of education in 1971, said that a northern curriculum had been developed and was being introduced in schools across the Arctic.

One such school was the Gordon Robertson Education Centre, a $3-million junior and senior high school that opened in Iqaluit that year. Students there were taking a number of "cultural inclusion" courses in addition to "normal" courses. They studied Inuit language and folklore and learned how to build a sled or an igloo, how to carve stone, how to make a harpoon and hunt a seal. The school offered an outdoor education course consisting of snowmobile drives, camping, and hiking.[83] The Inuit had good reasons for wanting such courses in the school curriculum. Caleb Apak, president of the Education Society in Igloolik, told a reporter from the native-language paper *Inuktitut*: "We have been concerned about the lack of traditional Inuit educators for many years now. The climate in the north is not going to get any warmer. It will always get cold during the winter season. We are now hearing more and more about young people dying while they are out on the land in different places in the North. This is due to their lack of knowledge of survival skills out-of-doors. This was our main concern."[84]

The teaching of these skills at Gordon Robertson is one of the few good things the Inuit have to say about this school. Its history has been unhappy, as Hugh Brody shows in detail.[85] The government's biggest mistake was placing a residential school in Iqaluit in the first place. Among the smaller communities on Baffin Island the town has "a black reputation for drunkenness, violence and prostitution." Even the white people consider it "a hotbed of iniquity and the embodiment of all that is wrong in northern development and administration."

And yet the children from many of the smallest and most remote settlements were sent to Iqaluit. During the school's planning and construction – 1967–71 (it was originally proposed but abandoned in 1961) – the government held "a bare minimum" of consultation with those families whose children would be expected to attend. When teachers in one of the Arctic settlements heard of the proposed school in 1969 they submitted a petition in protest and received a reprimand from their superiors for doing so. The authorities held no open discussion on the school with the Inuit, even though Inuit parents had been complaining for years about a residential school in Churchill.

When the school opened in Iqaluit, parents in the small communities expressed anxiety about sending their children "to such a notorious place." "My personal opinion," said Caleb Apak, "is that I would rather see them go to southern schools to attain further education."[86] Between 1971 and 1973 total enrolment fell from 220 to 100, and the dropout rate and rate of truancy have remained high. On any school day, Bryan Pearson told the NWT Council in 1977, one could find 30 per cent of Iqaluit students "playing hooky."[87] His excuse was that one "can't force education on children: they will continue to stay away from classes because they don't like them." Ever since the school opened, certain students were plainly unable to fit in. They could not endure the socialization process that accompanied "going to GREC."[88] But by the end of the decade even good students were dropping out, and those who "managed to adapt to the education offered often found that they had increased difficulties in communicating with their families."[89] Families were more relieved when the students left Iqaluit than when they stayed. Pupils returned home with stories about drunkenness and violence within the residence. Girls told how they lay awake at night, their doors locked, fearing assault. The place was and remains unhappy. Each year at least one student there takes his own life.[90]

"Despite the Eskimo distaste for residential education," Hugh Brody writes, "the Frobisher Bay school was established with a complete disregard for what the authorities knew the Eskimo attitudes to be". This raises the point that the Inuit, like the Indians and the Metis in northern Canada, were never offered the chance to decide who would teach their children, in what language they would be taught, or indeed what the goals of their children's education would be. Not surprisingly, the disregard that educators have shown towards the participation of northern native peoples in their own schooling has led to a strong sense of disaffection among parents and students alike towards the value of education. Robert Paine quotes an NWT legislator as saying that "the kids who have been through the system either for any length of time or even a short period are the people who are unhappy, who are disillusioned, who are in the correction camp, who are the layabouts, the people whom you are trying to encourage to take on these jobs. These are the people who have a smattering of your so-called education."[91]

The highly motivated Inuit Cultural Institute (ICI) objected to the fact that educational plans in 1976 allowed the Inuit no input into deciding what could be termed "satisfactory standards of instruction" and no choice of the language of instruction after the first few years of schooling. The NWT seemed to regard the Inuit as "of secondary importance" and refused to let them become "involved with the educational process at a responsible decision-making level." In view of these feelings, the ICI created in the fall of 1976 a National Inuit Council on Education (NICE) "to examine the feasibility of Inuit educational institutions in the north, planned and administered by the Inuit themselves." It sought to voice the regional concerns of Inuit people with regard to the educational system and to explore supplementary and alternate methods of making it meaningful, relevant, and challenging for the Inuit.

The first meeting of NICE an April 1977 discussed the current situation, in which "schools and formal educational training ... [were] a liability rather than an asset to Inuit youth." The meeting agreed that exposure to different environmental traditions, different educational methods, a new language, and the prospect of being sent out of their own community to attend high school in a city were only a few of the reasons why many Inuit children left school before completing even Grade 6.[92] The eleven members of NICE represented every region in the north, from the Mackenzie delta to Labrador. All agreed that there was a serious need in each of their geographical areas for cultural input in the schools, language training, job and training opportunities for native dropouts, and a general outlining of the advantages to staying in school. But that was NICE's only meeting. "Because of the shortage of funds they were unable to meet again and it no longer exists.[93]

The Inuit position is that the education of northern natives has continually ignored the need to integrate native values in the school curriculum:

Such things as joking behaviour, non-verbal communication, avoidance of confrontation, and parent-child relationships are determined by values which have been retained and in many areas strengthened, despite the onslaught of modernization. These values need not be taught since in most cases native children have learned them before their classroom education begins; instead they should be acknowledged and incorporated into the learning resources and curriculum so that the learning process in the classroom can extend and reinforce what has already been learned. Their use in the pedagogy of native schools would contribute immeasurably to a more comfortable and understanding teacher-student relationship and should eliminate previous impressions by observers that many northern teachers perceived native values in the classroom as a hindrance rather than an asset in the formal education of native young people.[94]

The greatest asset of the native people is their language. A people's language is one of the most powerful instruments for tightening the coherence of a community, for creating a feeling of national or ethnic unity. Language is the soul of the nation, as the Malaysian slogan had it. In the late 1970s many Inuit were expressing the desire to have Inuktitut schooling for their children. Countries like Greenland and Finland were expanding the use of the native tongue as the language of instruction in native classrooms, and Canada should do the same. In 1980–1 the Inuit language was taught in only 27 of 70 NWT schools.[95] The Inuit wanted a better ratio than this, but they realized that to provide more Inuktitut education required more Inuit teachers. In 1982 only 46 of 741 NWT teachers were of native origin.[96] For several years Inuit across the north had been acting as classroom assistants in their community schools. They acted as interpreters between pupils and teachers, made teaching aids, gave math or social studies lessons, and taught Inuktitut. The Inuit hope was that more of these classroom assistants could be trained as teachers themselves.

Disappointment and Dissatisfaction

As mentioned earlier, a teacher education program for NWT native people started at Fort Smith in 1969. An attempt to start a similar program in Iqaluit in 1977 foundered because of the number of dropouts and other problems there. A new Teacher's Education Project (TEP) in Iqaluit was organized in 1979 and started in September with 10 students,[97] a wholly inadequate number. Mick Mallon, who worked on the project, told *Inuktitut*: "The policy of the Department of Education is that in those communities where the local education authority wants instruction to be in the native language, instruction will be mostly in Inuktitut from Kindergarten to grade 3, and taught as a subject afterwards. Given that there is a specific number of teaching positions in Kindergarten to grade 3 in the east and dividing the number by the five students graduating each year from TEP, it would take 40–50 years at the same rate to train enough Inuit teachers for the positions there are at present."

In February 1982, McGill University announced a new program that would train NWT Inuit classroom assistants to become teachers within four years. With 13 courses and 45 credits, it was similar to an Inuit teacher-training program that McGill had been running in northern Quebec since 1975. Applicants had to be 21 years old, hold a full-time teaching assistant's position, be recommended by their supervisors, and speak Inuktitut fluently. Actual instruction was to be given in the north, with courses taught in Inuktitut by Inuit graduates of the Quebec program and by NWT-based instructors.[98]

"Until now there has been a chronic shortage of competent Inuit teachers," said Jack Cram, director of McGill's Centre for Northern Studies and Research. Although the cost of training teachers in the north was "astronomical," Cram maintained that results were well worth the price. "If Inuit children are to benefit from their schooling they must be taught by understanding, sympathetic and professional teachers from their own culture."

One institution that could serve as a model for others in the Eastern Arctic is Attagutaluk School in Igloolik. It is exemplary in many ways. As "Georgia" describes it for readers of *North*, it is "a beautiful collection of buildings with a gym that is the envy of many southern visitors. Self-contained trailer classrooms have been added to accommodate the school population which overflowed the main building, and exquisitely designed additions have such features as child-sized coat racks with tile floors and drains to catch the runoff from snow-covered parkas and boots." But the strength of the school is in its staff. Often exceptional and usually excellent, it sometimes has a majority of Inuit teachers and classroom assistants. "Next year we will have eleven Inuit teachers from Igloolik and eight teachers from the south," principal Jack Waye told Ulli Steltzer.[99] Several teachers came from the south a decade or more ago and have made their homes among the Inuit of Igloolik.

Through adult educators and principals who have worked hand in glove with elected education committees and boards, channels of communication have been forged and kept open between the community and the school. Not once, but time and again, Inuit challenges to Education Department policies and practices have been seconded by school officials acting in rapport with the community.

The strength of Attagutaluk School is in direct proportion to its relevance to the evolving community. Adults of all ages are increasingly aware of confronting an alien civilization and are consciously trying to determine which innovations are good, which are bad, which to accept and which to reject. The school, under sympathetic and wise guidance, has been subject to the same evolutionary process.[100]

"We are always breaking new ground up here in Igloolik," said Jack Waye. "For example, we do most of the teaching in our first three grades in Inuktitut. As far as local control in education is concerned, we are a lot more advanced than some other communities in the Northwest Territories."[101]

Regrettably, not all the schools in the Eastern Arctic are as progressive or exemplary. In spite of continuing developments, new programs, and increased financial investment, the school system in the Canadian Arctic in general has not worked. As the NWT minister of education himself declared, "Despite the efforts of a dedicated staff, our school system has not been successful."[102] Other territorial politicians have for several years been critical of northern education. Schools came under attack during the legislative assembly's debate on the proposed school ordinance in January 1977.[103] Councillors charged that, far from showing improvement, academic standards had declined. Tom Butters of Inuvik declared that in mathematics tests given to 400 Grade 9 graduates of various schools in the Territories, 74 per cent of the students failed to get a mark of 50 per cent.

A somewhat similar situation existed in Alaska. At Wainwright, a small Inuit village on the North Slope, a new high school opened in 1978 – 9 and a new elementary school was built in 1983. The total physical plant represented an investment of $15 million.[104] As a result, Wainwright had all the ingredients commonly considered essential for high student achievement: well-lit, spacious classrooms, a low student-teacher ratio, and a competent teaching staff. And yet in tests of basic skills, achievement, and proficiency, not a single Wainwright student rated above the seventieth percentile. Ninety-two per cent of the student body in grades 1 to 12 fell below the fiftieth percentile. High expenditure on education guarantees no commensurate academic results.

In the long-neglected Eastern Arctic the situation was so bad that for two years running the member for South Baffin, Bryan Pearson, called for an official inquiry into the standard of education in his region. He maintained in January 1978 that this was still unacceptably low and charged that employers were appalled to find young people who were incapable of doing such simple things as telling the time properly.[105] But Pearson's repeated call went unheeded. The territorial administration took no steps towards meeting his demand because council had voted down the issue.

Family circumstances may be one source of the problem of low educational standards. In the Eastern Arctic in particular there is no long tradition of school attendance, and parents often fail to understand what education is all about. As early as 1962 Frank Vallee was recommending a strong educational program to rectify this situation.[106] Six years later, A.M. Erwin, though writing about the Western Arctic, stated that "the only way of assuring the successful adaptation of the children is through reinforcement by adults at home.[107] If the adults at home have been left totally in the dark as to the goals of education, they cannot perform this vital role. David Born, doing field-work on the Belcher Islands in the 1960s, recorded the failure of adults to realize any benefits their children derived from school. They saw few young people go to school, hold down a good job, and then help their parents. "The adults state that the only thing which the children have learned which is of value ... are the chores which they performed as part of hostel living."[108]

Lynn Nash, a former headmaster at Iqaluit, lists other family circumstances that militate against the success of schooling in the Eastern Arctic.[109] One relates to the fact that children have to spend nearly 10 months of each of three, four, or five years in a student residence far from home. Local schools, even in a settlement like Rankin Inlet, offer no education beyond Grade 8, and students have to leave home to continue schooling in centres like Iqaluit. A report debated at the territorial legislative session that met at Inuvik in May 1982, *Learning: Tradition and Change in the Northwest Territories*, proposed expanding elementary schools to Grade 10 so that students could stay at home longer.[110] Nash's point, however, is that those students who have up to now been forced away from home return to their settlements alienated physiologically and psychologically from parental houses that are often overcrowded and draughty. Their interests now are different from their family's, and they know much more about modern technological society than their parents ever will. "The diet at home is different," Nash goes on. "Some students are unable, or prefer not, to eat raw meat any longer. This alienates the young people from their families even more. Some of their parent's habits or behaviour may seem almost uncouth to them and this devalues the parents in their children's eyes and tends to weaken the parent's position as role models. The consequences for many students are intense inner conflicts over self-image and feelings of inadequacy and hopelessness verging on anomie."

The NWT Special Committee on Education, author of the report referred to above, revealed what Nash and others had said often before: school alienates children from their families, traditional life skills, and native languages and yet leaves them ill-prepared to compete for jobs. The report documented an immense gap between the official school curriculum and what was actually taught in the classroom and alleged that the system lacked commitment to adult education and teacher training. Statistics underlined the failure of the territorial school system in spite of all the improvements of the 1970s. With 12,000 children going through the system in 1980, of whom 4,142 were Inuit, a mere 192 graduated.[111] "Our school goes to grade 9," said Jack Waye of Igloolik. "That's usually the end of formal education. We have very few kids who go away to Frobisher Bay for schooling – maybe two or three a year. And the numbers who stay to graduate are even smaller. Only two people from here have gone to college."[112]

The high dropout rate is a serious problem among Inuit high school students. "They leave school not only because of the gap between native culture and the curriculum, but also because they feel that academic preparation is unlikely to lead to employment and, accordingly, is not worthwhile ... Dropping out of school reduces employment prospects and adds to the despair and dependence that promote psychological disorders and a continuation of the cycle."[113] The Inuit themselves wanted to change that situation. ITC president James Arvaluk, in submitting the Inuit land claims proposal to Prime Minister Trudeau in 1976, called for, among other things, "a stronger voice in such fields as education."[114] One socioeconomic program that the Inuit advanced as part of their land claims settlement was "an Inuit Education Project to upgrade Inuit education, to assist Inuit in acquiring the necessary skills to manage their own affairs and preserve the vitality of Inuit culture."[115]

The Special Committee on Education agreed with the validity of the Inuit demands, and in order to give more control of the school system to the native people it proposed drastic decentralization of education in the Territories by calling for the setting up of 10 divisional boards of education. The only two existing boards were both in Yellowknife.[116] These boards would supervise program development, teacher training, and selection of native languages for use in the schools in their districts; in some communities English would become the second language. They would also schedule the length of the school year to jibe with the hunting and trapping season. Other proposals in the report, designed to meet the demands of the native people, included the one already mentioned, that education from kindergarten to Grade 10 be available in each community. In addition, grades 11 and 12 would come under the jurisdiction of an Arctic College, which would highlight vocational and adult education. Another proposal called for the minister of education to establish two centres for learning and teaching that would be responsible for curriculum development and teacher training.

These proposals won the endorsement of northern educators, who had been making similar recommendations for several years. For example, Del Koenig of the Institute for Northern Studies at the University of Saskatchewan, and a former teacher at Pelly Bay, suggested in 1975 that the government set up planning groups that directly involved northerners in the development of educational policies and programs.[117] In addition, she thought that the government should assist financially, and with the planning, for more programs to train northern people as classroom teachers at all levels of the elementary and secondary school system and argued that provision of community high schools should be a top priority of planning and budgets.[118] On the whole the proposals of the Special Committee on Education were well received. "If [they were] adopted," said Christopher Reid, president of the Northwest Territories Teacher's Association, "we would be well on our way to solving many of the problems with education."[119] Reid particularly welcomed the suggested teacher orientation, which would emphasize the different cultures and traditions, and local teacher training to increase the small number of native teachers.

Jack Waye of Igloolik was one of many who regretted the shortage of native teachers. "We would like to get certified Inuit teachers," he said, "but so far there aren't any. I can not pass on the Inuit cultural tradition; no southern teacher can. All we can pass on is our own tradition, our southern white values, and of course they don't fit here. Whatever blending of the two cultures there is should be of the Inuit's choosing, not the government's, as it was before we had organized local initiative. Igloolik people should have the balance of education they want. These are *their* children."[120]

The government agreed with its Special Committee on Education's recommendations for more organized local initiative and control. In September 1983 the legislative assembly made major changes to the Education Ordinance in order to meet some of these recommendations. The members approved an amendment to establish education divisions and to create divisional boards of education and community education councils. However, the formation of education divisions was not to be mandatory. Local education authorities would have to submit a petition requesting that a division be formed and that a divisional board of education be established. These divisional boards would permit communities to exert more control over their own schools.[121]

Higher Education

In 1980 only one Canadian Inuk was attending university out of a total Inuit population of 15,489. In Alaska 133 Inuit were at university out of a population of 36,800. That year only four NWT Inuit qualified for university out of 552 in high school.

The number of NWT students at university in southern Canada grew steadily after 1963, when government financial assistance was legislated. In its first 10 years, enrolment increased 6½ times, while costs grew 12½ times.[122] But the ethnic make-up of the students rushing to university in increasing numbers is unavailable. Records show that in the first year of assistance one Indian and one Inuk applied, and that in 1964 one Inuk enrolled. A study quoted by Del Koenig concluded in 1974 that "the majority of university students from the N.W.T. are non-native, and are residents of the larger population centres such as Yellowknife, Hay River, Fort Smith and Inuvik." On the whole the idea of "going south to school" appeals to young northerners, but for the majority the attraction of the south is short-lived.

Most respondents who either have been south, or who have spoken to others who have been there, speak of homesickness, loneliness, feelings of alienation, the difficulties of making new friends, feelings of inferiority, frustration with the size, speed and congestion of the city, life in a strange culture. In addition they feel that students are unprepared academically to cope with studies at southern institutions because "northern schools and teachers do not challenge them." Such students find themselves with a double handicap. Not only do they experience emotional and psychological dissonance, but they begin to fail at the job they came to do. The far off goal of academic success, which may or may not lead to a desired career in the north, becomes more elusive, and home and the north become more attractive. Those who stay out and achieve some success know that graduation guarantees nothing but more uncertainty. Northerners perceive that there are few jobs in the north for university graduates. Students feel that it will not be easy to return home, and to be accepted.[123]

"Bear this in mind," one NWT Council member said in 1975; "right now in Frobisher Bay today there are approximately one thousand kids in school. In Frobisher Bay today there are ten jobs available, ten jobs."[124] Here is one of the challenges to northern education. It becomes irrelevant. It guarantees no place in the labour market for those native students who struggle through the system against such overwhelming odds. This situation is not confined to Canadian Arctic education. It applies in Alaska as well. In Wainwright, for example, there are only about 60 permanent jobs, most of them unskilled and requiring no specific academic or technical training. This is what students know as reality. It stimulates no career goals, and without goals the young Inuit perceive no academic needs. Any relationship between education and future prospects is non-existent. High-school graduates and dropouts work side by side and draw the same pay or stand side by side among the unemployed.[125]

Another reason for the northern native students' failure to go on to higher education, at least as far as Canadian natives are concerned, may lie in their perception that they are "inadequately prepared in northern high schools to cope with the academic standards required in post secondary education."[126] To counter this criticism, Koenig recommends that "northern educational systems attempt to upgrade the standards required for those students who are granted high school diplomas. Several possibilities exist in this regard: more stringent requirements for high school completion; special tutoring assistance provided for students wishing to proceed into higher education studies; negotiation with universities for greater flexibility in entrance requirements; and financial assistance to provide tutorial staff for northern students who may be academically unprepared."

Koenig's data suggest a wide discrepancy between the expectations that northern people have of higher education and the realities of what is available at universities. In particular a noticeable difference exists between the types of studies that northerners want and those that the universities offer. Northern people are generally dissatisfied with the higher educational opportunities available to them in Canadian universities and technical training institutions, but to offer higher education in the north itself is a viable alternative only if it is of the highest quality. Current educational practice in the north makes one believe that this is unlikely.

The most serious discrepancies between expectation and reality appear in anthropology-archaeology and health sciences. In the first case, class offerings far exceed the expectations of northern students. In 1974, for example, Canadian universities offered 132 classes in anthropology, but only 23 northerners were interested in this discipline.[127] However, northern students forcefully expressed a need for work in the health sciences, but universities offered no classes designed specifically to train them in this field. The northern students' desire for training in health sciences undoubtedly reflects the state of northern health and wellbeing. "With a mortality rate f[a]r exceeding the national average, with sub-standard nutritional and housing levels, with sight, hearing and dental problems, and with mental illness becoming a serious condition, the northern concern for training in health sciences is not unexpected."[128]

Other fields where discrepancies appear are sciences, mathematics, and wildlife. Northern students want to pursue these studies, but Canadian universities offer too few northern-oriented classes to satisfy the demand. Instead the universities recommend education as a rewarding field for northern students, but few of these students list education as an area in which they would choose to study. Northern students' desire to study engineering is weak, but the number of students expressing it exceeds the number of courses that Canadian universities can offer them. In addition to the health sciences, this same curricular inadequacy occurs in political science and economics and in sociology and psychology.[129]

A new development has appeared in northern Canada that will answer many of the problems facing higher education there. This was the announcement in the summer of 1983 that an Inuit university, known to the native people as an Inuit Silattunrsavingat, expected to open in 1988.[130] This university will have students of all ages from across the Arctic, but instead of travelling to it, the students will receive their lectures at local centres by computer. The open-concept institution will cost a modest $2.5–3 million, cheap by university standards, but it will take five years to plan and put into operation. Describing the proposal as "unique and exciting," NWT Education Minister Dennis Patterson said that "it suits perfectly the character of the NWT and is much better than having a building that most of the population can't get to." As well as teaching Arctic survival, the new university hopes to ensure the survival of Inuit culture. Non-credit Inuit courses will include language, anthropology, meteorology, map-making, law, biology, nutrition, music, and games.

In the 1980s Inuit education is moving in new directions largely determined by the Inuit themselves. As Paul Welsman predicted in 1976, the educational system in the north has become much more than the "torch-bearer" for the invasion from the south. The northern schools, he said, would be "bastions of cultural identity for native peoples."

The northern school system is becoming the repository of cultural values, a vehicle of policial expression and an avenue of economic betterment, albeit a poor one at present. The decentralization of the system at both national and territorial levels, the emphasis on cultural relevance in curriculum development and teacher recruitment have combined to advance the state of northern education. The political implications of these developments are likely to be far-reaching. In all probability the educational system shall produce a new generation of students who are more articulate and aware of the problems inherent in native integration into northern society. This awareness may give greater impetus and direction to native rights movements and increased native participation in the political system.[131]

That prediction too is coming true.

CHAPTER FOUR

Providing a Living

TO 1945: MILITARY BASES AND INUIT ECOLOGY

Diamond Jenness argued that after the whalemen had "killed off most of the whales in the waters of Canada's Eastern and Western Arctic" and "destroyed the independence" of the Inuit, a new livelihood appeared that eventually replaced both the traditional self-sufficient hunting ecology and the more recent but rapidly vanishing occupations at the whaling stations. Fur trapping for private and corporate traders offered the Inuit a new and necessary economic base. So before they abandoned the native to his fate, Jenness wrote, the whalemen "supplied him with steel traps, and taught him to look to the small arctic fur-bearers for the income he needed to obtain the guns, the ammunition, the cloth and all the other goods of civilization that he could no longer do without."[1]

But most Inuit had always depended on the sea for their livelihood, and as a result they took some time to adjust to the new economy of trapping arctic foxes for the Hudson's Bay Company and other traders. Hunters by instinct and tradition, the Inuit generally regarded trapping as an occupation fit only for the women and children. "Although this indifference to trapping has broken down to a very considerable extent over the past forty years," James Cantley wrote in 1952, "and some communities and some individuals now trap extensively during winter months, the majority of the Eskimo men still remain essentially hunters and it is only when there is a good fur season and they have some definite important objective in view, such as the purchase of a boat or a rifle that they really concentrate on trapping. For the rest they are satisfied to combine their trapping with their hunting and to obtain enough in this way to purchase their ordinary requirements at the trade store."[2]

In addition to hunting and trapping, other forms of work newly introduced by the increasing white incursions into the Arctic were available to the Inuit. Each police station had a couple of Inuit families in residence, and the trading posts usually had a man who acted as interpreter and performed a variety of other jobs. Meteorological stations sometimes employed a few Inuit as housemen or odd-job men. When the summer supply ship arrived the Inuit worked as stevedores. Both women and men took part, and they enjoyed the opportunity of earning one or two days' wages. During the Second World War the US and Canadian forces established a number of air bases in the Arctic, partly manned by American crews. By the beginning of the 1950s almost all the bases were still functioning, and others had gone into operation since the war's end. These bases offered the Inuit certain chances of wage earning and employed some Inuit men permanently as day labourers or sometimes as chauffeurs.

The arrival of the US forces and other white men in the Arctic during the Second World War gave rise to problems concerning the ecological resources of certain areas. The newcomers began to hunt the local fauna, in particular the caribou.[3] Northern administrators viewed this activity with concern. It appeared to be contributing further to a decline in the size of caribou herds about which the Bureau of Northwest Territories and Yukon Affairs had been worried for some time. Its anxiety was understandable. Animals provided the Inuit not only with the food energy necessary to support life but in many cases with material necessities as well: in particular, the kind of clothing best suited to withstand the inclemency of the Arctic winter. In most cases too the local fauna provided through the fur trade the only source of income available to the Inuit with which to purchase the imported foods, rifles, ammunition, and equipment on which they now depended.

The fur trade was the only economic activity of any consequence, and it could function only where there were enough fur-bearing animals and healthy natives to harvest them. The cultural system in the Arctic rested on the welfare and abundance of the wildlife in the region. So the conservation of wildlife came to occupy an important place in the administration of the Arctic. All attempts to exploit the region's faunal resources for livelihood, financial gain, or sport had to be carefully scrutinized. The government established quotas, imposed hunting restrictions on the Inuit, and empowered the RCMP to enforce them. In 1942, on his return from the Eastern Arctic Patrol, an optimistic Maj. McKeand told the press: "The Es-

TABLE 1
Caribou per Hunter and per Person, Baffin Island, 1944

Region	Average Number of Hunters	Caribou Taken per Hunter	Total Annual Take	Approx. Number Dependants	Caribou per Person
Pond Inlet (including Clyde River, Home Bay, and Arctic Bay)	133	6	800	500	1.6
Pangnirtung	100	3	300	550	0.5
Lake Harbour (including Frobisher Bay)	90	0.6	50	450	0.1
Cape Dorset	80	0.13	10	330	0.03
Foxe Basin coast*	25	8	200	150	1.3

*Probably incomplete as to number of hunters and caribou taken.

SOURCE: J.G. Wright, "The Economic Wildlife of Canada's Eastern Arctic," manuscript in the Public Archives of Canada (RG 85, Vol. 955, File 13379A, Pt. 1) 1944, 9.

kimos are increasing due to the preservation of wild life on which they depend. This is a policy fostered by the Department of Mines and Resources and now coming into full effect."[4]

Of the local fauna on which the Inuit depended during the Second World War the state of the caribou herds caused most concern. Clothing was mainly of caribou and seal skins. Caribou skins were essential if the Inuit were to endure the rigours of hunting and travelling in the Arctic winter. Cantley claimed that clothing was more important to the Inuit than food.[5] Properly clad, he argued, the Inuit could persevere and usually obtain sufficient food. Poorly clad, they could not go far afield or stay out for any length of time.

Cape Dorset suffered most from the depletion of the herds, and in general the south of Baffin Island fared worse than the north. Table 1 shows the relative availability of caribou in different regions of Baffin Island as indicated by the number taken per hunter and per head of dependent population in 1944. The gross inadequacy of these numbers becomes apparent when one compares them with the earlier needs of the Inuit "when every Eskimo hunter required six caribou hides to clothe himself, an equal number for his wife, and three, four or five hides for each of his children."[6] Each season every hunter tried to kill at least two dozen caribou.

Northern administrators in the 1940s showed more concern over caribou than over any of the other fauna on which the Inuit depended for survival. Sea mammals were apparently not under any threat,[7] yet references indicate that government representatives were keeping a careful watch on them and on other ecological resources. The NWT deputy commissioner arranged for officers on board the Eastern Arctic Patrol to undertake "regular, periodic surveys on the wild life resources and native trading" at each port of call,[8] and these suggested to him that "the Eskimo native food supplies such as caribou, seal, walrus, white whale, etc. have become scarce in some areas."[9] Maj. McKeand referred to "the white man's wanton slaughter of sea, land and air animal life, during the past hundred years";[10] and Dr G.C.B. Gaulton, a medical officer recently returned from the Arctic, told an Ottawa meeting that the native food supply, by which he meant seals, had "undoubtedly decreased in recent years in some sections and the natives who live in such parts... are often short of native food."[11] As early as 1936 nutritionist W.A. Price warned that "unless a very radical change is made in the interference with the native supply of game and sea foods, the Eskimo population seems destined to have a rapid decline and an early extinction."[12]

Such was not to be the case, of course. The Inuit survived in ever-increasing – indeed too rapidly increasing – numbers. The problem became one of providing a living for this growing population. Imported food and clothing could and did augment any shortfall in local resources, but they, and all the other material necessities and luxuries to which the Inuit had become accustomed, had to be paid for. To find ways by which the Inuit could earn enough money to pay for everything they needed has been the central problem facing northern administrators since the Second World War.

1945–59: ECONOMIC ADJUSTMENT

Fur Trade Collapse

The Inuit's main source of earned income was the fur trade. This meant dependence on the one main furbearer of the treeless Arctic, the white fox. The use of this resource after about 1920 changed the economy and drastically turned around the way of life of most Inuit. To the Inuit's constant misfortune the white fox is a resource that fluctuates unreliably and therefore constitutes an unsound basis for a permanent dependable economy. It has an approximately four-year cycle of abundance, which causes the Inuit's annual income to veer wildly. The white fox is also a "luxury" product, the market for which is determined by factors outside the Arctic and beyond the control of Inuit. When the ladies of the southern cities decided after the Second World War that they preferred "short furs" such as muskrat and mink, the market price of white fox dropped disastrously.

In 1946 the Inuit were receiving between $15 and $20 for each white fox pelt; by 1949 they were receiving less than $5 and in some cases as little as $3.50.[13] Observers ascribed the all-time low to a lack of demand. For this they blamed "the fickleness of female fashions," exchange restrictions, and Russian dumping. The Soviet Union had dumped 35,000 furs on the European market at a cost of around $9 each, and these furs were apparently of better quality than the higher-priced Canadian.[14]

At the same time as the decline in fur prices deprived the Inuit of much of their income, the nagging suspicion remained that the traders were cheating them of more. Some years earlier, the government had received complaints from NWT residents and as a result amended the game regulations to provide that traders would issue a sales record to their trappers setting out the number and kinds of pelts traded and the type and value of goods exchanged for them. This amendment was to ensure that trappers obtained goods at fair prices. The system never worked. A sales record was useless to customers who could neither read nor write nor even speak English. And the use of syllabics on counter-slips was unfeasible because few traders could speak Inuktitut beyond the minimum necessary to carry on their business, and they seldom learned to write syllabics.

With income cut by four-fifths between 1946 and 1949 the Inuit had to face greatly increased prices on all their essential goods.[15] The cost in some cases almost doubled between 1946 and 1949.[16] Further, the Inuit had to pay a 15 per cent tax on rifles and ammunition that the federal government imposed nationally in 1950.[17] This tax was aimed at sportsmen who could afford to pay it. It was not intended as an extra burden on the Inuit, for whom rifles and ammunition were essential to obtain country food, but northern administration was unsuccessful in its attempt to have the Inuit exempted from it.[18] In addition to bearing high costs and unjust taxes, the Inuit had to pay freight rates to the Arctic that ranged between $90 and $150 a ton,[19] a crushing economic burden. As one observer explained: "The Eskimos must pay for their consumer goods with the factual price, that is the wholesale price paid by the [Hudson's Bay] company plus the cost of transportation to their rather inaccessible place of habitation, the cost of distribution and the company's

profit. Their own products are bought only with the price the company expects to get when selling them again, and subtracting cost
of transportation, cost of further distribution and the company's
profit."[20] Cantley, not surprisingly in view of this unjust economic
system, produced estimates "sufficiently accurate over all" to show
that Inuit income was "never much above bare subsistence level,
particularly when the very high cost of goods at Arctic posts is taken
into account."[21]

Concern for the Inuit and their financial plight was widespread,
not only in administrative offices in Ottawa but right across the NWT.
On 17 July 1949 a meeting of traders, government representatives,
and RCMP spokesmen in the office of J.R.E. Bouchard, the district
administrator at Aklavik, discussed "the conditions among the Natives in the Northwest Territories" and sought to arrive at "a solution
for their present financial difficulties." Insp. L.J.C. Watson of the
Aklavik subdivision of the RCMP, in his report of the proceedings of
this meeting, was scathing in his opinion of the traders and of their
role in the Arctic. They "have played no small part in being responsible for any financial difficulties in which the Native now finds
himself." In elaboration of this opinion he explained:

They have done very little, if anything, to encourage the Natives to develop
a habit of saving for hard times. On the contrary, they have encouraged
them to go into debt in the off-season for the purpose of compelling them
to bring their fur catch to them rather than a competitor. They have encouraged him to buy non-essentials with whatever money he has left over
after paying his previous year's debt.[22] They have neglected to take an
interest in seeing that he utilizes his spare time to good advangage and, in
general, have been quite satisfied to see him live a hand to mouth existence
as long as he serves their purpose – that is – brings in the fur. It is true that
there is the odd exception to this and that there are a few Native trappers
who have a few thousand dollars credit today. Yet, on the other hand, there
is a Native who has sold as much as $65,000.00 worth of white foxes in one
season who has today less than $100.00 in the bank. This same Native has
a movie camera sold him by his trusted merchant.[23]

The churches also came in for criticism from Watson: "This office
has no means of knowing how much fur is processed from the Native
by the Churches, but it is believed that the amount is enormous. It
is realized that Missions are permitted to accept furs wholly or in
part as donations and are required to conform with the Regulations
in regard to trading activities if dealing in fur." Watson then made
proposals for improving conditions among the Inuit:

If anything worthwhile is to be done for the Natives I am afraid drastic action must be taken, some of which is hardly in accordance with the policy of a Democratic Government. The following is submitted merely as a partial remedy to the many ails of the country:

(a) Churches to be permitted to remain in the country for Mission work *only* and under no circumstances be allowed to handle fur – as contributions or otherwise.

(b) The schools to be entirely undenominational.

(c) Merchants to be allowed to remain in business and sell articles and foodstuffs to the Natives and others at pegged prices.

(d) Pegged prices.

(e) The establishment of a Government Bank for the Territories with all licensed merchants acting as bank Agents, under Bond.

(f) Compulsory savings of a certain percent of the Native's earnings.

(g) The establishment of Fur Experimental Stations.

(h) Exploration of the possibility of outside markets for native handicraft and the encouragement of the Native toward this goal.

(i) Cancellation of hunting and trapping privileges presently held by whites not born in the N.W.T. with suitable remuneration to them for said cancellation to enable them to re-establish themselves elsewhere. This is not applicable to those over the age of 55 years.

The RCMP at G Division headquarters was not anxious to become involved in this controversy. In submitting Watson's report to the commissioner of the RCMP in Ottawa, Insp. L.S. Grayson, on behalf of the officer commanding G Division, wrote: "I concur with the Officer Commanding Aklavik Sub-Division that conditions amongst both Indians and Eskimos throughout the N.W.T. generally are becoming such that some drastic changes of policy might have to be put into effect by the Government as the natives in many parts of the Territories are becoming more destitute every year, but I think you will agree there are many reasons why we should not make any recommendations either one way or the other in respect to the recommendations above of the Officer Commanding Aklavik Sub-Division and I would suggest that perhaps you might wish to merely file this report."

Fortunately for the Inuit, not everyone concerned with the administration of the Arctic shared Grayson's laissez-faire attitude. The NWT commissioner himself proposed that "the economic position of the native people of the N.W.T. and the Yukon should be analyzed with a view to determining whether the time has arrived when the Dominion should take over the fur trading establishments."[24] The economic adviser to the deputy minister of mines and resources maintained in a confidential report that while this would be politically difficult, if not impossible, it might become easier "if the position of the fur trade gets worse and worse. At any rate, if conditions continue to deteriorate either some such action as this or a drastic moratorium and control of credit ... may well become the only alternative to the Government committing itself to unlimited relief (in other words a subsidy to the traders) for an indefinite period." Control of credit was essential:

The natives tend to spend any money that they have very quickly, and those who save any of their income from a good year are the exceptions. Consequently, in general they have no "cushion" to carry them through a period of low prices, and they get rapidly into debt. The competition by the traders for the furs which the natives bring in accentuates this process. When prices are low and a trapper has debts, he usually takes only a portion of his furs, say one-third, to the trader with whom his debts are, paying off only part of the debts. He takes the rest of his catch to another trader with whom he can then establish a new line of credit, thus getting himself further into debt.

"The whole trouble in a nutshell," wrote the district administrator at Fort Smith, "is too many traders. They compete for the trappers' business by extending credit. Now that works fine, and all is rosy, until the time comes when the trapper cannot pay his bills and have enough left to keep him and his family till the next harvest."[25] This situation was more prevalent in the Western than in the Eastern Arctic. In the latter region the Hudson's Bay Company had few competitors, the main rivalry being concentrated at Cape Dorset, where the Baffin Trading Company was still in operation. J.G. Cantley, once manager of the Baffin Trading Company at Cape Dorset and a former employee of its larger competitor, had high praise for the Hudson's Bay Company and considered the monopoly beneficial. The fact remains, he wrote, that the Inuit who were best off were those who had always lived under this monopoly. "It is true," he conceded, "that they have not received as much in return for their furs and other produce as natives in other areas and it is probable that the Hudson's Bay Company may have made larger profits out of them, but the natives have at least a large part of their native skills and independence and are in better condition today when the markets for all their saleable products have collapsed to make a living for themselves out of the resources of their own country."[26]

Consequently Cantley believed that the most self-reliant Inuit were those on Baffin Island, in the interior of Keewatin, and in the eastern sector of the Western Arctic. Elsewhere the Inuit had largely lost their native culture and ability to live off their own country; that is, those Inuit in the most accessible areas had been more affected by the encroachments of civilization than those in the more remote areas. The other side of this sophistic coin is that the most remote Inuit were the most naive with regard to the ways of the traders and thus the most easily cheated. Was it right for the Canadian government, which had accepted the responsibility of looking after the well-being and protecting the rights of the Inuit, to allow the trading companies to swindle them so blatantly on the excuse that non-interference allowed the Inuit to retain some semblance – for that is all it was – of their former self-sufficient life-style?

The Hudson's Bay Company and the Issue of Relief

A discernible mood of pessimism settled like a shroud over the northern administration, and a special meeting of the NWT Council on 27 October 1949 did little to dispel the gloom. The report of the meeting predicted: "Relief costs for Eskimos will rise particularly in areas where country food is scarce and the natives depend on store food. A number of independent traders will no doubt be forced out of business and if the low prices on white fox continue indefinitely, the Hudson's Bay Company may have to discontinue the operation of its Arctic posts as it did in Labrador a few years ago."[27] At this meeting the only positive step was to approve the appointment of a fur trade specialist to study and make recommendations for the improvement of the Inuit economy. The man appointed was James Cantley. His brief was to study such matters as stabilization of the Inuit income, co-operative enterprises, movement of population, and the development of new industries.

Two weeks later, the RCMP at Iqaluit reported that it had been informed early in September that effective from the last day of the month all Inuit employed at the base by the US government would be laid off.[28] Three weeks later the Americans asked for five Inuit to stay on, but the rest had to go. The cuts were part of an economy drive in the United States, but they came as a serious blow to the economy of Iqaluit. A total of 21 Inuit had been working at the air base permanently, and an extra 25 were hired during the summer.[29] The 21 permanent employees supported themselves and 79 dependants. The employees included one 13-year-old boy who worked in the laundry room to maintain himself, his younger brothers, and a younger sister. His mother and two other sisters were in hospital, and his father was dead. Another boy, aged 15, worked in the quartermaster's department to support himself and his mother. The layoffs were disastrous in view of the already depressed economic situation. Increased relief and other government assistance were imperative.

When the Hudson's Bay Company (HBC) started trading with the Inuit the company handled all relief, and only in rare cases did the government pay any bills for the natives. The company saw to it that none of its Inuit customers lacked the essentials to enable them to live and to trap the foxes from which the company received its return. Any unrecoverable advances were written off and considered as relief. "The Hudson's Bay Company ... take the view that a sick, undernourished or dead Eskimo brings no profit to the company and they do, in fact, take an active interest in the welfare of the native."[30] A memorandum dated 13 July 1944, which R.H. Chesshire, manager of the Fur Trade Department, wrote to the various district managers, stated clearly: "It is essential that all our post managers understand the Company's basic policy which, briefly stated, is 'to make sure that the native does not want at any time for the basic necessities of life.' "

The most obvious example of conditions beyond the control of the native are those circumstances of hardship arising from natural shortage of fur in the lean years, often accompanied by low prices, thereby forming a combination which can only lead to intense hardship. Failure of the walrus hunt – shortage of seals – and other natural food product shortages are other circumstances, which from time to time, all militate against the native being able to support himself ...

As already advised you, the rations, clothing, equipment, etc., issued in this way for relief to able-bodied natives is not to be handled as an advance which can be collected when conditions have improved. This is a legitimate relief charge and regarded as part of the normal operating costs of the post.[31]

But the company's altruism was already beginning to weaken. It "found it necessary to ask the government to pay relief costs to widows, orphans and infirm persons who did not produce any revenue for the Company."[32] Instructions to post managers from headquarters in Winnipeg reflected this change. "The relief for the maimed, the halt, and the blind, widows, etc., is the prerogative of the Government," the company now maintained, "and here again ... [the NWT commissioner] has quite clearly indicated that he does not expect a shortsighted and parsimonious attitude to be followed in caring for the requirements of these people. This does not mean that we should go to the other extreme and issue supplies indiscriminately, but rather that we follow exactly the same line of reasoning with these people as we do in the case of the able-bodied natives and active trappers whose welfare is our responsibility."[33]

The fact that the traders had control of the issue of relief gave them too much power over the Inuit. "Once the people living in hunting camps were short of basic foodstuffs," Hugh Brody writes, "a trader could effectively dictate his will to individual families by extending or refusing credit at the store. The 'reliable' or 'good' hunter would of course receive emergency rations; those hunters who were not 'good', who had resisted the pressure to shift from subsistence to exchange, would be left without rations. In regions where game was not abundant or in a bad season, this practice might lead to starvation."[34] That the situation did lead to starvation was known to the police, and even 30 years later the Inuit still talked of those hard times, as Brody heard them do in the 1970s. "Some Belcher Island Eskimos described to me the appalling conditions, with several deaths from starvation, which prevailed there during the early 1940s."

Newspaper reports based on interviews with people returning from the north were hardly reassuring. For example, Dr G.C.B. Gaulton, the medical officer at Pangnirtung, told the Ottawa *Citizen* on 10 October 1946 that natives who were unsuccessful in obtaining foxes were likely to starve because the traders refused to advance them ammunition, let alone supplies. This was directly at variance with the understanding the government had with the trading companies. Territorial Deputy Commissioner R.A. Gibson wrote to J.G. Wright of Arctic Division, "If any trader, either of his own volition or as a result of instructions which he has received from his company, either directly or through their inspector, is creating hardship, it is time we knew about it. It is such a policy that would bring into effect earlier than we had anticipated some system of government stores to replace the present system."[35] Gibson then wrote directly to P.A. Chester, general manager of the HBC, pointing out that such publicity reflected "unfavourably upon this Administration and upon the Hudson's Bay Company."[36]

Chester replied merely that it was not company policy to deny relief to the Inuit. Yet in his 1944 memorandum R.H. Chesshire had admitted that such policy was not always followed as intended. "One point is always stressed," Chesshire wrote, "and to a very large extent quite rightly so, namely, that in regard to relief measures nothing should be done which could in any way undermine the natives' self reliance and initiative. However, a too liberal interpretation of this objective has, I know, often resulted in a procedure being followed which merely amounted to supplying such meagre rations that it was all the natives could do to keep body and soul together."[37]

Chester unctuously assured Gibson: "No matter what is said to the contrary, I have no hesitation in saying, that good progress has been made in the past few years, and it must be remembered that this was accomplished in spite of the serious handicap and difficulties caused by six years of war, when scant consideration was given anything not related to the prosecution of that war."[38] "The war years were far from easy," Chester continued, "but due to the close co-operation among all of us with interests in that northern territory, the welfare of the natives was successfully maintained and even improved, so it distrubs me to see you and the rest of us rewarded for our efforts by misrepresentations and denunciations, which are made without knowledge of the facts." An unmistakable plaint of philanthropy maligned whines in Chester's letter, yet the charges that the traders were self-seeking in their dealings with the Inuit appear irrefutable.

The government did nothing. Northern administration was itself too dependent on the HBC to interfere on behalf of the Inuit. Meanwhile the company, through its close association with the federal government, gained considerably in its competition with rival traders. One of the points that observers on the Eastern Arctic Patrol in 1943 raised was that at those places where a trader was in opposition, only the HBC could dole out government relief.[39] At Port Harrison in northern Quebec F. Ford of the Baffin Trading Company estimated that the HBC gave out government relief of more than $1,000. According to his statements, reported to the Eastern Arctic Patrol and corroborated by the Church of England missionary, the HBC issued this relief only to those Inuit who traded with them. No one informed the Inuit that the government and not the HBC provided the money. In self-defence, the Baffin Trading Company had had to give $800 in relief out of its own pockets. F. Conrad of the Baffin Trading Company at Cape Dorset complained that the Inuit who received relief during the epidemic of the previous winter were told that it had come from the HBC. Government relief was thus a direct subsidy to this trading giant.

When economic hardship struck the Inuit, and the price paid to trappers for their foxes fell as low as $3.50, the HBC became anxious to divest itself of more of its responsibilities to the northern natives. The company regarded those who failed to bring in more than an average of 10 foxes a year over the previous five years as "inefficient trappers" and refused to support them.[40] They became instead "a subject for government assistance." In its own defence, "the Company revealed that it was budgeting for an expected loss of over $100,000 in the next four years on its Arctic operations and something had to be done to relieve the situation."

In spite of these changes, the HBC maintained the commercial philosophy of unquestioning optimism. In 1949 the general manager of the Fur Trade Department wrote to the NWT deputy commissioner:

At this time I do not think there is any great cause for concern, because we shall continue to outfit the Eskimos with their essentials, as we have always done.

While the low price for Foxes continues, the Eskimos will be able to buy little but the essentials of life, but this will not create any undue hardship. Actually, they have enjoyed a number of very good years in which they were able to buy and replace boats, engines, equipment and so forth, so that generally speaking they are in relatively good shape to withstand a less prosperous period.

We have experienced similar circumstances many times in the past and I do not think the Eskimos suffered. At the present time relief for needy cases is efficiently administered; and they also now have Family Allowances which provide additional protection for their families.[41]

Postwar depression of the market for Canadian fur, together with economic instability and lingering mistrust of traders, prompted many to recommend establishment of a crown company to do all trading with the Inuit and to replace all other traders. The NWT commissioner himself had considered this as a possibility.

For these critics of the private trading system in the Arctic the model of a better way to help the Inuit was the Danish system in Greenland. There the Danes had, for more than a century before the Second World War, excluded visits from non-residents other than government officials, whether from Denmark or elsewhere. They occasionally made exceptions for established scientists but firmly refused to admit casual visitors and fishing or trading boats. By closing Greenland as tightly as Japan under *sakoku*, the Danish authorities hoped to protect the native people not only from disease but also from economic exploitation:

The strict isolation made it possible to "manage" the economy. The limited natural resources of the country could be sold by the Greenlanders, so far as they were not needed for local use, and in return essential supplies could be purchased from the government stores. Prices remained constant for a year at a time and were so arranged that essential goods such as hunting gear were relatively inexpensive, while "luxury" items such as sugar, coffee, white flour (as contrasted with rye and whole wheat flour) were more highly priced.[42]

The feeling grew in Canada that the federal government could best protect the Inuit against commercial exploitation by setting up government stores and regulating the prices of produce on sale to benefit the Inuit rather than the traders. The RCMP, which had been advocating such a step for many years, believed that a crown company could be run without a loss and that the Inuit could get a better deal for their furs. No one would hound them out to concentrate primarily on trapping, Insp. H.A. Larsen argued; instead, they would have more time for hunting meat. The government trader at each post could keep individual credit and debit accounts for every Inuk and control the payment of credits so as to spread them over any length of time, as and when the Inuit needed them. The goods that the crown company sold to the Inuit could be only those that were beneficial to their way of life. Such payments as family allowances, allowances for the blind, and old age allowances could all go to the individual Inuk's credit account with the traders. The traders would be under no compelling necessity to show a large profit for the operation of their posts.[43]

Government advisers, in particular fur trade specialist James Cantley, remained unconvinced. Cantley held firmly to the view "that the formation of a Crown Company would not offer any advantage over the continuation of trade by private enterprise under wider departmental supervision."[44] He argued that a crown company would be no more responsible to northern administration than the present traders and that it was "extremely doubtful if a crown company could be operated as efficiently or as economically as a private concern." There was, too, the "vital question of staffing a crown company." If it were to retain the experienced men, of whom the RCMP had been so critical, then no advantage would apparently be gained. If it were to bring in new and inexperienced men, "the situation could be even worse."

H.A. Young, deputy minister of resources and development, agreed with Cantley and immediately discounted "the possibility of establishing a trading company owned and operated by the Federal Government."[45] However, he was "not in favour of utilizing completely the Hudson's Bay Company to carry out our Departmental responsibilities. For the time being at least I think we must continue with the function of welfare and family allowances being controlled by ourselves and the Mounted Police."

Like all other citizens of Canada, the Inuit had become entitled to receive family allowances in 1945. Opinions on the benefit of this form of social welfare varied widely. For example, Insp. Larsen thought little of it. "The amount that each family receives each month is so small," he wrote, "having regard to the high prices of foodstuffs and other commodities in the north, that it is, in my opinion, not worth the time of the Eskimos to go into the Posts so often. I estimate that the average Eskimo family (those families having children) would consist of two children eligible for Family Allowances, at an average of $6.00 per month per child, that is $12.00 per month per family. $12.00 does not buy very much in the north."[46]

However, the administrative officer of the Eastern Arctic Patrol in 1948 reported that the 350 Inuit in the Cape Dorset area "seem to be an independent group of people, who are appreciative of the help they are receiving through the Family Allowances credits. There is no hint at this settlement that Family Allowances is anything but a benefit to the children."[47] Alex Stevenson, officer in charge of the patrol in 1950, agreed. Although the fur market was exceptionally low, he reported, and there was a feeling that the standard of living conditions had gone down, nevertheless he thought "that with the help obtained from Family Allowances, Old Age Allowances and handicrafts, the average family now have, if not a better, at least a more consistent annual income than in former years."[48]

Family allowances were initially paid to the Inuit only in kind from carefully selected lists of items "designed to benefit the children."[49] Vouchers were issued to the Inuit who exchanged them for their choice of items at the nearest HBC store. Insp. Larsen believed "it would be far better if the Allowances were paid out ... not only in foodstuffs but in other authorized commodities, such as clothing for the children, rifles, ammunition, canoes and boats and camping equipment for the adults." His reasoning was that the children benefited "by the parents having better equipment with which to pursue their hunting and trapping."[50] But family allowances were more flexible than Larsen appeared to realize. Issues were left to the discretion of the district registrar, usually a member of Larsen's own G Division of the RCMP. The registrar could use his own judgement, provided he stuck to the authorized list of items. But the list itself allowed a lot of leeway. For example, Const. D'Aoust at Lake Harbour issued $108.95 worth of egg powder but no ammunition. He felt that ammunition should be issued, where possible, on company debt or company relief instead of on family allowances. Const. Barr at Pangnirtung was issuing large quantities of flour *and* ammunition on family allowances credits.[51]

James Cantley felt that while the decline in white fox prices and the rise in the cost of merchandise had undoubtedly affected the Inuit economy adversely, the receipt of around $300,000 a year in family allowances "should have lessened the impact and that, in the circumstances, if the available Eskimo income had been wisely used, there should not have been such a marked increase in relief costs."[52] Government relief to the Inuit cost $14,000 in 1946–7. It rose to $21,000 the following year, $47,000 in 1948–9, $90,000 in 1949–50, and $112,000 in 1950–1. Destitution relief was given only to persons incapable of earning their own living through physical disability or because of temporary shortage of local resources. All vouchers, both for family allowances and relief, were certified by the RCMP before being sent to Ottawa for payment, and no non-essentials were allowed.[53]

Northern Economic Problems

Since the Second World War the RCMP had been growing more and more unhappy with the rapidly deteriorating social conditions in the Arctic, especially in the settlements, where growing numbers of Inuit were concentrating. When Insp. H.A. Larsen, officer commanding G Division, wrote to his headquarters in Ottawa in 1951, complaining bitterly about the situation of the native people in the north,[54] he traced the source of the trouble back to the time when traders first entered Inuit territory and changed the whole way of life of the people, "from primarily hunters of meat to primarily trappers of fur." Larsen also held the government responsible for failing in its handling of Inuit affairs and argued that conditions in the Arctic called for the appointment of a commission to investigate fully "all matters pertaining to Eskimos." The commission should "travel into the country and visit the camps at different times of the year, summer and winter, and see at first hand how the Eskimos exist."

Larsen's suggestion appeared impracticable to the federal government's representative, James Cantley. But one other suggestion appealed to Cantley. "I think of all the recommendations Inspector Larsen has made, the one suggesting a meeting of persons concerned with Eskimo administration is the most practical and I would strongly recommend that it should be done as early as possible."

On 19 and 20 May 1952, in the board room on the fourth floor of the Confederation Building in Ottawa, representatives gathered from the departments of Resources and Development, National Health and Welfare, Citizenship and Immigration, National Defence, Transport, and Fisheries; from the NWT Council, the RCMP, Indian Health Services, and the Defence Research Board; and from the HBC and Anglican and Roman Catholic missions. The chairman was Maj.-Gen. H.A. Young, NWT commissioner. It was, as the director of Northern Administration and Lands Branch described it, "an informal gathering of those people who, ... from their experience ... could contribute something towards the solution of Eskimo problems."[55] The agenda included recent changes in the Inuit economy, the cumulative effects of government aid, the functions of the RCMP, suggestions for improving the situation, policy on employment of Inuit and on their education, and questions on health and welfare and on the scientific study, conservation, and use of wildlife resources.[56] With regard to these and related topics the conference was diplomatically stated to be in general agreement "that present measures for the care and advancement of the Eskimos were sound but efforts should be unified and intensified wherever possible."

The decline in white fox values, increased cost of merchandise and the apparent decline in the availability of food resources in some areas have all had their effect on the native population, as have also temporary employment at military bases, a seemingly greater incidence of disease, payments of family and other allowances, and increased relief issues. Greatly improved means of transportation and communication and the rapid opening up of the country by outside interests are constantly presenting new problems and emphasize the necessity of educating and preparing the native population to meet them. In view of the many divergent opinions held on what could or should be done to cope with changing conditions, it was felt that a collective approach by all those interested would be the most practicable one and it was hoped that everyone present would take advantage of the opportunity to express his views frankly.[57]

In view of the "many divergent opinions" and of the need for a regular forum in which to debate them, the conference agreed to set up a Committee on Eskimo Affairs and a special Sub-Committee on Eskimo Education. The members would represent those government departments, religious organizations, and commercial concerns that had an interest in the north and in the well-being of the Inuit. The first meeting of the committee took place on 16 October 1952 in Ottawa.

An Advisory Committee on Arctic Development had been in existence since early 1948; as set out on the authority of the cabinet dated 19 January 1948, it was to "advise the government on questions of policy relating to civilian and military undertakings in Northern Canada and to provide for the effective coordination of all government activities in that area."[58] This committee consisted of deputy ministers. It was intended not "to interfere in any way with the responsibilities or work" of the NWT Council but to deal with matters wherein the co-operation of other departments was essential or where help was needed to accomplish some plan in the general interest. It had held its first meeting on 2 February 1948, when the members hoped "that overall coordination and some comprehensive programme of northern development could be worked out."[59] It lapsed after a few sessions.

One would have expected the new Committee on Eskimo Affairs to have taken over its terms of reference, since the aims of both were similar, but northern administration works in strange and mysterious ways. It reactivated the Advisory Committee on Arctic Development under the new title of Advisory Committee on Northern Development. The first meeting of this newly revitalized body in February 1953 made it clear that its prime function was to feed information and ideas to the cabinet. The cabinet was apparently beginning to feel some concern about the Canadian north.[60] The ministers "had a genuine feeling of interest in this area but, unfortunately, incomplete knowledge of northern activities." At the same time the old bugbear of earlier cabinets and parliaments crept out: "an apprehension of seeming encroachment upon Canadian sovereignty." The cabinet wanted to be informed of all activities in the Arctic, to have periodic reports of proposed developments, to receive recommendations of what could be done to promote Canadian initiative, and to have Canada take the lead rather than let the United States set the pace in areas of joint participation.

The Ottawa *Journal* on 6 June 1953 reported that the cabinet had "moved quietly to set up a new brains trust to protect Canada's northern interests and co-ordinate all future economic and military planning in the Arctic ... Top military, science, financial and transport experts are included." The report ended on a note of optimism. The newspaper's informants emphasized the importance of the committee "with the possibility that the Arctic may be at the edge of an industrial boom, with new industries and new population speeding northward." But an editorial writer in the *Journal* on 12 June 1953 was sceptical:

Canada and her Parliament know very little about the North as a whole. They read of heroic missionaries, of uranium finds, of notable flights, of defence exercises in below-zero weather, of Eskimo ingenuity. But there is not one up-to-the-minute, comprehensive, official publication dealing with all the Far North although there are scattered papers on various regions and various undertakings such as the introduction of the reindeer and the ancient dwellings of long-dead Eskimos.

What we need at this time is much more than an advisory committee, helpful as that may be. What we must have is discussion of the North in Parliament, a public examination of its needs and its future. It is not enough for a modern nation to deal with problems as they arise, paint a piece of map red and say Canada's territory runs up to the North Pole. There should be imagination and foresight, and most of all, a public policy Canadians at large can study and approve.

There was truth in the *Journal's* editorial. Clearly no amount of information and ideas that the government's various advisory committees passed on would have any value unless they gave rise to imaginative and foresighted policy and to discussion of the north in Parliament. But Parliament heard little informative debate on the north. The public received more information from speeches made outside the House of Commons. The prime minister and various members of his cabinet made many public statements on the growing importance they attached to the north, not only for defence requirements but as the logical extension of the development of Canadian nationhood. Canada had developed in the east, the south, and the west, but the time and the conditions of peace and prosperity had not been present until then to allow the country to develop its northern areas.

So the future thrust of official policy was to be in the direction of northern development. The government admitted its past failings in that area but expressed its determination to make amends. One would like to believe that the new approach to the north, the sudden thirst for information on the region, and the unaccustomed government interest in its future were all due to a desire to improve the conditions of the Inuit whom the government had so long neglected. But the feeling comes through that nothing more than Canadian economic interests were responsible for the changed attitude. "Economic activity in the Yukon and the Northwest Territories continued to justify the country's accented interest [in the north]," said the annual report of the newly formed Department of Northern Affairs and National Resources in 1954. "Increased gold production from the three producing mines in the Northwest Territories sent the value of mineral production to more than a million and a half dollars above the 1952 figure."

As far as the people of the north were concerned, the government of Louis St Laurent displayed remarkable optimism, born either of ignorance or of political expediency. The prime minister himself said, in proposing the new department on 6 December 1953, "Of course the population of the territories is still small in relation to their area, but it is growing percentagewise quite rapidly. It is a healthy growth based upon proven resources that are being used and are providing a livelihood for the population." He spoke just 20 months after a government-sponsored conference spent two days discussing decreases in food resources, a "drastic decline" in white fox fur prices, "greatly increased" prices of store-bought goods, and the consequent "serious difficulties" that such economic stresses create

During that conference, in May 1952, representatives of Resources and Development revealed that in the seven years 1945–51 inclusive, relief to the Inuit had risen from $11,000 to $115,000 a year, and that altogether the government had paid out $405,000. During the same period, when fox prices dropped from $25 to less than $5 a skin, other forms of government aid, such as family allowances, brought the total northern outlay to $1,687,000. In the Baffin Island–Ungava Bay area, 53 per cent of Inuit income came from government sources; in the Western Arctic the figure was only around 25 per cent.[61] The 53 per cent had increased to 59 per cent when Cantley computed it in 1952. Family allowances then made up 31 per cent, and other forms of government relief the remaining 28 per cent. A further 13 per cent comprised unrecoverable debt and relief issued by the HBC. Only 28 per cent was earned.[62]

Something had to be done, with urgency, to improve the economic situation of the Inuit. In 1952 James Cantley proposed a number of "immediate steps that may be taken."[63] One involved the movement of people from economically depressed areas to locations where they might more easily make a living. Cantley's suggestions involved the transfer of three groups of about 10 families each: one from the Port Harrison area of northern Quebec to Ellesmere Island, where it could be looked after by the RCMP at Craig Harbour and by the proposed detachment near Cape Herschel; one from northern Quebec and / or the Cape Dorset area to Resolute Bay, provided arrangements could be made with the RCMP to station a man there "to look after the natives and enforce observance of Northwest Territories ordinances and regulations"; and one from northern Quebec and / or the Cape Dorset area to Clyde River in northern Baffin Island. Fur trading was to be the main economic support on Ellesmere Island. At Resolute Bay work could probably be found with the Department of Transport and the RCAF, while furs, handicrafts, and other produce "could be disposed of either locally to white employees and visitors at the base or brought to Montreal for sale." Near Clyde River, the US government was proposing to build a radar station at Cape Christian, and "most of the Eskimo men in this area could probably find employment on construction during the summer months."

Other proposals that Cantley made related to the "organization and improvement of hunting techniques," including those for walrus hunting at various centres in the Eastern Arctic, "to insure that herds are not killed off or driven away from their present haunts." Inuit everywhere should be encouraged to make greater use of nets for taking seals and white whales. Cantley considered nets to be more economical than rifles in view of the high cost of rifles and ammunition and the loss of animals shot, particularly in the summer when they do not float. Cantley suggested chartering a small whale hunting steamer for whaling and research in Hudson Strait and Bay. His argument was that the Inuit could kill whales and tow them to the nearest native settlement where they could store the meat and oil for local use and incidentally reduce the strain on walrus and seal.

As for "augmenting and conserving Eskimo earnings," Cantley made a number of proposals. He said, for example, that there should be a wider distribution of population during the winter months for trapping and hunting. To improve the trapping he suggested distribution of meat and fish caches, as a means of attracting white foxes, and provision of suitable box traps for taking ermine. To improve the products for sale or for use in local manufacturing, there should be investigation of dressing and tanning processes, not just for foxes but for white bears and sealskins. Cantley thought the Inuit should be encouraged to save and prepare hair sealskins better, so that they could command a better market outside or be used to make up saleable articles for disposal within the country. As for marketing, Cantley proposed the exploration of markets for walrus and white whale hides in Canada, the United States, and Europe and strongly urged both the investigation of methods of marketing white foxes and the role that Northern Affairs might play in promoting their use and obtaining a greater return for the Inuit. The average catch of white fox in Canada was about 45,000 a year. The only other producing country of any importance was the Soviet Union, and its foxes were under ban in the United States. "White foxes could conceivably be glamourized as a scarce commodity through control of the markets and the right kind of advertizing and promotion."

In addition to hunting and trapping, small fisheries could be organized to supply local settlements and the larger bases such as those at Iqaluit, Fort Chimo, Goose Bay, Padloping, and the one proposed at Cape Christian. In recognition of the belief that wildlife resources would be unable to support the growing population in the Arctic, Cantley urged the wider development of Inuit handicrafts and of other local industries whose product could be sold outside or used to supply Inuit requirements either locally or in other areas. Opportunities for employment of the Inuit were also to be provided by various agencies in the smaller settlements, at isolated radio stations, at High Arctic joint US-Canadian weather stations, and at US and Canadian army and air force bases.

In Greenland the Danish government went all out for industrialization. When Trevor Lloyd returned to Greenland in 1959 he found the scene "distressing" compared to the way he remembered it from before the war. The main reason was that the bulldozer was abroad in the land. "The amount of half-finished construction, the new roads loaded with trucks, factories erected, new wharves being built and houses crowding together ... [were] altogether too much like home to be enjoyed." These were the marks of an economic revolution that had begun a generation before with a slight rise in the temperature of the surrounding seas.

This modest change brought in the Atlantic cod and caused the seals and other arctic mammals to migrate further north. The Greenlander became of necessity a fisherman rather than a seal hunter, and an industrial worker with a pay packet rather than a proud and independent provider for his family. Since 1950 a determined effort has been made to make him efficient, if industrial worker he must be, by providing modern processing plants, better boats, and improved equipment. By 1958 the modernizing of the economy even spread to the rather inhospitable East Greenland coast when a ship supplied with salt and the necessary gear was stationed near Angmagssalik to enable local hunters to catch and process cod found to be present even in those chilly waters.

Beginning in 1959, the tempo of construction in West Greenland is to be increased. Several new fishing harbours, a number of filet factories and shrimp processing plants, as well as improved water supply, electricity and other services required by the new industries, are to be built. The decision having been made to industrialize Greenland, it is felt that this cannot be achieved too soon. Only by greatly increased production can the fishermen be given high enough wages and the government secure the funds to amortise its high installation costs. The recent approval by the Danish authorities of a plan to build a large transit harbour near Godthaab for shipment to Europe of iron ore received from Ungava in Canada, is an indication of the lengths to which Denmark is prepared to go in aiding development of Greenland.[64]

Canada was not prepared to go to the same lengths on behalf of its northern peoples in the 1950s, nor indeed has the federal government ever made the same degree of commitment to the Canadian Arctic as the Danes did to Greenland. Canadians have never had a clear, well thought out, and forcefully presented northern policy. Official attempts to do something about the Canadian north have been half-hearted and half-baked; they have lacked direction and determination, wavering from side to side in the fickle alternating winds of successive governments, political strategies, social pressures, and commercial interests. While the Danes pushed ahead with a well-defined economic policy for the development of Greenland, aided by an educated and wholly literate native population, the Canadian government pursued its piecemeal, stop-gap, butterfly measures in an Arctic social environment facing economic and demographic destruction.

On 23 May 1956 the Advisory Committee on Northern Development devoted almost its entire meeting to the "economic crisis in the north."[65] R.G. Robertson, deputy minister of northern affairs, stated that on 15 February the minister had reported to the cabinet on the economic problems facing the people of the north. The cabinet had approved establishment of a special committee to study ways of stimulating economic development. The committee had held several meetings to consider the employment that would be available in the north during the next few years and to evaluate various proposals for increasing economic activity. The advisory committee considered that the prospects for employment were "relatively good for the next three years owing to the high rate of government construction." But what then? Most government officials feared a repetition of the demoralizing situation when wartime employment ceased and the formerly employed Inuit and their families were forced back on to the land. After the initial three-year period of high labour demand foreseen in 1956, "the amount of employment would probably decline rapidly." Then the basic economy of hunting and trapping would no longer be able to "provide a suitable livelihood" for as large a proportion of the population as then lived off the land, and there were no prospects that this situation would improve. The advisory committee believed that current mining activity, based on gold and uranium and confined to the Western Arctic, would provide little additional employment.

The special committee set up by cabinet decision on 15 February 1956 was known as the Working Group on Northern Economic Problems. Research that a subcommittee of the working group undertook found that for the NWT and Arctic Quebec the potential male labour force, the 16-to-64-years age group, was about 2,600 out of a total population of 9,900. The number of Inuit in the two regions known to be working full-time for wages in 1956 was put at about 150 to 200. These included 23 special RCMP constables, 18 employees of the Department of Transport, 17 working with Indian and Northern Health Services, about 15 with Northern Affairs, and about 20 with the HBC. Another 23 worked full-time at various occupations in Iqaluit and 10 in Churchill, and 16 were herders at Reindeer Station. Accepting a maximum of 200 fully employed Inuit meant that 2,400 employable Inuit were without work. Large numbers of these were, however, either self-employed in trapping and hunting for at least part of the year or were engaged for varying periods in various kinds of wage employment: for example, on construction of the DEW Line and the Mid-Canada line, with the mining companies at Rankin Inlet and the Belcher Islands, as stevedores with the transport companies, and on survey parties. "It seems reasonable to assume that about 2,000 would constitute the employable unemployed category."[66] And this situation was likely to deteriorate. In the NWT in 1956 about 65 per cent of Inuit and 55 per cent of Indians were under 25 years of age, and the numbers in this age group were increasing. "With continued growth in population over the next few years," the working group's report pointed out, "both the male native labour force and the numbers of employable unemployed can also be expected to increase."

The government revealed its long-term plans for the Inuit in a report prepared in January 1957 for the Advisory Committee on Northern Development.[67] Where "primitive Eskimos in remote areas" were "relatively free from contact with white civilization," the suggestion was to leave their way of life as undisturbed as possible. In those areas where permanent contact was already established, integration of the Inuit with the white economy would be encouraged. The government and its advisers believed that, between these two extremes, employment of the Inuit was advisable so long as it did not "interfere unduly with their normal life." In the mean time the ploy of transferring families from unproductive to more promising lands would continue. The government in 1957 also planned to do what many later administrations have tried to do also: that is, to diversify the northern economy. Other plans included the expansion of rehabilitation facilities for that tenth of the Inuit population in hospitals in southern Canada and an adequate child welfare program for the long-suffering children of the Arctic.

In addition to these planned expedients, four important ongoing Arctic developments continued to provide opportunities for local employment, even if the outlook for full-time, permanent work was depressingly unpromising: the DEW Line project; the federal government's house-building and other construction programs, especially at Iqaluit; the appearance and growth of the co-operative movement; and the non-renewable resource industries.

Inuit Employment and the DEW Line

For the administrators of the Canadian Arctic the decision late in 1954 to go ahead with the construction of the DEW Line system came at exactly the right time. A new economic crisis was developing in the north. The population was increasing rapidly. The fur economy had sunk into a deep depression. The job market was lower than mid-winter temperatures. Family income, though fluctuating from year to year, was declining overall and dragging the people down into the slough of poverty. Demands for government relief and social assistance were increasing. In this bleak scenario the brightest hope for the future was seen to beam out from the stack of construction projects that were promised in the north.

And yet, at the same time, the Canadian government showed commendable caution about grasping too readily and indiscriminately at the straws of whatever jobs the fickle winds and currents of circumstance happened to waft to the shores of the Arctic. The lessons of the Second World War, when the Inuit were employed for a while and then returned to living off the land, were not easily forgotten. At a meeting of the Advisory Committee on Northern Development in November 1954, Dr O.M. Solandt, chairman of the Defence Research Board, asked if the Inuit should in fact be employed on the DEW Line. "During the construction phase there would be many well-paid jobs," he said, "but these would soon disappear."[68] A Sub-Committee looking into the administrative implications of the DEW Line expressed similar views a few months later. "The Sub-Committee considered that large-scale and indiscriminate employment of Eskimos was undesirable and all employment should be on a planned basis and carefully controlled. It was noted that under the Canada-U.S. agreement on the construction of the D.E.W. Line all employment of Eskimos would be arranged through the Department of Northern Affairs and National Resources. In general the Sub-

Committee recommended that Eskimos should be employed only when there was a likelihood of continuing employment beyond the two-year construction phase."[69]

The position of the department as expressed by its deputy minister was that it was "anxious to obtain employment for those who would benefit by it."[70] Political rather than social considerations obviously motivated this anxiety. But the deputy minister believed that various Inuit were at different stages of advancement. The extent of their contact with DEW Line activities might be modified according to their ability to adapt themselves. In any case negotiators would be sure to include in the DEW Line agreement regulations to protect the best interests of the native people.

Instructions issued to the northern service officers with respect to DEW Line activities incorporated most of the officially expressed viewpoints in a compromise package worked out by Northern Affairs. The northern service officer's primary responsibility was to the Inuit. Considerations of their welfare were to dominate at all times. Only Inuit who wished to be employed were to be hired, and only for such periods and in such locations as were suitable and acceptable to them. Northern service officers were to have constant regard to arranging continuous employment only for such numbers of Inuit as seemed likely to go on working after the construction phase was over, either on the DEW Line itself or on other operations for which the training they received would make them suitable.[71]

The number of Inuit working directly on the DEW Line was never high, but others found jobs as a result of spin-off from the main construction activity. The Federal Electric Corporation gave 94 as a firm figure for the initial requirement of Inuit labour.[72] These included four men at each of 4 main stations in Canada, two men at each of 18 auxiliary stations, two at each of 20 intermediate stations, and two at a relay station. But the contractors made it clear that more Inuit would doubtless be needed than the estimated 94, which represented only the minimum requirements for Inuit employees. More would be hired as conditions warranted, not directly by the Federal Electric Corporation but by subcontractors. For example, Northern Construction Company would need 28 Inuit for two months' work as stevedores. Then Federal Electric itself announced increases in its Inuit employment. Four extra men were wanted at the lower camp at Cape Dyer and two more at Broughton Island. And in 1958 the corporation announced an expected increase of 30 to 40 Inuit workers.[73] This was an optimistically premature announcement. Instead of increasing by 30 or 40, the number actually dropped by 10 in the western section of the DEW Line.[74] So although a total of 7,281 men were spread along the Arctic coast in construction work at the height of DEW Line activity in August 1956, the number of Inuit employed in all of Canada did not exceed 100 till July 1961. Then the total was 101. By September the number was back down to 96, which it had been in March, and in November it dropped again to 89.[75]

Even before 1961 many were openly expressing doubts about the benefit of DEW Line employment to the Canadian Inuit, and some considered the whole project to have been a mistake. There were those who had held this view from the start, but by the end of the 1950s such sentiments were widespread. The comments of the northern service officer at Tuktoyaktuk in August 1959 are typical. "I am unable to supply convincing arguments," he wrote, "as to where and how additional Eskimo help could be used on the DEW Line. Does anyone have any idea of the life expectancy of the DEW Line? With the Sunday supplements parading Super radars, missiles and bombs the old DEW Line is looking awfully decrepit. I can not help thinking that perhaps we should start wondering what to do with 100 newly jobless Eskimos. Should we not bend our efforts to shrinking rather than augmenting this number? If the DEW Line is good for even 10 more years is this a long enough term to base the economic future of a large segment of the Eskimo population on?"[76]

Like a descant to the main theme, almost inaudible but strongly sensed, was the frustration of technocrats whose urgent desire to get on and finish the job was thwarted by the irrational hang-ups of backward natives and the obvious biases of northern service officers. In words that almost blamed the Inuit for being there, the Federal Electric Corporation stated, "The presence of an Eskimo population residing in the area of the DEW Line presents health and sociological problems of mutual concern to DEW Line supervision and the Northern Service Officer."[77] The corporation quoted an agreement between the US and Canadian governments concerning the employment of Inuit on the DEW Line to illustrate the restrictions under which the corporation had to provide the labour for its construction work. "The Eskimos of Canada," the agreement read, "are in a primitive state of social development. It is important that these people be not subjected unduly to disruption of their hunting economy, exposure to diseases against which their immunity is often low, or other effects of the presence of white men which might be injurious to them."

The Canadian government expected the Federal Electric Corporation to hire Inuit as workmen and treat them like pampered children. When Adm. R.H. Cruzen, vice-president of Federal Electric, announced the anticipated increase of 30 or 40 Inuit in the 1958 labour force, Jameson Bond, the northern service officer on the DEW Line, remarked that because of strong family ties and kinship bonds most Inuit liked to remain in the general area where they were brought up. Although some were prepared to work for a few months in other parts of the Arctic, this was unlikely to prove feasible on a permanent basis.[78] Cruzen said that he preferred Inuit employees to remain "relatively permanent" in one location.

Another source of irritation to Federal Electric was the request for special holiday consideration that Bond presented on behalf of the Inuit. Two factors had to be borne in mind in timing holidays for the Inuit: first, the peak work periods that ordinarily occurred during the summer shipping season and during the period of winter storms; and, second, the productive periods in the annual hunting cycle that occurred in the late spring for seals and in late August and early September for fish. Many Inuit were still close to the hunting life, Bond maintained, and so would probably welcome holidays during these peak hunting periods, work load permitting. Negotiators agreed that the sector superintendent and the station chief could best work out the actual arrangements in consultation with the northern service officer for the particular area.

The work expected from the Inuit on the DEW Line was initially to be no more than casual labouring in snow clearance, the maintenance of roads, airstrips, and other ground areas, stevedoring, water hauling, ice crushing, waste disposal, and other jobs like handling supplies in exterior locations and unheated storage areas. As they gained experience or completed training courses they would earn promotion to maintenance work on mechanical equipment and on rigging and towers, and then to posts as assistants to maintenance mechanics.[79]

This scheme worked satisfactorily in the Western Arctic but not in the east. There were not enough Inuit in the Eastern Arctic of the calibre the corporation required. The reason was easy to find. Decades of neglect of the eastern Inuit had left them grossly underqualified to accept employment when the opportunities came along. Adm. Cruzen himself raised the matter with the deputy minister of northern affairs in April 1958. "I would like to take this opportunity to point out a specific problem which is of concern to the Corporation," he wrote. "This is the quality and availability of Eskimos in the Baffin Island area. I recognize that with this problem there are many extenuating circumstances. When we first started employing Eskimos in that area, we were aware of the lack of qualified personnel and were aware that we would experience difficulty in obtaining a full complement. However, we are still experiencing difficulty in getting sufficient qualified Eskimos to properly man our stations."[80]

The deputy minister replied at the beginning of May. "The Eskimos of Baffin Island area, to whom you refer have not had the advantage of gainful employment to the extent that Eskimos of the Western Section of the DEW Line have had. It has been more difficult to effect arrangements for Eskimos of the Baffin Island area to attend the vocational training courses, and for that reason they have not been as well qualified as Eskimos elsewhere. We are developing a plan of vocational training for these Eskimos and it is to be hoped that you will continue your policy of re-employing them when they return to their site locations."[81]

The administrator of the Arctic described the problem of finding qualified Inuit to work on the eastern section of the DEW Line as critical. He said that it was more difficult to train Inuit from the Eastern Arctic than those from the west because of the language barrier and the remoteness of the Eastern Arctic from civilization. He hoped that they could overcome the problem in the near future by making educational facilities available to the eastern Inuit. He went on to say that he had a few vacancies in the eastern section for some trainees and added that because of the critical situation "we must look to the West for some Eskimos who might accept employment in the East. It is known that this has not been too successful in the past, but I feel we must impress upon the Eskimo the advantage of accepting employment in the East and try to break down the feeling they have against travelling from one section to another for employment."[82]

The experiment was only a partial success. Men did come from the Western Arctic, but they did not come to stay. Even in the Western Arctic the Inuit regarded wage employment as a casual undertaking rather than a permanent way of life. Few of those who came from Tuktoyaktuk or Mackenzie remained in the east. Most of those immigrants who stayed "on a more or less permanent basis" were from the Cambridge Bay area of the Central Arctic.[83]

The failure to attract western Inuit to work on the eastern sector of the DEW Line was a blow to the Federal Electric Corporation and to some of the people in northern administration. The consensus was that "Western men" had "proved far more competent as DEW Line workers than Eastern men." The west had been "carrying the East for some time," and the assistant regional administrator at Frobisher Bay hoped that it would continue to do so till more trained men were available in the Eastern Arctic. "We are now in a serious position regarding DEW Line employment," he wrote, "in that we are not now able to fill our commitments to the Federal Electric Corp. The danger exists that the FEC might in future reject our programme as unfruitful. To overcome this situation we should have a constant source of trained Eskimos at our disposal."[84]

Administrators from Northern Affairs were in an unenviable position. The stresses of the postwar northern economic crisis and its recrudescence in the mid-1950s were most severely felt in the Eastern Arctic. Income was decreasing while energy and material needs were increasing and becoming more expensive. The obvious solution was to diversify the economy of the Inuit and overcome their dependence on a single commodity, the exchange potential of which was seriously declining. The DEW Line project appeared to offer opportunities for such diversification, but those who needed the new jobs most were the least able to accept them. The Inuit of the Eastern Arctic had no tradition of permanent wage employment. In the 1950s most of them were still hunters, largely dependent on country produce to supply their food and material requirements. Northern administrators faced the dilemma of trying to preserve what they could of the hunting way of life for the Inuit while encouraging them to join a modern, highly developed work-force with its own demands and standards of employment.

Requests for special consideration for the Inuit in respect to holidays, time off, casual work habits, and unwillingness to move permanently from home areas merely exasperated Federal Electric officials, who were more accustomed to the take-it-or-leave-it competition of American labour relations. The feelings of the American employers surfaced at a meeting between them and representatives from several Canadian government departments in July 1961. The corporation alleged that about 50 per cent of the Inuit then working on the DEW Line needed more supervision than was desirable "as they couldn't be counted on to do their jobs properly on their own." Then came the crunch. "Because of superior skill on the job and their better work attitude, requests had reached Federal Electric Headquarters recommending that Caucasians be employed instead of Eskimos. Some Eskimos were poor employees and some had worked out very well indeed, and at least some had advanced by leap-frogging over one classification. However, there were unfilled vacancies and rising standards of operational procedures which required prompt attention."[85]

Clearly the outlook for sustained economic development in the Eastern Arctic offered little encouragement to those whose task was to find ways to stimulate it. Experience with the DEW Line had shown beyond doubt that modern economic development depended to a critical degree on education. The Inuit of the Eastern Arctic were singularly ill-equipped.

Federal Electric flatly rejected the excuse of Canadian officials that "lack of English ... was the root of the problem," especially in the Eastern Arctic. In the blunt language of the Americans, "the factor was unreliability." Most unreliable of all were the Inuit of Iqaluit, who had established a poor reputation on the DEW Line and were considered bad prospects for employment.[86]

A quarter of a century later the DEW Line stations still keep an ever-watchful eye for enemy penetration of North America's polar skies. In Canada the four main sites are at Cape Parry in the west, Cambridge Bay in the Central Arctic, and Hall Beach and Cape Dyer in the east. Seventeen auxiliary stations report to these main sites and to their respective military commanders. Fifty-five Inuit still work on the line along with 20 Canadian military personnel, about 10 from the United States, and several hundred contracted civilians from the south.[87]

The Boom at Iqaluit

In addition to the US government's DEW Line, the Canadian government's house-building and other construction provided a welcome and much needed boost to local Inuit employment. One settlement that especially benefited was that chosen as the administrative and logistical centre for the eastern sector of the DEW Line: Iqaluit (Frobisher Bay). By 1956 it was "booming." The northern service officer stationed there described it as a "high employment, high income area." "We do not have sufficient Eskimos to fill all the positions that are available," he complained. "And quite a few Eskimos are not yet interested in employment on construction except for the summer period."[88] The RCMP elaborated on the burgeoning situation: "The economy of the Frobisher Bay Eskimos is one based largely on employment at the U.S.A. Air Force Base and the townsite which is being developed by the Department of Northern Affairs and National Resources. About thirty-five families are engaged in this full time, and during the summer months practically every adult male Eskimo is working with the unloading of supplies from the ships."[89]

But this "high employment, high income" situation demanded more of the Inuit than labour alone. The RCMP officer added another observation to his report. "Trapping," he noted, "plays a relatively unimportant role in this area now." Hunting suffered also. The men who were fully employed were also the good hunters, who, because of their work, were no longer able to pursue their former livelihood. As a result, their diet and that of their families deteriorated to what they could afford to buy from the far from healthily stocked shelves of the Hudson's Bay Company store. Inuit employees now had to work regular and full hours. They had little time not only for hunting, but also for collecting firewood, maintaining equipment, and looking after their houses. Earning between $115 and $140 a month[90] they were making insufficient money to buy fuel or furniture or luxuries. They were unable to improve their homes or better their lot in any way. For men with large families, wage employment brought a hand-to-mouth existence. Others could save very little. And yet this was what the Inuit appeared to want. A 1958 report estimated that between 200 and 500 Inuit would be interested in moving to Iqaluit, attracted by the opportunities for work in the many construction projects in the town.[91]

Although the Inuit wished to move to Iqaluit in search of jobs, a survey of those already working there in 1958 and 1959 showed that a majority would have been happier with more time off for hunting.[92] This preference reflected the Inuit's need to reconcile their obligation, as they saw it, to hunt and thereby to provide enough seal meat and other indigenous foods for themselves and their families and their desire to continue in wage employment to earn the money required to buy motor boats, guns, ammunition, and other manufactured goods.

Even after working continuously for 15 or 16 years an Inuk could decide to give it up and return to a life on the land:

This situation is not entirely the consequence of wage employment, although the latter lies at the heart of the problem. It also stems from the requirements of the whole new cultural order – sending children to school, observing modern health and sanitation measures, abiding by numerous government laws and regulations, ranging from the R.C.M. Police rule requiring the leashing of dogs to filling out federal income tax returns, and so on. It also stems from the restrictions the new social order has imposed on the Eskimo's traditional mode of life. Most notable in this regard is the limitation placed on his freedom. The wage employed Eskimo, for example, is no longer free to hunt when he pleases, to let his dogs roam unleashed, to pitch his tent wherever he pleases, nor to build winter houses from scrap lumber and other discarded materials. Even his home is no longer a private domain, for it is subject to periodic inspection by health officials. In many ways he has become a helpless captive of Western civilization.[93]

By the time of the 1959 survey, the boom had reached its peak. The demand for labour had already begun to drop, but the Inuit kept coming – at least for a while. The native village at Iqaluit became an overcrowded, unhealthy slum. The phenomenal rate of growth of the town between 1961 and 1966, described as "the most outstanding social feature in the whole Eastern Arctic,"[94] was thus due much less to natural increase than to unprecedented immigration from neighbouring communities. The Inuit population alone increased from 858 to 1,065 during this period, a jump of 24 per cent.[95] Lake Harbour contributed most heavily to this migration; Cape Dorset only slightly less so.

Paradoxically, Iqaluit, the town that earned the shabby reputation for workers among the Americans involved in the DEW Line, became the central area for a major changeover to wage employment that marked the 1960s in the Eastern Arctic. By 1969 only 5 per cent of the area's population was entirely dependent on the traditional way of life based on the fur trade.[96] The rest had tied themselves into the broader Canadian economy through some kind of paid work in addition to hunting and trapping. "It was wage labour which attracted Eskimos to Frobisher Bay," the director of Northern Administration Branch wrote in 1964, "and there is still a considerable amount of wage employment associated with the airfield, as well as with the provision of administrative services ... Although the opportunities for wage employment have contracted substantially since the airfield had a major commercial role, the expenditures on relief are perhaps less than one would expect."[97]

Some Inuit might have returned to the land "if there were a sound base," but northern administrators believed them to be few and far between. Official experience of helping native people to move back out of Iqaluit to areas of demonstrably good hunting in which they had formerly lived strongly underscored the reluctance of the Inuit "to return to the hard and uncertain life of the land when they have seen the kind of living to which other Canadians aspire."[98] So the majority stayed in the settlement and found full- or part-time jobs as carpenters, heavy-equipment operators, stevedores, cooks, helpers, and general handymen.[99]

1959–71: INUIT ART AND ARCTIC RESOURCES

Environmental Movement and the Fur Trade

Because of the government's refusal to guarantee fur prices, it became obvious by the mid-1960s that hunting and trapping were no longer able to maintain the majority of Inuit. The period of rapid economic expansion that began a decade earlier with massive governmental, military, and commercial involvement in the Arctic was winding down. At the same time the hunting and trapping economy was reaching a critical stage where, in almost all cases, income from the sale of native products was insufficient to cover current operating and depreciation expenses. Basic welfare income, social assistance, and whatever wage employment became available in each locality had to make up the difference. Hunting and trapping had been modernized technologically and commercialized economically, but they could not be freed from the dictates of a gladiatorial marketplace. For the sealskin and fur industry, fighting for its survival, the thumbs turned down.

For a while the beleaguered industry put on a good show after its earlier poor performance. To help it survive its postwar beating and come out fighting again, James Cantley in 1952 had suggested among other things the improved preparation of hair sealskins so that they could command a better market outside or be used to make up saleable articles for disposal within Canada. Ten years later his foresight proved itself. Beginning about 1962, advanced techniques in the preparation of hair seal pelts and the increased use of sealskin in clothing, especially in Europe, combined to create a rapidly expanding market for skins from all seal species. For the first time the ringed seal, or jar, reached market values that made Inuit seal hunting highly lucrative. Prices rose again from the low of $4 in 1955 to $17.50 in 1963. The best skins sold for well over $20 in 1963 and 1964.[100] Response to these improved economic conditions was immediate and widespread. In the NWT the number of sealskins traded rose from 10,470, valued at $48,689, in 1961–2 to 49,962, worth $691,707, in 1963–4.

Then disaster struck. The late Don Foote, an assistant professor of geography at McGill University, has chronicled what happened next.[101] Just when the market was going well for the Inuit in 1964, the Society for the Prevention of Cruelty to Animals "became increasingly concerned with the manner in which newborn harp seals were killed in the annual Gulf of St Lawrence and Newfoundland hunt. These critics contended that seal pups were skinned alive. Evidence in the form of television films and eyewitness accounts were widely disseminated in [much] of western Europe and eastern North America. A book, *The Last Seal Pup*, by Peter Lust, also focussed attention on the purportedly inhumane killing of whitecoats."

The result of the highly emotional campaign was that the average female consumer boycotted not just harp sealskin but all sealskin products. "By the spring of 1967," Foote relates, "the market for sealskins in Switzerland had dropped to 5 per cent of its former level, sales in West Germany were down by 50 per cent and one quarter of the Greenlandic skins placed on auction in April went unsold." The most catastrophic decline in prices was not for the harp seal fur but for other sealskins, especially those of the ringed seal. During the summer of 1967 most buyers in Alaska refused ringed seal at any price; in Canada the Hudson's Bay Company announced that it would buy pelts at $2.50 each "in order to prevent total economic collapse in many northern areas."

The situation is loaded with irony. The harp seal, *Pagophilus groen-landicus*, the subject of the southern protest movement, is only a summer visitor in northern waters and makes up no more than 3 per cent of the Inuit annual catch.[102] The Eastern Arctic Inuit depend heavily on the ringed seal, *Phoca hispida*, a year-round Arctic resident and one of the most numerous pinnipeds in Canadian waters. The ringed seal constitutes not only the main local source of food for many settlements, but its skin has traditionally provided, and indeed continues to provide, a major portion of the cash income of many Inuit. But the harp seal protest rebounded most strongly on the hunters of the ringed seal. As Don Foote explained, "Both the whitecoat and fur seal provide high quality pelts that undergo specialized tanning and dying [sic] processes to produce a finished product quite unlike the stereotyped version of a sealskin. The appearance of the ringed seal and other hair seal species, however, remains unchanged as a result of tanning. These skins, therefore, are easily rejected by perspective [sic] buyers influenced by any stigma surrounding sealskins in general." So the sale of harp seals was hardly affected while that of the ringed seals plunged disastrously. Those who suffered most were the Inuit of the Eastern Arctic. The campaign to stop the inhumane killing of newborn harp seals had its greatest effect on those hunters who used the most humane killing methods and who never even encountered a harp seal pup. They hunted the ringed seal with high-powered rifles and killed it instantly with a bullet in the head.

The drop in sealskin prices in the mid-1960s was a catastrophe for the Inuit. It meant the ruin of a viable industry in a region of chronic economic depression. In Greenland an estimated one-quarter of the population stood to lose its livelihood, with no alternative in sight. The proportion was probably much higher in the Eastern Arctic of Canada. Many of these Inuit suffered even more severely than others because they had invested the profits from their hunting in the purchase of modern equipment. In eastern Baffin Island, for example, most hunters used the gains of the early 1960s to buy canoes, flat-bottomed boats, outboard motors, snowmobiles, and low-calibre, high-powered rifles. Foote's data show that the Cumberland Sound region in 1962 had only 1 native-owned snowmobile; by 1964 the number was 17, and in 1966, 36. In the summer of 1953 the Inuit of the Clyde River area had only 2 small, unpowered wooden boats and 1 18-foot canoe with an outboard motor: in 1966 the same area boasted 25 canoes, 27 outboard motors, and 1 large powered whaleboat. Broughton Island in 1961 had 2 canoes and 3 whaleboats; in 1966 9 canoes, 12 rowboats, and 6 whaleboats.

Clearly modernization of Inuit seal hunting such as Cantley called for in 1952 meant greatly increased operating costs. Taking gasoline, motor oil, and ammunition expenses into account, the cost to the eastern Baffin Inuit for each sealskin sold in the year ending July 1966 was $6.29 in Cumberland Sound, $5.45 in Broughton and Padloping islands, and $4.46 at Clyde River. Obviously the depressed market value of the skins in no way covered the basic operating and depreciation costs. The lonely seal hunter of the Eastern Arctic could no longer earn enough from a basic way of life to support his family and pay for the running of his costly new equipment.

The drop in earnings and the increased costs of hunting in general affected all aspects of Inuit life. Hunting itself continued to provide many of the necessities of the traditional ecology and technology. Meat, for example, primarily seal meat, remained a staple of the Eastern Arctic Inuit. Among surviving camp Inuit, seal blubber continued to supply fuel for soapstone lamps, and sealskins the material for boats, dog traces, travelling bags, and rifle cases. In most Eastern Arctic settlements, however, traditional technology was giving way to the new methods of white Canadians. Oil stoves and free fuel-oil replaced the *kudliks* and the blubber store. Nylon, wool, duffel, and canvas ousted the skins of caribou and seal. Foods imported from the south and bought in the settlement stores diminished, but did not eliminate, dependence on the land and the country resources. The same applied to clothing: preference for imports diminished but did not eliminate dependence on local products. The RCMP reported in 1967: "With each passing year it is observed that the Eskimos are turning more to manufactured southern style clothing as stocked by the local retail outlets. This is more evident in Spring, Summer and Fall[. H]owever, winter wear still consists of their native made parkas and mukluks to a large degree ... The Teen-Generation continue to follow trends in their clothing emanating from the south, with several being observed in the latest of "MOD" fashions, complete with long hair which is quite unkempt. Luckily, few are able to grow whiskers long enough to be considered a beard."[103]

This adoption of southern life-styles was another admission of that inferiority of Inuit culture, vis-à-vis the white man, that underlay so much of the cultural change in the Eastern Arctic during the 1960s. Social, technological, and economic changes were all equally imbued with this failure of Inuit culture to challenge successfully the superiority ascribed to the culture of the new immigrants from the south. And all the desired elements imported from southern Canada had to be bought. Acceptance of a southern cultural system meant acceptance of its economic arrangements. The failure of the traditional Inuit economy to produce enough in exchange value forced the Inuit to turn more and more to the new employment opportunities that white incursion into the Arctic made available. The Inuit reached a stage in the 1960s when not one of them was untouched by the white man's ways or independent of the white man's economy. The Inuit could no longer live without the intervention of southern Canadians. Even in a relative stronghold of traditional life-styles like Cumberland Sound, wage earning became the single most important income source, and native ecological products took second place. "The shift in the region's economic base, from the sale of native products to wage employment, can not be over-emphasized."[104]

The shift in the economic base of the native people of the Arctic brought about a new regular pattern of life but one that still followed the changing of the seasons. In summer everyone who was able to left the settlements and headed for the old traditional camping areas on the coastal bays and inlets. Men and boys would hunt and fish; women and girls would prepare game and pelts for trade. As the short summer ended, the camps broke up and the Inuit started back to the settlements so that the children could attend school.

Then, in the settlements, another style of life began. The people would put away the tents and furs. The women would ready their homes for the long winter months of indoor living while their menfolk unloaded the last of the Hudson's Bay Company supply ships. Company employees filled the shelves in the stores, stocked the warehouses, and started trading again. School teachers returned from Ontario or England. Classes began again, and Inuit children switched to thinking in English and reading stories of Dick and Jane and life on the farm.

The traditional native pursuits of sealing, trapping, fishing, and hunting continued. They brought in supplies of country food, but they earned less money than they used to. A man needed regular work if he wanted to earn money, but jobs were less plentiful now too. Increasing the availability of work to maintain the Inuit's reliance on a wage economy depended on the government's ability to provide continuing development projects or to diversify the employment picture in the Arctic. The future economic stability of the whole region depended on this. When the construction boom on the DEW Line contracted in the 1960s, government building projects were able to take up some of the slack. Settlements like Broughton Island on the east coast, which had been a creature of the DEW Line, were able to survive, however precariously. When only three Inuit workers were required on the DEW Line at Broughton Island, others were transferred to alternative sites at Cape Dyer and Fox Four.[105] Very little year-round employment was available on the east coast, and seasonal jobs during the short navigation and construction period did little more than help to reduce social welfare costs. They were no answer to the problem of unemployment. In 1965 at Broughton Island steady wage employment involved only half a dozen or so out of a total estimated labour force of 35 to 40 adult males. The rest were dependent on native products like furs, skins, and carvings, augmented by federal government relief, welfare payments, and family allowances.

This enforced dependence on government aid does nothing to improve the self-esteem of the Inuit, to remove the feelings of inferiority, inadequacy, and inequality that caused so many social problems in the 1960s and that continue to dog the Inuit. Even when the Inuit are employed they work almost exclusively in low-status occupations. The white men are not only never unemployed but are the administrators and planners, the foremen and supervisors, the highly paid, luxuriously housed, expensively dressed leaders of communities in which they are in essence interlopers. The Inuit are the unemployed, the underemployed, the poor. Their housing was, and in many cases still is, inadequate, even unsanitary. Their clothing was until recently unsuitable for the harsh Arctic environment. Their diet was, and again still is in many cases, inferior. The major causes of the depressed living standards were poverty and ignorance, and these led to social problems as well as to poor living conditions.

The Co-operative Movement

A new avenue for Inuit labour that opened in the late 1950s was as artists working for local co-operatives. "The beginnings of the Arctic co-operative movement are submerged in the rush of the Federal health and educational activities of the 1950s," writes Jensen Delane.[106] He traces the "germ" of the movement to the Area Economic

Survey of Ungava that Jon Evans carried out in 1958, but its inception was inherent in the various measures that James Cantley proposed in 1952. Evans picked up on the idea of co-operation. He extended his report on Ungava beyond the limits of the standard inventory of natural resources to include ways of improving the economic situation. He emphasized Inuit ownership of new industries and singled out the co-operative as an organization that would best restore control to the native people.[107]

The co-operative movement needed a commodity that would serve as its economic base, and it found one in Inuit arts and crafts. The birth of the commercial interest in northern native art occurred a decade before the interest in northern native co-operatives. In the summer of 1948 a young Ontario artist, James Houston, went north to paint. The beauty of the Inuit carvings that he saw impressed him so much that he took a few home with him. The Canadian Handicrafts Guild was equally impressed when it saw the Inuit work, and it sent Houston back to the north to buy more carvings. It was especially interested in carvings in ivory, which was a medium familiar to southern buyers. But because soapstone was more readily available than ivory and easier for the Inuit to carve, Houston encouraged the Inuit to work in this material instead. The Inuit responded enthusiastically, and Houston returned home in the fall of 1949 with a collection of a thousand carvings. When they went on sale in Montreal the public snapped them up in three days.[108] Next year 10,000 were sold, and the boom in "Eskimo art" had begun.

All that remained was to wed the demand for Inuit art and crafts to the co-operative system of production and marketing. In bringing this perfect match about, the government acted as the marriage broker. In 1959, after the submission of Jon Evan's report, Northern Affairs introduced the community co-operative concept to the Ungava Bay Inuit at George River and Port Burwell. Representatives from the department encouraged the Inuit to organize producer co-operatives to harvest the arctic char that Evans listed in his inventory. At the same time Father André Steinmann was independently initiating a co-operative producers organization among the Inuit carvers at Povungnetuk.[109]

Carving was a vital part of traditional Inuit camp life. Soapstone lamps and cooking pots and snow goggles made of ivory are only a few of the better-know items from a range of tools, toys, amulets, and talismans that the Inuit carved from ivory, bone, and stone. "Anyone who has seen the tools and weapons of the Eskimo in a museum," writes Peter Farb, "knows how carefully, and often beautifully, they are made. That fact has interesting implications for theories about the beginning of art. In the far north, where man must face the constant threat of starvation, where life is reduced to the bare essentials – it turns out that one of these essentials is art. Art seems to belong in the basic pattern of life of the Eskimo."[110] The sale of Inuit artifacts to whalers and other white adventurers became important in the nineteenth century. As a result, "cribbage boards, canes, scenes of Eskimo life scored on walrus tusk, small-scale dog-teams and the like had found their place alongside other souvenirs in some southern homes long before the commercialization of soapstone carvings."[111]

That commercialization got under way in the 1950s, when soapstone – which had long been used for making cooking pots and blubber lamps – was urged on Eskimos as a medium for artwork that might have great value in southern markets. Some of the motifs of these soapstone carvings are distinctively Eskimo, but their size, and many of their forms, have been conditioned by the marketplace, if not by the somewhat idiosyncratic artistic sensibilities of one or two of the scheme's White pioneers. Eskimo carving, as it is now internationally known, is a consequence of southern domination of Eskimo economic life.[112]

The co-operatives that began in the small communities of Arctic Quebec and later spread to the NWT were completely subsidized by the federal government. Officials hoped that the enterprises would eventually be independent of government support, and to speed development of fiscal autonomy they sent co-operative development officers to the communities to train the Inuit in bookkeeping, purchasing, and almost all aspects of business life. In 1959 the NWT Council passed legislation allowing for incorporation of co-operatives. "This action, by recognizing and formalizing the importance of locally-administered economic development projects, illustrated the increased role natives would assume in the determination of their own future."[113]

Povungnetuk, on the west coast of the Ungava peninsula, became the centre of the co-operative movement in Arctic Quebec and sent its leaders out to other villages like apostles preaching the creed of co-operation. The new gospel converted Indian Affairs and Northern Development officials into zealots. In the 1960s they organized two conferences for the leaders of Arctic co-operatives, one at Iqaluit in 1963, the other three years later at Povungnetuk. "It is impossible to fully evaluate the positive stimulus these two conferences had on the rapid diffusion of Eskimo co-ops in the middle and late 1960s ... They obviously helped focus attention on the struggling movement by bringing together Eskimo village leaders from the far reaches of the Canadian Arctic for the first time. The enthusiasm and goodwill generated by the Eskimo participants was carried back to their home villages and to neighbouring villages not served by co-ops."[114]

The success of the Inuit co-operative movement was assured from the start, when the sale of arts and crafts provided the northern natives with an annual revenue of a quarter-million dollars. This income rose rapidly each year till it almost equalled the sales return from the fur trade in the Eastern Arctic.[115] The co-operatives were thus making a big contribution to economic development. In 1962 one in five of nearly 12,000 Inuit belonged to the movement, and more co-operatives were being established.[116]

An important aspect of co-operative development was the role of the Hudson's Bay Company (HBC). In the early 1960s it was a major supporter. In Coppermine the manager of the local HBC store financed a co-operative from December 1962 to March 1963. In Povungnetuk, an HBC trader, Peter Murdoch, set up an accounting system for the co-operative. Similar situations have occurred throughout the Arctic.[117] The apparent contradiction of the HBC's roles as both supporter and competitor of the northern co-operatives is easy to resolve. The original co-operatives were primarily producer-oriented, notably in arts and crafts. To encourage the establishment and expansion of co-operatives and thereby to increase the spending power of the Inuit was to the HBC's advantage. But many, though not all, co-operatives gradually became more consumer-oriented. This economic diversification led to direct competition between the co-operatives and the HBC in many communities. Cape Dorset is a good example.

Enterprising Cape Dorset was among the first communities to form a co-operative, the West Baffin Eskimo Cooperative, after the NWT passed the necessary legislation in 1959. Well-heeled by northern standards – hunting in the area is better than average, and the co-operative grossed more than $60,000 in 1961 from its second annual sale of prints – Cape Dorset was also the first to challenge the northern commercial supremacy of the HBC. It lured HBC manager Red Petersen to its side. Then it started to stack its shelves as a general store with flour, salt, lard, tea, canned food, dried beans, guns, ammunition, clothing, fuel, and knick-knacks. On top of all that it announced that it would handle furs too and sponsor tourism projects, a small bakery, and co-operative fishing.[118] As an extra bonus the co-operative acts as Shell Oil distributor and Bell Telephone and weather station operator.[119]

The federal government supports Arctic co-operation through the Cooperative Services section of Northern Affairs. This support proved indispensable during the difficult inaugural period, when new co-operative societies were forming among people more accustomed to political and economic domination. It took the form of auditing, inspecting, and supervising co-operatives in the Arctic as well as co-ordinating government assistance programs and providing feedback on the acceptance and desirability of such aid. One of the most successful of support services was the marketing agency Canadian Arctic Producers Ltd (CAP), established in 1965. The Department of Indian Affairs and Northern Development had itself been marketing the handicrafts and artwork for the northern co-operatives, but when volume began to outstrip the department's limited resources, the government asked the Cooperative Union of Canada to set up CAP. The agency receives a 10 per cent commission, and the governement provides it with enough funds each year to make up the difference between these receipts and its operating expenses. In addition the government provides equipment and loans to help individual co-operatives become established or expand their range of activities.

The main source of financial aid is through the Eskimo Loan Fund, from which a co-operative may borrow up to $50,000 for a ten year term at 5 per cent interest. This amount is sufficient for small ventures, such as building or stocking a co-operative store, or setting up a handicraft industry, but not for the capital-intensive requirements of establishing an integrated fishing industry, building tourist facilities of a quality to compete with white-controlled northern resorts, or purchasing equipment needed to exploit local resources and provide adequate transport. Jim Lotz drew attention to the discrepancy between government aid to native co-operatives and that to private enterprise. "Despite the world glut of iron ore, the Department stood ready in 1967–68 to help Baffinland Iron Mines come into production with a subsidy of $25 million. At the same time that talk of subsidizing this mine was going on, two Indian co-operatives in the Northwest Territories, at Fort Resolution and Rae, were refused further financial assistance from the government on the grounds that they were costing too much money."[120] Government equipment loans to northern co-operatives helped to ease the burden of insufficient capital. The most-requested items were fish-freezing plants, which cost about $50,000 when installed in Inuit communities. Unfortunately, such plants were often in short supply, and communities had to wait several years for delivery.

In 1969–70 the NWT government assumed responsibility for as-

sisting native co-operatives within its jurisdiction. Then on 22 February 1972 Canadian Arctic Cooperative Federation Ltd was formed
under the NWT Cooperative Association Ordinance (part II), with a
registered head office in Yellowknife and membership offered only
to NWT co-operatives.[121] The following year the Department of Economic Development established a Cooperative and Credit Union
Development Section, charged with helping communities and
groups to establish new co-operatives and credit unions. The section
also had a legal responsibility to provide information and advice to
established co-operatives and credit unions and to promote and administer various funds over which the NWT government retained
control.

By 1982 Inuit co-operatives, taken as a group, were the largest
single employer of native labour in the Arctic, with an annual volume
of business in excess of $24 million, one of the biggest sources of
Inuit revenue.[122] Individual Inuit, like the top carvers in Cape Dorset
and Lake Harbour, could make $60,000 a year. For medium-sized,
best-quality carvings, each Inuk received about $1,000 in 1980; in
southern markets these carvings fetched upwards of twice that
amount.[123] Co-operatives have, over the couple of decades since their
inauguration, become actively involved in the provision of municipal
services, construction, commercial fishing, and retail stores and the
production of crafts, graphic art, and sculpture. They function even
where the odds are stacked against them. Pelly Bay, for example, a
small settlement in the southeastern part of the Boothia peninsula,
is noted for its woven wallhangings and its delicate ivory carvings
that depict in miniature the life on the land. In the development of
this art and and craftwork the co-operative has been indispensable,
in spite of logistical difficulties:

To get a barge into Pelly Bay is impossible. It would have to go all around
Boothia Peninsula; it could get here, but not back, before the bay freezes
up again. Everything has to be flown in, even the fuel. That means that our
food is twice and three times as expensive as in other places in the North.
We balance the prices somewhat by changing more for sweets, pop and junk
food than for staple foods.

This co-op is run by the natives. We support ourselves through the sales
at the store, through contracts – hauling gas from the airstrip to the village –
and through the money that comes in from the fish plant. We pay the
fishermen by the pound, and the ladies who clean the fish, by the hour.
Once the fish is frozen and packed we sell it to various consumers in Yellowknife.[124]

In spite of the success of the co-operative movement, the Inuit have suffered from the economic recession. Sources of cash income that once helped them survive times of poor hunting have dwindled throughout the Baffin Region. The European market for sealskins has dwindled to almost nothing, and carvings are harder to sell. "The market is still good for high-priced works of art and for souvenir carvings in the $100 range," one Inuk has said, "but the middle market disappeared in the recession."[125]

The development of the commercial arts since the 1950s has had repercussions besides the purely economic. It has, for one thing, allowed the Inuit to make the transition from an insecure land-based economy, dependent on white traders, to a commercial-production and cash-consumer economy in which they have gained, besides an income, a sense of self-worth and a collective consciousness of identity. With the related spread of co-operatives and the formation of federations, this commercial arts "industry" served to foster Inuit socio-political institutions and thereby to prepare the Inuit for management of their own affairs. Through the co-operative system many Inuit have been introduced to the concept of free elections and the secret ballot. Native community leaders have emerged, first as directors of local co-operatives and later as leading members of Inuit councils. The co-operative movement in the Arctic has been a political as well as an economic force.

North Rankin Nickel Mine

The political development of the Inuit – to be discussed in the next chapter – has led them to the point where they are demanding a measure of self-determination in their own proto-province, Nunavut. A large part of the revenues necessary to fund Nunavut the Inuit see as coming through royalties from the exploitation of non-renewable resources. Ironically, the Inuit today are in somewhat the same position as the federal government in the mid–1950s: they are pinning their hopes on the mineral wealth of the Arctic. This includes possibly a thousand million tons – estimates vary – of high-grade iron ore at Mary River in northern Baffin Island and major amounts of lead, zinc, and sulphur in the Arctic islands, in addition to large copper reserves in the Coppermine area of the Central Arctic coast. Geologists have predicted that drilling will locate oilfields in the Canadian Arctic to rival those in Alaska. The discovery of oil in the Mackenzie delta and of natural gas in the Arctic islands gave the spur to exploratory drilling in 1970. Oilhungry interests, their attention focused on the great gypsum domes and basalt cliffs of Axel

Heiberg, see this island as the biggest claim-staking site in Canadian history. Gypsum domes can indicate the presence of oil. On Axel Heiberg they measure a mile, and in some cases up to three miles, in diameter, and they may mark one of the richest oil reserves in Canada. Ultimate recoverable reserves in the Arctic islands and the adjacent Arctic coastal plain have been conservatively estimated at 43 billion barrels of oil and 260 trillion cubic feet of natural gas; that is, twice the amount of oil and almost three times the amount of gas that will eventually be recovered from the entire province of Alberta.[126]

In the 1950s this estimated wealth of oil and gas was still untapped, and the only mining being done in the Eastern Arctic was at Rankin Inlet. The North Rankin Nickel Mine was opened to exploit a lode of nickel that prospectors had discovered in 1928.[127] The rise in world nickel prices during the Korean War of 1950–3 made the mining of the ore economically feasible. Inuit employment began with the initial development of the mine in 1953, when Inuit helped to unload the ship carrying men and equipment to the area. Those who proved to be good workers were kept on during the construction phase and later in the mine itself. The mine went into production in 1957 and attracted Inuit from many areas. More than 70 came to work at North Rankin, two-thirds of them from Chesterfield Inlet, a quarter from Eskimo Point, and smaller numbers from Repulse Bay, Baker Lake, and Arctic Quebec.[128]

Development of the mine gave rise to a fair-sized settlement where no Inuit labour force existed before. This settlement, now known as Rankin Inlet, became a permanent feature of its surrounding low, rolling hill country only after the mine was developed. Until then the area rarely supported more than 10 families. They lived by hunting, trapping, and fishing, but game in the area was never enough to support large numbers of people for any length of time, even if exploited to the maximum. Settlement of the area had to wait for development of its nickel deposits.

Some Inuit settled down to steady work and became relatively skilled at their jobs. "The [*Northern Miner*] found it hard to believe that without exception all the native operators of bulldozers, mucking machines, ore trains, drills, crushers, etcetera, were primitive hunters and igloo dwellers as recently as three years ago. At the time the only products of white civilization to reach Rankin Inlet were a few primus stoves and rifles."[129] Other Inuit abandoned their jobs after a short time and returned home, while some came only in search of temporary employment to augment their income from hunting and trapping.

North Rankin was the first mine in Canada to employ Inuit labour underground.[130] So in addition to being an economic venture, it was an experiment in training Inuit miners to become earners at relatively skilled jobs. Fortunately they showed special aptitude for mechanical procedures, and the training period was short. "The Eskimo's quick grasp of mechanics," said the *Northern Miner*, "and his ability to operate efficiently and safely all the equipment at the mine and in the mill has surpassed even the fondest hopes of management."

The satisfactory use of Inuit labour meant untold savings for the mine itself. A native work-force eliminated the cost of transporting southern personnel into and out of the Arctic and the additional economic burden of holiday travel. It also assured much greater stability of the work-force, whose pay averaged $15 a day plus bonuses. In order to disrupt the Inuit way of life as little as possible, the mine trained several people for one job wherever feasible. That way some of the men could be free part of the time to hunt and fish. Most of them were muckers, cage tenders, deckmen, and labourers, and the mine management expressed general satisfaction with their aptitude and ability to learn. But the Inuit's reluctance to live to a rigid time schedule caused problems of tardiness and absenteeism, which were never completely eliminated.

In April 1959, on the basis of completed drilling and development, the estimated ore reserves stood at 363,500 tons, enough for perhaps four more years' production.[131] Obviously the mine would have to cease operations after that time if exploration discovered no new deposits. Starting in 1959, surveys held out no such hope of rescue, and the mine closed in 1962, before the summer shipping season had even ended.

The closing of the mine was a disaster for the settlement. From June until November of that year the number of people drawing social assistance jumped from 88 to 264, the cost from $25 per head in 1961 to $174 in 1962.[132] Families relocated in Yellowknife, in Lynn Lake in northern Manitoba, and in settlements in Keewatin, but few of these moves proved successful, for a variety of sociological reasons. By 1965 the population of Rankin Inlet was down to 287 from 512 three years earlier, but since then it has moved up again. Arts and crafts industries attracted the Inuit back. The moving of the Daly Bay cannery to Rankin Inlet created more employment. Supporting activities such as whaling (until the early 1970s) and fishing added to the opportunities. The territorial and federal governments employed a large proportion of the local labour force, and the RCMP, the nursing station, and the Hudson's Bay Company hired

others. By 1983, with a population of 1,109, Rankin Inlet was Keewatin's regional centre, easily accessible by air from southern Canada
as well as from other parts of the Territories.

The story of the North Rankin Nickel Mine illustrates the precariousness of dependence on one non-renewable resource. Rankin
Inlet survived and went on to thrive, at least by the standards of
northern settlements. It was lucky. Northern mining is economically
tenuous, and mines are often short-lived. Private developers have
approached the Arctic with caution. In the past they have been
forced to invest not only in a particular commercial activity but also
in the infrastructure of the local area. Only a few large firms could
cope with this special problem common to most developing areas of
the world. These few large and wealthy corporations, faced with the
double investment of developing the resource and creating needed
facilities such as transport and power, would commit themselves only
to high-grade natural resources and, to minimize costs, pursued a
policy of integration in primary production, related processing, supply, and general transport operations.[133] North Rankin was proud
of "standing on its own feet." The company brought the mine into
production with no government assistance and continued to operate
it economically, despite extreme isolation, permafrost working conditions, and high costs of supply, transport, and operation.[134]

Since then, however, the government has, with an abandon close
to recklessness, poured out its coffers into diggings in the Arctic
earth. "What of the future?" Jean Chrétien asked at the opening of
the Fifty-first Session of the NWT Countcil. "The potential of the
north is surely limitless... I think of the mountains of rich ore at
Mary River... uneconomic today but not tomorrow. I think of the
lead-zinc deposits at Arvik on Little Cornwallis Island, at Strathcona
Sound and the Bathurst-Norsemines deposit at Hack River..."[135]
Senior members of the federal government assumed more confi-
dently than ever that in the far north they were standing on the
edge of a bonanza and about to take the first forward steps into
massive wealth.

AFTER 1971: ECONOMIC DILEMMA –
MODERN AND TRADITIONAL
OPTIONS

Development Policy for the 1970s

Poverty, and its related inferiority and social inequality, can be overcome only by providing work and restoring a sense of worth to the

individual. To help do both, the government established a Northern Economic Development Branch in 1969. This branch was responsible for the effective management of oil and gas, mineral, forest, water, and land resources and for developing the economy of Yukon and NWT.[136] Going into the 1970s the government pinned most of its hopes on the extractive industries, in particular on the exploitation of oil and natural gas. These hopes appeared to be justified, as the number of Inuit wage earners "increased significantly" during the first half of the new decade and a substantial contribution to this increase was ascribed to the activities of the Panarctic and Gulf Oil interests.[137]

But, wisely, the branch was not to confine its interests to the extractive industries. Its tasks were to seek out and identify all means whereby the economy of the north could be expanded at a more rapid pace, to develop a broad plan of economic progress, and to recommend – and in some instances to manage – specific projects and policies for bringing this plan to fruition. Its director saw three major objectives in the development of the north: "(i) to ensure that the region contributes to the total national output and to the sustained, long-run growth of that output, on the basis of the fullest and most efficient use of the human and material resources available to the region; (ii) to raise the standard of living of the inhabitants of the region; and (iii) to maintain effective occupation of the area."[138]

As if anticipating criticism, the director and his advisers stated: "In the context of alleviation and avoidance of poverty problems in the Territories, the means of attaining the second objective are of the most direct importance. The Branch has developed several methods of ensuring that economic development programs significantly help Territorial residents to raise their standard of living."

To this end a resource employment liaison officer was appointed to provide contacts between northern natural resource industries and those government departments and agencies responsible for the training and placement of northern residents in order to provide employment opportunities for the people of the north, particularly Indians and Inuit. This officer's responsibilities were to include the negotiation of special agreements for the employment and training of northern natives under the provisions of special incentives and of several federal programs. In helping to ensure that territorial residents derived optimal benefits from economic development, an Economic Staff Group surveyed manpower, evaluated and analysed the social benefits accruing from northern development projects, and became involved in formulating a systematic approach to regional development.

In 1971 the administration worked out a new policy framework to guide northern development for the decade. It committed both levels of government to stressing improvement of the social environment so that native residents would benefit from present and future developments.[139] Inuit participation in all sectors of the modern economy was, and continues to be, well below the potential. Lack of education and technical skills, high capital costs, small markets, and seasonal factors share responsibility for this. To help overcome at least financial obstacles, the new policy included the provision of credit facilities in areas of the Arctic not served by commercial institutions through a loan fund designed to meet the special needs of the Inuit and to further economic development among the Inuit through grants. Full participation in development was to be encouraged through co-operative ownership and enterprise, and resource harvesting improved through loans to trappers for the purchase of food and supplies. This new emphasis on the support of resource harvesting was welcome, but the level of support proved niggardly.

When looked at alongside the cost to the nation of subsidizing industrial advance at the frontier, the sums spent on maintaining Eskimo hunting and trapping – 'the traditional options' – have been negligible. Fur prices have never been guaranteed, nor has welfare been used in any systematic way to ensure a minimum income to those who choose to live by harvesting renewable resources. In January 1974, the superintendent for game of the Northwest Territories announced 'incentive grants' for licensed trappers. The incentives amounted to a $60 grant for a trapper who made $400 from sale of furs in one season, and $150 for a trapper who made $1,000. At the same time as that scheme was being formulated, the Federal Government was proposing to develop a multi-million dollar, non-economic, ill-considered mine site. It is hard to believe that the fine talk about guaranteeing the 'traditional' option has amounted to very much at all.[140]

Had the government guaranteed fur prices, the "traditional option" might have remained open to many more Inuit and the prolonged international campaign against seal hunting might have had a less disastrous effect on the people of the north. But instead the government poured money into industrial development projects like the "ill-considered mine site" – Nanisivik.

Nanisivik

An often expressed view is that the Canadian north does indeed contain vast quantities of minerals, oil, and natural gas, but that the wealth of these resources is no guarantee of their production. They must be rich enough to offset the extremely high costs of northern exploration, extraction, and transport. Should world prices change to make northern resources more attractive, as they did for nickel during the Korean War, those resources must still be able to compete successfully with similar but hitherto marginal resources that could be made available more cheaply in southern Canada. It is thus incorrect to assume that substantial increases in price will automatically lead to northern resource development.

K.J. Rea, however, has argued that the relatively high costs of production in all the activities carried on in the Canadian north "were possibly more the consequence of the relative lack of investment in large-scale and efficient 'social overhead capital' facilities than they were in consequence of such factors as distance and climate."[141] In short, while the physical nature of the north may often induce extremely high costs of development, this cost barrier can be breached. The question "Is it profitable?," Rea states, may be answered in the affirmative if the resources have a comparative advantage in the market-place. The geographer J.L. Robinson made this point many years ago: "If resources are found which are rich enough to compete with those closer to present markets climate will not be a principal obstacle impeding development of the Canadian Northwest." Presumably Robinson meant more than just climate, but remoteness and the physical nature of the north as well. Ultimately the eradication of remoteness entails an efficient, low-cost transport network connecting both the "exporting" industries and the "importing" sector of the north with southern markets; the creation of markets large enough to absorb much of the regional output, and the development of industries capable of meeting regional demands; and a public subsidy of the costs of operating northern transport, similar to the now defunct Crow's Nest Pass arrangement for prairie grain but extending over a broader range of goods.

So the Canadian government invested huge sums of public money in northern roads, transport, and electrical power, in addition to public health, education, and welfare. Private developers no longer had to suffer the handicap of "preparing" an economically backward area in the course of exploiting a particular resource. So projects like the Nanisivik mine are thrust upon the people of the north.

Nanisivik lies 12 miles north of Arctic Bay in northern Baffin Island. These are the only two communities in the Eastern Arctic to be joined by an all-weather road. The area round Nanisivik is unusually barren, devoid alike of vegetation and wildlife. No Inuit ever lived there. But during the 1950s deposits of lead and zinc were found in the area. Samples of the ore were examined in 1962, and 10 years later Mineral Resources International (MRI), a company with addresses in Calgary and Toronto, began to press the government to subsidize exploitation of the ore. And the government yielded. In 1974 it gave approval to an expenditure of $16.7 million dollars to provide ancillary support for the mine in the form of roads, a wharf, an airport, and townsite assistance.[142] And all this for a mine with enough ore on hand to last a dozen years.[143]

MRI maintained that the mine would prove profitable if initial subsidies were as high as those the government eventually paid. Economists denied this, arguing that, from Canada's point of view, the mine could only be uneconomic. Canadian processing and manufacturing facilities were too small, and the ore would have to be exported in crude form to West Germany and Holland. The advantages to shipbuilding would not be Canada's. The mine's proponents countered with social arguments, pointing out that the mine would provide employment for local Inuit. However, the area needed no employment. "It is claimed, it seems," wrote Father Guy Mary-Rousselière, the editor of *Eskimo*, "that this enormous expense is justified by the need to provide local employment. Now, precisely, since Panarctic uses Eskimo labour, there is no unemployment in this area. We were told recently that meat had to be brought in by plane from the south to a small settlement because there were no longer enough hunters to supply local game: a bewildering situation."[144]

The mine offered no economic gain to the people of Canada, no social advantages, no needed local employment. Yet the Canadian government rushed headlong into supporting it with millions of dollars, "helping private industry to ship approximately $820 million of Canadian ore to Europe."[145] The first ore left the mine in 1977 amid controversy over environmental questions and over the balance between the financial assistance that Ottawa gave the mine and the mine's likely benefits to the north, to the Inuit, and to the country as a whole.[146] "The mine was hurried into existence by persons determined to have development at any price. These same persons who had, at other times, insisted on the importance of alternatives to wage-labour failed to suggest that the national economy devote some of its surplus to subsidizing those alternatives. The Nanisivik mine illustrates how development can take place for development's sake."[147]

Panarctic Oils

The mining of northern resources, whether justifiable or not, receives less attention in southern Canada than the exploration for oil
and gas, perhaps because of the highly charged political nature of
the petroleum industry, both nationally and internationally. Like
the DEW Line, the Iqaluit construction project, the native co-operative movement, and the exploitation of minerals, the influence of
the petroleum industry in the north also goes back to the 1950s. In
February 1959 many oil companies applied for federal exploration
permits covering large areas within the Arctic archipelago. Subsequent exploration led to major gas discoveries on the Sabine peninsula of Melville Island, where the first exploratory oil well in the
Canadian Arctic was drilled in 1961, on King Christian Island, and
at Kristoffer Bay on Ellef Ringnes Island. Oil was discovered on
Thor Island and on the Forsheim peninsula of Ellesmere Island.[148]
Panarctic Oils in collaboration with other companies made most of
these discoveries between 1968 and 1972 after the oil find at Prudhoe
Bay, Alaska, put new pep into oil and gas exploration in the Canadian
Arctic.

Panarctic Oils used the settlements of Pond Inlet and Arctic Bay
as a labour pool that provided about 50 workers for drilling operations in the islands. Pond Inlet, splendidly situated in mountainous
fiord country, changed from a long-established hunting community
of 480 people, with a total annual income of no more than $40,000,
to a place where wages soared in 1972 to around $180,000.[149] Each
man's monthly earnings represented half of his annual cash income
from earlier years of living from the land. And still they were able
to live at least in part from the land. For central to Panarctic's plans
in the High Arctic was a schedule that rotated Inuit crews on a 20-
day-work, 10-day-holiday basis. The company ostensibly devised this
scheme in recognition of the Inuit's traditionally strong family and
community ties and in the knowledge that potential workers would
refuse to take jobs that meant months away from their wives and
children on frontier drilling rigs. A Panarctic Twin Otter plane rotated the native crews to and from the isolated villages of Pond Inlet
and Arctic Bay.[150]

Those eager to praise Panarctic have made much of the comapny's
altruistic approach to the hiring of native labour. Hugh Brody, however, states that in the early stages of Panarctic's operations, agents
based in Edmonton hired workers from southern Canada to man
the drilling rigs. Panarctic devised the 20-days-on, 10-days-off shifts
not to benefit Inuit who wanted to be able to continue hunting but

to meet the needs of a southern work-force whom the company agreed to fly out to Edmonton for the 10-day breaks.[151] Only later did the federal government discover that Panarctic drew none of its labour force from northern settlements. Officials put pressure on the company to take men from Pond Inlet and Arctic Bay and to extend the shift system to them. In order to ensure that Inuit could benefit from skilled work and not be left to do the most menial jobs, the government sent Inuit from the Eastern Arctic, five in 1968, to take a course in oil drilling at the Alberta Petroleum Industry Training Centre in Edmonton. The Administration Branch of the Department of Indian Affairs and Northern Development paid the $70-a-week tuition fees and living costs at the Edmonton YMCA plus pocket money. At the end of a four weeks' course the Inuit were guaranteed work as driller's assistants or "floor men" at $3.15 an hour.[152]

The two dozen or so men from Pond Inlet and Arctic Bay who eventually worked for Panarctic brought $400,000 into the two small communities. Panarctic's apologists tried to show that this money did nothing but good. Others, including the Oblate missionary in one of the settlements, reported a disturbing increase in alcohol consumption, as much as 15 cases of hard liquor a month where, a couple of years before, 2 cases a month were unusual. In January 1974 an irate NWT commissioner announced that he had received so many complaints about drunkenness in Pond Inlet that he had decided to cut off the supplies.[153]

Despite this and other problems that income from Panarctic had aggravated, if not caused, many men in the settlements continue to be eager to work on the oil and gas sites. They and their relations need money. If one hears but little protests against the wage-labour option, it is because there is no viable alternative. Men who live by hunting and trapping, or by a mixed economy, tend to be regarded as unemployed, and are listed as potential workers. So long as the lists of unemployed are long, industrial development can be said to be solving a local problem, as well as creating wider opportunities. The ideological commitment of developers provides its own justifications. Unfortunately the Federal Government has in practice and from the beginning allied itself with the corporations and their purposes.[154]

The promise of wage employment from industrial projects has been broken too often for most northern native people. During the 1970s and early 1980s four basic facts became apparent concerning resource development in the Canadian north. First, the income opportunities for native people in nearly all cases were short-lived, and the native people themselves were relatively poorly paid in comparison with other workers. For example, in 1970 in the Western Arctic, where major non-renewable resource development first began,

the mean income for skilled workers from southern Canada employed in mines, on oil rigs, in support services was estimated to be $10,000 a year. Inuit workers employed in the same enterprises earned $3,000 annually. In 1977, researchers working for the Mackenzie Valley Pipeline Inquiry led by Mr. Justice Thomas Berger, concluded that there was no reason to believe that there had been any significant change in the proportional distribution of income in the last eight years. Despite continual industrial activity in this area of the Arctic, the Pipeline Inquiry researchers determined that the money economy of the North continued to be centred in urban locations, government centres and mining towns, not in native-dominated communities.[155]

Second, the Inuit learned few, if any, new skills that they could carry over to or market in another area. Third, if any permanent positions were available when a major capital project ended, nonnative people filled them in almost all cases. And fourth, the economic and social effects of major industrialization projects on local native communities were often disastrous.

Because of exceptionally high rates of population growth in these native communities, fewer Inuit proportionately were able to rely on wage employment. "The increase in productive capital necessary to cope with demographic growth demands real investments, in addition to those required for the renewal of existing equipment. These investments are called *demographic investments*."[156] A study by Jacques Henripin of the University of Montreal has shown that the annual growth of personal income can be as high as 4.8 per cent in a stationary population and as low as 0.7 per cent where the population is growing at 2.3 per cent per annum. The higher the rate of demographic growth the lower the possibilities of economic growth. Most of the Third World is experiencing growth rates much in excess of Henripin's selected threshold of 2.3 per cent. The NWT population grew almost twice as quickly. "Deterioration of the standard of living must appear when the annual maximum growth rate of the population of 2.3 per cent ... is passed."[157]

Those responsible for northern development policies were thus fighting a war they could only lose. They were using the wrong weapons and the wrong strategy. They were channelling vast sums into industrial development when they might better have deflected some into measures designed to bring down the high native birthrate and diverted more into supporting traditional subsistence activities.

Tourism, Job Creation, and Outpost Camps

In 1972 an old but hitherto relatively meagre source of income and employment – tourism – received a powerful boost. On 22 February Jean Chrétien announced that the federal government had set aside more than 18,500 square miles of land in Yukon and NWT in order to create three new national parks: Kluane, South Nahanni, and Baffin Island's Cumberland peninsula. The last-named area was known simply as Baffin Island National Park until February 1975, when Parks Canada, in consultation with the Inuit of the local communities, chose a new name, Auyuittuq, Inuktitut for "the place that never melts." The Penny Ice Cap, an ice-age remnant, covers just over a quarter of the 8,290 square miles of the park's pre-Cambrian granite mountains and dramatic glacier-gouged valleys.

The establishment of Auyuittuq has drawn attention to the recreational potential of the Canadian Arctic. The lonely challenge of the 6–7,000-foot mountains of Baffin Island has drawn the adventurous for decades. J.D. Soper crossed Pangnirtung Pass in 1925, and the Baffin Island Expedition studied the Penny Ice Cap and the Highway Glacier in 1953. Since the late 1950s, fishing camps have lured sport fishermen to Baffin's cold waters to pit their wits against the slender, black, and speckled arctic char, one of the world's tastiest and hardest-fighting fish. Between mid-July and August the arctic char, a member of the trout family, begins its annual inland migration beyond the reach of the soon-to-be-frozen sea. One fishing camp, Camp Dorset, was an all-Inuit venture, complete with tents and plastic igloos, which the fledgling West Baffin Eskimo Cooperative managed about seven miles from Cape Dorset.[158] The Baffin Region now has four fishing camps, Keewatin eleven, and the Central Arctic four also. The world's most northerly fishing camp is Lake Hazen Lodge on Ellesmere Island, 570 miles north of Resolute.

Demand for the type of tourist experience possible in the Canadian north will doubtless continue to grow. The numbers of visitors to the NWT, especially since 1967, have increased steadily, reflecting greater awareness of, and interest in, the Arctic as one of the few relatively unspoiled areas left in an overcrowded, horribly littered, jarringly noisy world. Some major developments will have to take place with respect to facilities in the near future before any large expansion of tourism can occur. What would be required is not only an actual increase in the number, and perhaps quality, of services, but also wider distribution of services to allow tourism to expand spatially instead of only quantitatively. This is particularly true in the Eastern Arctic, where settlements such as Iqaluit, Pangnirtung, Resolute Bay, and Chesterfield Inlet could certainly win increased tourist traffic and revenue if they had suitable additional facilities.

Most tourists head for the Western Arctic, attracted in particular to the Mackenzie delta and to the three hunting and fishing camps on Great Slave Lake. This traffic is likely to increase, but the Eastern Arctic and the northern islands could experience more rapid expansion of tourism if facilities were provided to meet the demand. Auyuittuq is now one of the major NWT attractions and is relatively assured of at least some development by the federal government. On 15 July 1982 John Munro, minister of Indian affairs and northern development, and John Roberts, minister of the environment, signed an agreement setting aside part of the northern tip of Ellesmere Island as a future national park. This will further enhance the attractiveness of the Eastern Arctic. Further, the Eastern Arctic is known to the general public in both Canada and the United States for its involvement in the development of Inuit art and handicrafts, especially at such settlements as Cape Dorset.

Relatively good air service to Iqaluit, and to a lesser degree to Resolute Bay, makes the Eastern Arctic reasonably accessible. In fact the Eastern Arctic is in a stronger competitive position than the west in relation to the large metropolitan markets of North America.[159] So given the general attraction of North Americans to national park areas, people will probably come in growing numbers to visit Auyuittuq and any other parks established in the region.

The importance of national parks for the Inuit lies in the revenue they generate and in the employment opportunities they afford. The Inuit can expect to benefit from the need to provide additional services outside the park, especially accommodation and local transport, as is happening in Pangnirtung. The only threat to the Inuit may arise from the effect of national parks on traditional subsistence activities. The seriousness of this threat will depend on whether the Inuit are allowed to continue their traditional activities within the park area. It will also depend on the behaviour of visitors in and around the parks. Jim Deyell, chairman of the community council in Broughton Island, has said that Auyuittuq will be a financial asset to the settlement. "As long as it does not interfere with native land claims and hunting rights, the Eskimos want the park."

The economic benefits and employment opportunities that arise from providing services to visitors is one step towards the government's goal of easing as many Inuit as possible off welfare and into productive employment. Job creation was the top priority of the

1970s, and the territorial government joined the crusade in April 1976 with a Subsidized Term Employment Programme (STEP), its first major job-creation project. STEP was designed to reduce the number of employable people on welfare by creating work for them, providing them with on-the-job training, or directing idle manpower into worthwhile community projects. By 31 March 1977, STEP had created 4,768 man-weeks of local employment: 2,511 in Mackenzie, 874 in Inuvik, 761 in Keewatin, and 622 in Baffin regions.[160]

At this time the Inuit themselves were aiming a number of their own proposals at the improvement of socioeconomic problems in the Arctic. For example, under the terms of the February 1976 agreement in principle between the federal government and the Inuit Tapirisat of Canada an Inuit Development Corporation was to be set up "as a business corporation pursuant to the laws of Canada."[161] The corporation was to perform two main functions: collect royalties earned from the development of subsurface oil, gas, and minerals, and with this wealth to help the Inuit take part in business subsidiaries at the community level through financing and providing managerial expertise to community businesses.

A second proposal associated with land claims was a "Hunting and Trapping Assistance Program to promote the viability of hunting and trapping as an alternative to wage employment" and "a financial assistance program to allow local Hunters and Trappers Committees to play a more active role in the hunting and trapping economy." Another was "a program to assist in the construction and mainte-nance of outpost camps."[162]

The appearance of outpost camps in the mid-1970s made southern Canadians, and even the Inuit themselves, aware that not all Inuit were susceptible to the blandishments of organized communities. Some were determined to preserve their own culture, language, and independence. Many of these Inuit believed that the only way to restore the integrity of their native communities was to return to traditional ways of life on the land and the sea-edge. They wanted to have nothing more to do with the competitiveness, aggression, and alcoholism that were major ingredients of what the white men called civilized life. The Inuit had watched the dissolution of family ties, the loss of fluency in the language, and the abandonment of traditional values. These Inuit had managed to retain pride in their past, confidence in themselves, and determination to fight against being recruited as labour for the extractive industries.

The NWT government, recognizing the longing of many Inuit to return to traditional ways, departed from its earlier policies of ac-culturation and urbanization and allowed this longing to find release in an officially assisted Outpost Camp Programme.[163] Under it, camp residents judge their own needs and apply for financial assistance from the Department of Renewable Resources. The department makes no attempt to raise the camps to any predetermined government standard. It merely outlines the maximum levels of assistance for transport to and from camp, building materials, heating fuel, two-way radio and first-aid kits, periodic visits by Fish and Wildlife service officers, and repayable loans for food supplies and equipment. Camp residents earn their money from the sale of furs, country food, and occasionally carvings. They may receive help in these efforts either directly from the government or through the Hunters and Trappers Association in the home community. The territorial government has imposed no kind of bureaucracy on outpost camps beyond requiring financial accounting of the grants received and the repayment of loans. Otherwise the government leaves the outpost camp populations to function as their leaders see fit. The camp residents are often exempt from the standards, norms, or regulations imposed on the inhabitants of the organized settlements. School attendance, for example, is not required of the children in the outpost camps.

The average outpost camp numbers about 20 Inuit, or four families. The traditional camp leader takes the place of an elected council, and decision-making is by the time-honoured consensus method. As in earlier times, the camps are located in areas with plentiful fish and game. This means that they are sometimes difficult to reach. Most of the camps are in the Baffin Region, 25 altogether in 1982, involving 350 Inuit.[164] This is, of course, only a small minority of the Inuit in the region, but to those concerned about erosion of traditional culture, the outpost camps are a significant alternative for which the kind of non-intrusive government assistance described above should be continued.

Fur Trade under Fire Again

At the close of the Sixty-fourth Session of the NWT Council, on 13 February 1978, Commissioner Stu Hodgson warned the members that job opportunities would become a key issue that council would not be able to avoid.[165] His view of the future of renewable resource harvesting, a mainstay of the native population, was pessimistic. An old threat to the industry was appearing again, like a periodically recurring blight. Pathogens from the Newfoundland seal-hunt protest were drifting northwards to the Arctic coasts, threatening to cripple yet again a livelihood that was none too hardy to begin with.

The symptoms of a new outbreak were already evident. The demand for sealskins was declining, and prices were falling. As Hodgson pointed out, "an entire community can be financially ruined because of some international incident that has no relationship to the area."

Little had been heard from the animal protectionists for a decade. Then in 1976 the protests rose again. Several environmental protection groups located in southern Canada, but with ties to European and American activists, began an intensive campaign aimed at a ban on the Newfoundland seal hunt. It was a more violent strain of the same epidemic that swept along the coasts of the Eastern Arctic in the mid-1960s. Its source was the anti-sealing propaganda of southern-based protectionists who made skilful use of television and other popular media to horrify the public into revulsion from all seal products. As before, the campaign had less impact on the harp seal hunt of the Newfoundlanders, against which it was directed, than on the ringed seal hunt of the Inuit, who were not involved. Like the earlier protest, the outbreak of the mid-1970s brought about a marked decrease in the value of northern ringed sealskins, and, unlike during the earlier, less virulent attack, the market available to the Inuit rebounded much more slowly.

As Don Foote had recorded the effects of the 1960s anti-sealing campaign on the Eastern Arctic Inuit, so McGill University anthropologist George Wenzel kept track of the ravages of the same campaign in the 1970s.[166] Wenzel's data show that by 1971 the price the Inuit obtained for their ringed seal pelts had risen throughout the Eastern Arctic region. At Chesterfield Inlet it stood at $13. At Clyde River it averaged $14 over the years 1971–4. But in the wake of the 1977 seal-hunt protest in the Gulf of St Lawrence, the one that Brigitte Bardot turned into an international media extravaganza, the demand for ringed seal pelts began a downward trend and prices plunged. They sank from $14 in June to $10 in August. By November the price in eastern Keewatin was down to below a dollar; in northern Quebec to $1.25. Communities on Baffin Island and in other parts of the Eastern Arctic reported a corresponding drop. These were the lowest prices paid for sealskins since the Black Fridays of the early 1950s. At a time when Inuit depend heavily on increasingly expensive imported equipment and material goods, any decline in income, but especially one so steep, poses a serious threat not only to sealing itself but to all other types of subsistence hunting as well. And food provided by marine mammals is vital for the nutritional health of the Inuit. As Wenzel puts it, "Members of Inuit communities may, as a result of these factors, have no other choice but to abandon hunting, despite the consequences for themselves and their families in terms of health and traditional culture."

Alarmed by the success of the southern-based animal welfare groups and by the catastrophic effect of their campaign on the well-being of the northern native peoples, Peter Ernerk of Keewatin, the member responsible for the NWT Department of Economic Development and Tourism, suggested that the government take a lead in counteracting the southern campaigns by calling an international meeting of representatives from Greenland, northern Quebec, Newfoundland, and the NWT.[167] The result was the first international conference of the sealing industry, a three-day event that opened in Yellowknife on 31 July 1978. But L.R. McIntosh, assistant to the Hudson's Bay Company's general manager of furs, told the members that the prime culprit was not the seal-hunt protest. "The fashion trend, in our estimation, has had more to do with the drop in the sealskin market than anti-sealing publicity ... The publicity aggravated a situation that was already bad as far as the market is concerned."[168]

But fluctuations in the price of sealskins since 1977 have coincided too closely with the Newfoundland harp seal protest for the protest to be ruled out altogether. Ironically, the price paid for harp sealskins, the subject of the protest, has scarcely varied. Ringed sealskins, however, after dropping to less than a dollar, recovered to $16 by 1980, then fell again to an average of about $5 a skin at the time of the European ban on sealskins in 1983.[169] For the first time the outbreak of anti-sealing propaganda was accompanied by the voluntary compliance of European governments with the preservationists' call for action against seal hunting. Political pressure, of the kind operating on the Europeans, is a much more potent force in the sealskin market than any vagaries of fashion. Fashion makes little use of hair sealskin nowadays in any case; most of these skins go to the leather goods industry.

Unfortunately the Eastern Arctic Inuit have little to put in the place of sealskins as an economic asset. Other traditionally marketable commodities, like polar bear hides or narwhal and walrus ivory, were either generally unavailable or their availability was already regulated by Canadian and international law. But unlike sealskins in the fickle world of fashion, white fox was still in demand and fetching high prices, as much as $50 for a good fur. One trapper on Banks Island, the world's largest reserve of white fox, caught 1,600 foxes in 1974, making a record income of approximately $80,000.[170] White fox was a resource that the more eastern Inuit had not fully exploited on Baffin Island, and so the territorial government encouraged seal hunters to switch from uneconomic and unpopular sealskins to the more lucrative luxury fur of the arctic fox. Expert trappers came from Banks Island to teach the Eastern Arctic Inuit the old and well-tried tricks of their trade.[171]

Economic Ill-health

The economy of the Eastern Arctic was clearly still unwell, and only the most optimistic held out hope of a recovery to full health. Its constitution was weak, depending on non-renewable resources that were uneconomically expensive and heavily subsidized and on renewable resources that were unfashionable, politically threatened, and not subsidized enough. The only significant sources of employment were government offices, both federal and territorial, and the Inuit co-operatives, whose major activity, the production and sale of native arts and crafts, was menaced by economic recession. Minor sources of employment lay in a small tourism and services sector.

The physical and social environment of the north provided yet more impediments to full economic health. These were the age-old, chronic afflictions of immensity of land, extremes of climate, sparse but now rapidly growing population, and high rates of unemployment and underemployment. Demographic projections encouraged little optimism. The number of working-age people, those in the 20-to-59-years age group, was expected to double by the end of the century.[172] The total population growth rate to 1988 would probably almost triple the national average: 3.5 per cent compared to 1.3 per cent for the country as a whole. The national population had already been growing at 1.3 per cent a year from 1971 to 1976. During the same period the NWT population increased annually at an astonishing and frightening 4.6 per cent.[173] The large proportion of young people in the Inuit population had kept the short-term growth rates high despite a lowering of fertility. In 1983 Statistics Canada recorded the impact of these figures on the labour force. Between 1971 and 1981 the national labour force increased by 40 per cent. The NWT showed the highest regional increase: a disastrous 76 per cent.[174]

One need only glance across the NWT to see significant regional disparities in physical environment, social conditions, and economic activity. A closer look will show that in most comparisons with the favoured west, the Eastern Arctic comes off worse. The 1981 census returns record, for example, a male unemployment rate of 5.8 per cent in the Fort Smith Region compared with 11.8 in Baffin; the total unemployment rates were 6.0 and 12.8 per cent respectively. In 1983 unofficial figures put the Baffin Region unemployment rate in the 20-to-40 per cent range, depending on the season.[175] The large proportion of young people threatened even higher unemployment in the next two decades unless development plans created more jobs and the government made more training available. Even the official returns of Statistics Canada put unemployment among the young, the group of 15-to-24-year-olds, at 22.8 per cent in the Baffin Region, but only 10 per cent in Fort Smith.

A two-nation dichotomy was latent not only within the NWT. Within each of the two potential nations, the Western and the Eastern Arctic, two separate economies coexisted: the traditional livelihood tied to the land, and the more recent way of life based on wage employment. Hitherto government had devoted most of its effort and expense to increasing opportunities for wage labour among the Inuit, while conspicuously ignoring the traditional pursuits. Hugh Brody charged the government with plotting to drive the Inuit away from the hunting and trapping grounds and into the labour market. The goad was the threat of hunger and poverty because of too rapid growth of population:

So the trap is set. Northern development is good because, among other advantages, it gives native people a greater range of choice: they will, with education and industrial advance at the frontier, be able to choose between a life on the land and wage employment. But, we are also told, a life on the land is no longer possible – the population is too large and the renewable resources are insufficient. So federal policy must be directed at creating jobs. Therefore economic development is urgently needed – in order to solve, of course, the Eskimos' problems. With this circular and self-justifying argument policy-makers effectively narrow down the alternatives: Eskimos must become wage-labourers. And as long as federal investment in or support of the hunting and trapping alternative is minimal, Eskimos are under direct and heavy pressure to accept the wage-labour option. They need the money, and must go where money can be earned.[176]

The Inuit fell for the subtle ploy, became its victims. "When you don't have a regular job," Celine Ningark of Pelly Bay told Ulli Steltzer, "it is hard to raise a family, to buy all the clothes for school. Even with an income it is hard. We can't get away from the problems. I guess we are hooked on the white culture."[177]

In the 1970s government's attitude began to change. When Peter Usher proved that the federal government had colluded with oil interests in order to overwhelm opposition from the prosperous trapping community on Banks Island, it caused an uproar that shook the Department of Indian Affairs and Northern Development.[178]

Criticism from Arctic specialists mounted, fuelled by the publication of studies like those of Hugh Brody and Doug Sanders[179] and by the well-publicized demands of the Inuit Tapirisat of Canada under its land claims negotiations. The prevailing opinion was that the remedy of injecting overdoses of cash into the weak industrial veins of the northern economy was threatening the traditional heart. Unless that heart kept beating strongly, giving its indispensable life support to the native communities, that economy would die. Hunting societies were dying in other parts of the world that were undergoing economic resuscitation, but in the Arctic, where agriculture was impossible, the persistence of hunters not only seemed assured but was deemed essential. The sick economy of the north depended on it.

Those concerned tried yet again to put some pep into the cataleptic body. On 4 April 1979 the NWT government and the federal departments of Regional Economic Expansion and Indian Affairs and Northern Development signed a five-year general development agreement. Both levels of government pledged to work in unison to promote economic growth and development in the NWT. Officials on both levels had come to realize the wisdom of striking a balance between the demands of economic growth and those of ecological health – and between renewable and non-renewable resources. Economic planners saw little reason why resource harvesting should be incompatible with wage employment. A marriage of the two could be arranged, as the Science Council of Canada suggested, "by wage employment schemes which are sensitive to the components of the subsistence cycle and which accommodate seasonal events like hunts, maintenance of trap lines, etc."[180] Panarctic Oil's rotational scheme of 20 days on and 10 days off, for example, allowed for this kind of flexibility.

To give the general development agreement's interim strategy the boost required to get it off the ground, an interim subsidy agreement provided $3.8 million over two years to community groups and government agencies for community-oriented development activities, including promotion of tourism and long-overdue expansion of the use of renewable resources. Some of the money was earmarked for work-rotation programs, community-based planning, and development of yet another economic strategy for the NWT.

The future of the Inuit thus rests on the continued operation of a mixed economy in which the people will derive their income from full-time and seasonal wage employment, government transfer payments, and hunting, fishing, and trapping. But the success of a northern mixed economy depends on the ability or willingness of the federal government to carry out the remedies it has agreed to.

Its record of past squeamishness when faced with the need for firm action in the north leaves some observers with little confidence. Thus the only cloud hanging over the future health of the Arctic economy is that the long history of government weakness to pressure from industrial and commercial corporations puts the option to hunt and trap and fish in jeopardy.

In a report released on 30 March 1983 a Senate special committee under Sen. Earl Hastings charged that the federal government had failed to establish clear priorities for northern resource development and warned that the policy vacuum could hurt the environment and escalate social costs. While billions of dollars worth of activity in the oil and gas industry was gearing up, priorities for frontier development remained vague. Unless planning measures were formulated and clearly and unequivocally stated before work advanced much further, the options for alternative types of land use, resource exploitation, and environmental management would be lost.[181]

This persistent erosion of the Inuit's traditional option and strengthening of the federal-industrial designs on the north could be countered by a land settlement that recognized the Inuit's right to political self-determination and territorial control. Inuit Tapirisat of Canada president James Arvaluk has dismissed the term "land claims." The Inuit, he said, were "claiming" nothing. "Rather, we are offering to share our land with the rest of the Canadian population in return for a recognition of rights and a say in the way the land is used and developed."[182]

The way the land is used and developed must include guarantees for the protection of those traditional pursuits that are still a powerful force in Inuit culture and potent symbols of Inuit identity, unity, and uniqueness. Hunting, fishing, and trapping, as Gurston Dacks forcefully points out, are more than just ways to earn a living. They return the Inuit to those older ways of life in which the land, the sea, and the wild animals take up again a central place in native religion. Hunting, fishing, and trapping thus reaffirm the Inuit's place in the spiritual world and link them with their ancestors who lived on the land before, providing that feeling of continuity with the past in which all human beings find psychological security. Wage employment cannot provide such deeply rooted satisfaction. In whatever form it takes, it is alien to the Inuit and puts them in a subordinate position with regard to white employers, foremen, supervisors, and co-workers. "Hunting, fishing and trapping ... are activities in which native people can take part free of the feeling of powerlessness and inefficacy that have made contact with white society so alienating for them. In this way, these activities are not only psychologically satisfying because they embody elements of tradition. More significantly, they are psychologically satisfying because they are controlled by the native person himself, and organized in a fashion that makes sense to him, not according to some alien logic."[183]

CHAPTER FIVE

Relinquishing Authority

TO 1945: POLITICAL TAKEOVER

Within the structure and organization of any society the political system is that part of the total social system involved in "the articulation and implementation of public policy, ... the means by which groups and individuals achieve and, more precisely, use power."[1] Politics is about power, in the dual sense of authority – the ability to control others by virtue of office – and of influence – the ability to control others without the benefit of office. The way in which power is enacted, distributed, and exercised is the basis of the political organization of society, the network of social relationships that allows for the co-ordination and regulation of behaviour related to the maintenance of public order. Political organization is specifically concerned with the organization and management of the public affairs of a society.

In traditional Inuit society political organization had evolved no further than the level of the extended family, the group that lived together and hunted as a single ecological unit for the greater part of the year. Leadership of this group generally fell to the oldest male, to the father of adult sons, or to the oldest among a group of brothers. He gave the signal for the start of hunting or fishing, and he decided matters relating to migration and camp selection. But the leader took all decisions informally, gently, and usually in consultation with other members of his extended family. In late summer, when the arctic char were moving back up river, and later still, when the caribou were heading south, a number of extended families would meet at some well-known campsite to pool their resources for the good of all. In winter the largest aggregation of Inuit took place in order to increase their chances in the hunting of seals through breathing holes in the ice. Traditionally, then, the most important area of co-ordination and decision-making was in the realm of ecological activities involving the extended family, the summer fishing group, and the winter sealing camp as ascending units of co-operation and food distribution, each with attendant systems of authority based on the *isumataq*, or headman.

The traditional Inuit hunters were men of influence and authority. Experience and personal ability had equipped them to make decisions that affected both the community as a whole and their own families within it. They expected, and they usually received, obedience; they did not assert their authority forcefully but presumed that the rest of the group would accept it. Younger persons and dependants were never bullied into accepting the experienced hunters' authority; they were simply expected to recognize its value for themselves. "Probably the move from camp to settlement, together with other disruptive changes," Brody suggests, "have combined to create a situation in which opposition and discord within families is much more frequent and in which the authority of older men and women is systematically called into question."[2]

Their age-old political organization, like all other components of Inuit culture, broke down under the influence of high-status, non-Inuit immigrants: trader, missionary, policeman, and government administrator. The Inuit accepted a new outlook on authority – institutionalized, formal, and impersonal, imposed by recognized lawmakers. In other words, Inuit society acquired a new political dimension. It did so, not by evolution of its own structure and complexity, but by having an evolved political system grafted on to its own social trunk. This new state-level political structure – its legal system, land tenure, resource ownership regulations, communications networks, military organization, and system of individual rights and privileges – was Euro-Canadian and not in the least Inuit. Outsiders, strangers from another culture, held the high-status positions. In the developing native communities these outsiders wielded supreme power. Their roles, as one observer pointed out, were "central to the process of change engendered by culture contact and the subsequent re-orientation of indigenous society toward a cash economy."[3]

As a consequence, most Inuit abdicated their responsibility for decision-making. High-status positions in every settlement came to be held by various non-Inuit representatives of powerful outside organizations: government agents, clergy, commercial personnel. Regardless of the personal qualifications or of the way in which they carried out their roles, by virtue of their position in the native community they held sovereign power. Indigenous leadership waned in light of the growing prestige of the external, non-Inuit leader. The danger in this situation is that as the number of outside status leaders increases, and the number of institutions they represent also increases, and no overall authority is granted to any one of them, "leadership in the community is chronically unstable, relying as it must on each crisis situation for specific leadership to emerge."[4]

In 1942 the Canadian Arctic was a "collection of solitudes" where 13,600 people lived in small, isolated settlements and hunting camps.[5] The Canadian government's sole representative in most of the settlements was the RCMP officer, and the only long-term, non-Inuit residents were the missionaries and the trading company employees. There was no local government. The only municipal-type structure was the "local administrative district" of Yellowknife, and regional structures of any kind were unknown. The "government" of the NWT consisted of an interdepartmental committee of federal civil servants who met not in Yellowknife or in any other location in the north but in Ottawa. There they made their recommendations in consultation with those federal departments that had a vested interest in the north. Those charged with putting the recommendations into effect were in the main the officers of the RCMP.

1945–59: SOUTHERN SUPREMACY

One Step Forward, Two Steps Back

During the years after the Second World War the RCMP became increasingly unhappy with the social conditions under which the Inuit were living. As a result of a severely critical report from Insp. H.A. Larsen, commanding G Division, a conference was convened in Ottawa on 19 and 20 May 1952. As mentioned in the previous chapter, it brought together representatives from all those government departments and agencies, commercial interests, and religious institutions that were involved in any way in Canada's Arctic. But the people most involved had no representation at all: the Inuit themselves. "The only reason why Eskimos were not invited to the meeting," the director explained, "was, apart from the difficulties of transportation and language, that it was felt that few, if any, of them have yet reached the stage where they could take a responsible part in such discussions. There is ... no tribal system among the Eskimos and no leaders other than those of small family groups. It would therefore be quite impossible to select any individual – or even a small group – which could speak authoritatively for all the Eskimos."[6]

Thus the government recognized the difficulty of involving local Inuit in planning policy at levels higher than the community. In terms of political development the Inuit had yet to reach the stage where they could take a responsible part in the discussion of their own problems. They were still at the family level of political organization, still in the infancy stage of dependence on government representatives, missionaries, and traders. So it was left to these southern Canadians to settle the future of the people of the north.

Two years later a new government department, Northern Affairs and National Resources, was set up to oversee the future development of the north. It quickly realized that exploitation of the north presented a greater challenge in the human environment than in the physical. Its second annual report contained a special article on "Human Problems in the Canadian North." The writer admitted that it "was not till the Second World War – which made the Canadian Arctic far more accessible than before and brought many Eskimos into contact with large defence undertakings – that the problems of these people were brought forcefully to the attention of the government and of the country as a whole." So only in the relatively recent past did the government and people of Canada become aware of their responsibilities to the Inuit and of the need for a program that would enable the native people "to participate fully in the national life."

With this in mind the new department sought to establish a local administrative system that would allow native northerners to manage their own affairs and to assume responsibility for their decisions. Obviously the northern administrators wished to avoid a repeat of the embarrassing situation of 1952 when they were asked why no Inuit were taking part in a conference on Inuit affairs and had to admit that they did not believe the Inuit had "yet reached the stage where they could take a responsible part in such discussions." The minister of northern affairs wrote that a new social order was supplanting the primitive life of the Inuit:

In the new order, however, direction is given by the various white men on the scene. The Eskimo inevitably tends to lose initiative individually and collectively in such a regime. It seems obvious that an effort to place the direction of local affairs in the hands of the Eskimos is desirable. In this matter we can learn from the Indian Affairs administration which in both Canada and the United States have had conspicuous success with band councils and other community activities that centre in the people themselves rather than in superimposed leadership. We can learn also from studying programs with similar objectives among Eskimos in Greenland and Alaska.[7]

However, the native Greenlanders were literate; they were competent in managing local councils and the business of the country in general; and they took part in Danish national affairs through elected members of the Danish parliament. In 1953 Greenland had ceased to be a "colony" and become an amt or county of the homeland, electing two members to the national Folketing.[8] Greenlanders were thus remarkably further advanced than the illiterate Canadian Inuit who still had to take directions from white men in their own communities and who had only just been given the right to vote in federal elections. Incredibly, Eastern Arctic Inuit were unable to vote in territorial elections till 1966.

Obviously special training was imperative if the Inuit were to move any way towards participation in the national life of Canada. The emphasis of the program, as Northern Affairs envisioned it, was to be on citizenship training and on mobilizing the Inuit into a local bureaucracy. The eventual goal was political participation at the local level by the northerners themselves. From 1954 a new breed of government official was to help the Inuit reach this goal, a band of northern service officers (NSOs), "the first non-military public servants to take up residence *en masse* in the Northwest Territories."[9] These officers would live among the Inuit in the more important centres and help them adapt to current conditions of life in the north. The administration intended not that the NSOs would take over the functions of the RCMP or of others in the field but rather that they would try to co-ordinate the activities of all field organizations with a view to making the greatest possible use of all available resources and to improving both economic and social conditions among the Inuit in the areas to which they were assigned.

Unfortunately the educational and community-development functions of the NSOs were quickly overshadowed by the pressing need to administer the federal commitments included in a new Northern Administration Programme that embraced health, welfare, education, housing, and justice. The NSOs soon ceased to exist as such and became area administrators through whom the various federal projects continued to grow and expand.

What developed then was a rigid, bureaucratic structure which the government introduced to communities where traditional flexibility and consensus had previously governed Inuit decision-making. This was the first step in a long process of imposing a southern model of decision-making. "Thus it came about," Hugh Brody notes, "that Canadian interest in the eastern Arctic had a typically colonial aspect: land and people were incorporated into a growing political entity without regard to the people's own wishes. Eskimos would indeed have found it hard to express wishes in the matter, for they had heard little of the institutions and less of the nation that was carrying out the process."[10]

Local administration became invested in the area administrator, who accepted input from the native people only at his own discretion. This alienation of the local population led to apathy and to Inuit distrust of local government ideas that lasted at least until the 1970s. For under the domination of the area administrator the local people received only marginal control of their own affairs. An inflexible hierarchy of decision-making evolved that "included the local residents only as confused observers."[11] The good intentions of 1954 with respect to Inuit participation in local government received a setback from which it took more than a decade to recover.

Racial Segregation

In spite of the political alienation and apathy of the Inuit, in the economy and technology the mid-to-late 1950s saw unprecedented development in the Eastern Arctic: the DEW Line, the Iqaluit administrative centre project, and opportunities for work opening faster than administrators and employers could find Inuit to fill them. Not only did droves of hopeful Inuit flock to the Eastern Arctic settlements and construction sites, but large numbers of southern Canadians and Americans moved in with them. The situation was one to gladden the hearts of northern officials. Like any caring parents or guardians they wanted to see their charges settled in suitable jobs and able to earn a living for themselves. And yet they showed concern too. The Inuit for whom they were responsible were, like callow adolescents, still simple and innocent and inexperienced in the ways of the world. Could they handle themselves in this new situation, into which they were running with the blind faith of the young?

The northern administrators could not bring themselves to let go of the Inuit entirely. They felt that they had to continue to keep an eye on these unsophisticated natives and in particular to protect them from the hard-bitten immigrants from southern Canada and the United States. At the twenty-first meeting of the Advisory Committee on Northern Development in November 1954, Dr O.M. Solandt, chairman of the Defence Research Board, suggested that "it might be salutary during this phase to adapt the Danish policy of prohibiting contact between the Eskimo and construction personnel." R.G. Robertson, deputy minister of northern affairs, said that the Inuit were at various stages of advancement "and the extent of their contact with the D.E.W. Line activities might be varied according to their ability to adapt themselves. The Department ... was anxious to obtain employment for those who would benefit by it. Regulations to protect the interests of the Eskimo would be included in the D.E.W. Line agreement."[12]

This was in fact done. The following year a list of instructions to NSOs included the following, as section 12: "The contractors will prohibit non-Eskimo employees from visiting Eskimo villages, houses, or tents, or having other close contact with Eskimo other than project employees, since this is dangerous to health and often an inconvenience to the Eskimos. The contractors will also prohibit Eskimos, other than those employed on the project, from visiting buildings in the contractors' camps."[13]

The political implications of the regulation were raised in Parliament. On 30 May 1955 George Drew, leader of the opposition, drew the House's attention to the fact, reported in the New York *Herald Tribune* of the previous day and "given wide publicity in the United States," that for those constructing the DEW Line "all contact with Eskimos is to be avoided except in cases of emergency." Drew wanted to know what department gave the order, under what circumstances, and why. Jean Lesage, the minister, replied: "Every precaution has been taken so the normal life of the Eskimos shall not be disrupted but that so far as possible and whenever possible work would be given to them." "We believe," he went on, "and I think with justification, that according to our past experience it would be a very bad thing if those who are now working on the D.E.W. Line were allowed to visit Eskimo villages frequently. The experience of the past, particularly so far as the health of the Eskimos is concerned, has been very bad indeed when people have been allowed to visit the Eskimo settlements. I am speaking about health at the moment, but here are other problems too." Everyone knew what was on the minister's mind, but it took six years and a change of minister before the previously unmentionable could be stated frankly in the House of Commons: "the possibility of improper relations," as Walter Dinsdale boldly said on 22 May 1961; and he added, "I stress that word improper."

Segregation sullied ethnic relations in northern communities other than Iqaluit. Perhaps in an attempt at benevolent paternalism, the mining company at Rankin Inlet in the latter half of the 1950s kept the Inuit miners and their families segregated from Euro-Canadian residents. It did so with the approval if not the insistence of Northern Affairs.[14] Most of the white population had no idea of how the Inuit lived. The mine administration forbade them to enter the Inuit settlement without the permission of the superintendent and gave warning to any Inuit woman who seemed at all "familiar" with the white men. This social separation of the two populations continued after the mine closed in 1962. The same situation pertained in Resolute Bay. Another settlement artificially created in the 1950s by bringing Inuit from Pond Inlet and Spence Bay to service Department of Transport facilities and Royal Canadian Air Force bases, Resolute Bay had a policy of severe and policed segregation imposed on it. Even outside the NWT racial segregation became the order of the day. In Churchill, Manitoba, for example, the Inuit lived in Akudlik, a residential area separated from the main townsite. The only non-Inuit allowed to live there were Northern Affairs personnel.[15]

The government's concern in keeping white and Inuit separate had a moral as well as a medical basis. In 1953 venereal disease was reported in the Iqaluit area, and the administration had to take steps to restrict its spread. Four years later a medical observer warned the government that venereal disease might become a problem in the Iqaluit area as there were already at that time "a few recognized prostitutes."[16] To contain the spread of venereal and other diseases, the government imposed its controversial restrictions on Inuit and non-Inuit contact, but to enforce these was a practical impossibility. The director of Northern Administration and Lands Branch, B.G. Sivertz, realized that "any Eskimo girl who has reached the legal age of consent cannot be supervised twenty-four hours a day and clandestine meetings are likely to occur with some of the personnel at the airport."[17]

So the authorities in the north allowed the restrictions to lapse, and what some regard as moral standards lapsed with them. One of the reasons cited for increased promiscuity in Inuit girls was their "casual attitude to matters on which white men place moral influence."[18] Among their own people many Inuit marriages originated in the simple arrangement of living together, and sex was a fact of life to be met as simply or as honestly as hunger or thirst. Inuit girls had "expressed determination to marry non-Eskimos," and their agreeing to sleep with white men was the first step towards the realization of that goal. Other factors were involved. The mortality rate in the Eastern Arctic was inordinately high. This often left girls without parents, and the problem of sexual promiscuity could have been due almost entirely to individual emotional deprivation, often caused by the death or prolonged illness of one or both parents. The long Inuit tradition of female meekness and submission to men's wishes may also have been a factor.

Iqaluit was the main centre for Inuit-white contact in the Eastern Arctic and the place where prevention or reduction of the effects of that contact was most difficult. In June 1955, when construction was under way on the new townsite of Iqaluit, less than 200 Inuit lived there, compared with 275 US Air Force personnel plus 20 from the Canadian forces, 22 federal government employees, 12 representatives of private enterprise, and 2 police officers.[19] Two years later the permanent population was around 900, of which only 250 or so were Inuit.[20] In 1960 seven main groups made up Iqaluit's immigrant community: Department of Transport personnel in charge of the airport and air route operations; Eastern Arctic regional administrative staff belonging to Northern Affairs; social service officers from that department and Health and Welfare; the US Air Defense Command at the Pinetree base; the US Strategic Air Command then under construction; various commercial and related activities like the Hudson's Bay Company, banks, and oil companies and depots; and finally a miscellaneous group made up of the RCMP, the Northern Canada Power Commission, customs officers, and the like.[21] For the first time non-Inuit groups made up the majority in an Arctic settlement. And the Inuit themselves were a mixture of people from the Eastern, Central, and Western Arctic. Out of 53 Inuit working on the eastern sector of the DEW Line in 1959, 27 were from the western and central regions.[22] Yet there appears to have been no friction among the native groups. "All of the Eskimo families on the Dewline are getting along together very well," the RCMP reported, "and the writer had no complaints from any of these families regarding their neighbours. It is indeed quite a thing to see all of these people getting along so well, as these families come from all over the Eastern Arctic as well as the Western Arctic."[23]

But relations between Inuit and non-Inuit were less congenial. In the settlements, especially larger ones like Iqaluit, observers began to notice stresses in the newly developing social structure. Early in 1959 they reported that "working relations between whites and Eskimos at Frobisher are becoming noticeably strained," and they foresaw "possible friction this coming summer when construction activity increases."[24] A few years later the area administrator at Cape Dorset reported that the settlement was the first Arctic community he had seen "where there is virtually no rapport between the Eskimos and non-Eskimos, save that demanded by duties and responsibilities of one sort or another." Cape Dorset had changed "into a 'we' and 'they' kind of society."[25]

It was the classic situation, endemic in all colonial areas throughout the underdeveloped world, that led to political unrest and the upsurge of nationalistic demands after the Second World War: social inequality between the dominant white culture and the native majority. In the Canadian Arctic this familiar brand of ethinc confrontation, contrast, and potential conflict became a social force in the late 1950s and intensified through the 1960s. Some of the issues raised have not been settled even yet.

1959–71:ANARCHY TO ORDER

Social Inequality and Differentiation

In 1959 reports suggested that the Inuit population was beginning to feel that with all the activity, construction, and planning going on, or rumoured to be going on, they were receiving little consideration.[26] The Inuit failed to see where they fitted into it all and nourished a sense of insecurity and frustration. They were mostly employed as labourers and as such were not in a position to receive any explanation of what was happening or planned for their area. They were the plebs in the land that belonged to them.

By contrast the new immigrants from the south quickly established themselves as high-status patricians. They were the administrators, planners, decision-makers; they were the men of skill and knowledge and expertise; they were the source of credit and money, healthcare and learning, law and order, and all the material goods of modern technology. The developing sense of inferiority and inadequacy among the Inuit was understandable. Concrete manifestations of inequality fostered and fed it. Housing, in particular the difference in the level of housing, "was an indication of a lack of progress and a constant reminder of the social inequality of the Eskimo."[27]

The planners of the new townsite at Iqaluit walked the high wire of idealism but could not avoid toppling into hypocrisy. "It has been stated elsewhere," wrote the chairman of the Frobisher Project Office, "that all housing in the town is to be of the one standard. Only that portion of the Eskimo population who can meet the financial requirements of rent, etc. will live in the town and it is intended that they shall occupy houses or apartments similar to those of the white population. There is to be no special Eskimo housing."[28] In that case, the new townsite was being planned as a reserve for the well to do. Few Inuit could "meet the financial requirements of rent, etc." What was to be the residential lot of the majority? The office of the administrator of the Arctic had already researched that question:

At present there are about 50 Eskimos in full time wage employment in Frobisher Bay. They are employed in a variety of occupations, skilled, semiskilled, and unskilled, ranging from carpenter to handyman. A few of these are reported to have annual incomes of $4,000 a year or more, but most earn between $2,000 and $3,000 a year. These employed Eskimos and their families live for the most part in ... houses, many of them reasonably well furnished, and in general they enjoy a much higher standard of living than those Eskimos who do not have full employment.

Heads of Eskimo families without full employment still outnumber those working full time. Most of the unemployed and partially employed live in shacks and tents at the old Eskimo village near the air base. A few live in tents near the Apex Hill townsite. As job opportunities increase, most of these people will probably be absorbed into the present community. However, it is likely that for years to come Eskimos will drift to Frobisher Bay from surrounding areas, and continue to live in tents on the fringe of the settlement.[29]

Gene Rhéaume, MP for the NWT, brought home to the House of Commons on 7 November 1963 the glaring discrepancy in housing standards and living conditions between the Inuit and the non-Inuit residents of the north. "I for one," he said, "cannot feel happy when confronted, as I have been on numerous occasions in my travels throughout the Northwest Territories, with the anomaly of superheated, fresh-vegetable-filled D.E.W. Line sites, put there at fantastic cost to the Canadian government, in the very presence of our Eskimo people, who spill their tattered and ragged lives digging in D.E.W. Line garbage dumps, attempting to survive under the worst living conditions on earth." This may have been exaggeration for political effect, but a basis of fact underlay it. Living standards varied widely in the Arctic settlements between the white newcomers and the native population, and this material evidence of inequality received reinforcement from the Inuit "inability to compete for better jobs because of the lack of education and the consequent lack of equal opportunities."[30]

The cleavage within the population of the northern settlements was most exposed in Iqaluit. In 1962 one observer remarked that there were "two distinct cultures and social groupings in Frobisher." That the settlement was divided into three equally distinct geographical sections – Apex Hill, Ikaluit, and the airport – seemed "to be relatively less important."[31] What was more disturbing was that there was apparently "no impelling desire on the part of either adult group to integrate." This lack of social integration, or lack of willingness to integrate, had been latent since at least 1959. That year the secretary of the Frobisher Bay Development Group pointed out to the administration in Ottawa that there were possibly "800 to 1,000 construction workers and stevedores in Frobisher Bay in August, September and October and only slightly smaller numbers in April, May, June and the latter part of the construction season." New areas of entertainment would be available – a contractor's bar, canteens, and so on – and the Inuit would be excluded.[32]

By 1963 two separate recreational associations had evolved in Iqaluit. The Department of Transport provided three buildings at the airport for the Frobisher Airport Recreational Association (FARA), a society organized by and for the employees of the department. "The fact that the lion's share of the existing recreational facilities were provided by members of FARA and the fact that membership in FARA was restricted by the Association's constitution to the employees of the Department of Transport has meant that very few Eskimos have been able to avail themselves of the facilities provided."[33] This was simply recognizing the established state of affairs. "It is perhaps unncessary to point out that there has always been a de facto separation between the two races at Frobisher Bay. The physical separation of the main Eskimo communities from the non-Eskimo has fostered this development." The Inuit had their own recreational association at Apex Hill, where about 450 Inuit lived. It organized community entertainment each week, including movies, dances, and bingo sessions. But another 500 Inuit at Ikaluit, the village near the airport, had no facilities for recreation, except by travelling three miles to Apex Hill.

By this time the restrictive regulations against racial contact had been allowed to lapse, and the government had executed a full about-face. As Walter Dinsdale told the House on 22 May 1961, "Conditions in the Arctic have changed remarkably in the past six years. As an indication of the government's current attitude, in 1959 a letter was sent to all government departments that have employees in the north, dealing with the questions of relations with the indigenous population. There was no attempt whatever to curtail fraternization; indeed, the reverse is the case. The Department of Northern Affairs and National Resources has a number of employees, both male and female, who are Eskimos married to white persons or white persons married to Eskimos."

In order to encourage social mixing, the administration at the end of 1963 planned a new recreational association at Iqaluit that would be open to any Baffin Island resident. R.L. Kennedy of the Arctic District Office at Iqaluit reported optimistically: "Should the aims of the new association be realized the long standing problem of racial exclusiveness in recreational facilities will have been largely overcome."[34] But Kennedy's optimism was misplaced. On 18 December 1963 he told the Committee on Social Adjustment "that original hopes for a merger of the Frobisher Airport Recreational Association into the new Frobisher Bay Recreational Association had been set aside because of the unfavourable attitude on the part of some D.O.T. employees."

Racial discrimination had become part of the social environment of Iqaluit. This worried A. Simpson of the Education Division, who "suggested that a rider clause should be attached to all agreements made with community organizations subsidized by the Government that there must be no discrimination on the basis of race, colour or creed in selection of members." But the committee slunk away from this suggestion. It argued weakly that "it was hard to set down rules when we de not know how successful the new organization is going to be." Everyone was undoubtedly aware of the discrimination, but each was satisfied with allowing Kennedy time to review the situation at Iqaluit, with making his feelings known to the territorial government, and with postponing Simpson's proposed rider clause for consideration at the next meeting. The minutes give one an unmistakable impression of the committee's desire to sweep the whole business under the carpet. At the next meeting the members again held over Simpson's rider-clause proposal, this time until the completion of Kennedy's full report.[35] Thereafter the proposal and the report both vanish.

Discrimination against the Inuit was a denial of their social equality and ran counter to official policy in operation since the late 1950s. The deputy minister of northern affairs had written in 1958: "First, it is most important at this time to do everything within our power to raise the social status of the Eskimos. Our objective must be the full dignity and responsibilities of Canadian citizenship for these people, in fact as well as in name. Quite clearly they have not enjoyed such status."[36] One aspect of the differential status, which the deputy minister recognized, was "the easy relations between persons from the south and Eskimo women." He said that it was "necessary to make it as clear to the Eskimos themselves as to others that it is no longer possible to take advantage of Eskimos, as has so often been done in the past."

Such relations were not only symptomatic of the difference in social status but instrumental in furthering the development of social inequality among the Inuit themselves. The ultimate cause was failure – or unwillingness – to apply the restrictive racial contact regulations indiscriminately. Exceptions had been made for selected Inuit girls whom their selectors considered to be more sophisticated and more socially acceptable than their peers. Federal government personnel and employees of the Hudson's Bay Company and other agencies encouraged these girls to mix socially with comparative freedom. "I hope, but I am very far from certain," commented the area administrator at Iqaluit, "that it was the intention of those who supported the policy to assist the process of integration by gradually admitting more and more Eskimo girls into this 'select' group as they 'qualified' for entrance."[37]

The results of the practice, however, were not so successful. Two of the Inuit girls in the select group formed relationships with non-Inuit men. They cut themselves off to a great degree from the Inuit community but were not by any means generally acccepted by the non-Inuit group. They were consequently in the unpleasant position of being suspended between the two, which must have caused a lot of personal distress for them. Unfortunately the consequences did not end there. A number of less fortunate, less accomplished girls, by being denied access to the group favoured by the white Canadians and Americans, were impelled to compete in the most practical way possible: by promiscuity. The girls who became promiscuous, or who were actively prostituting, formed another unhappy group, generally condemned by the Inuit community and hardly less so by the non-Inuit. They placed themselves in this group by a mixture of envy and rebelliousness. "It cannot be denied," the area administrator stated, "that the girls who have freedom to attend private non-Eskimos parties and go out with non-Eskimo men constitute a group that is widely envied by teen-aged Eskimo girls. The favoured group are more sophisticated, dress better and have more fun. Furthermore, they typify a rejection of traditional Eskimo values, and this seems exciting and attractive to girls at a rebellious age who are caught in a cultural conflict."

The worst part of the problem resulted from nubile girls placing too heavy an emphasis on the social accomplishments considered necessary to compete in the frequently frivolous race for the favours of young white men. The inevitable result was gradual but general disintegration of the traditional values of Inuit life. This had serious implications for the survival of Inuit culture and, on a personal level, must have had a destructive effect on the girls involved, for they rejected indiscriminately much that was good in Inuit society. These developments were bound to have repercussions on the young Inuit men. Like the less fortunate females, the young men were placed at a disadvantage by the inordinate admiration of non-Inuit society. That they reacted with bitterness and hostility was only natural.

In this situation the parents of girls and boys alike seemed unable to cope with their children or with their attitudes.[38] Traditional familial bonds were loosening rapidly, and the controls that were elemental to the family-level political structure were vanishing. Part of the blame may be attributed to education for a completely different kind of life-style. As Stuart Hodgson, NWT commissioner, explained:

The younger generation has been educated in the schools and know little or nothing about the skills of hunting and trapping. They are being educated towards a wage employment economy and away from a hunting economy[. However, when they go back to their settlements there is little or no wage employment and they don't know how to go out on the land. Something is lost between the older and younger generation. Parents and children no longer understand each other and it is difficult if not impossible to communicate. The older generation used to be respected. Today children tend to take their parents' guidance with a grain of salt.[39]

Hugh Brody saw this happening in the Eastern Arctic. The heads of households had become

embattled, surrounded by shifting difficulties which confuse and threaten to engulf them. The older generation struggle with the young, and they urge whites to be more committed in their support. The younger generation try to find a way of life for themselves, independent of the family, beyond the manipulation of outsiders. The final irony is of course to be discovered in the result: the Eskimo family has begun to experience the family life that is normal to and typical of the dominant society – private, tense and unsatisfying. It is in this newly constituted family that every Eskimo feels most acutely the disadvantage of the changes that the south has brought to the north.[40]

John Honigmann saw the young men from these newly constituted families as one of three special groups of people making up what he called "the skeleton of a social-class system" that was forming in Iqaluit.[41] This young group was oriented towards neither town nor land. It showed "a fairly strong vector toward European culture" but manifested "no consistent syndrome of that culture, partly because their access to certain elements was blocked as much by their youth and limited economic means as by their inadequate personal resources." For one thing, they lacked discipline. In them the value that the Inuit placed on happiness became "an intense pursuit of excitement." Those who could afford to drink did so excessively. Hence the police were apt to know them unfavourably.

The young men making up this social grouping – Honigmann excludes women from his three embryonic social classes – were considered to be less "steady" than those of the other two classes. One of these classes was a "category of men ... strongly attracted to Eurocanadian middle-class standards of living." They wore European business suits, lived in middle-class furnished homes, and sampled a wide range of Euro-Canadian material culture, including high-fidelity stereograms and cars. They were willing to speak English, even though they often lacked fluency. They drank with restraint. They sent their children to school because they saw value in formal education. They went hunting in their spare time but depended very little on the land. They were the most urbanized of Eastern Arctic Inuit, "the most accomplished townsmen in Frobisher Bay."

Somewhere between the westernized townsmen and the unsteady youth came a class of Inuit who revealed fewer aspirations to the material wealth of Euro-Canadian culture even though some of them were permanently employed. Socially they were "steady, church-going men who also value[d] education for their children." But they were more land-oriented than the westernized townsmen "and more inclined to hearken back to selected aspects of former Eskimo culture." They were non-drinkers, unlike the other two classes, and Honigmann attributed this to "their prominent roles in church affairs and their sincere religiosity."

The egalitarian homogeneity of Inuit society was breaking down. The catalyst was southern Canadian cultural elements, the rapid influx of which kept the traditionally quiescent Inuit cultural system in ferment. Iqaluit was a primary crucible for this social catalysis. Here the Inuit from the smaller settlements or from the abandoned camps, accustomed only to a trading post and maybe a school, a medical station, or a small police detachment, found shops, recreation hall, administrative offices, social welfare offices where they received their monthly family allowances and other payments, liquor store, tavern, air terminal, and rehabilitation centre. As Honigmann puts it, "The openness of Frobisher Bay augments its dynamic potential. The stores import new goods, administrators arrive with new ideas, teachers come with new concepts, comic books bring new heroes, the radio injects new songs, and Eskimo return from schools, hospitals, jails and reformatories with new technical skills and, sometimes, new zest for delinquency."[42]

Inuit society was subject to differentiation as well as to integration, a sure sign of strong modernizing change. But socio-political change was not confined to Iqaluit or even to the other smaller settlements. Among the more conservative camp populations the former egalitarian hunting and trapping societies were showing signs of incipient stratification. Rules of food-sharing and partnerships had maintained the egalitarian nature of Inuit hunting society,[43] but the trapping economy tended to enhance the autonomy of the individual trapper. Trapping required no corporate effort, and its returns "were usually not subject to the elaborate rules of sharing that were applied to game obtained through group effort."[44] Trappers distributed the money or store goods they obtained for sealskins and fox pelts among members of their own nuclear or extended families but not among the entire camp group. Where individual trappers collected money, the more hard-working and conscientious could buy more material goods. The result was a wide variation in possessions among hunters and trappers in the same camp.[45] Social egalitarianism was a thing of the past.

Rapidly developing political and economic inequality marks Inuit society in the 1960s. This inequality was most noticeable between the Inuit and the white Canadians and Americans who increasingly shared their Arctic environment. But among the Inuit themselves it became apparent in their ability to obtain and hold a steady job, to acquire more personal and domestic possessions, to win acceptance by the white society, and to compete for its favours. Such a breakdown of the formerly egalitarian nature of Inuit society was bound to have other social consequences. One was resort to alcohol.

Drinking and Delinquency

In 1959 the secretary of the Frobisher Development Group warned the administrator of the Arctic that with the large immigration of white construction workers, stevedores, and other southern Canadians and the consequent increasing use of alcohol, it was "too much to hope that some of the Eskimos will not be able to obtain liquor, probably the more restless element as is generally the experience in situations of this nature."[46] Not only were Inuit able to obtain drink, but just over a year later they were able to do so legally. In May 1960 a court order stated that the Inuit, like any other Canadian citizens, had the right to consume alcohol.[47] Alcoholic drink, mainly beer, was bought from the local licensee and either drunk on the premises or taken home. In the summer of 1961 a territorial liquor store opened in Iqaluit. This outlet provided only beer at first; later it sold hard liquor but with a waiting period of three weeks.

Within a short time drinking became a big problem in the Eastern Arctic; not alcoholism, as Dr J.S. Willis reminded an Ottawa meeting in 1961, because the Inuit had not yet had time to become alcoholics, but excessive use of alcohol.[48] Where beer was not available as freely as at Iqaluit, the Inuit resorted to home-brewing. Cape Dorset in particular was well-known for this practice. The area administrator there reported to his superior in 1964 that home-brewing "reached the stage, in the fall of 1962, where it was being fortified with methyl hydrate and sold to other Eskimos. Brewing originated with older Eskimos and was quickly taken up by the younger single group."[49]

The Inuit themselves recognized alcohol as a problem but were apparently "unable to exercise sufficient will power and self control to solve it."[50] One Inuk at a council meeting in Iqaluit in 1964 "expressed the feeling that the people were not ready to consume liquor, when it was made available to them ... He stated that the Eskimo people do not have the inner values or the organizational power to protect themselves from liquor."[51]

Excessive drinking as a serious problem in Arctic communities was recognized by Inuit and non-Inuit alike. The most worrisome aspect of the problem, however, was not drunkenness itself but an escalating crime rate that was clearly associated with it. In 1960, when drinking was legally permitted in Iqaluit, the number of criminal convictions rose to three times the number in 1959. It rose again by almost 20 per cent in 1961, when the government liquor store opened. The criminal statistics for Iqaluit from 1957 to 1961 are as follows:[52] 1957, 19 convictions; 1958, 25; 1959, 53; 1960, 155; and 1961, 190. Ninety-five per cent of convictions under the Criminal Code were related in some way to the use of alcohol.[53] In the four months to January 1962 these convictions had increased again by 47 per cent.

Statistics showed "an exceedingly high incidence of total criminal activity in the general population, nearly thirteen times the national average."[54] This high rate of indictable offences did not represent simply a lot of crimes committed by a small number of people. In fact, 20 times as many people were convicted of indictable offences in Iqaluit, in proportion to total population, as in the country as a whole. Search of the court statistics also showed that the proportion of convictions for indictable offences to those for summary offences was significantly higher in Iqaluit than in the rest of the nation. The great majority of summary offences in Iqaluit were liquor violations, so that other types of petty crime were correspondingly low.

If crime occurrences are pictured as a continuum extending from the less to the more serious, the offences at Frobisher Bay seem to be grouped at each end of the scale, i.e. a heavy concentration at the minor extreme (liquor violations) and a similar heavy concentration at the major extreme (indictable offences) but relatively little between the extremes. This absence of median activity, i.e. of petty crimes such as occur in southern Canada could be accounted for in a number of ways. First, the community is relatively loosely organized, and it may have a greater degree of tolerance for behaviour which does not, like public drunkenness or indictable offences, obviously and directly affect the public peace. Second, the relative lack of sophistication among the general population may limit the expression of anti-social be-haviour to the grosser forms (offences such as gaming and betting, for example, obtaining money under false pretenses, or income tax violations, occur generally in a more complex society). Third, the opportunity for the median-type crime may not exist (with few retail outlets, shop-lifting is more easily controlled, and with no Unemployment Insurance office offences against the Unemployment Insurance Act do not occur, and so on).

T.D. Stewart of the welfare division of Northern Administration Branch advised caution in reading too much into Iqaluit's crime statistics. At a meeting in March 1962 he stressed that the tabulation of court statistics did not provide definitive information on the mag-nitude and causation of crime in the town: the sample was too small to be compared effectively with the larger provincial and national samples. But, he was quick to agree, the figures did indicate that concern over crime was well warranted. "In this connection Mr. Stewart pointed out that, in the same manner, medical authorities frequently compared national and international infant mortality rates with the number of infant deaths in particular towns or villages to provide a rough index of child and maternal health."[55]

The statistics failed to bring out, and no available records of the meetings of the Committee on Social Adjustment refer to, the break-down of responsibility on an ethnic basis. The assumption under-lying discussions of Eastern Arctic crime was that the Inuit were responsible for the high rates recorded there. However, an RCMP report dated 29 August 1959 observed that in Iqaluit during the previous 18 months there had been the following offences by group: 45 theft and pilfering, 47 liquor, 2 sex, 10 Customs Act, 4 juvenile delinquency, 3 attempted suicide, 7 motor vehicle, and 2 Fisheries Act, and 14 other serious offences.[56] That makes a total of 134, almost double the number of convictions for 1958 and 1959. Either someone's statistics are at fault, or the police won a low proportion of convictions in relation to crimes committed. But, according to the RCMP, "Approximately 40% of the total crime rate is credited to the

Eskimo population and the remaining 60% to the other groups."
According to the same RCMP report, the Inuit proportion of the total
population was only 45 per cent – 740 Inuit, about 900 Caucasians.
These figures do not, however, include transient Inuit passing
through the rehabilitation centre, or transient DEW Line employees,
stevedores, and so on. Nevertheless the Inuit were apparently responsible for less than their share of crime at Iqaluit.

An increase in the crime rate was only one of the undesirable
consequences of excessive drinking. F.J. Neville, superintendent of
welfare at Iqaluit, noticed that the pattern of drinking had changed
during 1961. Not only were more Inuit indulging, but they were
doing it more in their own homes than in public places. This exposed
the children to drinking and thus helped to ensure perpetuation of
the practice.[57] Children suffered more directly from parental consumption of alcohol, at home or elsewhere. For example, Neville
found that "a very high proportion" of total income went on liquor,
leaving less for necessities. The Hudson's Bay Company reported
that after the opening of the liquor store at Iqaluit sales of clothing
and of small luxury items dropped. But food sales remained constant. Children often suffered neglect because their parents drank.
They were left alone at home "hungry or without anyone to supervise
them."[58] At times their fathers beat them up. Children tended to
lose respect for their parents and refused to accept their supervision
when they saw them drinking. This loss of respect, added to the
alienation that education caused, helped to create that gulf between
parents and children that was part of the fracturing of the formerly
integrated Inuit society.

Another consequence of excessive drinking was that adults would
miss work on the day after a drinking bout or be sent home because
of poor performance. Some would actually lose their jobs and have
difficulty finding other work. Often these men would be unable to
look after their families, would fail to keep up payments on the
homes they were buying, and in many cases would have to live off
relatives or friends who were still working.

At Cape Dorset, liquor, "in both racial groups, was regarded as
the greatest general influence for discord."[59] And the problems
blamed on liquor increased as more of the camp Inuit moved into
the settlement.[60] One of the biggest, the association of home-brewing
and delinquency, was concentrated among teenagers and older
youths. The area administrator reported in 1964 that teenage delinquency in particular had "increased sharply" during the previous
two years.

There have been many thefts of articles from the homes of non-Eskimos, thefts of watches (2) from Girl Guides by other Girl Guides, "gas-sniffing" parties, break-ins during the night at the Federal School, petty thefts from both stores, use of vacant government buildings for immoral purposes, theft of food from the Anglican Mission, vandalism at the vacant Roman Catholic Mission, etc. etc. ... The Hudson's Bay store was broken into once and money stolen from the till, the Anglican Mission was broken into several times, and the Church collection, food and other articles taken. The lock on the Government warehouse has been forced on at least two occasions and the Co-op warehouse and the Anglican Mission warehouse broken into once. Government oil, gasoline and kerosene has [sic] been pilfered.[61]

This kind of lawlessness came to a head in January 1964. After a number of home-brew parties in Inuit homes during the Christmas season, one large party on 4 January ended in a "public free-for-all" in the community hall. The local justice of the peace broke up the disturbance and then wired for the RCMP at Lake Harbour to come and lay charges. Four convictions were obtained, including one against the "main brewer, who had been responsible for many of the drinking bouts during freeze-up." He was caught at last with enough evidence against him for a conviction, and the court fined him $100. The area administrator's report added: "The problem group of young teen-agers, some of whom are still in school, continued their prowling in the settlement during the night, syphoning gasoline into empty coke cans and 'sniffing' it for its intoxicating effects, sleeping in porches, breaking into empty buildings, stealing carvings and re-selling them, etc. This group became quite promiscuous during the freeze-up period and at least three of the teen-age girls are now pregnant. Most of the teen-age activity stopped with the arrival of the R.C.M.P."[62]

But convictions and fines and even the impending return of the RCMP failed to curtail teen-age delinquency for long:

One young man obtained money for his fine by stealing a carving from the Co-operative and selling it to the H.B.C. Another obtained more money than necessary for the fine from his father's Old Age Pension and spent the balance on the wherewithal for more brewing. This lad and his tent-mate have taken to terrorizing other youths in the settlement, way-laying them as they return to their homes, threatening them with knives and other dangerous weapons. Both have been brewing regularly; one of them committed an indecent assault against a young teacher in the early hours of the morning while she was asleep in her own home. The fact that they are now facing new charges when the R.C.M.P. arrive has had no effect on them, in fact, they have been brewing and drinking almost daily since the night of the assault and bragging that they are not afraid of anything the police could do to them.[63]

This was what the new administrator, who came to Cape Dorset in the summer of 1964, preferred to call "uncertainty and unease rather than flagrant contempt for law and order."[64] Like his fellow administrators in Iqaluit and Ottawa, he blamed the situation on excessive consumption of liquor. Why did the Inuit drink so much? The new administrator tried to answer this question too. Liquor, by which he meant "beer, methyl hydrate, molasses brew and the like," was "fast becoming a panacea for boredom and discontent among the young people, most of whom have rejected a life on the land for one of loafing miserably around the settlement." His predecessor had agreed, but on a more general level than that of the young people. Cape Dorset, she had said, was not a model community as depicted in some official correspondence but "a normal northern settlement undergoing the social problems connected with any transition period between small-camp existence and large-community living in which the traditional controls have broken down."[65] On this level the explanation for Inuit overindulgence was regional rather than local. It applied to all Inuit suffering social and economic dislocation and related to their feelings of insecurity and inadequacy. The superintendent of welfare for the Iqaluit region commented:

It is generally agreed that excessive drinking is caused by the person's insecurity, an unsatisfactory environment, and the problems in his relationship with others about him. It has been said that the Eskimos drink excessively because they are losing their familiar way of living and now have to adapt to the white man's way of life. He drinks to escape the pressures which have been put upon him and with which he is unable to cope adequately. Liquor is an escape from the realities of the world in which he is expected to adapt himself and it is a recreation to take the place of the enjoyments and excitements he had when he was a hunter.[66]

If excessive drinking was a response to a changing environment, it also caused many problems. It was hindering the changeover from the Inuit's traditional way of life to their new life-style in a complicated urbanized society. This prompted the acting director of Northern Administration Branch to ask if the Inuit with a drinking problem were in fact the "typical God-fearing people of formerly placid communities, or were they the ones who left their homes because of incipient problems of social adjustment?"[67] The area administrator replied to this question with regard to Iqaluit:

Most of those in Frobisher Bay had immigrated there from elsewhere and we could reasonably conclude that they represented a selection of certain elements from a number of other communities. Immigrants usually displayed certain characteristics such as greater aggressiveness, greater willingness to seek change in their life, less of a bond with other members of their original community, and less of a tie with traditional values of their original communities. For the most part, the sound stable members of a community did not immigrate. They tended to be well connected to the community and to have sound sources of income and to be well satisfied with conditions. From this point of view we could expect those who had moved to Frobisher Bay to be persons who were not "typical Eskimos."[68]

This reads like an attempt to blame the serious social problems of the 1960s on a minority of unstable, atypical Inuit. But the problems were not confined to Iqaluit. They were found equally among Inuit who migrated and those who stayed at home. They were obviously the result of a more widespread, more pervasive social malaise that most observers ascribed to a fundamental breakdown of the traditional fabric of society and the consequent disorientation of bewildered people. Compared to the urbane southern Canadian leaders of the new society then developing in the Arctic, the Inuit were unsophisticated, uneducated, incompetent natives, living in tents or shacks or other substandard houses, dirty, ill-dressed, and existing on government handouts or other forms of social charity. The Inuit were clearly inferior in their own eyes to the white Canadians who now controlled almost every aspect of their lives. Drinking was an escape, a way of forgetting the realities of their lives. "Alcohol was thus perhaps not so much the problem as one of the symptoms of deeper emotional disturbances."[69]

In contrast to the shack-town conditions in which they lived, the environment of a bar or a tavern gave the Inuit a feeling that they had achieved equal status with southerners, especially when being waited on by southerners. Drinking, as Dr J.S. Willis suggested, was "an indication of status seeking." V.F. Valentine, chief of the Northern Co-ordination and Research Centre, disagreed. He doubted that stratification and social inequality were contributing to excessive drinking. His main argument was that the kind of involvement with the law attributed to drunkenness was not that great among blacks in the United States, yet they too were subject to segregation and inequality. Valentine preferred the counter-suggestion that drinking problems had arisen "not so much as a result of social differences or repression as of the current breakdown of Eskimo society."[70]

One aspect of social breakdown was the loss of traditional means of control of social behaviour. In times past the nuclear or extended family and the strict observance of taboos were responsible for such control. Then the missionaries came and took on the role of arbiters of socially acceptable behaviour. The Church built a protective tent around the people, giving them an etiquette of right and wrong, a code of morals and ethical standards. Then, almost suddenly, the Church lost its hold over the people, and the tent was removed. In the resulting exposure of moral conflict, the new and strong temptation of alcohol could and apparently did prevail. The moral control of the Church and the social control of the family gave way to the legal control of the police. Legality succeeded morality; and one aspect of the problems of drinking and delinquency was that in the areas most affected, the numbers of available policemen were too low. Valentine made this point in regard to Iqaluit when he observed that there was only one policeman to every 60 Inuit. "This could account for the apparent high incidence of offences being brought before the court," he said.[71] At Cape Dorset there was no police presence at all. The RCMP inspector and Const. Wilson of Lake Harbour were strongly of the opinion that Cape Dorset definitely required a resident policeman. The residents of the settlement, Inuit and non-Inuit alike, shared this view.[72]

The people of Cape Dorset had first requested a police detachment in a petition to the NWT Council when it met at Cape Dorset in 1962.[73] It took two more years of public and administrative pressure plus "one final report" by J.G. Hughes, the new area administrator, before the NWT commissioner finally agreed. The administrator of the Arctic was jubilant. "Our representations during the past year or two have finally borne fruit. The Commissioner has authorized the establishment of an R.C.M. Police detachment at Cape Dorset."[74]

Great benefits were expected to accrue from the police presence. Not only would it go a long way to reduce much of the disregard for law and order, but it would also give a greater sense of security to the community at large, something it appeared to lack. As the regional administrator at Iqaluit once pointed out, loss of security "seems to have a cumulative effect because as the community feels increasingly insecure, those who wish to take advantage of it are emboldened to the point of outright indifference for the consequences of their actions."[75]

But the administration recognized that the establishment of a police detachment at Cape Dorset was not the final answer to the sort of problems that it encountered there. The area administrator was aware of this and had other measures in mind:

> Just as it is impossible to legislate for morality, so, it seems to me, it is impossible to expect police involvement in the settlement to change the trend very much. I have spoken to the missionary, Mr. Gardner, about a counselling programme, and we are going to meet with the young people and some of the older Eskimos every week. I hope that this programme is going to be carried out in a friendly rather than a punitive atmosphere and I am intending to follow it up with a kind of probationary service for some of the young offenders. For the most part there is still a great deal of respect for my position and I am hoping that the programme will be successful because of this and the involvement of the church.[76]

The involvement of the Church, however, did little for the age group most concerned: the young people of Cape Dorset. In 1967 the RCMP reported that whereas the local church had "good influence and direction with older folk," it had "lost communication with the 16–22 year olds."[77] This age group appeared "too lazy to do anything other than loaf about," and the older people expressed concern over its lack of ambition. Nevertheless the RCMP considered "the spirit and happiness of the population generally" to be "high." The troubles of the early 1960s appeared to have receded into history. The Inuit of Cape Dorset, the police observed, "enjoy a high standard of living as compared to other settlements having a similar size of population, and appear content and happy with matters as they presently exist."

Drinking continued to be a serious problem in Iqaluit, and more and more people took up the idea of restriction. This heatedly debated issue involved political, economic, and ideological attitudes, all charged with inescapable racial overtones. In 1961 Insp. Lysyk of the RCMP broached the subject with the Committee on Social Adjustment.[78] He thought, despite views often expressed to the contrary, that restricting the availability of alcohol in the north had obvious merit. But exercising control at the then current stage of liquor-outlet development was hard. The administration could withhold licences from establishments, but only with extreme difficulty could it cancel an existing licence. A referendum might test public opinion on the issue, but W.G. Brown, chief of the Territorial Division of Northern Administration Branch, said that there was no legal basis for a local referendum to determine community opinion on the granting or cancelling of liquor permits. However, the administration introduced restrictive measures with the approval of Inuit community representatives. In August 1962 the Frobisher Bay Eskimo Council accepted a decision that "there would be no liquor sales over the counter at the Rustic Lodge [airport bar] starting September 1st and that there would be a three week waiting period for buying liquor and beer at the Beer Store."[79]

By 1964 "a notable sentiment" was developing among members of the Committee on Social Adjustment in favour of interdiction, even though some were opposed to it on the grounds that it could be successful only if backed by strict and severe punishment of offenders.[80] But they did nothing beyond discussing the problem to make sure that it was fully understood and that the right action was taken to solve it.[81] In the absence of any forthright policy, the problem got worse. In 1970 Health and Welfare recognized that alcoholism was not only a deteriorating social menace but also a health problem, "which is increasing in importance every year." In 1971 it reported that the association of alcohol consumption with deaths from injuries, accidents, and violence "has been estimated at between 40 to 50 per cent of the total episodes." One such death, described as "the final outrage," occurred in 1976, "when six-year-old Levi Inuqtaqau was thrown from a snowmobile driven by his intoxicated father and killed."[82] As a result, a petition from 300 citizens of Iqaluit brought about the closing of the government liquor store, "the busiest in the eastern Arctic."

In Frobisher ... RCMP Staff Sergeant Dick Vitt says every liquor-related crime in the book has dropped off substantially. The local jail's "drunk tank" is virtually empty and the Baffin Correctional Centre, usually overflowing with Frobisher prisoners, is only half full. School principal Lynn Nash says school attendance in Frobisher has zoomed, fights among students have stopped and no longer does he see kids coming to school beaten or exhausted. Adds Nash: "In the library now, rarely do we see a kid dozing on the floor. We used to have a dozen kids hiding in the book stacks having a sleep because they were kept up all night by drinking and fighting adults.

But the situation overall is still not encouraging. Iqaluit's incidence of juvenile delinquency, drug use, and suicide remains high, and Bryan Pearson, territorial councillor for South Baffin, fears that this might be "just the beginning of what could occur across the North."[83] The NWT Department of Social Services responded by creating a psychiatric social worker position in Iqaluit.

Another response was to restrict or ban the sale of alcohol. The Inuit of 15 NWT communities have voted in plebiscites to prohibit the possession of all alcohol within a 15-mile radius. The settlements include Hall Beach, Pangnirtung, and Lake Harbour in the Baffin

Region; Repulse Bay, Coral Harbour, Eskimo Point, and Sanikiluaq in eastern Keewatin; and Gjoa Haven and Pelly Bay in the eastern part of Fort Smith Region. But to prohibit or restrict the sale and possession of alcohol is not to attack the underlying causes of excessive drinking. Prohibition left untouched the social inequality, or possibly enhanced it. It did nothing to relieve the atrocious housing conditions, the unpromising economic prospects, the low educational attainment, the haunting spectre of racial discrimination. These were the real social problems. Excessive drinking and delinquency were merely symptoms, not causes.

Community action on the vexing issue of alcohol abuse was a good example of the success of a new government approach to the social ills of the Arctic. For in confronting the evil consequences of excessive drinking, the Inuit took it upon themselves to find a way to fight and overcome them. Agitation for plebiscites and prohibition came from the Inuit and not from the élite groups of the southern Canadian enclaves. In many cases the white immigrants were openly hostile to any restrictions on the sale of alcohol, though others came out strongly in support of what the Inuit were trying to do. Obviously other problems could be tackled by the Inuit themselves if they were encouraged, like adolescents approaching adult maturity, to knuckle down and accept a greater share of the responsibility for running their own affairs.

Community Leadership

Decision-making and social policies and programs could no longer be centralized processes issuing out of Ottawa but had to arise indigenously from among the local populations concerned. Who would be the leaders and decision-makers in such a situation? In earlier times the Inuit pattern of behaviour was regulated by the nuclear and extended family groups to which the individual belonged. With Inuit migration from camps to settlements, the influence of these family groups weakened, and consequently a new set of sanctions and standards, which often the Inuit did not understand, governed the conduct of their social affairs. Under these circumstances the Inuit frequently did not know what to do. One pertinent example was "the limited power of the Eskimo ... to control the conduct of the youth at the present time." "Part of this limitation," wrote the secretary of the Frobisher Development Group, "results from the general breakdown in intra-familial relationships, which in turn stems from the new and confusing demands made upon the Eskimo by a wage economy. Partly too, it results, perhaps, from the fact that an Eskimo community is not equipped by custom to apprehend or to deal with such large – though subtle – social problems."[84]

The fault lies in the lack of organized community leaders. In the new settlement conditions, in which most Inuit now found themselves, residents often had no idea who the actual community leaders were. The prestige of a hunter could linger long after his direct influence on a community had ceased with the disappearance of the old way of life. In many cases these family patriarchs controlled opinion and behaviour only within their own groups and did not necessarily influence community thinking and were merely spokesmen for their own interests.

Throughout the Arctic those Inuit of mixed blood were considered to be "more aggressive and readier to speak up at group meetings." But the half-breeds in their impetuous career often ran up against the "resentful attitude of the more conservative older hunters determined to be uninfluenced by the white man."[85] Another group with political potential was the young. The young had wandered furthest from the old ways; they had taken the newest paths and came closest to understanding them. But their youth and inexperience, together with their lack of any traditional leadership status, weakened their effectiveness as community spokesmen. Involved in this political awakening was the widening philosophical and psychological estrangement between the younger and the older generations and a noticeable loss of respect for each other. In some settlements, it was true, the younger, better educated Inuit, with a more advanced understanding of the changing world, did express views carrying weight and in some ways acted as a bridge uniting old and new. In general, however, few Inuit went beyond the role of spokesmen for the interests they represented and in no way shaped community opinion.

A start had to be made somewhere. Many argued that the Inuit had relinquished, or simply failed to accept, responsibility for their own affairs, preferring instead to leave it in the hands of the non-Inuit minority. In the new settlement conditions, and increasingly as the settlements grew in size and complexity and as the problems associated with this growth became more and more troublesome, recognition of the Inuit's lack of political power became an important factor in inter-ethnic and intra-Inuit relations. Northern administration came under growing pressure to motivate the Inuit into playing a more conspicuous role in running their own affairs. "There is ever increasing pressure on us," the administrator of the Arctic wrote in 1962, "to encourage any type of group action which will give the Eskimo people experience in self-government and develop in them a larger sense of responsibility for their common welfare." This had been the function of the original northern service officers in the 1950s.

It is true that for most of the time the Eskimos trading into the scattered Baffin Island settlements live in small hunting camps and, as a rule, have no need to organize for any larger purpose. There will always be times during the year, however, when they congregate at the nearest permanent settlement and immediately community problems develop concerning such matters as dog control, water supply, waste disposal and so on.

If our administrators, and our teachers as well in the smaller settlements, can in any way influence the need for concerted collective action by the Eskimo people to meet even the temporary problems arising from occasional en masse meetings then the seeds will have been sown for shared community action and this growth will be invaluable as each settlement gradually urbanizes and permanent community problems must receive organized attention.[86]

The key to opening the doors of Inuit political awareness was obviously education, but education, especially in the academically retarded Eastern Arctic, needed time. Limited functions could be turned over to local groups in the early stages of political evolution, and experience could be allowed to create more and more qualified people, able to take upon themselves more and more responsible decision-making. In 1961 northern administration stated in a policy directive:

Until now it has been unrealistic to consider asking the local people to take even an advisory role in many of the programmes which have determined the shapes of communities. Local councils or individuals might comment on certain aspects of plans but local advice frankly has been of little use in much of the initial building programme required to lay down roads, secure water supplies, build generator plants, and so on. We are, however, entering a new phase with our attempt to bring community facilities in the north in line with those in the south, in kind if not in degree. New municipal services are being established, such as the provision of electricity, oil, water and sewage disposal. The operation of some of these facilities may provide new opportunity for genuine local consultation. In the case of sewage and water local consultation will be given an added reality by local contribution to the service provided. They are services which affect the daily lives of local residents, and as in any southern community, excite local opinions. We must now take a new look at the extent to which local advisory groups can participate in the operation of such community facilities.[87]

A start had been made in setting up local community councils in the late 1950s. In Cape Dorset, for example, an Inuit council had been operating around 1957, but the area administrator at Cape Dorset in 1961 did not know when it had last met or why it had ceased to meet.[88] In 1958 a council composed of Inuit and whites had been established at Iqaluit, "but it ceased to function when the white people moved away and were not replaced on the council."[89] Northern administration adopted the policy of encouraging the reconstitution of these defunct councils and the founding of new ones. No subject received more attention in 1961.

Iqaluit took the first step to form a new Inuit council on 10 January 1962, when 13 Inuit met with some interested non-Inuit to discuss the purpose of a council. They agreed that it would be beneficial to have one and suggested that it should have five representatives from Apex Hill, two from the Butler apartments at the air base, and either five or ten from Ikaluit.[90] They were "quite vocal" in their opposition to having women on the council "and gave the reason that women are not knowledgeable in the affairs of a community as the men are. They did suggest that the women could form their own council." But women were in fact elected: one along with five men from Apex Hill, one along with five men from Ikaluit, and one along with one man from the Butler apartments. Two civil servants were elected as the white representatives on the council.[91]

At Cape Dorset the officers of the West Baffin Eskimo Co-operative represented the senior leadership of the Inuit community. While they dealt in a co-operative way primarily with economic activities and the use of resources – hunting, fishing, and trapping – they often discussed matters pertaining to the community as a whole. A community association also existed to oversee recreational facilities and functions. Between the two, "most phases of the work of councils in other settlements" were reasonably well covered.[92] Unfortunately the two groups failed to meet the challenge posed by rebellious youth to their ability to maintain order and stability in the community.

Pangnirtung, Lake Harbour, and Broughton Island, like other Eastern Arctic settlements such as Igloolik, Arctic Bay, Clyde River, and Pond Inlet, had only small permanent populations, with most of the local people scattered around in hunting camps. They served mainly hunting areas, and the camp Inuit came to visit only occasionally or seasonally, for trading or for other reasons. "Nevertheless," wrote the administrator of the Arctic, "we are suggesting to our teachers at these settlements that they can promote the idea of group discussion and action on matters affecting the interests of the

Eskimo groups.[93] At Pangnirtung early in 1962 an "embryo council" was formed that consisted of permanent Inuit residents of the settlement, the camp bosses, and the white residents.[94]

Where councils were operating, the problems of immediate concern included dog control, with a demand for compounds in many communities; community clean-up, which developed out of the consideration given in some places to improved sanitation: morality, a special problem in areas where external influences aggravated any established tendencies towards degeneration; employment practices, a subject of increasing interest as wage employment expanded; and home-brewing, another explosive issue in some places. Other subjects suitable for local advisory groups to consider were relief assistance, where an advisory group could counsel the local administrator or welfare officer on the validity of relief applications; the assignment of housing; community planning, where erection of government buildings or expansion of townsites was contemplated; and settlement services, like water delivery and sewage and garbage collection, which were too often organized on behalf of the Inuit.

Progress towards political awareness was thus under way but slowed by the tardy improvement in education. Another retardant, related to education, was "the difficulty of introducing into the Eskimo way of life the new idea of sitting together and discussing problems of the community."[95] Even so, the Inuit were making their voices heard at more than just the community level. Since May 1959 four Inuit delegates had been attending the Ottawa meetings of the high-level, interdepartmental Committee on Eskimo Affairs. They were Abraham Ogpik, aged 30, of Aklavik; George Koneak, 29, of Fort Chimo; and John Ayaruark, 52, and Sheenuktuk, about 55, from Rankin Inlet. In 1962 the chairman welcomed members to another session of the committee "and most particularly ... the four Eskimo delegates. Since the Tenth Meeting of the Committee, when Eskimo delegates first appeared at the meetings, the other members ... have come to rely on them more and more for their intimate knowledge of Eskimo ways, and the insight which they can give into the problems peculiar to the Eskimo. I do not believe this Committee could function without their advice."[96]

Local Government

Inuit participation in political affairs at any level is a recent development. Only in 1950 did the government repeal that section of the Dominion Elections Act that disqualified the Inuit from voting in federal elections. The first time they were permitted to vote federally was in the election of 10 August 1953. The NWT Council never met in the Eastern Arctic until June 1957, when the Thirteenth Session convened at Iqaluit.[97] Even more reprehensible, residents of the Eastern Arctic had no vote in their own territorial elections until Parliament approved a change in the Northwest Territories Act in 1966. During an earlier attempt to enfranchise the Eastern Arctic Inuit, in March 1962, Sen. Thomas Crerar, who had been a cabinet minister under Mackenzie King, stated that most Eskimos were unable to speak English and wouldn't be able to cast an intelligent vote. It had been a mistake, he maintained, to grant the franchise to the "ignorant" Eskimos in the Mackenzie riding. The error should not be extended.[98] Four years later that "error" was indeed extended. The Northwest Territories Act in 1966 added three seats to the council. Simonie Michael won one in the Eastern Arctic. The other two were won by acclamation. Robert Williamson of Rankin Inlet, an anthropology professor at the University of Saskatoon, took Keewatin, and Duncan Pryde, a Hudson's Bay Company store manager in Cambridge Bay, Central Arctic.[99]

Before that election the council consisted of nine members, four elected and five appointed. The appointees were not and never had been residents of the Territories. They had, almost to a man, been citizens of Ottawa. The commissioner himself had always been a senior Ottawa civil servant, a deputy minister of northern affairs. He was not a representative of the Queen like a lieutenant-governor. Further, there had been no representation from the Eastern Arctic. The four elected councillors had all come from the west.

It was at the local level that the government concentrated its efforts to raise the political consciousness of the Inuit in the 1960s. Part of this process was the passing of three municipal ordinances. The Municipal District Ordinance provided for local councils that were partly elected and partly appointed, though with the growth of a municipal district the trend was away from appointed towards elected members. Financing of a municipal district depended mainly on a property tax, and the powers granted to it included control of local business, building construction, roads, public health, and similar matters, together with the raising of taxes and expenditure of money for municipal purposes.

The Local Improvement District Ordinance enabled the territorial government to designate areas of land where it could carry out improvements and impose a limited amount of taxes on real property in order to recover part of the cost from local residents. The NWT commissioner established these local improvement districts where he considered that conditions warranted participation by landowners in improvement expenditures. The representative group of citizens was called the local advisory committee. This body had no legal status or decision-making power, though it was the policy of the administration "to follow the recommendations of the Committee 'as far as possible' ... This in turn has increased the prestige and influence of the Local Advisory Committee to the point where membership carries some distinction locally."

Where the commissioner foresaw growth in a community and the need for establishing control regulations, he could declare it a development area under the Area Development Ordinance. The purpose of inaugurating development areas was simply to provide control, mainly over building, from the point of view of health, safety, engineering, economic, and aesthetic considerations. Here again planners used the local advisory committee to help win local support.

In these development areas one difficulty that planners experienced was control of building standards. Standards acceptable in terms of health, engineering, and aesthetics were usually in conflict with what the Inuit could afford. "In dealing with the problem," wrote the head of the new Municipal Affairs Section of northern administration, "an effort has been made to insist upon adequate safety standards for all buildings of public resort, while tolerating a lower standard in private residences. Control is essentially a local matter vested in the appointed Territorial control officer. This officer will deal with applications for construction of small buildings himself and will refer applications or plans for larger buildings to higher authority for review by engineering staff and Fire Marshall [sic]."[100] The relevance of this policy to poor housing in the Eastern Arctic is obvious.

"One thinks of orderly progression from development area to local improvement district to municipality," says a Northern Administration Branch policy directive, " ... but in most of the Northwest Territories development is too new for this progression to have taken place."[101] In most remote northern communities the population had not had the resources to pay for any significant proportion of local services. Consequently the three new categories of municipal organization covered only six communities, and only one of these, the Frobisher Bay Development Area, was in the Eastern Arctic. Yellowknife and Hay River in the Western Arctic had reached the status of municipal districts.

Through the 1960s the Inuit made slow but steady progress in political development, educational improvement, and local autonomy. In 1963 the federal government appointed a full-time commissioner to set up a territorial civil service. In 1965 he received the assistance of a full-time deputy. That same year the first Inuk was appointed to the NWT Council. Having paved the way for local government and a territorial civil service, the council then recommended appointment of a commission to examine and recommend on the future of the north economically, socially, and politically. On 3 June 1965 Order-in-Council PC 1005 established the Advisory Commission on the Development of Government in the Northwest Territories – the Carrothers Commission. This was the first body of inquiry to travel the length and breadth of the Territories, talking to and getting the views of native residents. The following year the commission's report came out.

The report marked a major change of approach to local government. When the territorial government took over the federal northern bureaucracy in 1967, it assumed the local government problems that came with it. These were mainly a lack of native participation in decision-making and an inflexible attitude to training and educating the native northerner in the politics and administration of local government. The Carrothers Commission recommended development of a process of political maturation leading to full local autonomy within the territorial government. The process involved the growth of local control as the area progressed through various stages on the road to political maturity. "We consider that the continuing and intensified program for the development of local government in which all residents can be offered the opportunity of a meaningful role which they can understand is crucial to the economic, social and political development of the North."[102] Anthropologist Toshio Yatsushiro had advocated such a role for the Inuit four or five years earlier:

A properly instituted self-governing Eskimo body could serve as a most effective instrument of administration. It could function as the main channel of communication between the administration and the Eskimo residents. Important policies and regulations relating to work and other matters could be communicated effectively to the entire community through the duly elected assembly. Such a body would have the opportunity to initiate discussions concerning any matter and arrive at appropriate group decisions in a democratic manner. Through this representative leadership the administration could keep in close touch with the problems and desires of the Eskimo community, and thereby be in a better position to administer wisely. And in addition to legislative and communication functions, the representative assembly could assume judicial and administrative roles.[103]

Despite the difficulty of mobilizing community involvement without the community's initial support and the far-reaching social changes required to enable northern natives to become involved in imported southern structures, the transition from a centralized to a decentralized approach to local government, as envisioned in the Carrothers report, has progressed steadily since 1967 and been a major force in accelerating local autonomous development. Small, widely dispersed, and isolated communities makes transportation and communication extremely difficult and costly. Centralized political control becomes expensive to maintain and inherently removed from individual settlements in terms of both distance and dialogue. The functional isolation that this communications barrier creates can help develop and maintain local autonomy because of lower costs resulting from less direct input from the central government and the absence of excessive delays through having to wait for "permission" from the senior government.[104]

The north is now tending towards long-term establishment of a hierarchy of decision-making from the local through to the federal level. As part of this trend the territorial government in 1969 passed the Hamlet Ordinance, "a landmark piece of municipal legislation in Canada."[105] The earlier Municipal Ordinance, passed in 1963, had followed the standard Canadian model in linking corporate municipal status to a property-tax base. But most Arctic and Subarctic settlements lacked any economic or property-tax base; they would attain no local autonomy for many years, perhaps never. And yet greater political economy depended on healthy development of local government. In recognition of this fact, the council passed the Hamlet Ordinance, which allowed incorporation of communities without a tax base as so-called hamlets, the first level in the municipal hierarchy. This measure, incorporated into an amended Municipal Ordinance in 1972, has succeeded in bringing local autonomy to small and predominantly native communities. Eight of the twenty hamlets created are in the Baffin Region; one, Sanikiluaq hamlet, requested a transfer to Baffin from Keewatin Region.[106]

It is important to define carefully the *degree* of control hamlet councils have over their communities. Under the present Municipal Ordinance hamlets are incorporated municipalities, and the major differences between their powers and those of the tax-based municipalities lie in their revenue-raising ability and the Commissioner's power to veto certain hamlet bylaws prior to their passage by the councils. The hamlets cannot raise money through property taxes, nor borrow money through the sale of debentures or other means, but they can raise money through municipal service charges, building and equipment rentals, license fees, building and development permits, and where they are the sole owners of construction equipment in the community, through government contracts.[107]

AFTER 1971: THE ROAD TO NUNAVUT

Increasing Local Autonomy

The territorial administration developed the municipal structure as a new type of local government more in line with the 1970s. Based on town, village, and hamlet, it was intended to give the communities more say in running their own affairs. "What we are doing wherever possible," wrote the NWT commissioner, "is electing people from and by the community to the various forms of local government."[108] The result of this kind of encouragement, together with the universal availability of education and the growing urbanization of the Inuit, was that by the mid-1970s native people were increasingly coming to hold elected office "at all levels of government" and making their voices "frequently heard in national debates."[109]

The strategy of developing local autonomy before increasing autonomy at higher levels proved successful. But it led to frustration on the part of territorial councillors, "who contrasted the great ferment of action at the local level with their own somewhat futile efforts to influence the federal government."[110] When the NWT government moved to Yellowknife in 1967 on the recommendation of the Carrothers Commission and the size of the council increased from 9 to 12 members, it reversed from 5 federal appointees and 4 elected persons to 7 elected and 5 appointees. Only in 1975 did the council become a fully elected body. Then it grew to 15 members, most of them Inuit, Indian, and Metis. In a further growth spurt in 1979 the council, commonly referred to as the legislative assembly (though the federal government has yet to accept this terminology), increased to 22. Fourteen of these were natives. The council regarded political developments in the yeasty years of the 1970s with a certain nervousness lest the increasingly active leaven of political enlightenment bubbled over out of control.[111]

The council's political power is limited. Its executive committee is made up of the commissioner, the deputy commissioner, and five elected members of the legislature, each of whom is appointed by the commissioner and given ministerial responsibility for one or more government departments. The scope of the territorial government is almost as wide as that of a provincial government, with active roles in health, education, local government, game resources, public works, social and economic affairs, and other provincial fields of endeavour. But the NWT have at best only a quasi-provincial government. Its powers are fewer, the commissioner is responsible to the federal minister of northern affairs, and the federal government retains control over land and most resources and many provincial-type programs. Ottawa dominates the territorial budget through grants and transfer payments, and by means of the Northwest Territories Act it has ultimate control over any executive and legislative decisions made in Yellowknife.

Increased participation of Inuit in local government since the passing of the Hamlet Ordinance has been noticeably at the lowest settlement level.[112] Evidence suggests that at higher levels the degree of Inuit involvement falls, but not because of apathy towards local affairs. The Drury report described governmental structures as "incomplete, inappropriate and in many cases imported southern models."[113] Aside from the obvious obstacle of language, other significant barriers are "electoral procedures and decision-making styles which are inconsistent with traditional ways of doing things." As "the structures of decision-making in municipal government become more complex and increasingly irrelevant to the traditions native people are struggling to maintain, ... they turn to organizations which create an environment more conducive to the expression of their most pressing concerns."[114] These are in effect non-governmental political bodies. One example is the hunters' and trappers' associations that act in an advisory role in many communities but with limited administrative functions. They are concerned with the source of livelihood for many people and are central to the maintenance of a viable land-based economy. For that reason they feel that they should have more say in community affairs as well as at higher levels of government.

The municipal structure of local government in the north discourages many Inuit. The degree of responsibility vested in any municipality varies with size and with ability to pay for services. The smaller settlements have to obtain territorial approval more often than larger municipalities, and the unincorporated municipalities have no jurisdictional power at all. As a result several municipalities as far back as the mid-1970s began to question certain of the restrictions and regulations of the Municipal Ordinance. The feeling was that though there were instances when it might be desirable for the commissioner to be the watchdog of a municipality and to sign some of the bylaws, his powers were "a little too wide."[115] Municipalities had insufficient control over the development of their own bylaws, and the territorial government, in holding on to too much power, prevented local areas from exercising their own judgement and responsibility. This curtailed the ability of a municipality to develop on its own and retarded the growth of the local government system. "The Municipal Ordinance of course, is necessary," F.W. Henne, former president of the Northwest Territories Association of Municipalities, said in 1972. "However, in my opinion, it can become very burdensome and very heavy with restrictive measures."[116]

In November 1976 the Department of Local Government attempted to meet some of the criticism by sponsoring new training programs for the development of both the political and administrative arms of local government, including the training of settlement secretaries and the education of elected councillors. "The major responsibilities for community administration and development that government agents have assumed in the past," said Howard McDiarmid, head of the Training Section in the Research and Development Division of the Department of Local Government, "are now being transferred to the communities themselves ... As communities become more complex, new skills and abilities are required so local affairs may be controlled by the people."[117] Seminars on principles and practices focused on local government concepts and how they applied to governing bodies; development workshops dealt with such things as social change and community planning, organization and development; and administration courses concentrated on abilities required to run community affairs through the municipal structure.

But it was the ordinary citizen, more than the settlement secretary and the elected councillor, who appeared to need instruction in local government affairs. Many municipalities believed that the government was making too little effort to encourage education for those confused settlement dwellers who were often ignorant of the way their own councils worked. "People in the community do not know very much about what the Council is supposed to be," one local councillor said. "It is very difficult to make them understand that the Council represents them and it is there to govern the settlement. They think you are putting yourself forward if you speak. When we became a Hamlet, all help from the Government was cut off, and this made it even harder. What is needed now is a programme about Councils and Government. If a person from the settlement was hired and trained as a development specialist, he could go around the community making them aware of what is Council's role."[118]

Other hindrances to local involvement included a perception of bureaucratic indifference and wastage, resentment at the control of funds spent in communities, and discontent arising out of Yellow-knife's authority over social policy.[119] The sense in many communities was that the territorial council was a powerless body with members unrepresentative of local populations and unaccountable to constituents. Local councils became increasingly frustrated by the insensitivity of territorial officials who made decisions without considering their needs and wishes. "The people of the far north may be told that the resolution of their social and economic problems will become their own affair," Brody notes, "but the degree of autonomy that such a suggestion implies is not at present countenanced by the persons who continue to make the rules."[120]

The government had decentralized the responsibility for most "hard" services but had failed to do so with social programs. Many municipalities contended that this seriously inhibited community involvement because the problems that affected them the most were those over which they had virtually no control. They charged that the territorial council was effective only in so far as the federal government agreed to implement what it recommended. This was the case also with the development of a settlement council. There seemed to be a fear of allowing people to make mistakes: "The feeling of power is given, but not the actual power. This is built-in frustration."[121]

A viable economic base is necessary for the development of local government in the NWT as it is anywhere else. There is no point in local councils making decisions if they lack the financial backing to carry them out, and the conditions that the territorial government has placed on financial support merely constrain local political autonomy and add to the "built-in frustration." Obviously a healthy local financial situation makes possible the placing of greater responsibility and accountability on the well-heeled council. This in turn generates more interest in local decision-making. In this regard the larger municipalities are better off than the smaller because their powers of taxation are stronger and more independent. By contrast the hamlets and the unincorporated settlements receive their finances from conditional and unconditional grants from the senior government. However, this system allows for little control or flexibility in the determination of priorities. Those who decide local priorities are in practice those who allocate the grants; in other words, the territorial and, to a lesser extent, the federal governments, those bodies furthest removed from and often the least sensitive to local issues.

Richard Hunter comments: "Because the development of fiscal responsibility at the local level will be difficult to attain for many settlements, local autonomy will continue to be a distant ideal. The difference between those municipalities with a financial base and those without will become increasingly apparent. Those with fiscal autonomy can develop local government autonomy; those without will continue to be dependent upon the senior level of government for programme funding."[122] In spite of all the difficulties and setbacks Hunter concludes optimistically: "The organizational structure is evolving into a northern form of local government suited to the needs of the people in northern communities. With the decentralization of decision-making to the 'grass-roots' level, political autonomy will eventually be achieved by the local population. Finally, development of local autonomy implies the development of a proper balance of decision-making capabilities between the three levels of government. It is this balance which is presently being sought in the Canadian North."[123]

The Inuit Tapirisat Proposals

The political ferment of the 1970s in the Canadian north was stirred into agitation by the sudden growth to maturity of the Inuit Tapirisat of Canada (ITC). This was a development parallel, if slightly delayed, to what was happening in Greenland and Alaska, where political groups had formed to protect and advance the interests of the native people and proved "surprisingly powerful and effective."[124] The conception of a national native organization for Canada resulted from a July 1970 meeting at Coppermine, where Inuit from all over Canada gathered to discuss mutual problems. In August of the following year, at a conference held at Carleton University in Ottawa, the ITC was born. An organizing committee of Inuit "decided it was time for the native people of the Arctic to speak with a united voice on a host of issues concerning development of the North, education of their children and preservation of their culture."[125]

In an application for a $30,000 grant to continue the work started at Coppermine – all of ITC's funding comes from the federal government – the newborn organization told the minister responsible for citizenship, Robert Stanbury: "It was said at Coppermine that the only way we could get strong is to support each other; to organize; to have an organization with a name in our own tongue; that such an organization would develop pride in our young people, save our environment, determine what alternatives are best for our people faced with the combined problems of the old way of life and modern technology; and that we must control our own future if we are to survive as Inuit."[126]

A number of regional native people's political organizations have become affiliated with the ITC, including the Northern Quebec Inuit Association, the Labrador Inuit Association, and the Baffin Region Inuit Association, all representing areas of the Eastern Arctic. The Committee for Original People's Entitlement (COPE), representing the Western Arctic, the Kitikmeot Inuit Association, representing the Central Arctic, and the Keewatin Inuit Association also allied themselves with the ITC, though COPE has since backed out. "The affiliated organizations look after day-to-day problems and concerns in their communities and regions, but their presidents also sit as members of the ITC board of directors. The national organization concentrates on national issues, but helps out with community or regional problems when requested to do so."[127]

On 27 February 1976 the ITC presented to Prime Minister Trudeau and his cabinet in Ottawa a wide-ranging document entitled an "Agreement-in-Principle as to the Settlement of Inuit Land Claims in the Northwest Territories and the Yukon Territory between the Government of Canada and the Inuit Tapirisat of Canada." The first basic goal of the proposed settlement was to "Preserve Inuit identity and the traditional way of life so far as possible." Achieving this goal meant, among other things, creation of a new territory to be known as Nunavut – "Our Land" – "in respect to which, through numbers and voting power, the Inuit will have control for the foreseeable future." The second goal of the settlement was to enable the Inuit "to be equal and meaningful participants in the changing North and in Canadian society." This meant high Inuit involvement in all government activities, including land use planning and management. The Inuit envisioned an extensive social and economic program and an Inuit Development Corporation funded through royalties from development. Another part of these royalties was to go towards the financial support of national, regional, and local Inuit cultural organizations and activities. The Inuit made it clear that they were asking for no cash transfers from the government, only for such "monetary compensation or benefits ... [as came] through royalties arising from development. The Inuit will share fully the risks in respect to the benefits of development. The Inuit do not want handouts."

What they did want was control over their own territory, or rather Territory.

In brief, the basic idea is to create a Territory, the vast majority of people within which, will be Inuit. As such, this Territory and its institutions will better reflect Inuit values and perspectives than with the present Northwest

Territories. The Inuit should have actual control through their voting power, at least for the foreseeable future. No new or different powers are requested, other than voting requirements ... trilingualism ... and police ... than exist at present for a Territory. That is, "separate status" is not contemplated. The Federal Government cannot object on this point of legislative powers of the new Territory. The creation of Nunavut should mean that the Yukon and Northwest Territories will more quickly be able to become provinces, leaving Nunavut as a Territory relatively undeveloped for the present, and as a federal jurisdiction. This feature may well appeal to non-natives in both Yellowknife and Ottawa.[128]

Within this Territory the "Nunavut Territorial Government will be responsible for all matters in respect to which the governments of the Northwest Territories and Yukon Territory have responsibilities." The main differences would be, first, that Nunavut would be "so far as practicable, a trilingual territory whereby Inuktitut, English and French have an equal status" and, second, that it would have its own police force similar to the provincial police forces of Ontario and Quebec.

The ITC has continued to move towards its clearly defined political goals on two levels. On a regional level, the affiliated organizations are actively working for the preservation of the Inuit language and culture, "articulating the needs, aspirations and interests of Inuit people, developing strong Inuit leaders, providing information and educational resources, facilitating communications and encouraging unity and cooperation among various organizations established for the well-being of native people. These organizations conduct programs on land claims, economic development, wildlife management, social and recreation development, housing, health, alcohol prevention, education and job training."[129]

On the national level the ITC represents the broader interests of Inuit in all regions of Canada, including their newly awakened political ambitions. "We are asking Canada to help us take the first step in the direction of regional self-government," said James Arvaluk, president of the organization, "the kind of self-government that will be responsive to the needs of the Inuit who at present make up the majority of the population ... We want a stronger voice in such fields as education, housing, health and welfare, social and political development and the running of our communities."[130] Peter Ittinuar elaborates on how the ITC carries out this plan:

It studies, considers and recommends alternatives in renewable and non-renewable resources development. It provides impetus for Inuit participation in business through the Inuit Development Corporation. It also makes funds available for the study and implementation of legal, housing and health services. Inuit Tapirisat of Canada's Inukshuk Project is a path-breaker in the development of communications in northern communities. Similarly, the Inuit Cultural Institute has done invaluable work on the Inuit language and education. Finally, and most importantly in terms of political activity in the national context, Inuit Tapirisat of Canada articulates the Inuit position on land claims and constitutional development.[131]

The land claims issue is perhaps the most important in which the ITC is involved. After three years of study of renewable resources, land use, and occupancy,[132] more than 100 voting delegates attended a conference at Pond Inlet from 28 October to 2 November 1975 and passed a resolution authorizing the ITC to begin land claims negotiations with the federal government. Four months later the Inuit presented their land claims proposal, asking for rights to approximately 750,000 square miles of land north of the treeline and 800,000 square miles of ocean. This area, they maintained, represented the limits of the traditional use and occupancy of northern lands and waters. Within this vast area the Inuit asked for outright control over 250,000 square miles on the basis that this was the absolute minimum that would enable them to preserve what was left of their culture, identity, and way of life and, at the same time, to integrate into Canadian society as equal participants. On the remainder of the land the Inuit asked for hunting, fishing, and trapping rights, a degree of control to protect both the environment and the wildlife of the north, and a 3 per cent share of the revenues from non-renewable resources: "We drafted the Nunavut proposal, a political development paper for the creation of a separate territory within the Northwest Territories. Realizing that land claims will not leave us much land, we feel that our Nunavut government would be able to exercise a certain amount of political control. Since territories don't control land or resources, we hope at least to be able to assert more political pressure than the Northwest Territories government does."[133]

The glowing hopes of February quickly dimmed. In September 1976 James Arvaluk, president of ITC, announced the withdrawal of the Nunavut proposal after extensive consultations with the people of the north. The ITC wanted time to discuss changes in the suggested political structures for their new Inuit territory and in those proposals that dealt with protection of future rights for the native peoples. The Inuit leaders were forced to realize that much of their original Nunavut proposal was unworkable. Norman Ward of the University of Saskatchewan, retained by the NWT Council to study the implications of the proposal, reported that in his opinion the proper operation of the health, educational, cultural, and administrative agencies, in addition to the community and territorial corporations envisioned in the proposal, would need a group of skilled and experienced administrators far beyond the numbers that the poorly educated and inadequately trained Inuit population could supply. John Amagoalik, the ITC claims director, admitted on a CBC interview that estimates showed that the Nunavut proposal would have created 2,800 jobs by 1980, while no more than 1,400 native people could be available to fill them.[134]

The withdrawal of the Nunavut proposal signalled the start of a long and difficult period for the ITC. The first trouble came when COPE, which had given enthusiastic support to the original proposal, applied to Ottawa for funding to prepare its own land claims covering the western part of what was to have been Nunavut. Public name-calling on radio and in the native press widened the breach between COPE and ITC, and shortly afterwards James Arvaluk resigned as ITC president, his health reportedly damaged by the intolerable pressures.

Shaken but staunch in its resolve, the ITC presented to the federal government in December 1977 a new proposal in the form of 11 broad principles "for the establishment of Inuit rights between the Inuit of Nunavut and the Government of Canada."[135] But negotiations proceeded with glacial slowness. Growing more and more unhappy with the lack of discernible progress, the board of ITC abolished its land claims commission in February 1979 and embarked on a massive reorganization. The ITC feared that the land claims commission was beginning to take over decision-making power from the ITC itself. The fear was justified to some extent, for the commission had certainly become the most aggressive native group in the Eastern and Central Arctic.[136]

A month later Tagak Curley, executive director of the ITC, announced that the Inuit had abandoned the former strongly defended principle that nationhood be negotiated as part of any land claims settlement. The Inuit, he said, wanted more control and input in areas that affected their lives. Though they still intended to push for an Inuit-run nation, though one that stressed democratic rights for all, they were prepared to put off demands for nationhood in return for some guarantee that they would not be swallowed up in the rush to exploit the Arctic's natural resources.[137]

Meanwhile the Inuit were preparing a new discussion paper, largely in response to complaints from the federal government that their position in the past had been too vague to serve as a basis for serious negotiation. At the close of its annual meeting in Igloolik in September 1979 the ITC released details of a new comprehensive political development scheme for the north in a document entitled "Political Development in Nunavut." The Inuit demands remained largely unchanged: a new territory of Nunavut to cover all of the land north and east of the tree-line, a territorial government, and the attainment of provincial status within 15 years.[138] But even these proposals were still largely undefined on the issues of land and compensation.

At this time negotiations between the Inuit of Nunavut and the government of Canada were at an impasse. The talks, after two empty years, were slated to resume at the end of July 1980, but the government postponed them indefinitely while its northern affairs minister, John Munro, mulled over his list of potential negotiators. The bone in Ottawa's gullet, which the government could neither swallow nor dislodge, was the Inuit demand for political autonomy. Federal negotiators had argued that they had no mandate to discuss political change and could bargain only on land and money. The government in fact wanted to use the James Bay settlement, by which the Cree and Inuit of Quebec surrendered claim in return for $225 millions and a range of rights and privileges, as a model for the settlement of all native land claims. But many native leaders regarded James Bay as a sell-out, and, learning the lesson of their brothers in Quebec, the Inuit of the NWT steadfastly declared that they would never trade past, present, and future rights for land and money.

Late in 1980 land claims negotiations between the ITC and the federal government quietly resumed, and when they did the Inuit arrived armed with one of the most significant documents yet released by a native group. The 80-page *Parnagujuk*, "A Plan for Progress," contained a summary of the Inuit philosophy, a set of basic principles on which they sought agreement, and a preliminary list of implementation proposals. The document clearly revealed the Inuit's newly acquired political sensitivity, most noticeably in a major reinterpretation of the ITC's earliest unsatisfactory proposals. Gone was the uncompromising – some might even say offensive – language of the first agreement-in-principle. Instead *Parnagujuk* restated the Inuit position in a tone that was much more reassuring. For example, 1977's bold demand for self-determination had matured into a reasoned argument for the granting of a kind of municipal and provincial mandate to decide local and regional affairs. Further, in a startling but far-sighted move the Inuit renounced all proprietary claims to oil and gas resources. However, they made this renunciation on certain conditions, including revenue-sharing and the clear dedication of the resources for Canadian use. With one spirited sweep the Inuit had removed a virtually insurmountable barrier to agreement and showed a commendable degree of political realism. A hard-line stance on a claim to all proprietary rights to oil and gas would have stopped negotiations dead at the outset because the federal government, backed by the rest of the country, regarded energy issues as matters of national importance.

Through *Parnagujuk* the Inuit made it clear that they were in favour of economic and industrial development in the north and that they wanted to participate fully in the modern evolution of their territory. They welcomed future development so long as it was under Inuit political control and in harmony with Inuit needs:

Unlike some native groups, the Inuit contemplate a future squarely within the Canadian federation. Furthermore, that future is to be one of progress, in recognition of the complexities of modern Canadian society. Some traditional pursuits must be safeguarded. But isolation, leading to economic dependency and cultural and social decline, is to be avoided. The document's consistent focus on the future, and its moderation in referring to past grievances, will help make its principles acceptable to the majority of Canadians.[139]

In fact there was much of a general nature in *Parnagujuk* with which most Canadians could agree. Rapid progress could have been made on this settlement and the process of negotiation of native claims revolutionized. But such progress required clear thinking on the part of the federal government, and that kind of clear thinking has been conspicuously absent in Ottawa. A crippling inertia, a maddening refusal to move forward with the times, has paralysed the northern administration. The federal government has come up with no solution to the land claims issue, and many Inuit, even many white northerners, are becoming impatient and angry.

The use of the term "land claims," while emphasizing that native concern was primarily over land, has tended to obscure the fact that the Nunavut proposals are about much more than just the land and the uses to which it might be put in the future. They are, perhaps more importantly, about Inuit self-determination in an Inuit-dominated northern territory. "It should be emphasized that self-determination, in and of itself, does not automatically mean the division of a pre-existing polity," Kirk Patterson has observed. "The principle of self-determination means simply that peoples (by whatever definition) should be allowed to determine, without external pressure, their own political future. It could be that, given such a right, a people may decide to uphold the *status quo*, to maintain their existing political position."[140] One political scientist quoted by Patterson has written: "Self-determination can be an instrument for integration and unification, which, of course, must be based on the freely expressed wishes and desires of the people claiming the interest or the right in question." About the Canadian Arctic specifically, another author has written:

The movement for native self-government is directed toward creating a new system of responsible government for the native population to replace this present government from afar over which they have little control. The intention is that the new self-government would be responsible in two senses: first, it would be responsible and accountable to the native population, and second, the native population itself would be responsible *for* decisions. The obstacles facing these efforts are immense. The native population is small and scattered. It does not have at present the knowledge resources, skills and technical competence needed in modern government or administration. Without a concerted, coordinated, systematic effort to provide these resources, native self-government will not be able to create the kind of educational, cultural and economic development programs necessary to meet the challenge. The problems of Metis and non-status native populations, with their relationship to provincial rather than federal governments, need to be resolved. Federal-provincial conflicts and divisions of jurisdiction are formidable problems.[141]

But the greatest problem remains economic. The tax base of native communities is too small to support local government services. Education, wildlife, social services, housing, and the development of local government are now all firmly under the control of the NWT legislative assembly, each presided over by an elected minister. Economic development is also nominally under the assembly's control but only in a very limited or local sense. The main economic drawback is that ownership of non-renewable resources remains in Ottawa. This causes frustration in the north, which in turn helps to unite the different northern groups and to strengthen their resolve to have more say in resource development. The feeling is that the federal government views northern resource development mainly in terms of its benefits to southern Canada. Equally frustrating is the fact that while the government in Ottawa has asserted its primacy in resource management, it has yet to establish a policy framework for exercising this responsibility. One possibility that would be of great benefit to native government in the north would be a statutory requirement for a large part of the economic rents from resource development to be returned directly to the communities with no control or restrictions by the senior levels of government. Another would be statutorily guaranteed funding of native government. Settlement of land claims through grants or resource-rich tracts of territory, accompanied by the allocation of capital funds, might alleviate some of the economic problems facing potential northern native governments.

For most native peoples, a claims settlement has a better chance of success if it gives them a measure of control over the many features of their lives that influence their self-definition as a people. The Inuit believe that to succeed in the society now evolving in the Canadian Arctic they must build on that strong sense of identity as native people that gives meaning to their lives. White society's denial of that sense of identity has degraded the Inuit as a group. To appreciate what this means, it is crucial to remember that the Inuit identity is multi-dimensional and touches on most aspects of their lives – ideological, economic, political, even aesthetic and familial. Fostering this threatened identity requires claims settlements that will provide a total cultural support system, one that will give native cultures a reasonable chance of adapting with integrity to the new realities of the Arctic. The Inuit realize that, to succeed, this adaptation will require an economic base. Economic success entails sufficient capital to finance it. Moreover a significant portion of this capital must belong to the Inuit themselves if they are to avoid continued dependence on non-Inuit. While they may borrow from non-Inuit, the Inuit's capital supply "must be sufficient to enable them to make decisions that emphasize their own needs rather than the priorities of others. Claim settlements present the obvious – indeed the only – source of this supply of capital."[142]

Arctic Regionalism

The ITC was not the only soda being stirred into the frothy mix of NWT politics in the 1970s. On 14 April 1977 the elected representatives of 14 Baffin communities, chosen by the respective village, hamlet, and settlement councils, voted to form the Baffin Regional Council. The council is made up of mayors and chairmen of the region's community councils. Those councillors from the legislative assembly who represent the Baffin Region, together with the president of the Baffin Region Inuit Association and a representative of the ITC, are ex officio members; they take part in debates and act as resource persons but have no vote.[143] They also provide a permanent link with the territorial government and with the native organizations who represent the Inuit of the region. This organizational structure of the Baffin Regional Council recognizes the importance of the community as a unit of interest and of the local council as the elected body that legitimately represents that interest.

The renewed surge of political activity at the regional level, which the Baffin Regional Council represented, caused alarm in the territorial government. Its position paper on constitutional development, approved early in 1979, clearly stated that there was no place in the NWT "for a regional level of government with its law-making powers and administration."[144] But Lucasi Ivvalu, Speaker of the Baffin Regional Council, reassured the House on 30 March 1979 that at present his council sought no legislative powers but only more involvement in the development of the Baffin Region. "It wants to be involved in decision-making as a decision-making body," he said, "for instance on the decentralization of power from Yellowknife to Frobisher Bay." C.M. Drury, the prime minister's special representative on NWT constitutional development, said that the assembly need not fear the growth of regional government within its jurisdiction. The Baffin Regional Council, and similar developments then being proposed for the Western Arctic, were simply "limited forms of authority meeting regional needs."[145] An appeased territorial council went on to pass a motion recognizing the "legitimate aspirations" of the Baffin Regional Council.

This motion constituted tacit recognition of one of the most fundamental facts of NWT life: regional differences. The immense expanse of the Territories and differences in history, culture, and economic activities have created an enduring sense of regionalism. Regionalism as a socio-political movement seeks to foster or protect an indigenous culture in particular regions or to decentralize government to an intermediate level between that of the state and the traditional units of local government. The movement has been particularly strong in France and Spain and has become of increasing importance in Great Britain, with the establishment in the 1960s of regional economic planning councils. The growing strength of regionalism in the Canadian Arctic is thus no isolated phenomenon. Nor is it different in its goals and wishes from examples elsewhere. Like them, the regionalism of the Canadian north is more than just awareness of differences among its separate regions; it gives rise to a strong feeling that the differences make it unlikely that a single body can effectively govern all of the disparate regions together. It then becomes a belief that a regional government would better serve the interests of the people than a territorial government.

C.M. Drury was known to favour regional government in the NWT. On 20 October 1978 he had praised the Baffin Regional Council not only as a good idea but as one that was proving itself successful. "It grows from the bottom up, instead of the other way round," he said. "I have been impressed ans have no hesitation in commending its adoption elsewhere."[146] Retiring Commissioner Stuart Hodgson added his prestigious support. On a farewell tour of the Baffin Region, he told an audience in Cape Dorset on 24 March 1979 that, unlike some people opposed to the Baffin Regional Council, he did not see it as a dividing force. It was a unifying force for the people of the Baffin Region. "This regional council has only been in existence for a year and a half," he reminded the members present, "but already people are beginning to take notice of you. In all sorts of ways, you are having a strong influence in Yellowknife and with the government in Ottawa."[147]

Regional councils can have a major influence on the way in which territorial and federal governments deliver programs and services. Education, social development, health services, fish and wildlife management, and community planning are what a regional council should be concerned about. It should also look at the social and economic effects of resource developments, like off-shore drilling, and at what will happen to communities as a result of such developments. "As regional councils are established they will exert greater and greater pressure on the administration to respond to regional priorities and needs rather than to territorial policies formulated without regional input. Indeed, to judge from the example of the Baffin Regional Council, regional councils may take the initiative in formulating government policy and legislation, especially when those are directly relevant to their communities or regions."[148]

Regionalism is the political philosophy of the Nunavut proposal and the driving force of the Baffin Regional Council. Both of these developments are founded on recognition of the distance separating the majority of Inuit in the Eastern Arctic physically from Yellowknife and figuratively from the needs and aspirations of the Mackenzie valley, which has tended to dominate the government. Many Canadian Inuit villages are much closer to Greenland than to Yellowknife. Distance was one of the basic arguments in favour of Nunavut. A legislator from Iqaluit might commonly take two days and have to make air connections through Montreal simply to attend a legislative assembly meeting in Yellowknife.[149] Simonie Michael, the first Inuk elected to the council, charged that the lack of lateral air transport between Iqaluit and Yellowknife caused hardship for people like him and made it very difficult for one man to represent his far-flung constituents adequately.[150]

Because of the distance separating the Eastern Arctic from Yellowknife, the Inuit of the region accused the territorial government of being unresponsive to their needs. The accusation had a certain justification. With respect in particular to the basic needs for individual growth and development – adequate shelter, health care, education, and livelihood – the Eastern Arctic Inuit had always suffered greater neglect at the hands of successive administrations in Ottawa and Yellowknife than had the native people of the Western Arctic. This unpleasant truth lay behind the Baffin Regional Council's aim of achieving the decentralization of powers from Yellowknife to Iqaluit. It prompted the territorial councillor for Iqaluit, Dennis Patterson, to say that it was impossible for officials in Yellowknife to administer the Eastern Arctic, 2,000 miles away. "They are completely out of touch," he declared, "and we are constantly getting the short end of the stick." He added that provincial status for the NWT would only make matters worse.[151]

Dividing the Territories

The Inuit occupied that vast area of Canada that stretched north from the tree-line. Despite their small numbers, in the far-flung region of treeless tundra they were the majority population and would for long remain the majority of the permanent residents. Yet despite this, the Inuit were nowhere a majority in political structures. They had "no voice or opportunity to promote their culture and hopes except as minorities pleading for the generosity of the dominant majority."[152] But the small numbers in the Eastern Arctic posed a political threat in that Ottawa might consider it unjustifiable to transfer to Nunavut the substantial powers that the ITC claimed for it. Division of the NWT, as Gurston Dacks points out, could freeze Nunavut into a junior position in Confederation.[153]

The Eastern Arctic's desire to appear politically mature and independent, together with its frustration with Yellowknife, lay behind Tagak Curley's announcement on 13 November 1979 that the members of the NWT legislative assembly who came from the area above the tree-line would appoint six "shadow ministers" to keep executive committee members informed about their views and to see that government departments were acting in the best interests of the people of Nunavut.[154] Himself the member for Keewatin South, Curley made it clear that the decision was in no way an attempt by the Inuit to divide or split the House or to vote as a party – party politics are as yet non-existent in the NWT, though by 1980 several lines of party development were beginning to appear possible.[155] The arrangement that Curley announced was simply aimed at giving members the opportunity to make proposals for change to government structure so that it would better reflect the needs of the remote areas than did the existing system. Curley urged the assembly to take a "long serious look" at the Nunavut proposal. The Eastern Arctic people strongly supported it, he said; they felt isolated from Yellowknife. The distance separating them was too great.

The Eastern Arctic Inuit, in pressing their claims for a separate, self-governing Territory of Nunavut, were not alone in considering the NWT too large and diverse for effective administration from a single centre. The federal government itself had long recognized this fact, and regional divisions of one kind or another have always been part of the Territories' administrative and political history. The earliest divisions, dating from the late nineteenth century, consisted of the districts of Mackenzie, Keewatin, and Franklin. Franklin included the Boothia and Melville peninsulas and the Arctic archipelago. The federal government established the Arctic Islands Game Preserve as a separate administrative unit in 1926 and expanded it in 1929 and again in 1942. It survived till 1966, when the NWT Council abolished it and brought this area for the first time within the same framework as the rest.

Six years before, in January 1960, Councillor K.H. Lang, who represented the Mackenzie delta, suggested that the District of Mackenzie be separated soon from the districts of Keewatin and Franklin. It is worth emphasizing that this proposal came from a white politician in the Western Arctic and not from an Eastern Arctic Inuk. The suspicion is strong that the proposal was related to the racial segregationist philosophy then prevailing in the Canadian Arctic. But the idea appealed to the pro-Western Arctic government. Commissioner Gordon Robertson confirmed that the Department of Northern Affairs and National Resources was actively considering the step. In fact the federal government went along with the proposal to the point of presenting bills to that effect in Parliament. In July 1961 Prime Minister John Diefenbaker was in the north, seeing "at first hand something of the achievements of the past, something of the things that have already been done" and promising that anything the northerners suggested in the way of "increasing the field" of their responsibility and, "to a measure not before known, of self-government" would receive his "warmest approval and support." Diefenbaker used these words in a speech to the NWT Council on 20 July, and he added, "When you mentioned that you hoped there would be, not too far away, a division of this vast northern area into two districts, I think that too is something that deserves the most sympathetic consideration on the part of the federal government."[156]

True to his word, Diefenbaker included in the Speech from the Throne on 27 September 1962 the government's intention to place before the House measures "to provide for the division of the Northwest Territories into two territories, and to provide more self government for the residents of that area as a step toward the ultimate creation of new provinces in Canada's great north."

Diefenbaker's government fell to Lester Pearson's Liberals before he could make good his promise. But Pearson was as sympathetic as his predecessor to the northerners' expressed desire to divide the north. In the House of Commons on 21 May 1963, the minister of northern affairs and national resources, Arthur Laing, introduced bills C-83 and C-84, which would amend the Northwest Territories Act and create two separate territories, one to be named Mackenzie, the other Nunassiaq, "the beautiful land." The House debated the bills in July and November. On 8 November the minister declared that he had no qualms about Mackenzie. "I am satisfied," he said, "that this particular area is quickly going to be able to take care of itself." Not so Nunassiaq.

In so far as the eastern Arctic is concerned, I must say at once that, due to the fact it is above the tree line, due to the fact that so far, in spite of investigations we have made, there do not seem to be comparable resources to those existing on the western side of the Arctic, the outlook for the future is more difficult. The fact is that, in spite of investigations made by our fisheries department and other departments, the amount of resources in the country seems relatively low in proportion to the people who are living there. Communication is exceedingly difficult. It is for this reason that in the bill respecting that part, in other words the residue of the territory left when we pass the Mackenzie bill, we have decided to retain the centre of government in Ottawa.

"I am content in my own mind that the future of the western part of the Arctic is secure," Laing said later in his speech. "I think our chief interest for some years to come is going to be in respect to the eastern Arctic."

Yellowknife lawyer Mark de Weerdt has pointed out that the lack of Eastern Arctic representative in the NWT government had been so obvious that those Mackenzie delta politicians who favoured division of the Territories argued not that such representation should be improved but rather that the need for it could be sidestepped by cutting off the Eastern Arctic from their area of responsibility.[157] If the proposed division of the Territories became law, Mackenzie would get its resident commissioner but Nunassiaq would not; and Mackenzie would have five elected as against four appointed councillors, whereas Nunassiaq would be permitted two elected and five appointed, of whom four would be non-residents and three of whom might form a quorum. This was obviously no way to introduce the Eastern Arctic Inuit to the working of democracy.

But the proposed division never became law. On 15 November 1963 the House agreed to refer the bills to the Standing Committee on Mines, Waters and Forests for consideration. They never came back. The year of Canada's centennial, 1967, came and went. That was to have been the year for greater autonomy and responsible government for the Western Arctic district. But they failed to appear.

What appeared instead was an administrative restructuring of the NWT, one that could pave the way for an easier political separation at a later date. The districts of Franklin and Keewatin were amalgamated into a new Arctic District. The boundary separating Arctic District in the east from Mackenzie in the west was a northward extension of ̅the Manitoba-Saskatchewan border. Mackenzie thus contained most of the populated centres: Yellowknife, Fort Smith, Port Radium, posts along the Mackenzie River, and Aklavik. It also contained most of the operating mines in the Territories, the Great Slave Lake fishery, the inland waterways system leading to the Arctic Ocean, the Norman Wells oilfield, the Pine Point mine, some timber, small areas of arable land, furbearing regions, and potential reserves of untapped mineral wealth. Mackenzie could thus reasonably expect to attain provincial status much sooner than the eastern districts.

The amalgamation of the two much less richly endowed and less financially secure eastern districts to form the new Arctic District, and Arctic District's administrative separation from Mackenzie, were de facto recognition of the NWT division that today's proponents of Nunavut are requesting. In administrative terms the big difference between Mackenzie and Arctic districts was that whereas Mackenzie had its headquarters in the north at Fort Smith, Arctic District was administered directly from Ottawa. Ironically, many Eastern Arctic Inuit maintain that things were better then than when they were brought under Yellowknife in 1967, because it was easier to attract the government's attention to Arctic problems.[158] But the general feeling in the north was that "Ottawa's army of whites [was] getting the most out of Ottawa, not the Eskimos. The Eskimos get houses when politics make that a good move. The whites, meanwhile, get free travel to and from Frobisher, subsidized housing, northern allowance, trucks to travel about in, bright, airy offices in which to write reports and all the glory of bureaucracy in the Arctic ... Until there is self government here, Ottawa's northern missionaries are wasting their time and huge sums of public money."[159]

But there was to be no self-government yet. Carrothers effectively squashed that hope when his commission came out against any division of the Territories for at least another decade. On the contrary, the government handed the Eastern Arctic over to Yellowknife like an unwanted orphan. This was in compliance with the Carrothers report, which recommended that the NWT should remain, at least for the time being, a single political entity, with Yellowknife as its capital, replacing Ottawa as the seat of the territorial government. A strong, officially appointed commissioner, holding the rank of deputy minister, should chair the council and head the executive. As Carrothers saw it, this position would evolve in future into a lieutenant-governorship. At the same time a deputy commissioner, eventually to be chosen from the council, would become a premier. An Executive Council, initially appointed and given cabinet-type powers, would in time consist entirely of elected members. This council, to be referred to henceforth as the legislative assembly, should see its size increased to 14 elected and 4 appointed members. In keeping with these recommendations, there should be a territorial civil service, and provincial-type responsibilities should be devolved to a decentralized territorial administration. At a lower political level, professional advisers and adult educators should encourage and strengthen the growth of local government activities. Within this new structure the central government should concentrate on economic development, with input from regional citizens' groups. Finally, all of the commission's recommendations should be reviewed in 10 years time.

The overall intent of the recommendations was to allow the NWT a means of growth towards provincehood as a single political unit, though provincial status itself was a matter to be held in reserve till some distant future date, contingent mainly on the attainment of a level of economic development capable of providing a much higher degree of fiscal autonomy for the Territories. This lack of fiscal autonomy remains the impassable obstacle to provincial status. In a 70-minute introduction to territorial government plans for the 1980s, Commissioner Stuart Hodgson said on 19 January 1979 that northerners had to be prepared to face economic realities and recognize the size of contributions from outside the NWT. About 80 per cent of the money needed to help the north grow came from the rest of Canada. In the 1960s and 1970s this totalled about $2.4 billion from federal sources. Annual federal and territorial spending worked out at more than $7,500 for every man, woman, and child in the NWT. This was more than the per capita spending in heavily populated Ontario, a province that had the political and financial clout "to decide who forms the federal government."[160] Evolution to provincial status, a long-standing aim of the Advisory Committee on Northern Development in the 1950s and early 1960s, ceased to be an objective of the federal government after the establishment of the resident territorial government in 1967.[161]

The idea of dividing the NWT sank out of sight, if not entirely out of mind, in the ocean of government business, both federal and territorial. Then it bobbed back to the surface in a new guise, having undergone something of a sea change. In 1976 a special Electoral Boundaries Commission published a report recommending division of the huge NWT federal electoral district into two ridings. "The proposed division is the closest division that can be made so as to as much as possible give recognition to the traditional life and cultural patterns of the majority of the indigenous peoples while at the same time paying deference to the other factors" – ease of transport and communication within the electoral districts, and their size and shape relative to one another.[162]

The name of Mackenzie was to be changed to Western Arctic; the Eastern Arctic became not Nunassiaq but Nunatsiaq. "The centre of communications and influence for Nunatsiaq, or the Eastern Arctic," Walter Dinsdale said in the House on 5 April 1976, "will be Baffin Island, at Frobisher Bay."

The idea we are discussing has long been in abeyance, but has come to the fore because of the persistence of the native peoples. They have evinced a desire for greater independence and responsible government. Although this move will not bring about two separate territories as was originally proposed in 1962, at least it is the beginning of a move in the right direction and, as such, all members of this House should support it warmly and heartily. I hope that in due course the division recommended by the Electoral Boundaries Commission will become two new territories. We look forward to the day when the great expectations of that area of Canada will come to pass, that the 3.5 [sic] million square miles of territory rich in resources, human and natural, will eventually come into its own.

Nunatsiaq's first MP was Peter Ittinuar, who won the seat for the New Democratic Party in the general election of 1979. Ittinuar was the first Inuk to take a seat in the Canadian House of Commons. In 1982 he defected to the Liberal party, but in the general election of 4 September 1984 the Nunatsiaq Liberal organization rejected him as a candidate. He ran as an independent and lost.

Electorally the NWT were painlessly divided. But the political bi-
section has yet to be performed. The Carrothers Commission of
1966 came out against immediate division. In deciding two years
later to keep the NWT intact, Jean Chrétien was following the urgings,
not only of the Carrothers Commission, but also of Commissioner
Stuart Hodgson. Hodgson, a big, burly man whom the Inuit called
Umingmak – the musk ox – [163] was known to be so violently against
the idea that even his closest advisers in Yellowknife hesitated to
bring the matter up. "If he's got a closed mind on anything," said
one of his close aides, "it's division."[164] "But the fact remains," journalist Stuart Lake commented, "that the Eastern Arctic is not sharing
in the huge amounts being spent on private development in the
North. Most of it is spent in the Mackenzie."

The Carrothers Commission had recommended a review of the
division question in 10 years time. Ten years later saw the birth of
the electoral riding of Nunatsiaq, but its twin, Nunavut, appeared
to have been aborted soon after conception. In 1977 the Prime
Minister's Office let it be known that the idea was dead:

In the North, as in the South, the Government supports cultural diversity
as a necessary characteristic of Canada. However, political structure is something quite different. Legislative authority and governmental jurisdiction
are not allocated in Canada on grounds that differentiate between the people
on the basis of race. Authority is assigned to legislatures that are repren-
sentatives of all the people within any area on the basis of complete equality.
Jurisdiction is placed in the hands of governments that are responsible
directly or indirectly to the people – again without regard to race. These
are the principles that the Government considers it essential to maintain for
any political regime or governmental structure in the Northwest Territories.[165]

Gurston Dacks argues that this Liberal rejection of Inuit self-government as a racially motivated demand is itself racially motivated;
it implies a desire to prevent that situation from developing in which
a non-native minority might find itself governed by natives.[166] In
fact, the Inuit – and the Déné – proposals establish no racially defined governments. On the contrary, they go out of their way to
affirm the political and other rights of all the residents of the respective areas. The Inuit desire for control of their own affairs is
no more an example of ethnic government than the white control
over the governments of the Northwest Territories or Yukon.

Ideas are hard to kill, as politicians the world over have discovered to their cost. In August 1977 Prime Minister Trudeau appointed C.M. Drury to head a commission charged with investigating if any life was left in the idea to subdivide the NWT. Two and a half years later Drury decided that there was. But this northern Sleeping Beauty, like the original Belle au bois dormant, was surrounded by a wood that Drury considered impenetrable. The *Report of the Special Representative for Constitutional Development in the Northwest Territories*, presented to the prime minister on 6 March 1980, rejected division of the Territories as a solution to the conflicting interests of white residents, Inuit, and Indians. The longer-term external consequences of division had not yet been adequately considered, Drury argued, as if the people of the north should wait the stipulated hundred years before sending in their prince to rouse their heart's desire to life again. In the mean time, Drury made suggestions for changes in government at the territorial and community levels. While these included the much desired devolution of federal and territorial responsibilities, the move to full autonomy for the NWT, or for any part of them, was out of the question. The thorniest obstacle, as Drury saw it, was the gnarled old snag of fiscal dependence on Ottawa. Having reared its territorial offspring to maturity, the federal government was loath to let it go out into the world for fear it could not support itself.

But any headstrong youth yearning for independence will resist parental attempts to keep him at home. Peter Ittinuar, then working for the Inuit Tapirisat of Canada, had told the Task Force on Canadian Unity in April 1978 that through the settlement of outstanding land claims the Inuit were "determined to become full-fledged citizens with the degree of political self-determination necessary to take responsibility once again for running our own affairs." The Inuit, like the Indians and the Metis, were "asking for recognition of our right to survive as a unique group of people within the Canadian mosaic through constitutional guarantees for the preservation of our language, culture and society."[167]

The Eastern Arctic Inuit were pinning their hopes on winning control of the Arctic's rich natural resources. With the authority to license companies and collect royalties, the new government of Nunavut would be able to support itself once the land claims were settled and the resource revenues came pouring in. The Inuit realized that to talk of self-government without revenues was impossible. This is what their land claim was all about. Drury's opposing contention, however, was that regardless of the potential of the NWT as a revenue producer, either for Canada or for Nunavut, huge investments would have to be made to bring the resources into a revenue-producing position. His inference was that such investments would be well beyond the means of any fledgling territory.

The most that Drury could offer NWT residents, though he considered the step inadvisable at the time, was a process for deciding themselves whether the Territories should be administratively divided or not. Warren Allmand, one-time minister of Indian affairs and northern development, showed his contempt for Drury's hesitancy. Less than two months after the special representative's report was published, Allmand put himself forward as the northerners' champion by introducing Private Member's Bill C-254, An Act to Create the Territories of Nunavut and Déné-Mackenzie. Not to be outdone, the more likely prince of the north, Nunatsiaq's own Peter Ittinuar, introduced Bill C-431, An Act to Create the Territories of Nunavut and Mackenzie. Both bills received their first reading on 2 May 1980, but neither was ever debated.

By this time, however, the focus of the controversy had shifted to Yellowknife. The legislative assembly was no longer opposed to changes that by the end of the 1970s began to appear inevitable. In November 1979 it had set up a Special Committee on Unity "to determine the means by which political consensus would be generated amongst the people of the North." The committee presented its final report and recommendations at Iqaluit on 22 October 1980. It found "no significant support" for the current governmental format and called for a referendum on dividing the Territories. Thus emboldened, the assembly "gave commitment in principle to the division of the existing N.W.T. into an Eastern and a Western Territory, recommended a plebiscite on division to be held in the N.W.T. and that a constitutional development committee be established to investigate future constitutional and political development in the Western N.W.T."[168] In May 1981 the assembly voted 12 to 0 in favour of a plebiscite on the question: "Do you favour the creation of a Nunavut Territory?" In November it adopted the Plebiscite Ordinance and amended the question to: "Do you think the Northwest Territories should be divided? Yes or No?"

On 14 April 1982 all northerners aged 19 and over with at least three years' residence were called to the polls to answer this question. Only a little over half of them responded, 9,891 out of 18,962 eligible voters. Of those, 5,560 (56.65 per cent) answered yes; 4,331 (43.35 per cent) answered no. But the Inuit of the Eastern Arctic voted solidly in favour of division. They flocked to the polls in turnouts exceeding 80 per cent in some communities and averaging more than 60 per cent. There could be no doubt about their feelings. The Western Arctic, with communities having a substantial white population, voted just as solidly against division. Political leaders in the east claimed a victory; those in the west were less certain. The minister responsible for the north, John Munro, said that a decision on dividing the Territories could come within two or three months.[169] The federal government took six months to reply. On 26 November 1982 Munro announced its willingness in principle to divide the unwieldy NWT into two separate political entities. Such division was contingent on a number of conditions "that northerners have no trouble accepting." They had to forge a consensus on "such crucial issues as boundaries, future locations of any new administrative centres and the distribution of powers with respect to local, regional and territorial levels of government."[170]

But Munro made clear that nothing would be done until the land claims were finally settled. This displeased the impatient Inuit of the Eastern Arctic. "Any suggestion that division of the Northwest Territories requires prior settlement of land claims," said ITC president John Amagoalik, "appears at complete odds with past federal policy that political change and land claims are not directly related."

The Inuit in their struggle with the sluggish, foot-dragging federal government continued to receive support from Yellowknife. The 1980s have been marked by the growing influence of the legislative assembly, which has acquired a more northern orientation and won the co-operation of Indian and Inuit leaders. On 19 May 1982 members of the legislature voted by 19 to 0 to ask the federal government to divide the Territories in two and to appoint a commission to determine where the border should be. The proposed three-man commission should visit the communities most affected by a border and decide on a boundary between east and west. The Nunavut proposal called for a boundary along the tree-line from the Mackenzie delta to the NWT-Manitoba border near Hudson Bay. The Déné nation wanted to be part of a western territory it would call Denendeh, which, like Nunavut, means "Our Land" in the native language. Denendeh would include Yellowknife and most of the Teritories' Déné, Metis, and white populations. The Western Arctic Inuit, who were close to forming a regional municipality of delta communities, excluding Inuvik, were noncommittal about whether they wanted to be part of Nunavut or part of Denendeh.[171] This independent-minded delta group of about 3,000 Inuit, living within the proposed Denendeh region but claimed for Nunavut by the Eastern Arctic Inuit, have refused to make alliance with either of the proposed new territories and had in fact broken away from the Inuit Tapirisat of Canada (ITC).[172]

Involved in this contentious issue is the fact that the delta business community of Inuvik, with its ties to Yellowknife, Edmonton, and Calgary, clearly preferred to be part of a western territory.[173] The Inuit proponents of Nunavut realized that the inclusion of Inuvik within the boundaries of their eastern-oriented and native-dominated territory was unrealistic. Their suggestion was to set up a new Inuit settlement in the Western Arctic to replace Inuvik so long as a sufficient number of Inuit – at least 400 – wanted to move there.[174]

For two years the Nunavut political leaders wooed the Inuit of the west, the Inuvialuit, and vowed to fight "tooth and nail" to keep all the Inuit together. At the same time the other native groups in the west wanted the Inuvialuit to take their place in the proposed new western territory, for without them the Déné and the Metis would find themselves outnumbered by the white population. The Inuvialuit, however, have maintained their stubborn independence, going their own way in terms of their land claims and leaving other political questions to be decided later. In December 1983, represented by COPE, they signed with the federal government the draft of a final agreement that replaced the 1978 agreement-in-principle that Ottawa had refused to ratify.[175] This Western Arctic claim process culminated on 28 March 1984 when the federal cabinet approved the settlement. The government will pay the Inuit represented by COPE the equivalent of about $90 million in instalments through 1997, the actual sums to be adjusted to take account of inflation. COPE will also receive $10 million for an Economic Enhancement Fund to help develop Inuit industries and businesses. In addition the federal government will finance a $7.5 million Social Development Fund to be used for housing, maintaining the native language, health care, and care of the elderly. With respect to the lands side of the settlement, the Inuit will receive full ownership rights, including ownership of petroleum and other mineral resources, in 13,000 square kilometres, plus title, but without mineral rights, to an additional 78,000 square kilometres.[176] In June 1984 the House of Commons passed the Western Arctic (Inuvialuit) Claims Settlement Act, which approved and made valid the agreement between the federal government and COPE, the first agreement reached under the federal comprehensive land claims policy announced in 1973 (the James Bay agreement was negotiated separately).[177]

A long-contended issue was the boundary between the Eastern and the Western Arctic, between Nunavut and Denendeh. The choice of the tree-line presents difficulties that a boundary commission would have to settle. The tree-line is often hundreds of miles from Inuit communities, yet only one or two miles from Déné communities, and the Déné have hunted in these nearby barren lands for as long as they can remember. A further difficulty arises from the fact that the tree-line, like many river boundaries, is not permanently fixed but has actually moved westwards and continues to change. There are also political difficulties. In January 1985 the two sides working out the division of the Territories reached a tentative agreement on a boundary line running roughly north-south and putting six Mackenzie delta Inuit communities firmly within the western territory. But the 3,000 Inuvialuit feared that they would become submerged by the 17,000 whites and 14,000 Déné and Metis if this proposed new division became permanent. "We are going to end up like the Arabs in Israel," said Mary Lyons, a Western Arctic Inuit teacher. "We are going to be a minority in our own country, the land we were born into. Nunavut speaks to the soul of the Inuit. It's like a promised land for the Eskimos."[178]

Continuing negotiations by a constitutional alliance of Inuit and Déné has led to agreement on a boundary between their respective territories (see endpaper maps). The agreement, reached at Iqaluit on 14 January 1987, was presented to Indian Affairs Minister William McKnight, who described it as "historic, not only in Canada, but in North America ... Aboriginal people have sat down and made a division on a map of their own choosing, not something that was imposed on them by another form of government."[179]

The future of Inuit participation in the political life of Canada, in local, regional, national, and international domains, depends on the resolution of the fundamental issue of dividing the Territories between the Déné west and the Inuit east. The ITC rejects the position that political development can be discussed outside the context of land claims. It disagrees with the view that a decision on territorial division is premature, that it can be postponed indefinitely and then settled by some territorial council mechanism at a future date. What the ITC fears is that the incremental transfer of powers to Yellowknife before the federal government comes to a decision on division of the Territories will reinforce the status quo and prejudice the ultimate decision. While the Drury report failed to recognize the growing support for the creation of a new northern territory, the ITC maintains that various sources are now in agreement on the establishment of Nunavut.

The facts of the case support the Inuit. The NWT are not a single homogeneous unit, either geographically or ethnically. Even their imposed political unity is more apparent than real. At a seminar held in September 1983 to discuss the management of the Canadian north, "it became clear that many of those who study or deal with the Canadian North do not conceive of it as an entity: such a view of the North as a whole has always been undermined by the regional (rather than transnorthern) experience of those people as well as by the separate federal, provincial and territorial political structures. The sectorial division of the northern regions is an obvious feature and the personality of each one of these areas must be respected."[180] Sooner or later the federal government will have to give overt political expression to the regional differences within the present NWT. Division is inevitable.

When division comes, few northerners will object, mainly because the NWT lack above all a sense of historical continuity:

In some respects it can almost be described as the residue of the Canadian province forming process. Its political boundaries have changed several times in the history of our country, and each time as a result of what was taken out, rather than that which was included in. It faces other changes in the future as residents begin to focus on distinctions of geography, transportation and communications patterns, economic potential and political aspirations. In working through for themselves this process of defining the real communities of interest, they wil not likely feel confined by any sense of the historical continuity of the Northwest Territories.[181]

Political Maturity

In 1979 the Inuit's claim to ownership of the land they called Nunavut received a setback. In the spring of that year 113 Inuit hunters from Baker Lake, backed by the community council, the Hunters' and Trappers' Association, and the ITC, took the government of Canada and six mining exploration companies to court. The Inuit claimed aboriginal title to the land and testified that mining exploration was disrupting caribou migrations, making it difficult for the native people to find a traditional source of meat. They wanted the court to establish Inuit ownership of the land and demanded a permanent halt to the mining exploration which, they charged, was a threat to their livelihood. Lawyers for the mining companies – Noranda Exploration, Urangesellschaft of Canada, William Mince, Cominco, Essex Mining Company, and Pan Ocean Oil Ltd – and for the government of Canada argued that aboriginal rights had never existed or, if they had, had been extinguished by federal legislation following the acquisition of the then Northwest Territories from Britain in 1870.

In his decision, handed down on 15 November 1979, Mr Justice Patrick Mahoney ruled that the herds of caribou were indeed declining, but he added that on the basis of probabilities presented to him, he was unable to find that the mining exploration companies were significantly responsible. Nor did he think that exploration activity would change general migration routes. He held that the lands were "subject to the aboriginal right and title of the Inuit to hunt and fish," but he also ruled that these rights should in practice be reconciled with federally established mineral exploration rights that had been granted to the defendant mining companies. Aboriginal hunting rights did not mean ownership, nor did they constitute a good reason for prohibiting the work of the mining companies.[182] On the bright side, as far as the Inuit were concerned, the judgement represented an important affirmation of their aboriginal rights, but Mr Justice Mahoney cast it in terms so favourable to the mining companies that the Inuit were deeply dissatisfied.

The Inuit are not implacably opposed to non-renewable resource projects. The Inuit Development Corporation, for example, has been willing to take part directly in non-renewable resource development by becoming a partner in the Cullaton Lake gold mine in Keewatin. It also agreed in 1980 to supply labour for the construction of Cominco's Polaris Mine on Little Cornwallis Island. Rather, the Inuit oppose projects that would jeopardize the renewable-resource base, the indispensable source of their own independent livelihood and well-being. One of the greatest threats to the Inuit's renewable-resource base lurks in the activities of the powerful multinational oil companies. Panarctic Oils has continued its drilling in the High Arctic, though Canterra curtailed its drilling in the Davis Strait after its exploration yielded disappointing results.[183] Imperial and Aquitaine Canada have also drilled in south Davis Strait. Altogether, geophysical exploration and independent scientific activity in the Eastern Arctic increased tenfold in the latter half of the 1970s. The region "changed from a forgotten backwater to a hub of political interest."[184]

The threat to the Inuit's renewable-resource base from all this activity lies not only in the potential marine pollution from the drilling itself but from the way by which any oil and gas discovered in the Arctic is transported to southern markets. This threat has been hanging over the Inuit since at least 1969, when Humble Oil converted its 150,000-ton supertanker *Manhattan* for Arctic navigation and sent it on a trial voyage through the Northwest Passage to Prudhoe Bay. A decade later the bogey of the north became the Arctic Pilot Project. This project brought together the daunting power of the federal crown corporation Petrocanada and the largest Canadian energy corporation, Dome Petroleum, in an alliance with a number of lesser partners. It would have seen natural gas produced from a field on northern Melville Island, carried through a pipeline to a harbour at the island's southern end, to be liquefied there, transferred to tankers, and shipped through Barrow Strait and the ecologically vital Lancaster Sound to ports on the east coast. Fortunately for the Inuit the project was shelved in 1984, two years before it was due to go into operation.

At community discussions and more formal hearings in Resolute in April 1980, the Inuit made their opposition to the Arctic Pilot Project very clear. Since then they have signalled to the federal government that they have no intention of sitting by and watching any industrial development destroy the source of their hunting and trapping livelihood or of standing idly on the shore and watching oil from tankers pollute the waters on which so many of them depend. Inuit view their own use of the seas and the land as a fundamental right that is woven into the fabric of their lives. They view their environment and their own place in it as an indivisible entity. The inability of outsiders to grasp the Inuit perception of their own world is at the root of most of the present conflicts between the Inuit and their governments. The ITC discussion paper "Building Nunavut," published in May 1983, proposes that the land-fast ice zone is useful as a management area because of its coincidence with the area that Inuit have traditionally used and continue to use offshore. It recommends

that a Nunavut government have particular powers in relation to the fast ice zone, its management, exploitation within it and benefits from its development, and that a functional division of powers respecting the offshore be worked out with the federal government, taking into consideration the marine nature of Nunavut, the revenue requirements of a Nunavut government, the dependence of Inuit on the arctic seas and the health of the marine environment, and the employment and economic benefits which could accrue to the people of Nunavut from offshore development.[185]

Of course, Nunavut has yet to come into existence, let alone acquire the powers it is asking the federal government for. Aware of their limited influence on policy-making, even concerning the land and ocean on which they depend, the native people have reacted to the threatened destruction of their traditional life-style and culture by demanding land settlements before any further development proceeds.

Apart from the domestic political issues involved in the land claims negotiations between the Canadian government and the northern native peoples, the fact that Indians in Alaska and northwestern

Canada and Inuit in Alaska, Canada, and Greenland all faced the same problems tended to bring the native peoples of all three countries together in a recognition of shared interests. Because many of the northern issues could not await official domestic and international recognition or resolution, the native people of the circumpolar countries – including Russia – came together at an Arctic peoples' conference in Copenhagen in 1973. Sponsored by the ITC the conference brought together Canadians, Greenlanders, Saami, and Yuit but yielded no concrete results.[186] However, two later circumpolar conferences confined to Inuit peoples took place, one in Barrow, Alaska, in 1977, and another in Nuuk, formerly Godthaab, in Greenland in 1980. At these conferences the Inuit set up a number of forums for self-help, study, and co-operation. Many executive and working-group meetings have taken place since then, and in Nuuk the delegates laid a solid foundation for a continuing organization called the Inuit Circumpolar Conference (ICC). The ICC met again at Iqaluit in July 1983. Canada, Alaska, and Greenland each sent 18 voting delegates, but the Soviet Union refused permission for any Yuit to attend.[187] The principal goal was the drafting of a comprehensive Arctic policy to be urged on the governments of Denmark, Canada, and the United States. The resolution that the meeting adopted declared boldly that the "Inuit have a right to protect, to manage, to benefit from and to retain access to the arctic environment and its resources, the whole based upon their historical and current use and occupancy of the arctic environment."[188]

The Inuit of Canada, particularly of the Eastern Arctic, have stepped with confidence onto the world political stage. The activity of the multinational oil companies in the Arctic, backed by the political muscle of their respective governments, has helped to stimulate not only an increase in the pace of national native political growth but the pioneering of permanent northern international relations. This development is likely to proceed most rapidly and strongly where relations between the Inuit in the Canadian Eastern Arctic and those in Greenland are concerned. Since 1979 Inuit in Greenland have been busy assuming the responsibilities of home rule, reorganizing functions and developing a unique Inuit society in what had long been a Danish missionary and trading post colony. Self-government for the Inuit in Greenland and the increasing political effectiveness of the Canadian Eastern Arctic Inuit have strengthened the historic cultural affinity between the two groups and encouraged closer co-operation between them in matters of environmental control and resource management.[189] Both, for example, were threatened by the implications of the Arctic Pilot Project. The strengthening of relations between the Canadian and the Greenland Inuit poses new challenges for native diplomats on both sides. One such diplomat is Peter Ittinuar, who, at the Greenland conference in 1980, "displayed the diplomatic and political skills which have made him an invaluable and increasingly acknowledged spokesman for his people both in Canada and overseas."[190]

In these international political developments the role of the Eastern Arctic Inuit has been crucial. A distinct people who speak a unique language, they have values and hopes different from those of the Mackenzie valley. The rejuvenation and growing strength of the Inuit language and culture are evident everywhere in the Eastern Arctic. The sense of social inferiority that clouded the 1960s has dispersed. A new, blue-sky mood of self-confidence and purpose has taken its place. Dramatic changes have occurred in the Eastern Arctic since 1966, when the Carrothers Commission considered the Inuit too unsophisticated politically and too depressed economically to be worthy of self-determination.[191] Today they have shown that they have acquired not only the political sophistication that was lacking in the mid-1960s but also energy, confidence, and a sense of purpose that will help them meet the economic, political, and environmental challenges that face them. They are keenly aware of "the contradiction between the frequently stated southern views that on the one hand, they are too few and too poor to support full government, and on the other, too rich in lands and resources to be allowed control of these for themselves."[192]

The system of government of the NWT is threatened by the political developments of the 1970s and seems unlikely to survive in its present form. Native claims advanced to date have included demands for political control, the setting up and delivery of social programs, preferential treatment in economic activities, and control of land use and wildlife. All of these demands, aside from land and money, impinge on the Northwest Territories Act, which is the territorial constitution.

In the fluid political situation in the north one must never lose sight of the fact that serious differences divide the various groups involved. On the one hand there is the native population, itself divided into the two very different racial and linguistic groups of Inuit and Déné; on the other hand is the non-native population, an extension into the north of the southern culture and economy. Between, and even within, each of these two major groups the political objectives and economic profile differ widely:

As in the Yukon, the native population tends to reside in the smaller and more isolated communities, while the non-native population is concentrated in a few large urban centres. Unlike the Yukon, the minority population does not appear to have that minority position reflected within the political, social and economic structure of the Territory. Non-native residents tend to be highly transient and there is little sign of the emergence within the Northwest Territories of a sizeable, permanent non-native population with ongoing ties to the Territory.

The allocation of political power within the two territories tends to reflect these differences. In Yukon the distribution of legislative seats clearly favours Whitehorse, allowing that centre and its population to dominate the territorial political scene. In the Northwest Territories the situation more closely reflects the southern Canadian pattern, in which the allocation of electoral ridings is weighted towards the rural areas. In addition, and perhaps related to this electoral distribution, native organizations within the Northwest Territories appear to be able to exercice s great deal of political influence directly within the political system at both the federal and territorial levels.[193]

In all the discussions related to the evolution of responsible government in the north, the federal government has to take into consideration two main political points of view. One is that of the territorial government, which claims its legitimacy and growing influence from the northern electorate. One problem here arises from the fact that the political objectives of the territorial government and the Department of Indian Affairs and Northern Development (DIAND) are growing further and further apart. Mike Moore and Gary Vanderhaden argue that the north's political gains during the first half of the 1980s have been won "despite the advice of DIAND and not because of it. This discrepancy between the political objectives of the GNWT [government of the NWT] and DIAND owes much to DIAND's interpretation of its responsibility for managing 'northern development.' DIAND's approach to managing the north poses, in our view, the major stumbling block in the constitutional development of the north."[194]

The second point of view is that of the different native organizations to which the government is bound by the need to negotiate a settlement of comprehensive claims within a constitutionally accepted concept of aboriginal rights. The constitutional conference of 1983 recognized the principle of native rights, but so far these have remained undefined, though the process of trying to tie them down goes on:

In the process of defining and entrenching aboriginal rights, NWT representatives at the constitutional conferences can be expected to advocate a broad interpretation of aboriginal rights to include guaranteed permanent representation for aboriginal people in national, territorial and even in local political institutions, economic catch-up measures, and special rights regarding the harvesting of fish and wildlife. So far, Ottawa has shown the least interest in making concessions on guaranteed representation in political institutions. Groups such as the Dene Nation and Inuit Tapirisat will have the most to say on political guarantees for aboriginal people; they will assert that the NWT offers a unique opportunity to protect and nurture aboriginal rights in Canada – which might be the basis for an ideology.[195]

Peter Ittinuar charges that the development of a political ideology in the north has so far been based on a southern-style model that evolved gradually in response to the needs of southern Canadians. But this development is inappropriate to the needs of the Inuit and constrains their participation in decisions of vital interest to them. The risk is that a constantly frustrated northern native people might suffer severe and irreversible disillusionment and withdraw completely from the federal and territorial political process:

If the trend continues, it is possible that Inuit participation in government will not increase as substantially as it has in the recent past. People naturally seek an arena which is conducive to the most effective expression of their views. At present Inuit are more likely to find such an environment within their own organizations. The inevitable increase in participation in Inuit organizations will have positive consequences in terms of obtaining experience and working out solutions to northern problems. However, disproportionately greater participation in non-governmental and exclusive native organizations may result in the development of a set of parallel institutions with a clear voice for Inuit interests but no power to implement their positions. The optimal situation is one in which Inuit participation is encouraged in all types of political institutions.[196]

Ittinuar argues: "The key to sustained and effective Inuit participation in politics does not lie in further elaboration and consolidation of existing structures, nor in tinkering with existing mechanisms for decision-making. It lies in the formal constitutional recognition of the Inuit's fundamental right to determine their own future and to develop the institutions and procedures most appropriate to the expression of their deepest concerns." So the Inuit themselves are helping to draw up a constitution for their new northern territory of Nunavut. Early in 1983 the Nunavut Constitutional Forum was inaugurated under the chairmanship of Dennis Patterson, the NWT associate minister for aboriginal rights. This forum is the vehicle through which the elected leaders of Nunavut are developing their proposals for the creation of a government. At Rankin Inlet on 4 October 1983 the forum started a tour of 20 Eastern Arctic communities to gather opinions from the residents as to how the future government should be run and where the new territorial capital should be. Suggestions for the site of the capital have included Iqaluit, Rankin Inlet, Cambridge Bay, and Baker Lake.[197] Wherever the seat of government might eventually be, the creation of the new, predominantly Inuit territory would guarantee the Inuit a majority government whose official language would be Inuktitut. The Subcommittee on Division tabled in the NWT legislative assembly in September 1983 a 400-page study on how the administrative changeover would be effected.[198]

All of this feverish activity may be premature. Ottawa has given no indication that it is prepared to concede more than an advisory role to a Nunavut government. In its announcement of approval in principle in November 1982 the federal government remained silent on the question of resource revenue sharing and on all other resource issues. This silence has been a focus of criticism from northern leaders, both native and non-native. The federal government, however, can be under no doubt about the political motivation of the northern native peoples. At the NWT election of 21 November 1983, for which the size of the council had been increased the previous June from 22 to 24, with a new riding each for the Western Subarctic and the Eastern Arctic,[199] a huge turnout – 70 per cent on average in most ridings, with 95 per cent in some – returned 13 native people out of the 24. A handful of these new members spoke only Inuktitut.[200]

Commissioner John Parker predicted on election night that the new Eastern Arctic members might want to flex their political muscle more in the new assembly. In the previous legislature only two had stood for election to the Executive Committee. But the Eastern Arctic members had grumbled about "Western ministers" being unable to understand the nuances of life in the vast other reaches of their treeless territory and had shown a strong desire to gain more governing experience, especially after Ottawa's decision to partition the NWT eventually into two self-governing regions.

Further, the Eastern Arctic Inuit now had the support of the legislative assembly for their Nunavut proposals. Since at least 1980 the two foci of NWT political activity, the assembly and the native groups, had been working together. The assembly had come to recognize the interests of the majority of the population, but this in itself was threatening to become another source of dissension. The assembly's support for the native cause was creating unease among non-renewable-resource developers and non-native businessmen in the NWT. In this sense, as Gurston Dacks observes, "it is not completely accurate to define the evolving situation as one of unity." But there is ample evidence that the native people are quite willing to accept non-traditional forms of economic development once they achieve the security of claims settlements. "With this assurance and the recognition of the inevitability of a majority in the Assembly sympathetic to the native claims," Dacks goes on, "the tone of territorial politics is changing. It is no longer fashionable to openly attack the claims. Rather, most people are attempting to come to terms with the philosophy and to work out the details of the claims. So long as no provocative event occurs to deflect this process, the N.W.T. for the first time in its history will be able to address the real political question, which is its relationship with the South. Whatever the outcome of this struggle, at least it can be said that the N.W.T. will approach it much more united than at any time in the past."[201]

Notes

ABBREVIATIONS

DINA   Library, Department of Indian and Northern Affairs, Hull, Quebec

PARC   Public Archives Record Centre, Ottawa (temporary storage only; material is periodically transferred from PARC to RG 85.)

RG 85   Public Archives of Canada, Ottawa, Record Group 85 (Northern Affairs)

RCMP   Historiad Section, RCMP Headquarters, Ottawa

PREFACE

1   Climatic information in this section comes mainly from J. Brian Bird, *Physiography of Arctic Canada* (Baltimore: Johns Hopkins University Press 1967), 14–21.

2   Henry B. Collins, "Bering Strait to Greenland" (Montreal: Arctic Institute of North America 1962), Technical Paper No. 11, 126–39.

3   William E. Taylor, "Hypothesis on the Origin of Canadian Arctic Thule Culture," *American Antiquity* 28 (1963): 459–62.

4   Jorgen Meldgaard, "On the Formative Period of the Dorset Culture" (Montreal: Arctic Institute of North America), Technical Paper No. 11, 92–5.

5   Taylor, "Hypothesis," 459.

6   Diamond Jenness, "Eskimo Administration II: Canada" (Montreal: Arctic Institute of North America 1964), Technical Paper No. 14, 47.

7   Margaret Atwood, *Survival* (Toronto: Anansi 1972), 32–3.

8   Ulli Steltzer, *Inuit: The North in Transition* (Vancouver: Douglas and

McIntyre 1982), 43.

9 In a plebiscite on 10 December 1984 the people of Frobisher Bay
   voted by 310 to 213 to change the name of the town back to the
   original Inuit name of Iqaluit, which means "fish." The change
   became effective on 1 January 1987. The name of the former Inuit
   camp and the latter Inuit village that occupied the site was usually
   spelt Ikaluit. I have retained this spelling to distinguish the old
   camp and village from the modern town (Iqaluit).

10 Doug Wilkinson, "A Vanishing Canadian," *Beaver* 289 (1959): 25.

INTRODUCTION

1 Harwood Steele, *Policing the Arctic* (London: Jarrolds 1936), 226.

2 Hugh Brody, *The People's Land* (Harmondsworth: Penguin Books
   1975), 18.

3 Morris Zaslov, "Administering the Arctic Islands 1880–1940: Policemen, Missionaries, Fur Traders," in *A Century of Canada's Arctic
   Islands, 1880–1980*, edited by Morris Zaslov (Ottawa: Royal Society
   of Canada 1981), 66–7.

4 Diamond Jenness, "A Demographic Enquiry into the Eskimo Population," *Geographical Review* 19 (1929): 336–7.

5 Diamond Jenness, "Eskimo Administration II: Canada" (Montreal:
   Arctic Institute of North America 1964), Technical Paper No. 14,
   32–3.

6 Richard J. Diubaldo, "The Absurd Little Mouse: When Eskimos
   Became Indians," *Journal of Canadian Studies* 16, No. 2 (1981): 35.

7 Quoted by Jenness, "Eskimo Administration II," 37.

8 See Diubaldo, "Absurd Little Mouse."

9 Zaslov, "Administering the Arctic Islands," 75.

10 Herbert Patric Lee, *Policing the Top of the World* (London: John
    Lane 1928). See also the *Annual Reports* of the commissioner of the
    RCMP, the annual issues of *Scarlet and Gold*, and the original patrol
    reports in the Historiad Section, RCMP Headquarters, Ottawa.

11 Zaslov, "Administering the Arctic Islands," 78.

12 Trevor Lloyd, "Changing Greenland," *Beaver* 289 (1959): 42.

13 Harold Adams Innis, *The Fur Trade in Canada* (New Haven: Yale
    University Press 1930), 370.

14 RG 85, Vol. 1069, File 251–1, Pt. 1, Gibson to Chesshire, 11 May
    1943.

15 Ibid, Gibson to McKeand, 29 July 1943.

16 Ibid, McKeand to Gibson, 19 October 1943.

17 Ibid, Gibson to McKeand, 18 October 1943.

18 Ibid, Gibson to Chesshire, 11 December 1943.

19   Ibid, Chesshire to Gibson, 20 December 1943.

20   Ibid, Gibson to Commissioner, RCMP, 1 February 1944.

21   Ibid, McKeand to Gibson, undated.

22   Jenness, "Eskimo Administration," 76.

23   RG 85, Vol. 1069, File 251-1, Pt. 1, Deputy Commissioner, NWT, to Manning, 11 May 1943.

24   Ibid, unsigned memo for McKeand, 30 April 1943.

25   RG 85, Vol. 955, File 13379, Pt. 1, J.L. Robinson, "Preliminary Report and Recommendations for the Administration of Canada's Eastern Arctic," 26 October 1943.

26   Jenness, "Eskimo Administration," 77.

CHAPTER ONE

1   Franz Boas, *The Central Eskimo* (Lincoln: University of Nebraska Press 1964), 11.

2   Edward Moffat Weyer, *The Eskimos: Their Environment and Folkways* (New Haven: Yale University Press 1932), 112.

3   Harold E. Driver, *Indians of North America* (Chicago: University of Chicago Press), Map 15.

4   RG 85, Vol. 1002, File 16480, Pt. 1, J.L. Robinson, "Settlements in the Canadian Eastern Arctic," 1946.

5   DINA, N.O. Christensen, "Some Information on Canadian Eskimos" (1953), 7.

6   Hugh Brody, *The People's Land* (Harmondsworth: Penguin Books 1975, 167.

7   Ibid, 131.

8   RCMP Patrol Report: Native Camps in Frobisher Bay Area, 4–6 December 1952.

9   Gontran de Poncins, *Kabloona* (Chicago: Time-Life Books 1965), 60.

10   RG 85, Vol. 1119, File 1000/167, Pt. 1, Cape Dorset Welfare Teacher's Report, January 1951.

11   RG 85, Vol. 1120, File 1000/167, Pt. 2, Cape Dorset Welfare Teacher's Report, February 1955.

12   RG 85, Vol. 1119, File 1000/167, Pt. 1, Cape Dorset Welfare Teacher's Report, March 1951.

13   Ibid, Cape Dorset Welfare Teacher's Report, January 1951.

14   RG 85, Vol. 1234, File 251-1, Pt. 2, Larsen to Commissioner, RCMP, 30 October 1951.

15   Ibid, Cantley to Wright, 20 November 1951.

16   RG 85, Vol. 1267, File 1000/169, Pt. 7, Memo re Eskimo houses at Frobisher Bay, 4 June 1956.

17   RG 85, Vol. 1349, File 1000/167, Pt. 5, RCMP Report, Cape Dorset, 27 April 1958.

18   RG 85, Vol. 1360, File 252-5/166, Pt. 1, RCMP Report, Lake Harbour, 11 May 1959.

19   PARC, N233, File 1000/170, Pt. 2, RCMP Report, Pangnirtung, 24 March 1960.

20   RG 85, Vol. 1360, File 252-5/166, Pt. 1, RCMP Report, Lake Harbour, 11 May 1959.

21   PARC, N233, File 1000/170, Pt. 2, RCMP Report, Pangnirtung, 24 March 1960.

22   Canada, Department of National Health and Welfare, *Annual Report* (1960), 8.

23   RG 85, Vol. 1349, File 1000/167, Pt. 5, RCMP Report, Cape Dorset, 27 April 1958.

24   RG 85, Vol. 1360, File 252-5/166, Pt. 1, RCMP Report, Lake Harbour, 11 May 1959.

25   RG 85, Vol. 1120, File 100/167, Pt. 2, RCMP Annual Report, Lake Harbour, year ending 31 December 1955.

26   RG 85, Vol. 1267, File 1000/169, Pt. 7, Memo re Eskimo houses at Frobisher Bay, 4 June 1956.

27   Ulli Steltzer, *Inuit: The North in Transition* (Vancouver: Douglas and McIntyre 1982), 92

28   Lyn Harrington, "Nursing in the Near North," *Family Herald and Weekly Star*, 29 September 1948, 34.

29   R.A.J. Phillips, "Slum Dwellers of the Wide-open Spaces," *Weekend Magazine* 9, No. 15 (1959): 22.

30   Harrington, "Nursing in the Near North," 34.

31   RG 85, Vol. 1349, File 1000/167, Pt. 5, RCMP Report, Cape Dorset, 27 April 1958.

32   RG 85, Vol. 1119, File 1000/167, Pt. 1, Cape Dorset Welfare Teacher's Report, January 1951.

33   RG 85, Vol. 1349, File 1000/167, Pt. 5, RCMP Report, Cape Dorset, 27 April 1958.

34   RG 85, Vol. 1120, File 1000/167, Pt. 2, Cape Dorset Welfare Teacher's Report, February 1955.

35   Ibid, November 1954.

36   RG 85, Vol. 1071, File 251-5, Pt. 1A, Sivertz to Cunningham, 21 November 1955.

37   RG 85, Vol. 1234, File 201-1-8, Pt. 5, Dr J.A. Hildes, "Report on Visit to the Eastern Arctic," 24 October 1957.

38   RG 85, Vol. 1267, File 1000/169, Pt. 7, Memo re Eskimo houses at Frobisher Bay, 4 June 1956.

39   Ibid, RCMP Annual Report, Frobisher Bay, year ending 31 Decem-

ber 1956.

40 Ibid, Memo re Eskimo houses, 4 June 1956.

41 RG 85, Vol. 555, File 1009/3, Pt. 8, Report re development at Frobisher Bay, 29 November 1955.

42 RG 85, Vol. 1473, File 201-1-8, Pt. 4, Report of the Eastern Arctic Patrol, 13 September 1958.

43 RG 85, Vol. 1349, File 1000/167, Pt. 5, RCMP Annual Report, Lake Harbour, year ending 31 December 1958.

44 RG 85, Vol. 1289, File 303/166, Pt. 1, Marsh to Sivertz, 23 March 1959.

45 RG 85, Vol. 1349, File 1000/169, Pt. 12, Memo from head of Projects Section, 12 February 1959.

46 RG 85, Vol. 1349, File 1000/167, Pt. 5, RCMP Annual Report, Lake Harbour, year ending 31 December 1958.

47 RG 85, Vol. 1349, File 1000/169, Pt. 12, Administrator of the Arctic to Chief, Arctic Division, 23 September 1958

48 RG 85, Vol. 1360, File 207-3, Pt. 7, Director, Arctic Division, to Administrator of the Arctic, 8 November 1961.

49 Ibid.

50 Canada, Department of National Health and Welfare, *Eskimo Mortality and Housing* (1961), 67.

51 RG 85, Vol. 1349, File 1000/167, Pt. 5, RCMP Annual Report, Lake Harbour, year ending 31 December 1958.

52 Canada, Department of National Health and Welfare, *Eskimo Mortality and Housing*, 69.

53 RG 85, Vol. 744, File 207-2, Pt. 4, DEWLine Order 30–44: Canada Eskimo Plan, 1959.

54 RG 85, Vol. 674, File 207-2, Pt. 2, Minutes of meeting, 22 April 1958.

55 RG 85, Vol. 630, File 207-3, Pt. 3, Packwood to Doyle, 9 January 1959.

56 Ibid, Report on 1958 construction operations: DEW Line housing for Eskimo employees, 17 December 1958.

57 Ibid, Robertson to Miller, 24 December 1958.

58 RG 85, Vol. 630, File 207-3, Pt. 4, Bolger to White, 9 September 1959.

59 RG 85, Vol. 630, File 207-3, Pt. 3, Stevenson to Bolger, 2 June 1959.

60 RG 85, Vol. 630, File 207-3, Pt. 4, Packwood to Regional Administrator, Frobisher Bay, 2 December 1959.

61 Ibid, Delaute to Bolger, 9 December 1959.

62 RG 85, Vol. 1360, File 207-3, Pt. 6, Memo from Bond, 14 October 1960.

63 RG 85, Vol. 1360, File 207-3, Pt. 7, Memo from Connelly, 16 No-

vember 1961.

64 RG 85, Vol. 1885, File NR2626-1, Pt. 10, Fournier to McDowall, 2 October 1969.

65 RG 85, Vol. 1911, File NR4/2-8, Pt. 1, Report of the Subcommittee on Eskimo Housing Programs, 25 June 1964.

66 RG 85, Vol. 1382, File 1012-9, Pt. 5, Minutes of meeting, Committee on Eskimo Affairs, 10–11 April 1961.

67 PARC, O-64, File 1000/167, Pt. 7, RCMP Annual Report, Cape Dorset, year ending 31 December 1967.

68 RG 85, Vol. 1382, File 1012-9, Pt. 5, Minutes of meeting, Committee on Eskimo Affairs, 10–11 April 1961.

69 RG 85, Vol. 1911, File NR4/2-8, Pt. 1, Minutes of meeting, Committee on Social Adjustment, 30 June 1964.

70 RG 85, Vol. 745, File 250-5, Pt. 1, Minutes of meeting, Eskimo Community Council, Frobisher Bay, 31 October 1963.

71 Ibid, 10 September 1964.

72 RG 85, Vol. 1911, File NR4/2-8, Pt. 1, Report of the Subcommittee on Eskimo Housing Programs, 25 June 1964.

73 Ibid, Minutes of Meeting, Committee on Social Adjustment, 30 June 1964.

74 Ibid, Report of the Subcommittee on Eskimo Housing Programs, 25 June 1964.

75 Ibid, Minutes of meeting, Committee on Social Adjustment, 4 November 1964.

76 RG 85, Vol. 1890, File 108-4, Pt. 6, Community Planning: topic introduced by W.G. Cleghorn, Northern Conference, Ottawa, 7–14 April 1964.

77 RG 85, Vol. 1885, File NR2626-1, Pt. 10, Hodgson to Deputy Commissioner, NWT, 25 August 1959.

78 Ibid, Hodgson to Chrétien, 25 August 1959.

79 PARC, O-64, File 1000/167, Pt. 7, RCMP Annual Report, Cape Dorset, year ending 31 December 1967.

80 RG 85, Vol. 1885, File NR2626-1, Pt. 10, Davidson to Hodgson, 29 May 1970.

81 PARC, O-64, File 1000/167, Pt. 7, RCMP Annual Report, Cape Dorset, year ending 31 December 1967.

82 *Edmonton Journal*, 21 April 1969.

83 RG 85, Vol. 1885, File NR2626-1, Pt. 10, Hodgson to Chrétien, 25 August 1969.

84 D.K. Thomas and C.T. Thompson, "Eskimo Housing as Planned Culture Change" (Ottawa: Department of Indian Affairs and Northern Development 1972), Social Science Notes 4, 11.

85 RG 85, Vol. 1885, File NR2626-1, Pt. 10, Hodgson to Chrétien, 25

August 1959.

86 Thomas and Thompson, "Eskimo Housing," 11.

87 Ibid, 15.

88 G. Anders, editor, *The East Coast of Baffin Island: An Area Economic Survey* (Ottawa: Department of Indian Affairs and Northern Development 1967), 9.

89 Brody, *The People's Land*, 179–80.

90 Canada, Department of External Affairs, "The Eskimos of Canada," (1975), Reference Paper No. 71.

91 *Edmonton Journal*, 11 February 1975.

92 Northwest Territories Housing Corporation, *Annual Report* 1977.

93 Gabriella Goliger, "Arctic Housing Update," *Habitat* 24, No. 1 (1981): 26.

94 Government of the NWT, Information Release No. 79-075, 15 February 1979.

95 *Native People*, 16 May 1977.

96 Goliger, "Arctic Housing Update," 28.

97 Gaby Perrault-Dorval, "L'habitation nordique" *North/Nord* 29, No. 3 (1982): 39.

98 Government of the NWT, Information Release, No. 79-075, 15 February 1979.

99 Goliger, "Arctic Housing Update," 28.

100 DINA, "Notes on the Northern Policy Statement 1970–1980: A Mid-Term Look at the Native Situation" (n.d.)

101 Goliger, "Arctic Housing Update," 27.

102 Government of the NWT, *Annual Report* (1982), 68.

103 Perrault-Dorval, "L'habitation nordique," 40.

CHAPTER TWO

1 RG 85, Vol. 955, File 13379, Pt. 1, J.L. Robinson, "Preliminary Report and Recommendations for the Administration of Canada's Eastern Arctic," 26 October 1943.

2 RG 85, Vol. 98, File 251-1-2, Pt. 1, McKeand to Gibson, 10 February 1944.

3 RG 85, Vol. 1871, File 550-1, Pt. 2, Gibson to McKeand, 11 Jannuary 1944.

4 Ibid, "Report on Hospital and Medical Facilities of the Northwest Territories," April 1944.

5 RG 85, Vol. 1871, File 550-1, Pt. 1, List of mission hospitals, NWT, 6 December 1941.

6 Ibid, Tabular data re medical administration in the NWT: Medical District No. 7 – Pangnirtung, 9 December 1943.

7   RG 85, Vol. 1871, File 550-1, Pt. 2, "Report on Hospital and Medical Facilities of the Northwest Territories," April 1944.

8   RG 85, Vol. 1871, File 550-1, Pt. 1, List of mission hospitals, NWT, 6 December 1941.

9   RG 85, Vol. 1871, File 550-1, Pt. 2, McKeand to Gibson, 8 June 1944.

10 Ibid, Memo re proposed reorganization of the health and medical services in the Northwest Territories and Eastern Arctic, 16 November 1944.

11 RG 85, Vol. 1871, File 550-1, Pt. 1A, McKeand to Gibson, 28 December 1943.

12 RG 85, Vol. 1871, File 550-1, Pt. 2, McKeand to Gibson, 22 March 1944.

13 RG 85, Vol. 815, File 6954, Pt. 3, Gibson to Millar, 28 November 1941.

14 Ibid, McKeand to Gibson, 27 November 1941.

15 Ibid, McKeand to Gibson, 9 March 1942.

16 Ibid, McKeand to Gibson, 27 November 1941.

17 RG 85, Vol. 1871, File 550-1, Pt. 2, Fleming to Gibson, 15 January 1944.

18 RG 85, Vol. 1506, File 600-1-1, Pt. 2A, Extract from minutes, NWT Council, 3 December 1946.

19 *Albertan* (Calgary), 9 July 1945.

20 RG 85, Vol. 955, File 13379, Pt. 1, Lt T.H. Manning, "Preliminary Report concerning the Eastern Arctic," 1943.

21 *Citizen* (Ottawa), 15 July 1950.

22 RG 85, Vol. 1234, File 251-1, Pt. 2, Press Release, Department of Resources and Development, 22 May 1952.

23 DINA, N.O. Christensen, "Some Information on Canadian Eskimos" (1953), 43.

24 RG 85, Vol. 1234, File 251-1, Pt. 2, Letter from H.A. Larsen, 30 October 1951.

25 Ibid, Cantley to Wright, 20 November 1951.

26 RG 85, Vol. 333, File 1009-3, Pt. 5, Memo re Northern Health Services, Document ND-88 [1954].

27 RG 85, Vol. 365, File 252-5/170, Draft paper re Eskimo Health Worker Programme, July 1958.

28 RG 85, Vol. 333, File 1009-3, Pt. 5, Memo re Northern Health Services, Document ND-88 [1954].

29 RG 85, Vol. 376, File 1009-3, Pt. 6, Memo for Cabinet, 12 April 1954.

30 Canada, Department of Indian Affairs and Northern Development, "Eskimo Population of Canada 1941–1970" (unpublished).

31 J. Lewis Robinson, "Eskimo Population in the Canadian Eastern Arctic," *Canadian Geographical Journal* 29 (1944): 131.

32 RG 85, Vol. 1275, File 164-1, Pt. 5, "Northwest Territories Census–1951."

33 Canada, Department of Indian Affairs and Northern Development, "Eskimo Population of Canada 1951–1971" (unpublished).

34 RG 85, Vol. 555, File 1009-3, Pt. 8, Progress report re Northern Health Services, 20 October 1955.

35 RG 85, Vol. 1355, File 550-8, Pt. 1, Robertson to Cameron, 17 June 1957.

36 Ibid, Minutes of meeting, Permanent Advisory Committee on Northern Health, 26 June 1957.

37 RG 85, Vol. 555, File 1009-3, Pt. 8, Report of committee to consider the co-ordination of medical facilities in the North, 23 November 1955.

38 RG 85, Vol. 674, File 207-2, Pt. 1, Minutes of meeting, Federal Electric Corporation and federal government, 23 May 1957.

39 RG 85, Vol. 649, File 1009-3-8, Pt. 1, Minutes of meeting re co-ordination of health facilities in the North, 9 November 1955.

40 RG 85, Vol. 744, File 207-2, Pt. 4, DEWLine Order 30-44: Canada Eskimo Plan, 1959.

41 RG 85, Vol. 1360, File 207-5, Pt. 2, Memo re medical arrangements on the DEW Line, September 1961.

42 Ibid.

43 Ibid, Cruzen to Associate Director, Indian and Northern Health Services, 23 February 1962.

44 Ibid, Memo re medical arrangements on the DEW Line, September 1961.

45 RG 85, Vol. 649, File 1009-3-8, Pt. 1, Report on potential users of medical facilities in the North, 22 November 1955. The total number of 2,280 potential users was made up of 1,743 Inuit, 90 civilians, 16 Canadian military personnel, 325 US military personnel, and 106 DEW Line staff.

46 Chief Medical Officer, Government of the NWT, *Report on Health Conditions in the Northwest Territories* (1981), 3.

47 RCMP Disc Lists, Department of Indian and Northern Affairs, Hull, Quebec; Statistics Canada 1961 and 1971 census returns; data tabulated by Statistics Division, Department of Indian Affairs and Northern Development.

48 Milton M.R. Freeman, "The Significance of Demographic Changes Occurring in the Canadian East Arctic," *Anthropologica* 13 (1971): 230.

49 Ibid, 231.

50 Ibid, 234.
51 *Midnite Sun*, Summer 1969, 4.
52 Ibid, Spring 1970, 8.
53 *Drum*, 7 November 1975.
54 *Inukshuk*, 27 August 1975.
55 Ibid, 8 January 1975.
56 Government of the NWT, *Annual Report* (1982), 58.
57 Government of the NWT, Information Release No. 78-043, 3 February 1978.
58 Government of the NWT, News Release No. 79-184, n.d.
59 Information on Resolute Bay and its nursing station comes largely from Michael Dear, "Planning Community Health Services in Arctic Canada," *Musk-Ox* 19 (1976): 34.
60 Government of the NWT, Information Release No. 78-040, 2 February 1978.
61 Dear, "Planning Community Health Services," 35.
62 Geoffrey R. Weller, "The Delivery of Health Services in the Canadian North," *Journal of Canadian Studies* 16, no. 2 (1981): 75.
63 Chief Medical Officer, Government of the NWT, *Report on Health Conditions in the Northwest Territories* (1974), 18–19.
64 Ibid.
65 RG 85, Vol. 834, File 7387, Pt. 1, Dr A. Collins, Medical Report, Eastern Arctic Patrol, 1945.
66 Ibid, Dr G.S. McCarthy and Dr C. Laidlaw, Medical Report, Eastern Arctic Patrol, 1945.
67 RG 85, Vol. 834, File 7387, Pt. 2, Dr H.W. Lewis, Medical Report, Eastern Arctic Patrol, 1947.
68 RG 85, Vol. 984, File 15117, X-ray Survey of Eskimos," Eastern Arctic Patrol, 1946.
69 Canada, Department of National Health and Welfare, *Eskimo Mortality and Housing* (1961), 78.
70 RG 85, Vol. 1234, File 201-1-8, Pt. 5, Dr J.A. Hildes, "Report on Visit to the Eastern Arctic," 24 October 1957.
71 RG 85, Vol. 1355, File 1003-20-1, Pt. 2, *Indian Health Services Newsletter* (Christmas 1954): 12–13.
72 RG 85, Vol. 834, File 7387, Pt. 2, Sinclair to Moore, 26 May 1952.
73 RG 85, Vol. 1474, File 252-3, Pt. 6, Frazer to Cunningham, 25 November 1954.
74 RG 85, Vol. 1355, File 1003-20-1, Pt. 2, *Indian Health Services Newsletter* (Christmas 1954): 16.
75 Ibid.
76 *House of Commons Debates*, 21 March 1956.
77 Canada, Department of Northern Affairs and National Resources,

Annual Report (1955), 103.

78   Ibid (1957), 103.

79   RG 85, Vol. 649, File 1009-3, Pt. 9, "Annual Report of Government Activities in the North," January 1957.

80   RG 85, Vol. 1474, File 252-3, Pt. 6, Marsh to St Laurent, 10 November 1954.

81   Ibid, Cunningham to Robertson, 26 November 1954.

82   Corinne Hodgson, "The Social and Political Implications of Tuberculosis among Native Canadians," *Canadian Review of Sociology and Anthropology* 19 (1982): 50.

83   RG 85, Vol. 1474, File 252-3, Pt. 6, Cunningham to Robertson, 26 November 1954.

84   Ibid, Cameron to Robertson, 6 December 1954.

85   RG 85, Vol. 1903, File 1009-13, Pt. 1, Preliminary report of medical party, Eastern Arctic Patrol, 1955.

86   RG 85, Vol. 1911, File NR4/2-8, Pt. 1, "Report on Northern Housing," 18 December 1964.

87   Ibid.

88   Canada, Department of Northern Affairs and National Resources, *Report on Health Conditions in the Northwest Territories* (1965).

89   Government of the NWT, *Annual Report* (1982), 60.

90   RG 85, Vol. 1506, File 600-1-1, Pt. 2A, Gibson to Moore, 30 November 1946.

91   RG 85, Vol. 1127, File 201-1-8, Pt. 2, J.G. Wright, "Report of the Eastern Arctic Patrol," 1946.

92   RG 85, Vol. 815, File 6954, Pt. 4, Dr G.E. Gaulton, "Annual Report for Year Ending 31 August 1964."

93   *Daily Star* (Montreal), 9 July 1948.

94   RG 85, Vol. 834, File 7387, Pt. 1, Dr D. Jordan, Medical Report, Eastern Arctic Patrol, 1945.

95   RG 85, Vol. 1234, File 251-1, Pt. 2, LeCapelain to Acting Deputy Minister, Department of Resources and Development, 8 December 1952.

96   RG 85, Vol. 834, File 7387, Pt. 2, Dr H.W. Lewis, Medical Report, Eastern Arctic Patrol, 1947.

97   RG 85, Vol. 480, File 252-1-2, Pt. 3, Policy circular, 20 March 1948.

98   RG 85, Vol. 1127, File 201-1-8, Pt. 2A, "Report of the Eastern Arctic Patrol," 1950.

99   RCMP, Patrol Report: Lake Harbour to Cape Dorset and return, 25 March to 14 April 1949.

100   RG 85, Vol. 834, File 7387, Pt. 2, Dr H.W. Lewis, Medical Report, Eastern Arctic Patrol, 1947.

101   Otto Schaeffer, "When the Eskimo Comes to Town," *Nutrition To-*

day 6, no. 6 (1971): 15–16.

102   Canada, Department of Northern Affairs and National Resource, *Report on Health Conditions in the Northwest Territories* (1961), 6.

103   RG 85, Vol. 1119, File 1000/167, Pt. 1, Cape Dorset Welfare Teacher's Report, October 1950.

104   RG 85, Vol. 1514, File 1012-1, Pt. 7, Minutes of meeting, Committee on Eskimo Affairs, 26 May 1958.

105   Ibid, Sivertz to Assistant Deputy Minister, Department of Northern Affairs and National Resources, 30 June 1958.

106   Canada, Dominion Bureau of Statistics, *Canada Yearbook* (1960), 237.

107   RG 85, Vol. 365, File 252-5/170, Pt. 1, Draft paper re Eskimo Health Worker Programme, July 1958.

108   Canada, Department of Northern Affairs and National Resources, *Report on Health Conditions in the Northwest Territories* (1962).

109   Chief Medical Officer, Government of the NWT, *Report on Health Conditions in the Northwest Territories* (1978), 11.

110   Ibid (1979), 9.

111   Ibid (1981), 5.

112   *Globe and Mail* (Toronto), 1 February 1980.

113   *Daily Star* (Montreal), 9 July 1948.

114   RG 85, Vol. 1036, File 20696, Pt. 1, Memo re Fur Trade in the Canadian Arctic, 23 September 1949.

115   RG 85, Vol. 815, File 6954, Pt. 3, Dr J.A. Bildfell, General Medical Report for the Year September 1940 to September 1941–Pangnirtung.

116   RG 85, Vol. 815, File 6954, Pt. 3, McKeand to Gibson, 18 February 1942.

117   RG 85, Vol. 815, File 6954, Pt. 1, RCMP Report, Pangnirtung, 30 June 1929.

118   RG 85, Vol. 815, File 6954, Pt. 2, McKeand to Gibson, 14 March 1942.

119   RG 85, Vol. 98, File 251-1-2, Pt. 1, Winifred Hinton, "A Study of Food Habits and Supplies in the Northwest Territories," February 1944.

120   RG 85, Vol. 1069, File 251-1, Pt. 1, McKeand to Gibson [February 1944].

121   RG 85, Vol. 98, File 252-1-2, Pt. 1, Gibson to Cameron, 16 January 1947.

122   Ibid, Gibson to Chesshire, 7 March 1947.

123   RG 85, Vol. 815, File 6954, Pt. 3, McKeand to Gibson, 24 November 1941.

124   RG 85, Vol. 480, File 252-1-2, Pt. 3, Sivertz to Beaton, 30 May 1955.

125   Ibid, Margaret Lock and L.B. Pett, "Better Bannock," 17 July 1952.

126 Ibid, Policy Circular: Issue of Milk and Pablum on Family Allowance Credits, n.d.

127 Ibid, Lock and Pett, "Better Bannock."

128 Ibid, Pett to Moore, 8 December 1954.

129 RG 85, Vol. 684, File A680-1-14, Pt. 2, Anne Berndtsson, Memo re home economics programme, 20 October 1961.

130 *Drum*, 22 February 1974.

131 Government of the NWT, Information Release No. 77-055, 17 February 1977.

132 Robinson, "Eskimo Population," 142.

133 RG 85, Vol. 1871, File 550-1, Pt. 1A, Memo for the Northwest Territories Council, January 1944.

134 RG 85, Vol. 834, File 7387, Pt. 1, Dr A. Collins, Medical Report, Eastern Arctic Patrol, 1945.

135 RG 85, Vol. 815, File 6954, Pt. 3, Thom to McKeand, 23 October 1941.

136 Ibid, McKeand to Gibson, 5 February 1942.

137 Ibid, McKeand to Gibson, 18 February 1942.

138 Ibid, Dr J.A. Bildfell, Medical Report for the Year 1941–42–Pangnirtung.

139 RCMP, Patrol Report: Lake Harbour to Cape Dorset district, 19 February to 16 March 1943.

140 "Cape Dorset," DINA, May 1955.

141 RG 85, Vol. 1679, File 405-5-1, Pt. 6, Chesshire to Gibson, 8 June 1943.

142 RG 85, Vol. 834, File 7387, Pt. 1, Dr A. Collins, Medical Report, Eastern Arctic Patrol, 1945.

143 RG 85, Vol. 1127, File 201-1-8, Pt. 2, "Report of the Eastern Arctic Patrol," 1 August 1945.

144 RCMP, Patrol Report: Lake Harbour to Cape Dorset, 27 March to 25 April 1946.

145 PARC, N233, File 1000/170, Pt. 1, Pangnirtung Community Teacher's Report, February 1959.

146 RG 85, Vol. 1234, File 201-1-8, Pt. 5, Dr J.A. Hildes, "Report on Visit to the Eastern Arctic," 24 October 1957.

147 RG 85, Vol. 1120, File 1000/167, Pt. 2, James Houston, "Report re Conditions of Eskimos – Cape Dorset" [Autumn 1954].

148 RG 85, Vol. 1903, File 1009-13, Pt. 1, Preliminary report of medical party, Eastern Arctic Patrol, 1955.

149 Canada, Department of Northern Affairs and National Resources, *Report on Health Conditions in the Northwest Territories* (1962).

150 Weller, "The Delivery of Health Services," 71.

151 Government of the NWT, *Annual Report* (1980), 28.

152 Government of the NWT, News Release No. 79-238, 16 November 1979.
153 Dear, "Planning Community Health Services," 31.
154 W.J. Wacko, *Observations and Recommendations respecting Alcohol and Drugs in the Northwest Territories* (Yellowknife: Department of Social Development 1973).
155 Chief Medical Officer, Government of the NWT, *Report on Health Conditions in the Northwest Territories* (1975), 43.
156 DINA, "Notes on the Northern Policy Statement 1970–1980: A Mid-Term Look at the Native Situation," (n.d.).

CHAPTER THREE

1   RG 85, Vol. 1505, File 600-1-1, Pt. 2, Data re schools in the NWT, August 1944.
2   RG 85, Vol. 1506, File 600-1-1, Pt. 2A, Fleming to Gibson, 19 November 1946.
3   Ibid, Wright to Gibson, 19 November 1946.
4   Trevor Lloyd, "Changing Greenland," *Beaver* 289 (1959): 42.
5   RG 85, Vol. 1505, File 600-1-1, Pt. 2, Gibson to Fleming, 4 December 1945.
6   W.T. Larmour, "Eskimo Education," *Arctic Circular* 3, no. 5 (1950): 51.
7   Paul Welsman, "Education of Native People in the Northwest Territories," in *The North in Transition*, edited by Nils Orvik and Kirk R. Patterson (Kingston: Queen's University. Centre for International Relations 1976), 27.
8   RG 85, Vol. 1506, File 600-1-1, Pt. 2A, Extract from minutes of meeting, NWT Council, 23 May 1947.
9   Ibid, Extract from minutes of meeting, NWT Council, 30 June 1947.
10 Dr Moore was unable to complete his survey in the Eastern Arctic because of the loss of the patrol ship *Nascopie*, which foundered off Cape Dorset on 22 July 1947. An education officer of the administration made a partial review in 1948. Then in 1953 education officers from both the Eastern and Western Arctic patrols carried out an extensive review in the field. Similar surveys and inspection trips were thenceforth made annually, the policy being to visit all schools at least once a year. See RG 85, Vol. 1506, File 600-1-1, Pt. 6, J.O. Jacobson, "Report on Eskimo Education," 27 October 1954.
11 RG 85, Vol. 1506, File 600-1-1, Pt. 3, Minutes of meeting, Subcommittee on Eskimo Education, 15 October 1953.
12 RG 85, Vol. 300, File 1009-3, Pt. 1, Memo re administration of the branches of the Department of Resources and Development in the

northern portions of Canada, n.d.

13 RG 85, Vol. 1513, File 1012-1, Pt. 1, Report of meeting, Subcommittee on Eskimo Education, 26 September 1952.

14 Fred Bruemmer, "The Best of Both Worlds," *Weekend Magazine* 24, no. 37 (1974): 2.

15 Larmour, "Eskimo Education," 54.

16 Dermot R. Collis, Review of *The Use of Greenlandic and Danish in Greenlandic Schools 1950–1978* by Brent Gynther, *Inuit Studies* 7, no. 1 (1983): 166.

17 RG 85, Vol. 1507, File 600-1-1, Pt. 7, "Education in the Northwest Territories: Policy Recommendations," 4 January 1955.

18 Ibid, "Report on Education in Canada's Northland," 12 December 1954.

19 Reported in the *Calgary Herald*, 6 January 1966.

20 Hugh Brody, *The People's Land* (Harmondsworth: Penguin Books 1975), 186.

21 Charles W. Hobart, "Some Consequences of Residential Schooling," *Journal of American Indian Education* 7, no. 2 (1968): 7–17.

22 David Omar Born, "Eskimo Education and the Trauma of Social Change" (Ottawa: Department of Indian and Northern Affairs 1970), Northern Science Research Group, Social Science Notes 1, 24.

23 *Edmonton Journal*, 28 August 1973.

24 RG 85, Vol. 1507, File 600-1-1, Pt. 7, "Report on Education in Canada's Northland," 12 December 1954.

25 RG 85, Vol. 414, File 1009-3, Pt. 7, Memo re administrative implications of the DEW Line, 2 March 1955.

26 RG 85, Vol. 1507, File 600-1-1, Pt. 7, Memo for the Cabinet, February 1955.

27 RG 85, Vol. 645, File 1009-3, Pt. 12, "Report of Government Activities in the North," 1958.

28 RG 85, Vol. 1513, File 1012-1, Pt. 1, Report of meeting, Subcommittee on Eskimo Education, 26 September 1952.

29 RG 85, Vol. 1506, File 600-1-1, Pt. 5, Directory of schools in the NWT, September 1953.

30 RG 85, Vol. 1514, File 1012-1, Pt. 3, Minutes of meeting, Subcommittee on Eskimo Education, 1 April 1953.

31 RG 85, Vol. 1513, File 1012-1, Pt. 1, Cunningham to Deputy Minister, Department of Resources and Development, 8 October 1952.

32 Ibid, Minutes of meeting, Committee on Eskimo Affairs, 16 October 1952.

33 RG 85, Vol. 1507, File 600-1-1, Pt. 7, Memo for the Cabinet, February 1955.

34   RG 85, Vol. 1207, File 201-1-8, Pt. 3, "Report of the Eastern Arctic Patrol," 1951.

35   R.A.J. Phillips, "Slum Dwellers of the Wide-open Spaces," *Weekend Magazine* 9, no. 15 (1959): 20.

36   *Calgary Herald*, 29 January 1959.

37   RG 85, Vol. 1507, File 600-1-1, Pt. 7, Memo for the Cabinet, February 1955.

38   Ibid, "Proposed Projects for the Eastern and Western Arctic Covering a Period of Five Years," January 1955.

39   W. Ivan Mouat, "Education in the Arctic District," *Musk-Ox* 7 (1970): 4.

40   Robert Davis and Mark Zannis, *The Genocide Machine in Canada: The Pacification of the North* (Montreal: Black Rose Books 1973), 103–4.

41   Welsman, "Education of Native People," 31.

42   David Finley, "Why Eskimo Education Isn't Working," *Phi Delta Kappan* 64 (1983): 581.

43   Georgia, "Arctic Schooling Alternatives: Assimilation or Adaptation," *North/Nord* 27, no. 3 (1980): 10.

44   Mouat, "Education in the Arctic District," 6.

45   Welsman, "Education of Native People," 29.

46   Mouat, "Education in the Arctic District," 6.

47   D.W. Simpson, D.K.F. Wattie, et al, "The Role and Impact of the Educational Program in the Process of Change in Canadian Eskimo Communities," in *Proceedings of a Symposium on the Educational Process and Social Change in a Specialized Environmental Milieu* (Edmonton: University of Alberta, Boreal Institute 1968), 13.

48   Born, "Eskimo Education," 24.

49   Bernard C. Gillie, *Survey of Education, Northwest Territories* (Yellowknife: Government of the NWT, Department of Education 1972), 8.

50   Collis, Review, 166.

51   RG 85, Vol. 744, File 207-2, Pt. 4, Superintendant of Schools to Administrator of the Arctic, 6 April 1961.

52   RG 85, Vol. 744, File 207-2, Pt. 5, Minutes of meeting, Federal Electric Corporation and departments of the government of Canada, 24 July 1961.

53   RG 85, Vol. 744, File 207-2, Pt. 4, Cruzen to the Deputy Minister, Department of Northern Affairs and National Resources, 21 March 1960.

54   RG 85, Vol. 1435, File 600-1-5, Pt. 3, Merril to Phillips, 26 May 1960.

55   RG 85, Vol. 744, File 207-2, Pt. 4, Administrator of the Arctic to

the Superintendent of Schools, 21 April 1961.

56   RG 85, Vol. 1435, File 600-1-5, Pt. 3, Stevenson to Phillips, 8 April 1963.

57   Ibid, Bolger to Phillips, 10 July 1961.

58   RG 85, Vol. 1435, File 600-1-5, Pt. 5, "Memorandum for the Cabinet: A Five-Year Education Plan for the Northwest Territories and Northern Quebec, 1965–1970," 9 February 1965.

59   RG 85, Vol. 1435, File 600-1-5, Pt. 3, Phillips to Thorsteinsson, 8 January 1963.

60   RG 85, Vol. 1435, File 600-1-5, Pt. 5, Memorandum for the Cabinet, 9 February 1965.

61   Ibid.

62   Robert E. Johns, "History of Administration of Schools, N.W.T.," *Musk-Ox* 18 (1976): 50.

63   Simpson, Wattie, et al, "The Role and Impact of the Educational Program," 5.

64   Canada, Department of Indian Affairs and Northern Development, *Education Review* (1966): 6.

65   Del M. Koenig, *Northern People and Higher Education: Realities and Possibilities* (Ottawa: Association of Universities and Colleges 1975), 158.

66   RG 85, Vol. 1130, File 254-1, Pt. 1, Jenness to Camsell, November 1925.

67   RG 85, Vol. 1435, File 600-1-5, Pt. 5, Memorandum for the Cabinet, 9 February 1965.

68   *Whitehorse Star*, 15 July 1968.

69   *Edmonton Journal*, 14 July 1971.

70   Ibid.

71   *Lethbridge Hearld*, 15 September 1967.

72   *Globe and Mail* (Toronto), 24 January 1963.

73   Simpson, Wattie, et al, "The Role and Impact of the Educational Program," 13.

74   *Lethbridge Herald*, 15 September 1967.

75   *Globe and Mail*, 21 September 1966.

76   *Edmonton Journal*, 17 January 1963.

77   D.A. Davidson, "The People in the North," in *Policies of Northern Development*, edited by Nils Orvik (Kingston: Queen's University, Department of Political Studies 1973), 26.

78   *Edmonton Journal*, 8 September 1971.

79   Ibid, 22 August 1972.

80   Ibid.

81   Inuit Cultural Institute, Statement released at the NWT Council, Rankin Inlet, 26 October 1976.

82   *Edmonton Journal*, 22 August 1972.

83   *Calgary Herald*, 28 June 1972.

84   *Inuktitut* (July 1981): 9–10.

85   Brody, *The People's Land*, 188–90.

86   *Inuktitut* (July 1981): 12.

87   Government of the NWT, Information Release No. 77-015, 21 January 1977.

88   Lynn D. Nash, "Drop-out Rate among Senior High School Inuit Students in Frobisher Bay," *Multiculturalism* 2, no. 2 (1978): 11–12.

89   Science Council of Canada, "Northward Looking: A Strategy and a Science Policy for Northern Development" (Ottawa 1977), Report No. 26, 40.

90   *Calgary Herald*, 15 May 1982.

91   Robert Paine, editor, *The White Arctic: Anthropological Essays on Tutelage and Ethnicity* (St John's: Memorial University of Newfoundland, Institute of Social and Economic Research 1977), 33.

92   Inuit Cultural Institute, Press Release, 22 April 1977.

93   Tom Kutluk, "The Inuit Cultural Institute," *Inuktitut* (November 1980): 36.

94   Harvey McCue, "Native Values and Northern Education," *Journal of Canadian Studies* 16, no. 2 (1981): 2.

95   *Inuktitut* (July 1981): 4.

96   Anna Prodanou, "Failed Marks in the Northwest Territories," *Maclean's* (19 April 1982): 51.

97   *Inuktitut* (July 1981): 26.

98   *University Affairs* (Montreal: McGill University, February 1982).

99   Ulli Steltzer, *Inuit: The North in Transition* (Vancouver: Douglas and McIntyre 1982), 11.

100   Georgia, "Arctic Schooling Alternatives," 11.

101   Steltzer, *Inuit*, 10.

102   Prodanou, "Failed Marks," 50.

103   Government of the NWT, Information Release No. 77-011, 20 January 1977.

104   Finley, "Why Eskimo Education Isn't Working," 580.

105   Government of the NWT, Information Release No. 78-033, 31 January 1978.

106   Frank G. Vallee, *Kabloona and Eskimo in the Central Keewatin* (Ottawa: Department of Northern Affairs and National Resources 1962), 36.

107   A.M. Ervin, *New Northern Townsmen in Inuvik* (Ottawa: Department of Indian Affairs and Northern Development 1968), 23.

108   Born, "Eskimo Education," 21–22.

109   Nash, "Drop-out Rate," 11–12.
110   *Calgary Herald*, 15 May 1982.
111   *Inuktitut* (July 1981): 4; Prodanou, "Failed Marks," 50–1.
112   Steltzer, *Inuit*, 10.
113   Gurston Dacks, *A Choice of Futures: Politics in the Canadian North* (Toronto: Methuen 1981), 37.
114   *Whitehorse Star*, 12 April 1976.
115   Inuit Tapirisat of Canada, "Agreement-in-Principle as to the Settlement of Inuit Land Claims in the Northwest Territories and the Yukon Territory between the Government of Canada and the Inuit Tapirisat of Canada," 27 February 1976, 57.
116   Special Committee on Education, *Learning, Tradition and Change in the Northwest Territories* (Yellowknife 1982), 17.
117   Koenig, *Northern People and Higher Education*, 214.
118   Ibid, 213.
119   Prodanou, "Failed Marks," 51.
120   Steltzer, *Inuit*, 10.
121   Government of the NWT, *Annual Report* (1983), 48.
122   Koenig, *Northern People and Higher Education*, 64.
123   Ibid, 182.
124   Welsman, "Education of Native People," 38.
125   Finley, "Why Eskimo Education Isn't Working," 581.
126   Koenig, *Northern People and Higher Education*, 213.
127   Ibid, 171.
128   Ibid, 172.
129   Ibid, 173–4.
130   AMMSA, 17 June 1983.
131   Welsman, "Education of Native People," 44.

CHAPTER FOUR

1   Diamond Jenness, "Eskimo Administration II: Canada" (Montreal: Arctic Institute of North America 1964, Technical Paper No. 14, 15.
2   DINA, James Cantley, "Survey of Economic Conditions among the Eskimos of the Canadian Arctic" (1952), 21.
3   RG 85, Vol. 955, File 13379, Pt. 1, Lt T.H. Manning, "Preliminary Report concerning the Eastern Arctic," 1943.
4   *Globe and Mail* (Toronto), 24 November 1942.
5   DINA, Cantley, "Survey of Economic Conditions," 29.
6   DINA, Diamond Jenness, "America's Eskimos: Can They Survive?" Script of lecture delivered at Waterloo Lutheran University, Ontario, 16 October 1952, 9.

7   For example, J.L. Robinson in his preliminary report and recommendations for the administration of the Eastern Arctic refers to the decrease in the number of caribou as one of the current problems in the region but does not mention any shortage of sea mammals.

8   RG 85, Vol. 1069, File 251-1, Pt. 1, Gibson to Commissioner, RCMP, 1 February 1944.

9   RG 85, Vol. 98, File 251-1-2, Pt. 2, Gibson to Cameron, 16 January 1947.

10   RG 85, Vol. 1069, File 251-1, Pt. 1, McKeand to Gibson, [1944].

11   Ibid, Report of meeting, 8 October 1944.

12   RG 85, Vol. 98, File 252-1-2, Pt. 1, quoted by Winifred Hinton, "A Study of Food Habits and Supplies in the Northwest Territories," February 1944.

13   RG 85, Vol. 1036, File 20696, Pt. 1, Memo re Fur Trade in the Canadian Arctic, 23 September 1949.

14   RG 85, Vol. 1069, File 251-1A, Pt. 1, Wright to Sinclair, 1 November 1951.

15   RG 85, Vol. 1036, File 20696, Pt. 1, Memo re Fur Trade in the Canadian Arctic, 23 September 1949.

16   RG 85, Vol. 1069, File 251-1, Pt. 1A, Frazer to Gibson, 29 August 1949.

17   RG 85, Vol. 1069, File 251-1A, Pt. 1, Wright to Sinclair, 23 November 1951.

18   RG 85, Vol. 1069, File 251-1, Pt. 1A, Wright to Sinclair, 9 October 1951.

19   RG 85, Vol. 1036, File 20696, Pt. 1, Memo re Fur Trade in the Canadian Arctic, 23 September 1949.

20   DINA, N.O. Christensen, "Some Information on Canadian Eskimos" (1953), 20.

21   DINA, Cantley, "Survey of Economic Conditions," 38–9.

22   In carrying out a food survey on behalf of the NWT council in 1943 – part of Winifred Hinton's survey, note 12 above – Cpl. L.F. Willan of the RCMP's Coppermine detachment argued that the Inuit might spend more money on foods of high nutritional value if control were exercised not on food purchases themselves but on the sale of non-essentials like jewellery, watches, flashlights, silk handkerchiefs, fancy silks and brocades, gold chains, perfumes, fancy soaps, even silver tea services (a trader sold one to an Inuit family on Banks Island). "Traders will not refrain from selling these articles," Willan wrote, "as there is a demand created by the traders themselves putting these items on the counters. If one refrains from selling them, the opposition at any point reaps all

the profits, which are large." See RG 85, Vol. 98, File 252-1-2, Pt. 1, Report re nutritional investigation, NWT Council, 27 December 1943.

23   RG 85, Vol. 1069, File 251-1, Pt. 1A, Report of meeting, Aklavik, 17 July 1949.

24   Ibid, Confidential report to the Deputy Minister, 8 July 1949.

25   Ibid, Frazer to Gibson, 29 August 1949.

26   DINA, Cantley, "Survey of Economic Conditions," 23.

27   RG 85, Vol. 1069, File 251-1, Pt. 1A, Report of meeting, NWT Council, 27 October 1949.

28   RG 85, Vol. 1071, File 251-5, Pt. 1A, Jack to Officer Commanding G Division, 8 November 1949.

29   Ibid, Jack to Officer Commanding G Division, 18 October 1948.

30   RG 85, Vol. 1036, File 20696, Pt. 1, Memo re Fur Trade in the Canadian Arctic, 23 September 1949.

31   RG 85, Vol. 1069, File 251-1, Pt. 1, Memorandum of Instructions to District Managers, 13 July 1944.

32   RG 85, Vol. 1069, File 251-1, Pt. 1A, Wright to Sinclair, 9 October 1951.

33   RG 85, Vol. 1069, File 251-1, Pt. 1, Memorandum of Instructions to District Managers, 13 July 1944.

34   Hugh Brody, *The People's Land* (Harmondsworth: Penguin Books 1975), 22–3.

35   RG 85, Vol. 1069, File 251-1, Pt. 1, Gibson to Wright, 11 October 1946.

36   Ibid, Gibson to Chester, 24 October 1946.

37   Ibid, Memorandum of Instructions to District Managers, 13 July 1944.

38   Ibid, Chester to Gibson, 6 November 1946.

39   RG 85, Vol. 955, File 13379, Pt. 1, Lt T.H. Manning, "Preliminary Report concerning the Eastern Arctic," 1943.

40   RG 85, Vol. 1069, File 251-1, Pt. 1A, Wright to Sinclair, 9 October 1951.

41   RG 85, Vol. 1130, File 253-1, Pt. 3, Chesshire to Gibson, 13 May 1949.

42   Trevor Lloyd, "Changing Greenland," *Beaver* 289 (1959): 42.

43   RG 85, Vol. 1234, File 251-1, Pt. 2, Larsen to Commissioner, RCMP, 30 October 1951.

44   Ibid, Cantley to Wright, 20 November 1951.

45   RG 85, Vol. 1069, File 251-1A, Pt. 1, Young to Sinclair, 28 November 1951.

46   RG 85, Vol. 1234, File 251-1, Pt. 2, Larsen to Commissioner, RCMP, 29 February 1952.

47 RG 85, Vol. 1127, File 201-1-8, Pt. 2, "Report of the Eastern Arctic Patrol," 22 July 1948.

48 RG 85, Vol. 1127, File 201-1-8, Pt. 2A, "Report of the Eastern Arctic Patrol," 1950.

49 RG 85, Vol. 1234, File 251-1, Pt. 2, LeCapelain to Acting Deputy Minister, Department of Resources and Development, 8 December 1952.

50 Ibid, Larsen to Commissioner, RCMP, 29 February 1952.

51 RG 85, Vol. 1127, File 201-1-8, Pt. 2A, "Report of the Eastern Arctic Patrol," 1950.

52 DINA, Cantley, "Survey of Economic Conditions," 38–9.

53 RG 85, Vol. 1234, File 251-1, Pt. 2, LeCapelain to Acting Deputy Minister, Department of Resources and Development, 8 December 1952.

54 Ibid, Larsen to Commissioner, RCMP, 30 October 1951.

55 RG 85, Vol. 1513, File 1012-1, Pt. 1, Cunningham to Clyde, 16 June 1952.

56 RG 85, Vol. 1234, File 251-1, Pt. 2, Agenda for meeting, 19 May 1952.

57 RG 85, Vol. 1513, File 1012-1, Pt. 1, Summary of proceedings of meeting, 19–20 May 1952.

58 RG 85, Vol. 300, File 1009-3, Pt. 1, Terms of reference of Advisory Committee on Arctic Development, 19 January 1948.

59 Ibid, Memo by Cunningham, 4 February 1948.

60 Ibid, Minutes of meeting, Advisory Committee on Northern Development, 16 February 1953.

61 RG 85, Vol. 1234, File 251-1, Pt. 2, Department of Resources and Development, Press Release, 22 May 1952.

There was a big difference between the Western and the Eastern Arctic in regard to the traders, their relations with the Inuit, and their role in the unfavourable economic circumstances of the North. In the Eastern Arctic fur was the major item in the economy, and here the situation was much more critical than in the Western Arctic, especially the Mackenzie area, where muskrats were the principal source of native income. The district administrator at Fort Smith pointed out in a letter written in 1949 that "the least of our worries should be Aklavik. There, even with rat prices at 40 cents, a subsistence income is assured the trapper. The trader's concern is not for the native's welfare but for his own. A trapper with a family who takes 1,000 rats, is assured of $400.00 at a minimum, or say $40.00 per month. This, with family allowance, is at least a subsistence income. Most trappers in the Delta will take from 1,000 to 3,000 rats. One has only to ascertain the total rat take, divide it by the number of registered lines, and realize the substantial income of trappers in the delta area." See note 16 above.

62 RG 85, Vol. 1234, File 251-1, Pt. 2, Figures computed by Cantley from Hudson's Bay Company information, n.d.

63 Ibid, James Cantley, "Proposals re Immediate Steps to Improve Eskimo Economy and Welfare," [1952].

64 Lloyd, "Changing Greenland," 43.

65 RG 85, Vol. 510, File 1009-3, Pt. 11, Minutes of meeting, Advisory Committee on Northern Development, 23 May 1956.

66 RG 85, Vol. 1903, File 1009-19, Pt. 1, Report of subcommittee, Working Group on Northern Economic Problems, 18 December 1956.

67 RG 85, Vol. 649, File 1009-3, Pt. 9, "Annual report of Government Activities in the North," January 1957.

68 RG 85, Vol. 376, File 1009-3, Pt. 6, Minutes of meeting, Advisory Committee on Northern Development, 8 November 1954.

69 RG 85, Vol. 414, File 1009-3, Pt. 7, Memo re administrative implications of the DEW Line, 2 March 1955.

70 RG 85, Vol. 376, File 1009-3, Pt. 6, Minutes of meeting, Advisory Committee on Northern Development, 8 November 1954.

71 Ibid, Instructions for Northern Service Officers, March 1953.

72 RG 85, Vol. 674, File 207-2, Pt. 1, Sivertz to Deputy Minister, Department of Northern Affairs and National Resources, 21 December 1956.

73 Ibid, Minutes of meeting, Ottawa, 27 January 1958.

74 Ibid, Handwritten marginal note.

75 RG 85, Vol. 744, File 207-2, Pt. 5, Federal Electric Corporation: Eskimo Statistical Reports for March, July, September, and November 1961.

76 RG 85, Vol. 630, File 207-3, Pt. 4, Saunders to Templeton, 6 August 1959.

77 RG 85, Vol. 744, File 207-2, Pt. 4, DEW Line Order 30-44: Canada Eskimo Plan, 1959.

78 RG 85, Vol. 674, File 207-2, Pt. 1, Minutes of meeting, Ottawa, 27 January 1958.

79 Ibid, Federal Electric Corporation: Plan for the Employment of Eskimos in Canada [Summer 1957].

80 Ibid, Cruzen to Deputy Minister, Department of Northern Affairs and National Resources, 18 April 1958.

81 RG 85, Vol. 674, File 207-2, Pt. 2, Deputy Minister, Department of Northern Affairs and National Resources, to Cruzen, 5 May 1958.

82 RG 85, Vol. 674, File 207-2, Pt. 3, Administrator of the Arctic to Saunders, 23 April 1959.

83   Ibid, Bond to Administrator of the Arctic, 28 April 1959.

84   Ibid, Assistant Regional Administrator, Frobisher Bay, to Administrator of the Arctic, 1 July 1959.

85   RG 85, Vol. 744, File 207-2, Pt. 5, Minutes of meeting, Federal Electric Corporation and departments of the government of Canada, 24 July 1961.

86   RG 85, Vol. 744, File A207-6, Pt. 1, Report of the Northern Service Officer, DEW Line (Eastern Sector) for June and July 1961.

87   David F. Pelly, "The DEW Line: A Journalist's Visit to Military Isolation Posts," *North/Nord* 29, no. 1 (1982): 23.

88   RG 85, Vol. 1267, File 1000/169, Pt. 7, Memo re Eskimo houses at Frobisher Bay, 4 June 1956.

89   Ibid, RCMP Annual Report, Frobisher Bay, year ending 31 December 1956.

90   RG 85, Vol. 1071, File 251-5, Pt. 5, Van Norman to Chief, Arctic Division, 19 March 1955.

91   RG 85, Vol. 1349, File 1000/169, Pt. 12, "The Economic Prospects for Frobisher over the next 25 Years," [November] 1958.

92   Toshio Yatsushiro, "The Changing Eskimo," *Beaver* 293 (1962): 20.

93   Ibid, 23.

94   DINA, "Settlements of the Northwest Territories."

95   Data tabulated by Statistics Division, Department of Indian Affairs and Northern Development, Ottawa.

96   D.W. Simpson and K. Bowles, "Integration of Eskimo Manpower into the Industrial Society: Difficulties, Programs, Attitudes" (Fondation française d'études nordiques 1969), Report No. 32, 3.

97   PARC, Q-134, File 1000/169, Pt. 14, Phillips to Deputy Minister, Department of Northern Affairs and National Resources, 3 December 1964.

98   Ibid.

99   DINA, "Settlements of the Northwest Territories."

100 Don C. Foote, "Remarks on Eskimo Sealing and the Harp Seal Controversy," *Arctic* 20, no. 4 (1967): 267.

101 Ibid.

102 George Wenzel, "The Harp Seal Controversy and the Inuit Economy," *Arctic* 31, no. 1 (1978): 3.

103 PARC, O-64, file 1000/167, Pt. 7, RCMP Annual Report, Cape Dorset, year ending 31 December 1967.

104 G. Anders, editor, *The East Coast of Baffin Island: An Area Economic Survey* (Ottawa: Department of Indian Affairs and Northern Development 1967), 89.

105 DINA, "Settlements of the Northwest Territories."

106 Jensen K. Delane, "A Cultural Study of Domination, Exploitation and Co-operation in the Canadian Arctic," Ph.D. dissertation, Department of Geography, University of Michigan, 1975, 141.

107 Jon Evans, *Ungava Bay: A Resource Survey* (Ottawa: Department of Northern Affairs and National Resources 1958).

108 Fred Bruemmer, "Canada's Gold Mine of Stone," *Financial Post Magazine* (October 1980): 92.

109 Delane, "A Cultural Study," 141.

110 Peter Farb, *Man's Rise to Civilization* (New York: Avon Books 1971), 58.

111 Brody, *The People's Land*, 113–4.

112 Ibid, 134.

113 Kirk R. Patterson, "The Theory and Practice of Home Rule in the International North," in *The North in Transition*, edited by Nisl Orvik and Kirk R. Patterson (Kingston: Queen's University, Centre for International Relations 1976), 50–1.

114 Delane, "A Cultural Study," 143.

115 *Edmonton Journal*, 31 July 1962.

116 *Calgary Herald*, 1 May 1963.

117 Patterson, "The Theory and Practice of Home Rule," 53.

118 *Calgary Herald*, 8 November 1961.

119 Patterson, "The Theory and Practice of Home Rule," 59.

120 James Robert Lotz, *Northern Realities: The Future of Northern Development in Canada* (Toronto: New Press 1970), 136.

121 Patterson, "The Theory and Practice of Home Rule," 53.

122 Canada, Department of Indian Affairs and Northern Development, *Native Peoples and the North: A Profile* (Ottawa 1982), 93.

123 Bruemmer, "Canada's Gold Mine of Stone," 93.

124 Ulli Steltzer, *Inuit: The North in Transition* (Vancouver: Douglas and McIntyre 1982), 91.

125 *Lethbridge Herald*, 31 August 1983.

126 *Calgary Herald*, 29 January 1973.

127 John S. Matthiasson and Carolyn J. Matthiasson, "A People Apart: The Ethnicization of the Inuit of the Eastern Canadian Arctic," in *The Canadian Ethnic Mosaic: The Quest for Identity*, edited by Leo Driedger (Toronto: McClelland and Stewart 1978), 239–40.

128 Terence W. Foster, "Rankin Inlet: A Lesson in Survival," *Musk-Ox* 10 (1972): 33.

129 *The Northern Miner*, 7 May 1959.

130 Foster, "Rankin Inlet," 34.

131 Ibid, 33.

132 Ibid, 38.

133 K.J. Rea, "The Political Economy of Northern Development" (Ot-

tawa: Science Council of Canada 1968), Background Study No. 36, 197.

134 *The Northern Miner*, 7 May 1959.

135 Brody, *The People's Land*, 217–8.

136 RG 85, Vol. 1899, File 1003-32, Pt. 4, Contribution of Northern Economic Development Branch to department brief to the Senate Committee on Poverty, 5 May 1969.

137 DINA, "Notes on the Northern Policy Statement 1970–1980: A Mid-Term Look at the Native Situation," (n.d.).

138 Ibid.

139 Ibid.

140 Brody, *The People's Land*, 227–8.

141 Rea, "The Political Economy of Northern Development," 314.

142 Bob Gibson and Bill McLeod, "Nanisivik," *Northern Perspectives* 4, no. 2 (1976): 1.

143 Robert B. Gibson, "The Strathcona Sound Mining Project" (Ottawa: Science Council of Canada 1978), Background Study No. 42, 77.

144 Editorial, *Eskimo*, Summer 1974.

145 Brody, *The People's Land*, 227.

146 See Gibson, "The Strathcona Sound Mining Project."

147 Brody, *The People's Land*, 227.

148 *Calgary Herald*, 29 January 1973.

149 Ibid, 28 June 1972.

150 *Edmonton Journal*, 17 March 1972.

151 Brody, *The People's Land*, 222.

152 *Edmonton Journal*, 2 December 1968.

153 *Ottawa Journal*, 26 January 1974.

154 Brody, *The People's Land*, 224.

155 Richard Bushey, "Native Settlements in Arctic Canada: A Decade of Change," *Habitat* 26, no. 1 (1983): 30.

156 Roland Pressat, *Population* (Baltimore: Penguin Books 1971), 105.

157 Ibid, 107.

158 *Weekend Magazine* 10, no. 20 (1960).

159 W.M. Baker, *Overview Study of Tourism and Recreation in the Northwest Territories* (Yellowknife: Government of the NWT 1973), 120.

160 Government of the NWT, Information Release No. 77-087, 29 March 1977.

161 Inuit Tapirisat of Canada, "Agreement-in-Principle as to the Settlement of Inuit Land Claims in the Northwest Territories and the Yukon Territory between the Government of Canada and the Inuit Tapirisat of Canada," 27 February 1976, 44.

162 Ibid, 56.

163 Government of the NWT, *Outpost Camp Policy* and *What Is the Outpost Camp Program?* (Yellowknife: n.d.).

164 Government of the NWT, *Annual Report* (1982), 68.

165 Government of the NWT, Information Release No. 78-061, 4 February 1978.

166 Wenzel, "The Harp Seal Controversy."

167 Government of the NWT, Information Release No. 78-046, 6 February 1978.

168 Government of the NWT, Information Release No. 78-202, 2 August 1978.

169 Personal communication, George Wenzel, Centre for Northern Studies and Research, McGill University, Montreal.

170 T.G. Smith, "How Inuit Trapper-Hunters Make Ends Meet," *Canadian Geographic* 99, no. 3 (1979): 58.

171 Government of the NWT, Information Release No. 78-275, 8 November 1978.

172 Government of the NWT, Information Release No. 78-053, 8 February 1978.

173 Government of the NWT, Information Release No. 78-125, 9 May 1978.

174 *Canada News Facts* 17 (1983), 2,851.

175 *Lethbridge Herald*, 31 August 1973.

176 Brody, *The People's Land*, 221–2.

177 Steltzer, *Inuit*, 92.

178 Peter Usher, *The Bankslanders: Economy and Ecology of a Frontier Trapping Community* (Ottawa: Department of Indian Affairs and Northern Development 1971).

179 Douglas E. Sanders, *Native People in Areas of Internal National Expansion: Indians and Inuit in Canada* (Copenhagen: International Working Group for Indigenous Affairs 1973).

180 Science Council of Canada, *Northward Looking: A Strategy and a Science Policy for Northern Development* (Ottawa 1977), 46.

181 *Globe and Mail* (Toronto), 31 March 1983.

182 *Whitehorse Star*, 12 April 1976.

183 Gurston Dacks, *A Choice of Futures: Politics in the Canadian North* (Toronto: Methuen 1981), 170.

CHAPTER FIVE

1 David E. Hunter and Phillip Whitten, editors, *Encyclopedia of Anthropology* (New York: Harper and Row 1976), 309.

2 Hugh Brody, *The People's Land* (Harmondsworth: Penguin Books 1975), 137–8.

3   R.W. Dunning, "Ethnic Relations and the Marginal Man in Canada," *Human Organization* 18 (1959): 117–19.

4   Ibid.

5   F.A.E. Cserepy, "New Styles in Administration since 1945," in *A Century of Canada's Arctic Islands, 1880–1980*, edited by Morris Zaslov (Ottawa: Royal Society of Canada 1981), 276.

6   RG 85, Vol. 1513, File 1012-1, Pt. 1, Cunningham to Clyde, 16 June 1952.

7   Jean Lesage, "Enter the European V – Among the Eskimos," *Beaver* 285 (1955): 7–8.

8   Trevor Lloyd, "Changing Greenland," *Beaver* 289 (1959): 43.

9   Cserepy, "New Styles in Administration," 278.

10   Brody, *The People's Land*, 18.

11   Richard Hunter, "Development of Local Government in the Northwest Territories," in *The North in Transition*, edited by Nils Orvik and Kirk R. Patterson (Kingston: Queen's University, Centre for International Relations 1976), 76.

12   RG 85, Vol. 376, File 1009-3, Pt. 6, Minutes of meeting, Advisory Committee on Northern Development, 8 November 1954.

13   RG 85, Vol. 414, File 1009-3, Pt. 7, Instructions for Northern Service Officers, March 1955.

14   John S. Matthiasson and Carolyn J. Matthiasson, "A People Apart: The Ethnicization of the Inuit of the Eastern Canadian Arctic," in *The Canadian Ethnic Mosaic: The Quest for Identity*, edited by Leo Driedger (Toronto: McClelland and Stewart 1978), 241.

15   Ibid, 242–3.

16   RG 85, Vol. 1234, File 201-1-8, Pt. 5, Dr J.A. Hildes, "Report on Visit to the Eastern Arctic," 24 October 1957.

17   RG 85, Vol. 1064, File 1009-16, Pt. 1, Sivertz to Cunningham, 10 December 1958.

18   Ibid, Secretary, Frobisher Bay Development Group, to Bolger, 6 February 1959.

19   RG 85, Vol. 1120, File 1000-169, Pt. 4, Northern Service Officer, Frobisher Bay, to Chief, Arctic Division, 30 May 1955.

20   RG 85, Vol. 1120, File 1000/169, Pt. 9, Memo from Sivertz, 30 September 1957.

21   RG 85, Vol. 1289, File 303/169, Pt. 3, John L. Jenness, "Observations on Frobisher Bay with Recommendations regarding Its Present and Future Development," 1960.

22   RG 85, Vol. 674, File 207-2, Pt. 3, Northern Service Officer, Frobisher Bay, to Northern Administration, 30 October 1959.

23   Ibid, RCMP Report, 10 August 1959.

24   RG 85, Vol. 1064, File 1009-16, Pt. 1, Secretary, Frobisher Bay

Development Group, to Bolger, 6 February 1959.

25 PARC, Q-305, File 1000/167, Pt. 6, Report re social conditions, Cape Dorset, 13 July 1964.

26 RG 85, Vol. 1064, File 1009-16, Pt. 1, Secretary, Frobisher Bay Development Group, to Bolger, 6 February 1959.

27 RG 85, Vol. 1911, File NR4/2-8, Pt. 1, Minutes of meeting, Committee on Social Adjustment, 27 December 1961.

28 RG 85, Vol. 1479, File 303-169-5, Pt. 1, A.B. Connelly, Briefing paper for design consultants, 28 July 1959.

29 Ibid, "Eskimos: Their Status in the Frobisher Community," 1 April 1959.

30 RG 85, Vol. 1911, File NR4/2-8, Pt. 1, Minutes of meeting, Committee on Social Adjustment, 27 December 1961.

31 PARC, Q-134, File 1000/169, Pt. 14, Report on trip to Frobisher Bay, 24–31 January 1962.

32 RG 85, Vol. 1064, File 1009-16, Pt. 1, Secretary, Frobisher Bay Development Group, to Bolger, 6 February 1959.

33 RG 85, Vol. 1911, File NR 4/2-8, Pt. 1, Report on the availability of recreational facilities at Frobisher Bay, 18 December 1963.

34 Ibid.

35 Ibid, Minutes of meeting, Committee on Social Adjustment, 5 February 1964.

36 RG 85, Vol. 1064, File 1009-16, Pt. 1, Robertson to Jackett, 22 July 1958.

37 Ibid, Stewart to Chief, Arctic Division, 11 July 1958.

38 Ibid, Secretary, Frobisher Bay Development Group, to Bolger, 6 February 1959.

39 RG 85, Vol. 1885, File NR 2626-1, Pt. 10, Hodgson to Chrétien, 25 August 1969.

40 Brody, *The People's Land*, 211.

41 DINA, John J. Honigmann, "Arctic Townlife as a Stimulus to Eskimo Culture Change" (1965), 7–8.

42 Ibid, 5.

43 Asen Balikci, "Some Acculturative Trends among the Eastern Canadian Eskimos," *Anthropologica* 2 (1960): 140–1; "Development of Basic Socio-Economic Units in Two Eskimo Communities" (Ottawa: National Museum of Canada 1964), Bulletin No. 202, Anthropology Series No. 69, 36–7; *The Netsilik Eskimo* (Garden City: Natural History Press 1970), 117, 128, 176. See also David Damas, "The Diversity of Eskimo Societies," in *Man the Hunter*, edited by Richard B. Lee and Irven De Vore (Chicago: Aldine 1968), 113.

44 Charles C. Hughes, "Under Four Flags: Recent Culture Change among the Eskimos," *Current Anthropology* 6 (1965): 18.

45   G. Anders, editor, *The East Coast of Baffin Island: An Area Economic Survey* (Ottawa: Department of Indian Affairs and Northern Development 1967), 62.

46   RG 85, Vol. 1064, File 1009-16, Pt. 1, Secretary, Frobisher Bay Development Group, to Bolger, 6 February 1959.

47   Ibid, Report on the use of liquor by the Eskimo people of Frobisher Bay, 29 March 1963.

48   Ibid, Minutes of meeting, Committee on Social Adjustment, 13 December 1961.

49   RG 85, Vol. 1912, File A1000/166, Pt. 1, MacNeil to Orange, 19 February 1964.

50   RG 85, Vol. 1064, File 1009-16, Pt. 1, Minutes of meeting, Committee on Social Adjustment, 13 December 1961; RG 85, Vol. 1911, File NR4/2-8, Pt. 1, Minutes of meeting, Committee on Social Adjustment, 7 February 1962; RG 85, Vol. 745, File 250-5, Pt. 1, Extract from Frobisher Bay Regional Quarterly Report, January–March 1962.

51   RG 85, Vol. 745, File 250-5, Pt. 1, Minutes of meeting, Frobisher Bay Eskimo Community Council, 11 November 1964.

52   RG 85, Vol. 1064, File 1009-16, Pt. 1, Report on the use of liquor by the Eskimo people of Frobisher Bay, 29 March 1963.

53   RG 85, Vol. 1911, File NR4/2-8, Pt. 1, Minutes of meeting, Committee on Social Adjustment, 7 February 1962.

54   Ibid, Court Statistics, Frobisher Bay, 7 February 1962.

55   Ibid, Minutes of meeting, Committee on Social Adjustment, 21 March 1962.

56   RG 85, Vol. 1479, File 303/169, Pt. 2, RCMP report re Frobisher Bay development, 29 August 1959.

57   RG 85, Vol. 1911, File NR4/2-8, Pt. 1, Minutes of meeting, Committee on Social Adjustment, 7 February 1962.

58   RG 85, Vol. 1064, File 1009-16, Pt. 1, Report on the use of liquor by the Eskimo people of Frobisher Bay, 29 March 1963.

59   PARC, Q-305, File 1000/167, Pt. 6, Hughes to Orange, 11 August 1964.

60   RCMP, Patrol Report: Lake Harbour to Cape Dorset, 5–20 March 1964.

61   RG 85, Vol. 1912, File A1000/166, Pt. 1, MacNeil to Orange, 19 February 1964.

62   Ibid, Monthly Report for January 1964, Cape Dorset, 3 February 1964.

63   Ibid, MacNeil to Orange, 19 February 1964.

64   PARC, Q-305, File 1000/167, Pt. 6, Hughes to Orange, 11 August 1964.

65 RG 85, Vol. 1912, File A1000/166, Pt. 1, MacNeil to Orange, 19 February 1964.

66 RG 85, Vol. 1064, File 1009-16, Pt. 1, Report on the use of liquor by the Eskimo people of Frobisher Bay, 29 March 1963.

67 RG 85, Vol. 1911, File NR4/2-8, Pt. 1, Minutes of meeting, Committee on Social Adjustment, 27 December 1961.

68 Ibid, Minutes of meeting, Committee on Social Adjustment, 21 March 1962.

69 Ibid, Minutes of meeting, Committee on Social Adjustment, 27 December 1961.

70 Ibid.

71 Ibid.

72 RG 85, Vol. 1912, File A1000/166, Pt. 1, Monthly Report for January 1964, Cape Dorset, 3 February 1964.

73 Ibid, Fingland to Kennedy, 25 March 1964.

74 Ibid, Stevenson to Orange, 27 October 1964.

75 Ibid, Fingland to Kennedy, 25 March 1964.

76 PARC, Q-305, File 1000/167, Pt. 6, Hughes to Orange, 11 August 1964.

77 PARC, O-64, File 1000/167, Pt. 7, RCMP Annual Report, Cape Dorset, year ending 31 December 1967.

78 RG 85, Vol. 1064, File 1009-16, Pt. 1, Minutes of meeting, Committee on Social Adjustment, 13 December 1961.

79 RG 85, Vol. 745, File 250-5, Pt. 1, Minutes of meeting, Frobisher Bay Eskimo Community Council, 30 August 1962.

80 RG 85, Vol. 1911, File NR4/2-8, Pt. 1, Minutes of meeting, Committee on Social Adjustment, 5 February 1964.

81 Ibid, Report on Interdiction, 14 February 1964.

82 Nancy Cooper, "Getting off the Booze," *Maclean's* (24 January 1977): 18–19.

83 Government of the NWT, Information Release No. 79-033, 29 January 1979.

84 RG 85, Vol. 1064, File 1009-16, Pt. 1, Secretary, Frobisher Bay Development Group, to Bolger, 6 February 1964.

85 RG 85, Vol. 675, File A250-5, Pt. 1, Bolger to Phillips, 5 January 1962.

86 RG 85, Vol. 745, File 250-5, Pt. 1, Bolger to Orange, 12 January 1962.

87 RG 85, Vol. 675, File A250-5, Pt. 1, Northern Administration Branch Policy Directive No. 13: Community Development and Local Organization, 25 October 1961.

88 RG 85, Vol. 675, File A250-5/166, Pt. 1, Barry to Orange, 16 December 1961.

89   RG 85, Vol. 745, File 250-5, Pt. 1, Report on the election of a council at Frobisher Bay, May 1962.

90   Ibid, Orange to Acting Administrator of the Arctic, 26 January 1962.

91   Ibid, Minutes of meeting, Frobisher Bay Eskimo Community Council, 27 September 1962.

92   RG 85, Vol. 675, File A250-5/166, Pt. 1, Barry to Orange, 16 December 1961.

93   RG 85, Vol. 675, File A250-5, Pt. 1, Bolger to Phillips, 5 January 1962.

94   RG 85, Vol. 745, File 250-5, Pt. 1, Extract from Frobisher Bay Regional Quarterly Report, January–March 1962.

95   RG 85, Vol. 1382, File 1012-9, Pt. 5, Minutes of meeting, Committee on Eskimo Affairs, 10–11 April 1961.

96   RG 85, Vol. 1382, File 1012-9, Pt. 7, Opening remarks at meeting, Committee on Eskimo Affairs, 2 April 1962.

97   *Edmonton Journal*, 3 June 1957.

98   Ibid, 16 March 1962.

99   Ibid, 20 September 1966.

100 RG 85, Vol. 745, File 250-5, Pt. 1, General memorandum on municipal organizations in the NWT, 19 September 1961.

101 RG 85, Vol. 675, File A250-5, Pt. 1, Northern Administration Policy Directive No. 13: Community Development and Local Organization, 25 October 1961.

102 A.W.R. Carrothers, *Report of the Advisroy Committee on the Development of Government in the Northwest Territories* Vol. I (Ottawa 1966), 189.

103 Toshio Yatsushiro, "The Changing Eskimo," *Beaver* 293 (1962): 25–6.

104 Hunter, "Development of Local Government," 78.

105 Cserepy, "New Styles in Administration," 282.

106 Ibid, 286.

107 Ibid, 283.

108 RG 85, Vol. 1885, File NR2626-16, Pt. 10, Hodgson to Chrétien, 25 August 1969.

109 DINA, "Notes on the Northern Policy Statement 1970–1980."

110 J. David Flynn, "The Development of Autonomy in the Northwest Territories," *Musk-Ox* 17 (1975): 22.

111 Government of the NWT, Information Release No. 79-025, 23 January 1979.

112 Peter Ittinuar, "Inuit Participation in Politics," in *A Century of Canada's Arctic Islands, 1880–1980*, edited by Morris Zaslov (Ottawa: Royal Society of Canada 1981), 294–5.

113 C.M. Drury, *Report of the Special Representative for Constitutional De-*

velopment in the Northwest Territories (Ottawa 1980), 14.

114   Ittinuar, "Inuit Participation in Politics," 295.

115   Hunter, "Development of Local Government," 80.

116   Ibid, 81.

117   Government of the NWT, Information Release No. 76-263, 14 December 1976.

118   Hunter, "Development of Local Government," 86.

119   Ibid.

120   Brody, *The People's Land*, 123.

121   Government of the NWT, *A Paper on the Philosophy of the Department of Local Government* (Yellowknife 1975), 31.

122   Hunter, "Development of Local Government," 88.

123   Ibid, 91.

124   G.W. Rowley, "The Canadian Eskimo in 1971," *Arctic Circular* 22 (1971): 19.

125   Inuit Tapirisat of Canada (ITC), *An Introduction to the Eskimo People of Canada and Their National Organization* (Ottawa n.d.), 5.

126   *Albertan* (Calgary), 24 August 1971.

127   ITC, *An Introduction*, 5.

128   ITC, "Agreement-in-Principle as to the Settlement of Inuit Land Claims in the Northwest Territories and the Yukon Territory between the Government of Canada and the Inuit Tapirisat of Canada," 27 February 1976, 14–15.

129   Ittinuar, "Inuit Participation in Politics," 295–6.

130   ITC, "Agreement-in-Principle," 9.

131   Ittinuar, "Inuit Participation in Politics," 296.

132   Milton Freeman Research Ltd, *Inuit Land Use and Occupancy Project: Report* (Ottawa: Department of Supply and Services 1976).

133   Inuit land claims negotiator, Thomas Suluk, quoted by Steltzer, *Inuit*, 131.

134   *Toronto Star*, 6 April 1977.

135   *Native People*, 29 August 1980.

136   *Globe and Mail* (Toronto), 16 March 1979.

137   *Medicine Hat News*, 29 March 1979.

138   *Globe and Mail*, 10 September 1979.

139   Ibid, 5 February 1981.

140   Kirk R. Patterson, "The Theory and Practice of Home Rule in the International North," in *The North in Transition*, edited by Nils Orvik and Kirk R. Patterson (Kingston: Queen's University, Centre for International Relations 1976), 120.

141   C.E.S. Franks, "The Public Service in the North," *Canadian Public Administration* 27, no. 2 (1984): 236–7.

142   Gurston Dacks, *A Choice of Futures: Politics in the Canadian North*

(Toronto: Methuen 1981), 51.

143   Government of the NWT, Information Release No. 77-104, 18 April 1977.

144   Ibid, No. 79-106, 2 April 1979.

145   Ibid, No. 79-105, 30 March 1979.

146   Ibid, No. 78-255, 23 October 1978.

147   Ibid, No. 79-100, 26 March 1979.

148   Cserepy, "New Styles in Administration," 290.

149   *Globe and Mail*, 7 April 1982.

150   *Edmonton Journal*, 15 January 1970.

151   *Star-Phoenix* (Saskatoon), 2 October 1979.

152   Peter Jull, "Nunavut," *Northern Perspectives* 10, no. 2 (1982): 6.

153   Dacks, *A Choice of Futures*, 103.

154   Government of the NWT, News Release No. 79-228, 14 November 1979.

155   Dacks, *A Choice of Futures*, 110–11.

156   Quoted by Walter Dinsdale in the House of Commons, 5 April 1976.

157   *Edmonton Journal*, 28 January 1964.

158   Jull, "Nunavut," 2.

159   *Edmonton Journal*, 5 November 1966.

160   Government of the NWT, Information Release No. 79-022, 22 January 1979.

161   Mike Moore and Gary Vanderhaden, "Northern Problems or Canadian Opportunities," *Canadian Public Administration* 27, no. 2 (1984): 183.

162   Quoted by Doug Neil in the House of Commons, 5 April 1976.

163   Fred Bruemmer, "The Best of Both Worlds," *Weekend Magazine* 24, no. 37 (14 September 1974): 13.

164   *Albertan* (Calgary), 31 August 1971.

165   Quoted by Jean Morisset, "The Aboriginal Nationhood, the Northern Challenge and the Construction of Canadian Unity," *Queen's Quarterly* 88 (1981): 242–3.

166   Dacks, *A Choice of Futures*, 76.

167   *Native People*, 7 April 1978.

168   Government of the NWT, *Annual Report* (1980), 58.

169   *Canadian News Facts* 16 (1982), 2,679.

170   Ibid, 2,792.

171   *Calgary Herald*, 23 September 1982.

172   *Globe and Mail*, 7 April 1982.

173   *Canadian News Facts* 16 (1982), 2,703.

174   ITC, "Agreement-in-Principle," 20–1.

175   *Northern Perspectives* 12, no. 1 (1984): 5.

176   *Globe and Mail*, 29 March 1984.
177   *Northern Perspectives* 13, no. 1 (1985): 5.
178   *Medicine Hat News*, 23 January 1985.
179   *Globe and Mail*, 17 January 1987.
180   Louis-Edmond Hammelin, "Managing Canada's North: Challenges and Opportunities," *Canadian Public Administration* 27, no. 2 (1984): 166.
181   E.M.R. Cotterill, "The Territorial North," *Canadian Public Administration* 27, no. 2 (1984): 190.
182   *Albertan* (Calgary), 16 November 1979.
183   Government of the NWT, *Annual Report* (1983), 73.
184   E.J. Dosman and Frances Abele, "Offshore Diplomacy in the Canadian Arctic: The Beaufort Sea and Lancaster Sound," *Journal of Canadian Studies* 16, no. 2 (1981): 9.
185   Peter Jull and Nigel Bankes, "Inuit Interests in the Arctic Offshore," *Northern Perspectives* 11, no. 5 (1983): 4.
186   Jull, "Nunavut," 22.
187   *Calgary Herald*, 25 July 1983.
188   *Globe and Mail*, 1 August 1983.
189   Dosman and Abele, "Offshore Diplomacy," 8.
190   Peter Jull, "Diplomats of a New North," *Policy Options* 2, no. 2 (1981): 23.
191   Carrothers, *Report*, Vol. I, 143.
192   Jull, "Nunavut," 6.
193   Cotterill, "The Territorial North," 189.
194   Moore and Vanderhaden, "Northern Problems," 184.
195   Ibid, 185.
196   Ittinuar, "Inuit Participation in Politics," 297–8.
197   *Globe and Mail*, 8 October 1983.
198   Ibid, 4 October 1983.
199   *Canadian News Facts* 17 (1983), 2,889.
200   *Globe and Mail*, 23 November 1983.
201   Dacks, *A Choice of Futures*, 101.

Index

The Road to Nunavut

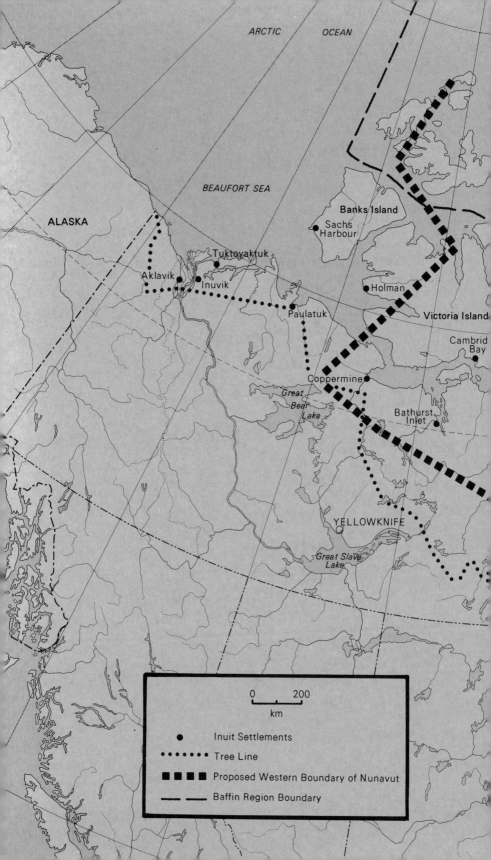

ARCTIC   OCEAN

BEAUFORT SEA

ALASKA

Banks Island

Sachs
Harbour

Tuktoyaktuk

Aklavik   Inuvik

Holman

Paulatuk

Victoria Island

Cambridge
Bay

Great
Bear
Lake

Coppermine

Bathurst
Inlet

YELLOWKNIFE

Great Slave
Lake

0   200
━━━━━━━
km

●   Inuit Settlements

● ● ● ●   Tree Line

■ ■ ■ ■   Proposed Western Boundary of Nunavut

━ ━ ━   Baffin Region Boundary

Ellesmere
Island

GREENLAND

Grise
Fiord

Devon Island

Baffin   Bay

olute

Namisivik
Arctic
Bay
Pond Inlet

Clyde River

Baffin Island
Broughton Island

ce
y
Igloolik
Hall
Beach
Pangnirtung
Davis   Strait

Pelly Bay

Repulse Bay
Circle
Iqaluit
(Frobisher Bay)

Lake Harbour

Coral
Harbour
Cape Dorset

er Lake

Saglouc
Koartac

hesterfield
Inlet
Ivujivik
Wakeham
Bay
Ungava Bay

Rankin Inlet
Whale Cove
Povungnituk
Fort Chimo

Eskimo Point

Inoucdjouac (Port Harrison)

Hudson Bay

Sanikiluaq
Belcher
Islands
Great Whale River